Ottoman warfare, 1500–1700

Ottoman warfare, 1500–1700

Rhoads Murphey

Rutgers University Press
New Brunswick, New Jersey

First published in the United States 1999
by Rutgers University Press
New Brunswick, New Jersey

First published in Great Britain 1999
by UCL Press Limited
Taylor & Francis Group
1 Gunpowder Square
London EC4A 3DE

Library of Congress Cataloging-in-Publication Data and British Library
Cataloguing-in-Publication Data are available upon request.

ISBN 0-8135-2684-1 (cloth)
ISBN 0-8135-2685-X (pbk.)

Printed in Great Britain

Contents

CONTENTS

List of illustrations

List of tables

Maps

1. *The Ottoman position in the West at the end of the seventeenth century*

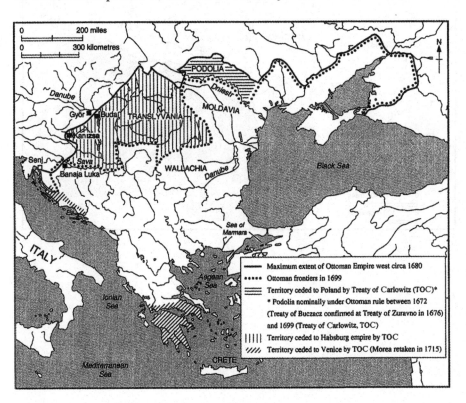

Legend:
- Maximum extent of Ottoman Empire west circa 1680
- Ottoman frontiers in 1699
- Territory ceded to Poland by Treaty of Carlowitz (TOC)*
  * Podolia nominally under Ottoman rule between 1672 and 1699 (Treaty of Carlowitz, TOC)
  (Treaty of Buczacz confirmed at Treaty of Zuravno in 1676)
- Territory ceded to Habsburg empire by TOC
- Territory ceded to Venice by TOC (Morea retaken in 1715)

2. The Ottoman position north of the Black Sea

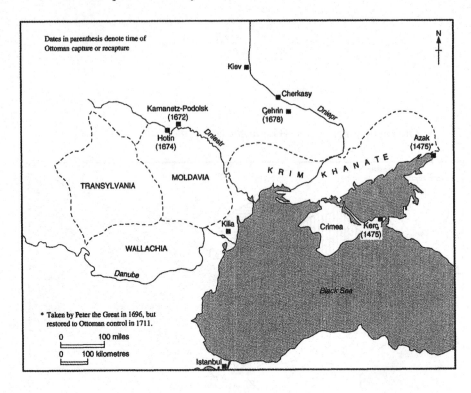

3. The Ottoman position in the East at the turn of the seventeenth century

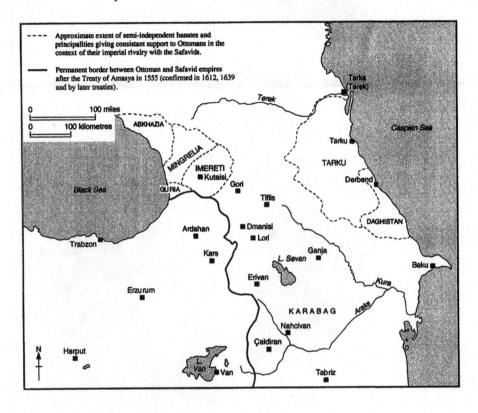

4. Distance of potential battlefields with reference to Istanbul

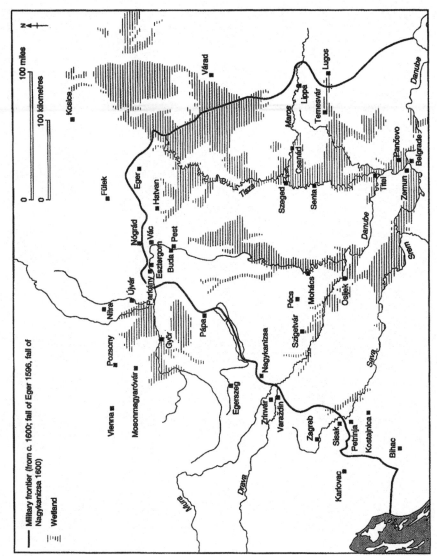

5. *River systems of Hungary*

Preface: Scope and purpose of work

The period 1500 to 1700 forms a period of Ottoman dynastic history when the Ottomans gave particular emphasis to their frontiers with Europe. While other fronts were activated against Iran in 1514, Syria and Egypt in 1517, and into the lower Tigris-Euphrates in the decade following the Ottoman capture of Baghdad in 1535, from the fall of Buda in 1541 to the close of the seventeenth century the Ottomans were most consistently concerned with the defence (and, periodically, the extension) of their trans-Danubian possessions. This channelling of Ottoman effort was the product (and an Ottoman response to) contemporary political circumstances. While the rise of the Safavid dynasty in the East from 1502 posed a potential threat to the Ottomans, the unification of the crowns of Spain and Austria under Charles V from 1519 posed a present and real danger to Ottoman strategic interests. Despite the redivision of territories at the abdication of Charles in 1556 and the succession of his brother Ferdinand (the First) to his eastern possessions and of his son Philip (the Second) to his western and northern possessions, the Ottomans had by that time irreversibly committed themselves to anti-Habsburg alliances and strategic positions of their own that kept them at the centre of Middle European politics until the end of the seventeenth century. While it will not be possible, given the wide scope of our coverage of general military developments over a two-century period, to focus in detail on developments in any one of the lands that formed the post-1540 Ottoman empire, a natural bias towards events on the northwest frontier represents the actual pattern of Ottoman military involvements in the period. Of the three most active fronts – the Caucasian, the Mesopotamian and the Hungarian – it was the latter which persistently claimed the lion's share of Ottoman resources and concentration of effort.

The sheer size of the post-1540 Ottoman empire necessitated such a balancing of interests and commitments. Resources and surpluses from one area were used by the Ottomans to good effect to subsidize and support military activity in another, and for most of the period the empire's size was a source, not of increased vulnerability, but rather of strength. From the mid-sixteenth century the Austrian military border along the northwest frontier, forming a 370-mile arch extending from Kosice on the north and east to Senj in the south and west, was guarded by a string of more than 50 forts and fortresses.[1] By 1600, with the addition of Kanice (Nagykanizsa) as the fourth province of Ottoman Hungary, the Ottomans were able to match the Austrians in number and kind, and the balance struck in the early years of the century was little changed until the 1660s. At the other extreme, although the Ottoman-Safavid frontier stretched over 600 miles from Batum on the Black Sea to Basra on the Shatt al-Arab, only a small proportion of the full extent was very heavily garrisoned or defended. Apart from confined periods of exceptional activity (as for example during the 1580s and again in the 1630s) the costs of maintaining the Ottomans' presence in this sphere could be offset by relying mostly on local resources. In view of these realities, the weight of evidence which we will draw upon for our narrative comes from the mid-sixteenth century onwards and predominantly from the European sphere of operations. References to events affecting other spheres and periods are unsystematic and included mostly to highlight parallel institutional developments or as illustrations of general phenomena.

In the book coverage of principal themes has been organized in accordance with the successive phases of warfare : before, during and after. The first part (Chapters 1–3) treats preparatory and planning aspects of warfare; Chapters 4–7 are concerned with operational matters; and a final chapter considers various aspects of the post-war impact of military activity. A unifying theme which links all three parts is constraints on and limitations of Ottoman warfare. This later preoccupation leads us to play down the importance of the planned and controlled aspects of Ottoman warfare, such as mobilization and finance, covered in the first part. These preparatory phases can be comprehensively quantified and verified from Ottoman archival sources, which record them in stunning detail. But it is the uncontrollable and unpredictable aspects of Ottoman warfare – in both its human and environmental dimensions – that will interest us most. The chapters which explore these dimensions are necessarily grounded (especially in the parts focusing on operational realities) in physical descriptions, operational reports, campaign journals and other Ottoman narrative accounts. The fiscal, technological, tactical and political dimensions of Ottoman military history have received considerable attention in print, but as yet little attempt has been made to recreate or evoke the physical and psychological realities of war as experienced by average Ottoman soldiers. Considering this former neglect and in hopes of providing a modest corrective, the balance of coverage in our book will favour operational matters. As an alternative to the all too common approach to Ottoman military history structured on the detailed post-mortem analysis of Ottoman success or failure in particular campaigns, we will place priority not on explaining outcomes but rather on the understanding of process.

In writing a book of this scope questions concerning the appropriate terms of reference and the consistency (as well as intelligibility) of terminology are bound to arise. In such matters I have been guided in the main by practical considerations rather than a doctrinaire concern for historical precision. For example, while the use of the modern term "Austria" to stand for the Habsburg domains in the eastern portions of their empire may be imprecise or historically inaccurate, its avoidance seems unnecessarily pedantic. Rather than insisting on finer distinctions between "imperial Austro-Habsburg standing army units" and regiments loaned to it by individual electoral states within the Holy Roman Empire, or by other sovereign states in alliance with them in particular campaigns, we have opted to subsume all participating groups under broader all-inclusive headings such as "Austrian army" or "coalition forces". Since no such ambiguity regarding the source of recruited soldiers existed in the Ottoman case (unless we consider the use of Tatars as auxiliaries for European campaigns or Kurds in campaigns to the East to be exceptions) we may, with considerably greater accuracy, refer to most military mobilizations as simply "Ottoman". While the dynastic term "Safavid" covers most cases of the Ottomans' relations with their neighbours along the eastern borders of the empire, the distinction between Imperial Austria (the hereditary lands), Royal Hungary and the Croatian borderlands – the latter enjoying a separate, semi-autonomous status as part of the *militargrenze* – defies simple classification as "Habsburg" or even such compromise alternatives as "Imperial". These levels of administrative and jurisdictional complexity in the "Austrian" case gave a characteristic stamp to Austro-Ottoman warfare. To describe it as a battle of wills between Vienna and Istanbul is misleading, since war was frequently waged using the personal resources of powerful local families of the borderlands such as (in the Austrian case) the Zriny, usually with the blessing of but often with only minimal input from "The State". By necessity we revert to the use of inappropriately monolithic terms such as "Austrian" as broad descriptors, but it is hoped that the analysis will serve to bring out some of the underlying complexities of frontier warfare along the Bosno-Croatian and Austro-Hungarian borderlands of the Ottoman empire. In this particular geographical environment local factors and particularisms decisively influenced the course both of inter-state and international conflicts.

The Ottomans' own way of referring to their Habsburg contemporaries was to call them Nemçe (Nemse) meaning German or Austrian.[2] Seemingly for them, too, finding a single term of reference for the confederation of Croatian, Czech, German, and Hungarian territories that made up the Holy Roman empire in the east was equally problematic. We have opted with them to reduce complex social and communal relations to a more comprehensible uniformity by the arbitrary use of more inclusive terms. We are prevented from applying a similar logic to the Ottoman or Safavid case by the fact that the closest equivalents of "Turk" and "Iranian" cannot be used without seriously distorting contemporary political realities. In the final analysis it seemed to us preferable that such inconsistencies in terminology should remain, than that our attempts to create a false symmetry should be allowed to become a source, not just of distortion, but (worse still for our purposes) confusion.

Tables of equivalents for weights, measures and standard coins in use during the sixteenth and seventeenth centuries are provided as appendices at the end of the book (*see Appendices III–VI*). Within our narrative it seemed preferable to stick as closely as possible to the original terms of reference used in the sources cited. In order to facilitate identification on modern maps, however, a list of place name equivalents is provided in Appendix VII. For example, references in the text to the important fortress on the banks of the Nitra river north of Komárom are made in the form most commonly encountered in Ottoman sources, i.e. Uyvar. For comparative purposes the modern Slovakian (Nové Zámky) and contemporary Hungarian (Ujvár) forms are both indicated in Appendix VII.

Acknowledgements

I am grateful to Dr Filiz Cağman, Director of the Topkapi Palace Museum in Istanbul, for permission to print reproductions of five miniatures from literary and historical manuscripts in the Topkapi collections as follows:

Hazine 1365, fols. 93a and 34b (Mustafa Ali, *Nusretname*); Bağdad Köşkü 200, fol. 100a (Seyyid Lokman, *Şehinşahname-i Sultan Murad Han*, Vol. 2); Hazine 889, fol. 14a (Nadirî, *Divan*) and Hazine 1124, fol. 54a (Nadirî, *Şehname-i Sultan Osman Han*).

I am also indebted to three readers all of whom graciously agreed to comment on my manuscript at successive draft stages. Virginia Aksan, Jeremy Black and William McNeill all offered probing insights which, in their turn, encouraged me to have a second think. If I have failed in the end result to rise to the challenge of their collective wisdom I assume full responsibility for the lost opportunity. I would also like to thank Caroline Finkel for her professional courtesy and general *politesse* in responding to what must have seemed tiresomely persistent requests for practical assistance connected with my research for the book.

I am deeply grateful to all the editorial staff at UCL Press for their patience and professionalism during the book's long journey, through co-operative effort, from editor's and author's pipe dream to handsome final product.

posterioribus

Chapter One

General political framework: the evolving context

Before considering the immediate context of specific Ottoman campaigns it is necessary first to develop a general sense of the enterprise within the framework of its limited political objectives (Chapter 1) and its physical and material constraints (Chapter 2). The Ottomans waged war at specific times for specific reasons. Both policies and strategies changed over time, and to reduce all Ottoman warfare to secular desires for world dominance or spiritual motives such as the triumph of Islam is a crude oversimplification of Ottoman thinking. While historians still debate over the purpose and timing of Ottoman offensives against Hungary in the 1520s, a recent reassessment openly challenges once standard views that Süleyman intended the conquest and annexation of Hungary from the very beginning of his reign, perhaps as early as 1521 after the capture of Belgrade.[1] Perjés is inclined to focus instead on the unforeseen dynastic crisis precipitated by the accession of a minor king (Janos II Zapolya) to the Hungarian throne in 1540 as the turning point, providing not just the opportunity and pretext but, more importantly, also the justification for Ottoman annexation of select districts of central Hungary (including the capital Buda). It can be convincingly argued that the Ottomans committed themselves to direct rule and annexation as opposed to rule by proxy in Hungary as a consequence not of preordained policy, but of fortuitous circumstance whose immediate effect was the removal of all other viable options. Individual sultans had particular views about the necessity or desirability of engaging in all-out war with the Austrians, and while Süleyman spent the last 25 years (1541–66) of his reign expanding and vigorously defending his new acquisitions north of the Sava and on both banks of the Danube, a succession of sultans who followed him in the eight decades between 1568 and 1649 entered into a series of extended and little-disturbed truces with the former enemy.[2] While the "Long War" of 1593 to 1606

1

provides an exception to the usual pattern of peace, it began and ended with localized disturbances, and in the intervening years it only exceptionally (as for example during the Ottoman offensives against Győr in 1594 and Eger in 1596) assumed proportions normally associated with full-scale imperial warfare. For much of the period following Süleyman's conquests the Ottomans were able to achieve their restricted political objectives – confined essentially to protecting the status of central Hungary as a buffer zone offering protection against further Habsburg expansion to the east – by the selective application of limited force. At the conclusion of Europe's Thirty Years' War (1618–48), during which the Ottomans had remained steadfastly neutral, the House of Austria entered a phase of their history which was to be dominated by post-war reconstruction efforts and confrontational politics, leading to a series of internal disturbances and local uprisings reaching crisis proportions during the decades between 1650 and 1680. Many historians agree in labelling this period the Habsburg "time of troubles".[3] During that period the Habsburgs were too distracted by wars on the western front (against France between 1672 and 1679) or internally (against the *kuruc* rebels in Hungary), or with both together, to mobilize the resources necessary to mount a serious attempt at dislodging the Ottomans from their well-entrenched positions in central Hungary. In the same period the Ottomans were in fact able to capitalize on such distractions, and between 1660 and 1664 undertook a serious offensive of their own aimed simultaneously against Transylvania in the east and Slovakia in the north. But at this time the Habsburgs were not prepared to become embroiled in a prolonged struggle in defence of their interests in Central Europe and a treaty was rapidly concluded at Vasvár in August 1664.

Local skirmishes, small-scale conflicts, the typical pattern of *klein krieg* did occur on a fairly regular basis during large parts of the extended period of general military quiescence that ensued after the death of Süleyman in 1566 and lasted until the resumption of full-scale war in 1683. But it would be a great mistake to judge the normal code and practice in Austria-Ottoman warfare across the whole period 1500 to 1700 by the yardstick set during the mass mobilizations of the mid-sixteenth century when the Ottomans were gearing up for their permanent installation in Hungary, or during the closing decades of the seventeenth century when they were pitted against a daunting international coalition of forces. Vigorous prosecution of war in the Central European theatre was (for both sides) a secondary priority during much of the period under study. From the Ottoman perspective the limited objective of maintaining the *status quo* in Hungary could be achieved by deployment of provincial forces.

Except in unusual circumstances the conduct of war and diplomacy in Central Europe after 1606 was left to the judgement and means of the

Ottoman governors of Buda. Mass mobilization armies led against the Austrian frontier by even a grand vezier, let alone the sultan, became a rarity in the seventeenth century. The typical pattern of engagement was rather the small-scale border raid which resulted in the exchange of minor forts or ended without substantial change to the existing border configuration. The confrontation of provincial units and of local forces mustered from several semi-contiguous border garrisons along a limited sector of the frontier and directed against a more important, temporarily vulnerable, fortress could also be organized locally without calling for input from outside sources. Prolonged encounters involving upwards of 40,000 combatants on either side involved central planning and finance, whereas brief clashes between local militias numbering some 6,000–8,000 on either side could easily be undertaken through local initiative. For example, the force mobilized by Toygun Pasha, the Ottoman governor of Buda, to subdue the stronghold of Fülek (Filákovo) in 1554 is described by reliable contemporary sources as consisting of only 3,000 of his own provincial forces, expanded to a total figure of no more than 8,000 with contributions from county commanders and castelans in nearby districts.[4] The escalation of such local conflicts into regional and occasionally international disputes depended on the favourable conjunction of political events and the reaching of a consensus among leading members of the *divan*. To think of the Ottomans' waging of war as a fulfilment of "the inherently bellicose character of the Turkish state"[5] greatly exaggerates the power of the state in this period. It is not at all clear either that the state possessed a monopoly on the use of military force or that they could always successfully channel and control the performance of those forces they did possess. How troops actually performed in battle involved a complex matrix of physical and psychological factors which we will examine more thoroughly in later chapters (see especially Chapter 2 on physical constraints and Chapter 7 on motivation and morale in the Ottoman army). In this chapter we confine ourselves to a consideration of political conditions and the role they played in determining the scale, intensity and duration of Ottoman warfare. Our survey analysis applies most particularly to the empire's two main land fronts on its eastern and western borders.

War on the Eastern Front

The prospect of ideological warfare aimed at the extinction of the enemy and complete absorption of his territories arose early in the sixteenth century, not as an objective of Ottoman war against the Christian infidel, but rather in the context of the Ottomans' relations with their heterodox Muslim neighbours in the East. During the eight-and-a-half-year reign of Selim I between 1512 and 1520 a hardline policy on religious conformity was for a time implemented, but the ferocity of Selim's attack against Iran in 1514 was conditioned in part by domestic considerations as well as his worries, still not fully resolved after two years on the throne, about the security of his succession. Selim's policies were repudiated, and eventually largely forgotten during the forty seven-and-a-half-year reign of his son and successor Süleyman.[6] By the time of the Treaty of Amasya (May 1555) the two sides had reached a mutual understanding concerning their respective zones of influence. The resumption of conflict after this date can be traced to a failure (by one side or the other) to observe the spirit of the Amasya agreements, which had placed Iraq (the southern perimeter) in the Ottoman zone of influence and Azerbaijan (the northern perimeter) in the Safavid zone of influence. The Ottoman offensive of 1578 aimed at the northern perimeter was timed to coincide with a period of severe internal turmoil and weakness within the Safavid state under the rule of Muhammad Khudabanda (1578–88). The removal (in 1555) of the Safavid capital from Tabriz at the heart of the area contested with the Ottomans to Qazwin midway between the Safavids' eastern and western military borders in Khurasan and Azerbaijan was a first step in the demilitarization of the area. These realities were only partially and impermanently altered by the Ottoman onslaught between 1578 and 1590. The re-removal (in 1597) of the capital from Qazwin to Isfahan served further to accentuate the Safavids' shifting of emphasis away from the priorities and security concerns of their northwestern frontier. From this date, especially after the recapture by Abbas I of the region's two main strongholds at Tabriz in 1603 and Erivan in 1604, the sub-Caucasian frontier between the two empires remained fairly quiet. The failed siege against Erivan in 1616 and Murad IV's "capture" of the fortress in 1635 both had the same net result: minimal impact on existing arrangements.[7]

In the seventeenth century the centre of gravity in the Safavid state shifted decisively and permanently south. The Ottoman offensives in Mesopotamia mounted in 1624, 1629–30 and 1638 were aimed simply at restoring the former balance of power in the region, which had been upset by the defection of the Ottoman garrison at Baghdad to the Safavids in 1623 during a period of Ottoman dynastic crisis. Since both Ottoman prestige and their commercial position in the Persian Gulf were linked with the retention of Baghdad as a base of operations, Sultan Murad IV (r. 1623–40) made its recapture a top priority of foreign policy, a concentration of effort that was made feasible by the embroilment of Christian Europe in internal wars of its own between

1618 and 1648. A restoration of equilibrium between the Ottomans and Safavids was achieved by the Treaty of Zuhab (Qasr-i Shirin) in May 1639, and its essential terms remained in force not just for the remainder of the century but until Mahmud Ghalzay's invasions from the east staged between 1719 and 1722 brought about the fall of the Safavid dynasty itself.[8]

The general trajectory of Ottoman-Safavid relations during the 220 years between 1502 and 1722 when their dynastic paths intersected was governed by a spirit of compromise and mutual recognition. The exceptions to this rule during the reigns of Selim I (1512–20) and Murad III (1574–95) and, to a lesser extent, Murad IV (1623–40) were the result of exceptional political circumstances and attempts to capitalize on fleeting opportunities. Such conditions were too ephemeral to provide a solid basis for the extension of Ottoman rule into Azerbaijan or beyond the Caspian. It is in the eastern theatre that we can see most clearly the limits of Ottoman warfare. If the distance of march, the inhospitable character of the terrain and the severity of climatic conditions were not in themselves sufficient to undermine the troops' determination to win at all costs, there was the added discouragement of negative Muslim public opinion. Although under exceptional circumstances the Ottoman ulema were willing to cooperate in the anathemizing of the heterodox "redhead" (kizilbash) supporters of the Safavids, a policy of continuous war against neighbouring Muslim states was unlikely to be sanctioned by them or, even with their sanction, to receive much popular support among the rank-and-file of the Ottoman army. Thus, if the conducting of "total war" on the western front was unnecessary (because of the internal divisions – both religious and dynastic – within the Christian camp during the era of the Reformation) restraint on the eastern front was dictated by the consideration that total war against a Muslim state was either undesirable or unthinkable. The use of military force against Muslim co-religionists to resolve specific disputes or to enforce treaty terms might be justified, but wars of conquest were another matter.

Large mobilizations such as those ordered and led by Murad IV in 1635 (against Erivan) and 1638 (against Baghdad), each involving in excess of 100,000 troops, made a symbolic show of Ottoman might, but neither of these armies remained very long in the field.[9] The historian Katib Chelebi who was present in the Ottoman army during Murad's offensive against Erivan in 1635 openly admits that, although the sultan managed to stage an impressive troop inspection at Ilica (15 km west of Erzurum) in July, only a small proportion of these forces remained at the sultan's side a month later when Erivan was put to the siege.[10] Because of the relative quiet on other fronts during the 1630s Murad was able to commit unprecedented manpower resources and treasury funds to his eastern wars. But his very successes only

5

served to reveal the vulnerability of the Ottomans' position, especially in the northern perimeter of the frontier. For a variety of reasons and most particularly because of the costs involved (see below, Chapter 3: Military Manpower and Spending) the Ottomans could manage such full-scale mobilizations for war in the East only once or twice per century. Murad's record-breaking feat of mounting back-to-back sultanic campaigns in 1635 and 1638 was so exceptional as to inspire the construction of matching commemorative pavilions in the Topkapi Palace compound at Istanbul.

War on the Western Front

European awareness of the Ottoman empire far predates the sixteenth century, and certain dramatic events such as the fall of Constantinople in 1453 and the Ottoman landing in the southern Italian peninsula at Otranto in 1480 could hardly be ignored. But, until the fall of Belgrade in 1521 (followed by Rhodes in 1522), the Ottomans remained a remote and somewhat academic concern for most of Europe. It was current events of the 1520s that sparked a retrospective interest in the earlier history of the Ottomans, reflected in works such as that published in 1528 by the Florentine Andrea Cambini on the origins of the dynasty.[11] Thereafter, the actual and potential military strength of the Ottoman empire became a lasting concern of the West. Venice in particular stood in awe of the sultan (*Gran Signor*)'s huge, by contemporary Western standards, reserves.[12] Such impressions of Ottoman military might were reinforced by image makers in the service of the Ottoman court who gave graphic demonstration of Ottoman invincibility in richly illustrated campaign histories commissioned by the sultan. Sultan Süleyman I (r. 1520–66) was the first Ottoman sultan to self-consciously produce a detailed pictorial record of his military achievements, thus ensuring the permanency of his legacy of greatness.[13] The reality of Ottoman military involvement in Europe during the sixteenth, and even more so in the seventeenth century, was less orderly than either the contemporary European or the artfully-presented Ottoman accounts would have us believe. Both accounts present the profile of the Ottoman army at maximum strength, mobilized for "great" campaigns and led by the sultan in person.

It is worth remembering that the outbreak of war was not always or only the result of sultanic initiative. As an example of the sometimes haphazard quality of Ottoman warfare in the European theatre the chain of events leading to the declaration of war on Austria in 1593 is particularly instructive. Starting from the summer of 1592 the Ottoman governor of Bosnia had already begun his own private war against the Croatian frontier by subduing the fortress of Bihac after an eight-day siege,[14] and constructing a new fortress at Petrinja on the southern bank of the Kulpa river facing the Croatian stronghold of Sisak on the opposite bank. Acting thus far only with provincial forces at his disposal and without open approval or assistance from the capital, Hasan Pasha's attacks, while a serious provocation, fell short of being an irreparable rupture of the peace. On the other hand, the dispatching of imperial troops from other provinces in support of such frontier raiding with the clear authorization of the Grand Vezier left no room for ambiguity about Ottoman intentions.[15] One of Koca Sinan Pasha's first acts upon his return (for the third time) to the Grand Vezierate in January 1593 was to appoint his son Mehmed commander-general of the Rumelian troops with responsibility for directing (and expanding) the attacks already under way against the Croatian frontier. Apart from providing the Austrians with advance warning of Ottoman mobilization plans, this achieved little, and the fall of Sisak to Mehmed Pasha in September 1593[16] was soon reversed by an enemy counter-offensive.[17] Thus, by the autumn of 1593, a condition of open war existed between the two sides that was not anticipated, nor yet very enthusiastically supported by wider court circles on either side of the conflict. The war that had begun in 1592 as the private war of Hasan Pasha was continued in 1593 as the personal war of the recently re-installed Grand Vezier whose judgement in embracing and whose competence for successful prosecution of the war were openly challenged.[18] During the gradual escalation from reciprocal border raids to open war over the 30-month period between July 1591 and the closing months of 1593 the burden of Ottoman defence fell heavily on the border districts,[19] and it was not before the summer of 1594 when Koca Sinan Pasha's offensive against Györ took shape that the Ottomans were able to mobilize a force of sufficient size to pursue the war with conviction. The Ottomans' unpreparedness for full-scale war in Hungary after more than two decades of relative inactivity in the north can be measured by the fact that, as late as May–June 1594 when the Austrians launched a determined assault against the Ottoman stronghold of Esztergom (measured, in traditional narrative style, as a "seventeen hundred shot siege"),[20] the only reinforcements the Ottomans could muster were 2,000 border guards and horse grazers (*voynuk*) from the frontier provinces of Semendire (Smederovo) and Bosnia who, soon after their arrival, defected to the enemy.[21]

While the Austro-Ottoman conflict of 1593–1606, also called the "Long War", should not be regarded as typical of Ottoman warfare in Europe, it is noteworthy that both its beginnings and its conclusion were closely connected with spontaneous events at the margins of the Ottoman and Habsburg empires. The Bosnian governor Hasan Pasha's raids against Croatia as the prelude to war in 1591 and Bocskai's rebellion in Transylvania in 1605 – which sparked a civil war in Hungary proper and a general breakdown of order in the Austrian borderlands – as the prelude to a negotiated settlement at Zsitva Torok in November 1606 were events that set off chain reactions, whose consequences and outcomes neither Istanbul nor Vienna could fully control. Such spontaneous events recurred periodically in the frontier lands between the two empires from 1521 onwards, but prevailing political conditions only exceptionally nurtured the unanimity of purpose required for cohesive and sustained military efforts. The halting pace of war in the fifteen years between 1591 and 1605 is one sign that even in periods of formal and declared hostilities such unanimity was not consistently or continuously present.

For their part, the Holy Roman emperors had only a modest number of standing troops they could call their own and relied heavily on units supplied, on a semi-voluntary basis, by the "armed provinces" consisting of (after 1648) the eight electoral states in Germany. Leopold I (r. 1658–1705) managed to coax as many as 34,000 troops from member states to supplement his own forces for an exceptional mobilization against Buda in 1686,[22] but such feats were highly unusual. Wartime mobilizations might temporarily swell the ranks of the standing army, but as late as the period of Montecuccoli's presidency of the Imperial War Council (*Hofkriegsrat*) between 1668 and 1680 the full strength on paper of the imperial army was still no more than 25,000.[23] The deployment of more than 12,000 of these at any given time to any single front was exceptional. If we put the 34,000 loaned troops together with the 12,000 mustered from the emperor's own regiments, the resultant figure comes close to what Montecuccoli had envisaged, remembering always that such numbers represent ideals that were rarely achieved in practice. Big armies, recruited, financed and provisioned from the centre never (as far as warfare in the Central European theatre was concerned) became the norm during the sixteenth and seventeenth centuries. For most of this period the Ottomans faced small "private" armies led (and to a very large extent recruited and even financed) by Hungaro-Croatian magnates of the border districts, such as the Nadasdy, Berceny, Batthany and especially the Zriny clans who themselves possessed extensive lands in the frontier zone and had a vested interest in the protection of their estates.

Accounts of the largest mobilizations and the sieges of key fortresses manned by considerable imperial garrisons which Ottoman sources record in greatest detail describe conflict of a scale and intensity that was by no means the norm. Most conflicts involved combatants numbered not in myriads but thousands. An accurate assessment of the overall scale of conflict will take on particular significance in the context of our analysis in Chapter eight which deals with the impact of Ottoman warfare. It is worth remembering that even when, in the context of wider conflicts, single campaigns might involve larger numbers of combatants, these were mounted against specific military targets and not directed in the form of free-ranging attacks against a wider territory. For purposes of comparison it may, therefore, be useful if we pause now to examine in some detail the political and financial context of the late seventeenth-century wars of the "Sacred Alliance" (*Sacra Ligua*). Once it is better understood how truly exceptional these wars were, we will be in a better position to judge the differences between international conflicts of that sort and the more localized pattern of single-front and single-adversary wars which predominated during most of the period from 1520 to 1680.

Wars of the Sacred Alliance, 1684–99

In the decades preceding the Ottomans' attempted siege of Vienna in 1683 Ottoman armies had successfully prosecuted single-front wars in Hungary (the sieges of Varad [Oradea] in 1660 and Uyvar [N. Zamky] in 1663), Crete (the siege of Candia [Heraklion] between 1667 and 1669], Poland (the siege of Kamanice [Kamanetz-Podolsk] in 1672 and Russia (the siege of Çehrin [Chyhyryn] in 1678). In each instance, when confronting a new technical challenge, the Ottomans had built upon their growing experience in siege warfare – accumulated in a variety of different theatres of war – to achieve success. Against Vienna itself in 1683 the Ottomans earned praise from Western observers for the efficacy and proficient engineering of their siege works.[24] On the political front, even as the Ottoman army was still massed in the vicinity of his capital, Leopold received word that France had mounted an invasion against the Spanish Netherlands with 35,000 troops,[25] and this force was soon expanded to 75,000 by the addition of 26,000 foot and 14,000 horse.[26] A flurry of diplomatic activity in the immediate aftermath of Vienna's eleventh-hour rescue, through the timely intervention of troops mobilized by extraordinary levies and led by senior commanders such as Charles Duke of Lorraine and Jan Sobieski King of Poland, secured France's agreement (at Regensburg in August of 1684)[27] to a 20-year truce with Leopold. But it was a short four years later (in October 1688) that this peace was again irrevocably shattered by France's invasion of the Palatinate. What followed, as far as the efforts of the Sacred Alliance were concerned, was a ten-year postponement (until the Treaty of Ryswick in 1697) of the joint offensive aimed at a permanent removal of the Ottoman presence in Hungary. Thus, even in the late seventeenth century, when the most serious and

9

best-supported war effort yet attempted against the Ottomans was finally realized, backed by generous war subsidies from Pope Innocent XI,[28] the Ottomans found themselves in a number of important campaigns (from the recapture of Belgrade in 1690 to the battle of Cenei in August 1696)[29] pitted against armies whose ranks had been seriously reduced by troop requirements on competing war fronts.[30]

The very fact that a league such as the *Sacra Ligua* was formed was itself a significant departure in seventeenth-century diplomatic practice. Venice, placing a priority on the defence of its commercial interests in the Levant, had remained mostly aloof from earlier attempts to create a strong anti-Ottoman coalition. Even after they and other semi-reluctant partners such as Poland had been persuaded to join, effective co-ordination of effort and concentration of resources was not easily achieved during the sixteen years of the League's existence between 1684 and 1699. Throughout this period the Ottomans continued to fight what were, practically speaking, separate wars against the four diplomatically-allied but effectively isolated powers: Venice, Austria, Poland and Russia. The Ottomans managed for the most part to confine the heaviest fighting to a single theatre at a time. Yet, despite the relative absence – with the exception of a brief Russian foray in 1687 and Selim Giray's successful defence of Or-Kapi (Perekop) in 1689 – of significant activity on the eastern front in the early phases of the war, Russia's membership in the alliance was enough in itself to discourage active participation of Tatar forces in the Ottoman defence of Hungary.[31] Thus, at precisely the point when the Ottomans faced what was – on land at least – an unprecedented quadripartite offensive alliance, they were deprived of their traditional source of auxiliary support which under "normal" circumstances would have ensured the active participation of between 40,000 and 100,000 Tatar troops.[32] Whatever the precise nature of the Ottoman ups and downs during a particular phase of the wars which stretched over the whole of the last decade and a half of the century, there is no doubt that the cumulative effect of the three-front war in the Aegean, Central Europe and the Northern shores of the Black Sea left the Ottomans exhausted.

Given the fluidity of the tactical as well as diplomatic situation faced by the Ottomans during the wars of the Sacred Alliance, it seems apparent that what most affected the Ottomans' position in Central Europe as the principal theatre of war at the close of the seventeenth century was not military, and still less technological, advances among Western European armies that left them lagging behind,[33] but shifting diplomatic patterns that forced them to confront a better-organized and financed, as well as more determined, adversary (or group of adversaries) than ever before in their century and a half as a fully-established power beyond the Danube. What had changed in Europe circa

1685 was that individual, entrepreneurial and private and semi-private initiative in the military sphere had begun to be replaced by collective action on a hitherto unprecedented scale.

It is both futile and methodologically unsound to indulge too much in speculation about the "what ifs" of the Ottomans' military and strategic position in the closing years of the seventeenth century or, with specific reference to the Vienna defeat, to speculate whether or not they should have foreseen the military consequences of Poland's last-minute participation in the pan-European alliance. It is, nonetheless, worth noting that the revival of the Sacred Alliance (which had by necessity lain dormant for much of the ten-year period during the war between Leopold I and Louis XIV in Flanders) after 1697 was by no means a foregone or inevitable conclusion. The century had provided plenty of other examples of the disintegration of such seemingly powerful leagues before they had fully achieved their purpose. The characteristic pattern of warfare in the period between 1566 and 1683 before the era of the Sacred Alliance had been one dominated by localized conflicts, small-scale engagements and the conduct of battle using fairly conventional methods. This scale and these methods had proved adequate to the task of confronting a Europe which was both politically and religiously divided through much of the post-Reformation era. The revocation of the Edict of Nantes in 1685 and the launching by a united Europe of a "Last Crusade"[34] inaugurated a new era in East-West relations that saw the Ottomans adopt an increasingly non-interventionist stance in European affairs. While the late seventeenth-century swing of the pendulum in Europe towards greater religious solidarity was by no means permanent, it served as a defining moment in the Ottomans' reappraisal of their position as a trans-Danubian military power.

To fill out our picture of the state of the art of Ottoman and European warfare in the sixteenth and seventeenth centuries, we turn our attention now to a description of the nature of "conventional warfare" (see above) and an assessment of the limits of the possible in the pre-Carlowitz era.

Chapter Two

Material constraints on Ottoman warfare: the immutable context

Some of the ways in which the changing political and diplomatic environment might sometimes impinge on the actual practice of Ottoman warfare were explained in the previous chapter. As the corollary to our treatment of the execution of (or resistance to) the sovereign's will, before we proceed to a discussion of the available means for the prosecution of wars, we should consider some general characteristics of the task itself. In the present chapter we will examine, in brief and introductory fashion, five constant variables that always played a role in shaping the course of Ottoman campaigns. While their effects might be mitigated, they could never entirely be escaped. The general constraints under which the Ottoman army operated are often forgotten or glossed over in accounts which consider the state's very being to have been bound up with its ambition for world conquest.[1] While it is certainly the case that the Ottomans were capable of mobilizing large armies, it is important to remember that size alone was not enough to guarantee success in military enterprise. *Five* contributory factors influenced in varying proportions Ottoman military performance in actual deployments: technological constraints; cost constraints; physical barriers and environmental constraints; motivational limits; limits of state power and coercion.

The limits of the possible for the Ottoman army were not noticeably different from those of other European armies of the time.[2] While we will need to consider most of these again in later chapters in greater detail, their combined weight and determining influence will be clearer if we explore some of their interconnections here.

Technological constraints

The use of the term "gunpowder empire" to characterize the Ottoman state has gained considerable, though arguably undeserved, currency in recent years.[3] A periodization that posits a causal link between the rise of the Ottoman state in the fourteenth and early fifteenth centuries and technological discovery, or between its demise in later centuries and technological atrophy places altogether too much confidence in the decisive effect, as well as the general reliability, of the weaponry broadly available in those centuries. While the Ottomans certainly knew of guns and gunnery and were able to deploy them effectively from the earliest stages of their imperium, they shared such capabilities with a number of contemporary states. In both the early and middle centuries of their state's existence between 1400 and 1700 guns remained an essential but in themselves insufficient part of the Ottomans' formula for military success. Although much is sometimes made of the innovations in gun design and in particular improvements made to standard firing mechanisms, the technology, because it was both relatively unsophisticated and at the same time readily transferable, gave no decisive strategic advantage to either the Ottomans or any of their usual adversaries. The maximum effective range of seventeenth-century field guns was, under optimal conditions, only some 200 to 300 metres.[4] The heavier siege guns had to be positioned almost on top of their targets in order to inflict any significant damage. Achieving this optimal position took weeks of careful preparation and was frequently, even with the most thorough of preparations, unachievable. Apart from such considerations, which in themselves were sufficient to ensure that the concentration by the attackers of overwhelming firepower was an unlikely event, there were the related questions of the standard of production and the inherent instability and perishability of gunpowder itself.

Without adequate quantities of high-quality and well-stored and preserved gunpowder the effectiveness of the guns was in any case negated. Achieving optimal results even from state-of-the-art weaponry was thus not just a matter of design, but highly contingent on the expertise in pyrotechnical matters and familiarity with metallurgical principles of those who were charged with their use.[5] Because of the decentralized nature of gunpowder production scattered between a number of locations throughout the empire from Buda to Konya, maintaining a consistent standard, both in terms of raw materials and quality of production, was virtually impossible.[6] But, perhaps even more critical than issues related to standards of production, was the question of the safe storage and transport of ready powder. The "shelf-life" of powder even under optimal storage conditions was limited, as is indicated by the existence of separate accounting categories used in Ottoman arsenal inventories for new and old powder.[7] Once the powder left central storage magazines to be transported for use on various fronts, the risks of its acquiring post-manufacture defects was still considerable. Even if the powder was transported overland in mostly dry weather conditions, the fording of rivers – an unavoidable fact of operational life in all possible theatres of war – presented a serious obstacle to the safe arrival of enough good powder to sustain consistent fire in the critical initial phase of siege. One example from the failed siege of Baghdad in 1630 shows how even a momentary lapse of attention during the fording of a minor river was enough to jeopardize the army's chances of success in a major mobilization.[8]

The reason for mentioning these vulnerabilities and inconsistencies connected with the technology of artillery warfare in the mid-to-late seventeenth century is to underline the fact that, whatever potential advantages were conferred by the possession of superior weaponry, this potential was rarely realized in full under actual conditions of use because of the interference of contingent circumstances. These might include adverse weather conditions, road accidents which led either to damage or delay in the delivery of ammunition, or other unforeseen obstacles.

Improvements in the design and construction of fortresses that were introduced in phases after the mid-sixteenth century played a further role in reducing the destructive potential both of cannon and standard mining techniques but, as will be discussed below (see below: Cost constraints), the expense of introducing these improvements removed in terms of the everyday practice of warfare any theoretical advantage such improvements might have conferred. Several of the fortresses, newly constructed or thoroughly upgraded to conform with the "modern style" and considered by then-current standards virtually impregnable, still succumbed in the face of determined Ottoman attack.[9] Overall the Ottomans kept pace with advances in military technology throughout the period 1500 to 1700 and in some areas (such as sapping and mining) emerged as standard-setters in their own right.[10] While the debate over the relative position in advancing technology of the Ottomans and their European contemporaries circa 1700 continues, the current consensus is that no serious divergence of methods and standards applied until after 1680.[11] During the period 1500–1700 both the Ottoman empire and the West demonstrated a marked continuity of practice, and very little perceptible, let alone rapid or transformatory, change was taking place. For virtually the whole period under study here the Ottomans maintained an enviable position both in terms of the weaponry deployed and the battlefield methods employed.[12] As was demonstrated during the siege of Buda by a coalition of Christian forces in 1686, success in siege might hinge on a lucky strike as much as it did on the predictability or accuracy of the siege guns.[13] Conversely, in other campaigns, progress to the final phase of siege was often halted by failure of land mines to detonate at the expected times.[14] In sum, it can be said that the technology employed by both sides was imperfect and fallible. Limits on the reliability of even the best grades of weaponry were such that the tactical advantage to be gained from superior hardware remained largely theoretical. In seventeenth-century warfare military equipment had not yet acquired anything like the same importance and determining influence on the outcome of battle as it later did in the era of modern warfare.

Cost constraints

The second fact limiting the scope of activities and level of performance achieved by pre-modern armies was expense. Although for most of the sixteenth century Ottoman treasury surpluses were successfully maintained,[15] the combined effects of increasing shortage of specie following the silver devaluation of 1586, and changes in the style of warfare dictating a heavier reliance on cash-paid, permanent, standing infantry troops as opposed to land-based, seasonally-mobilized, timariot cavalry made it increasingly difficult for the Ottomans to keep general state and, more particularly, centrally-disbursed military expenditure within sustainable bounds. Tables 2.1 and 2.2 show the growing importance both numerically and fiscally of infantry forces in the seventeenth-century Ottoman military.

One formula for limiting military expenditure that had been successfully applied in the sixteenth century was to restrict central treasury disbursements

Table 2.1[1] Increase in Janissary ranks shown as a proportion of all salaried staff

Date	Janissaries	Total salaried personnel	Proportion Janissaries (%)
1527	7,886[2]	24,146	32.7
1609	39,282	91,202	43.1
1660	53,849[3]	98,342	54.8

[1] Figures for 1527 and 1660 are taken from the budgets published by Barkan in *Ikitisat Fakultesi Mecmuasi* [IFM] XV (1953–4) and XVII (1955–6). The figures for 1609 are supplied in Ayn-i Ali's *Risale-i Vazife-Horan* (Istanbul, 1280), p. 88. According to Ayn-i Ali only 37,627 men were actives. The remaining 1,655 were sons (orphans) or retired or deceased members of the corps who were given minimal allowances and wages during their training for full inclusion in the corps. Because they were entitled to a bread ration they were called *nan-khwaran*, i.e. "eaters of the [daily] loaf".
[2] Just after the close of Süleyman's reign (by 1567) Janissary enrolment had dramatically increased to 12,798 men. See Barkan, IFM XIX: p. 305.
[3] Of these, 39,470 were barracked in Istanbul and the remaining 14,379 were assigned to provincial garrison duty; see Barkan, IFM XVII: pp. 263–4.

Table 2.2[1] Increase in salary payments to the Janissaries shown as a proportion of total salary payments

Date	Janissaries' wages	Total salary payments	Proportion Janissaries (%)
1527	15,423,426	65,882,938	23.4
1609	100,899,146	310,827,412	32.5
1660	133,424,896	285,905,688	46.6

[1] The sources for the data are same as in Table 2.1.

for the navy to a small proportion of general defence expenditure. Figures supplied by Ayn-i Ali for 1609 indicate that naval personnel accounted for only three per cent of manpower and four per cent of salary payments for the armed services borne by the central treasury.[16] For a contemporary European context we learn that the cost to France of waging land wars against the Protestants in the 1620s represented roughly one-half of all state revenues from direct taxation.[17] Because of the greater cost of equipment in naval wars, even apart from personnel considerations, land wars always represented the smaller burden. The French example, furthermore, represents an under-estimation of real costs, since in foreign wars transport and provisioning costs were at much higher levels. That the Ottomans were able through much of the sixteenth century to wage a semi-continuous series of land wars without heavy reliance on exceptional levies and campaign contributions was due in part to the absence of competing resource commitments within the central fisc for the waging of sea battles. In the sixteenth century cost-containment in the naval sphere was achieved through the co-optation by the imperial fleet based in Istanbul of corsair freelancers whose fleets operated out of Algiers, Tunis and Tripoli. The large armadas mobilized on both sides of the Mediterranean in the sixteenth century were the result of multi-party collaborative effort representing the combined capacity of privately-operated and state-subsidized fleets. By contrast, in the seventeenth century a growing share of the burden and expense of activism in the naval sphere was being borne by the state and taxpayers in the core provinces, especially western Anatolia.[18] Under exceptional circumstances the sixteenth-century fleet mobilizations of strategic importance for the Ottomans war-ranted treasury subsidy, but the short-term effect of such subsidies was to annihilate all surpluses accumulated by the treasury and curtail the Ottomans' readiness to mobilize quickly for land campaigns. As an example, it is estimated in contemporary Western sources that the cost to the Ottomans of outfitting the fleet sent to aid their French allies in 1543 was 1.2 million ducats, equivalent at current rates of exchange to 72 million akçes.[19] Ottoman treasury figures for that period show regular income of 198.9 million akçes against expenditure of 112 millions, leaving a positive balance of 86.9 million akçes.[20] But even under such comfortable balance of payments conditions as this, naval activity on any scale in successive years represented an unsustainable burden to the treasury. In the mid-seventeenth century a significant proportion of fleet expenses was met from off-budget sources and extraordinary levies.[21]

Another dimension of state military expenditure which, like the maintaining of a credible naval deterrent, formed an indispensable part of overall provision, involved both initial and ongoing costs for fortress construction and repair. Quite apart from the increased manpower demands and garrison forces' wage costs implied by Ottoman expansion into a new theatre of war, the cost of erecting the defensive shield itself was considerable. In the sixteenth and also in the seventeenth century the standard of construction for many of the forts both along the European frontier and in the East was relatively primitive: most consisted of little more than earthen ramparts reinforced by timber which could easily be set ablaze.[22] The construction of more elaborate, state-of-the art fortresses of stone masonry required not just the means, men and opportunity but also generous amounts of time. Regional strongholds such as Mosul, suitable for the safe storage and stockpiling of ammunition and other military equipment, had to be built to the highest standard, and for practical reasons ambitious construction projects were timed to coincide with the presence of the Ottoman army in a region.[23] The concentration of workmen, army engineers and a ready supply of funds at the commander's disposition all made it possible to complete the task with a minimum of delay. On another occasion when the army had been mobilized for an Eastern campaign in 1588 the army was able to complete an extensive overhaul of the 6,000 ells (approx. 2.8 miles) of wall surrounding the fortress of Ganja during a 40-day lull in the fighting between late August and mid-October.[24] But the completion of fortress construction and reconstruction work on this kind of scale, especially on the remoter frontiers, was possible only under exceptional circumstances. The distances between Ottoman supply bases in the interior and points along its military frontier with Safavid Iran were daunting enough in themselves, but the real obstacle to continuous state commitment to the improvement of its border defences was financial. The historian Ali notes that during the winter of 1584-5 alone sums amounting to a million akçes were expended to improve the defences of Erzurum, which was situated in a secure area a hundred miles inland from the active military frontier marked by the cluster of smaller fortresses concentrated around the Aras river boundary.[25]

On the Western borders of the empire the situation was similar. Writing of the period before the Ottoman victory at Mohacs in 1526, local Christian sources relate that in the absence of adequate state finance, the repair of strategic border fortresses proceeded only as far and as fast as the generosity of local patrons would take it.[26] Beginning in 1522, formal arrangement for a more cohesive[27] and better funded[28] frontier defence network had already begun, but available evidence suggests that these changes made little immediate difference at the local level and defence arrangements continued to rely heavily on local initiative.[29] The state's reliance on local initiative and input for the maintaining of border defences was not confined to Central Europe. In Western Europe too the formidable expense represented by the sudden need to conform to a new style of fortification meant that, here too, improvements were introduced so gradually that what emerged was a "medieval–early modern hybrid" rather than comprehensively redesigned and rebuilt structures.[30] Confirming the slow pace of progress, Gabriel de Guilleragues, French ambassador in Istanbul in the early 1680s, expressed his opinion of the Habsburg fortifications of his time which he said still *"resembled the [antiquated] French forts of Loches and Amboise"*.[31] For the Ottomans too fiscal realities dictated that only a few key strategic fortresses such as Belgrade, Buda and Esztergom could be fully staffed and maintained.[32] For the rest it was a question of moving men and material from one sector of the front to another when a threat developed.

A dispassionate assessment of the Ottomans' situation – whether in the spheres of naval activism and military construction reviewed above or in terms of their general strategic position – reveals that even in the sixteenth and seventeenth centuries, regarded as an unsurpassed era of prosperity and imperial success, the Ottomans had to prioritize, make choices and use their resources carefully. Rightly regarded as precocious by comparison with its European contemporaries because of its possession of a centrally-funded permanent standing army and an elaborate system for army provisioning, the Ottoman state still fell far short of an ability to exercise limitless military power, being always and inescapably confined to the fiscally possible. How far the state was willing or able to stretch the limits of the possible was tested in the seventeenth century, first in the Cretan war with Venice, whose indeterminate character and slow development over the quarter century between 1645 and 1669 was closely connected with resource problems, and later in the pan-European conflict with the forces of the *Sacra Ligua* between 1684 and 1699. Such wars of attrition were noted by contemporary observers as a particular Ottoman strongpoint[33] but, as the outcome of the Ottomans' second serial war of the late seventeenth century showed, even they had a breaking point.

19

Physical barriers and environmental constraints

Ottoman warfare in the seventeenth century – and even more so in the sixteenth century when the timariot forces made up the bulk of the army – was limited by the cyclically repeating pattern of the seasons. While conditions might vary between regions, out-of-season campaigning was generally avoided, not just by tradition, but because the logic that confined the efficient movement of men and animals on a mass scale to particular times of the year was irresistible. While the intense summer heat of Iraq required alteration of the usual pattern and dictated preference for winter campaigning in that sector,[34] the normal pattern of warfare in most theatres of war required strict adherence to a fixed timetable. The beginning of the campaigning season coincided with the growing season for crops (especially grass), and the onset of winter – when food and forage became not just less plentiful, but also very expensive – marked the conclusion of mass military activity in an equally definitive way. Fixed astronomical events such as the vernal equinox on 21 March which signalled the usual commencement of the pasturing season in the pastoral calendar and the autumnal equinox on 22 September which coincided with the harvest season for agrarian communities were events not just of ceremonial, but far more so of practical, significance for men at arms.

Throughout the period up to the end of the sixteenth century the composition of Ottoman armies (even without their Tatar and other auxiliaries who were accustomed to attend campaign with several spare mounts in tow) was characterized by a three- or even a four-to-one ratio of cavalry to infantry. This meant that the movement and deployment of any significant proportion of the total potential force was closely linked to the supply of forage for the horses. This link is made explicit in an anonymous Ottoman account of the battle of Varna in 1444 in which a speech attributed to the military leaders of the Christian coalition worried about the advance of the Ottoman host contains the following words:

> The Turk keeps constant watch for the appearance of the first grass shoots in Spring. As soon as the grass springs from the earth he will close the gap and be upon us.[35]

While there were some slight variations due to differences between the lunar and solar and Muslim and Christian calendars, the significant dates affecting army mobilization and demobilization were Hizir Ilyas Günü (corresponding to St George's Day on 23 April [O.S.]/3 May [N.S.]) and the Ruz-I Kasim (corresponding to St Demetrius' Day on 26 October [O.S.]/5 November [N.S.]). For military purposes these dates formed the two demarcation points around which all army activities were habitually organized. The first call to arms came at the vernal equinox which preceded the Day of Hizir by 40 days, but troops were by custom allowed April as a period of grace before reporting for active duty. This grace period was to be used, however, for the vitally important task of grazing the horses on the vitamin-rich spring grasses.[36] If circumstances demanded, the army's departure for the front could be pushed back to mid-March or forward to later in May, but in the former case this meant only a deferring of delays to a subsequent halting place better suited to the pasturing of the army herds. With regard to the formal closure of the campaigning season in early November there was far less flexibility. Maintaining armed forces (and their mounts) in the field for periods lasting longer than the usual 180 days between early May and late October was impossible, even for the Ottomans who ran a relatively efficient commissariat. The situation as far as the army's foraging requirements was concerned was not affected as dramatically as one might be tempted to think by the changes in the typical composition of the army at the close of the sixteenth century. Even infantry-dominated armies required large numbers of pack horses to carry supplies.[37] The magnitude of these supply requirements dictated an obligatory off-season period of total inactivity lasting at least four and preferably six months. These considerations determined a maximum range of operations that would allow an orderly advance to the front and return to base within a circumscribed time limit.

The nutritional needs of the horses were only part of what limited the army's movement and range of operations. While maximum capabilities of some breeds selected for endurance might, under exceptional circumstances, border on the supernatural,[38] the average walking pace of the horse in moderate terrain and road conditions was no more than three miles per hour. Moreover, the army on campaign encumbered by all its baggage trains could only manage about four and a half hours of march per day. The gradual nature of the army's progress towards its final destinations was perhaps the central factor that limited Ottoman warfare after the mid-sixteenth century since – as a result of the empire's rapid territorial expansion between 1450 and 1550 – all possible destinations were at or near the geographical limit of a single season's march out from and back to either Istanbul or an alternative central gathering point. Although the European theatre was, comparatively speaking, more accessible than the East, movement in the European sphere was hampered by other obstacles such as adverse weather conditions and terrain. Judged from the standpoint of distance alone, as shown in Table 2.3, operations in the East involving the crossing of the whole of Asia Minor required the army to remain on a mobile footing 61 per cent of the time as compared with 44 per cent for operations in the European theatre.

Table 2.3[1] Proportion of army's time spent in rest and march (comparison of European and Asian spheres of operation)

Itinerary for outward march	Days spent in march	Total of hours spent in march	Av. no. of hrs. p. day	Days spent in rest	Total days elapsed	% of time spent in march
Edirne to Esztergom (Europe)	52	231	4.44	67	119	43.7
Üsküdar to Baghdad (Asia)	121	544	4.49	76	197	61.4

[1] Sources for this table are: For Fazil Ahmed Pasha's 1663 itinerary en route to Hungary, a campaign journal copied into the margins of a seventeenth-century copy of Kemal Pasha-zade's *Tevarih-i Al-i Osman* (Vienna, ONB, H.O. 46a), fol. 124a, and for the 1638 Baghdad itinerary, Kara Çelebi-zade Abülaziz Efendi's, *Tevarih-i Feth-i Revan ve Bağdad* (Veliyuddin Library Ms 2424), f. 25a.

Campaigns undertaken to the East were not just physically more arduous: the distances involved made it inevitable that the army would have to remain in the field over two successive seasons. The slash and burn tactic employed by the Safavids to deprive the numerically superior Ottoman forces of their daily sustenance only compounded the difficulties inherent in operations on the empire's remotest and climatically harshest frontier.[39] See map no. 4, p. xiv.

Both distance and other geographical conditions strongly favoured a pattern of Ottoman military involvement oriented to the Balkans and Trans-Danubia in preference to the zone beyond the Euphrates. The limits to Ottoman expansion overland followed a similar logic to that which limited the Ottomans' involvement in wars on the sea in the sixteenth century. A study by Pryor focusing on the Ottomans' presence in the Mediterranean and contingent factors influencing the level of their naval activity has shown conclusively how physical, geographical and environmental constraints imposed by tides, prevailing winds and other natural forces defined the role they were able to play. Although Ottoman intentions in the Mediterranean had been signalled by the conquest of Rhodes in 1522, it was only through a patient and gradual building up of supply bases, especially in the Aegean – a process continued in phases over the course of an entire century between the late 1460s and the fall of Chios in 1566 – that they were able to position themselves to give adequate support to fleet operations in the mid-Mediterranean.[40] According to Pryor's study, position was of equal importance to advanced technology and seamanship in determining the limits of the possible on the sea.

The supply challenge in land wars, because of the exponentially expanded scale of operations, was orders of magnitude greater. According to calculations recorded by Katib Chelebi, a typical Ottoman fleet in the mid-seventeenth century consisted of only 46 vessels (40 galleys and 6 maonas), whose crew complement was 15,800 men, of whom roughly two-thirds (10,500) were oarsmen, and the remainder (5,300) fighters.[41] The numbers of armed soldiers and support staff committed to land wars needed to be in the order of four to five times greater than this. In addition, while at sea each ship tended to operate as a self-contained unit, whereas on land army forces shared a collective destiny. Stormy weather at sea affected the opposing fleets equally, and in extreme conditions forced both sides to retreat to their home bases without giving battle. By contrast, heavy rains or unseasonable weather affected attackers and defenders in siege warfare in disproportionate ways. The effect of unforeseen or freak weather conditions on land campaigns could be dramatic, turning imminent victory into sudden rout. One example of this can be seen in the 1664 campaign season when unforeseeable circumstances overwhelmed the Ottoman army near Szentgotthard (St Gotthard), marring an otherwise unbroken record of battle successes beginning the previous summer with Uyvar's fall to the Ottomans. In late July 1664 the Ottoman army was operating, largely unchallenged, well inside enemy territory northwest of the recently subdued fortress of Zalaegerszeg, in a sector of the frontier defined by the course of the Rába River. In early August, when the river was at its lowest ebb, a considerable Ottoman force was able to ford the river near St Gotthard undelayed by the usual need to pause for the construction of floats and bridges to secure their passage. Conditions at this time allowed the Ottoman vanguard to advance rapidly, but the path of retreat and communication with the main body of the army who remained on the near side of the river was effectively cut off. This position of temporary vulnerability was transformed overnight by exceptional meteorological events into the makings of a military disaster of major proportions. Western sources on the battle of St Gotthard make note of the decisive effect of freak weather conditions in the encounter. Rycaut's commentary includes the following statement:

> As soon as the Turkish army had (. . .) waded over the water, the night following so much rain, and such a deluge came pouring down from the mountains, that the river which was fordable the day before, did now overswell its banks and was not passible without floats and bridges.[42]

Ottoman sources confirm this account in its essential details.[43] The halting of military operations in August rather than October because of the onset of adverse weather conditions was highly unusual, but the underlying problem was endemic to Ottoman warfare in all theatres.

The standard methods for river crossings involved either the construction of semi-permanent structures which were vulnerable to enemy attack, or carrying enough material with the army to construct pontoon bridges at a chosen point or points which could be dismantled and re-used for the next river crossing. In his description of the 1696 campaign, culminating in an Ottoman victory at the battle of Cenei near Temeshvar, the Ottoman historian Nihadî describes how two bridges consisting of 15 pontoons each were erected in the space of three hours to allow the Ottoman forces to cross the Timis river using materials transported on 33 ox carts.[44] Wider rivers required longer bridges, and a year later during the Szenta campaign the bridge built to span the Tisza rested on 83 pontoon supports.[45] Whatever the weather conditions, the fragility and tenuousness of links forged in this manner put the army under serious threat of isolation and ambush. Ottoman accounts of the 1697 Szenta campaign relate that the advance of the forward units of the army only as far as Titel following their departure from the safe base at Belgrade had involved the fording of ten rivers and streams.[46] Each crossing was a slow, deliberate process, and ill-conceived attempts to hasten the army's progress put the flimsily-constructed structures under immediate threat of collapse.

The above discussion shows that, quite apart from the normal and predictable progression of the seasons which tended to confine the performance of certain basic military tasks to specific times of the year, Ottoman military activity was further restricted by the effect of a number of variable factors which differed according to the specific terrain and general operating conditions found in particular regions of the empire. Some areas were impenetrable to land armies because of the wetness of the soil or generally marshy conditions, others because the barrenness and sparseness of the vegetation provided insufficient natural support for the feeding of men and animals. Large tracts of northeastern Hungary, for instance, enjoyed a virtual immunity from attack because of the inhospitable quality of the countryside.[47] In the southern perimeter it was the desert margins, in the east the high peaks and narrow passes of the Georgian and Armenian borderlands, while in the northwest frontier of Hungary it was river boundaries, marshlands and bogs that determined the terrestrial limits within which the Ottomans could project their military power. While through extraordinary feats of will the Ottomans managed sometimes to exceed these limits in order to carry out brief forays, punitive raids or scouting missions into difficult terrain, to move and provision large armies for prolonged campaigning in such extreme environments was beyond Ottoman capabilities.

When they were operating within the radius of their own internal network of imperial supply stations (*menzil-hane*) or within practicable reach of central grain repositories supplied via navigable rivers, the Ottomans were able to support large armies in the field. But extended excursions beyond the confines of this supply system were problematic. Internal Ottoman sources estimate that when on march the sultan's household troops by themselves (excluding all timariot forces) consumed more than 5,100 bushels (5,000 *kiles*) of barley per day in fodder rations alone.[48] While the household troops were less numerous in the sixteenth-century army, available stocks of grain (whether for sale or free distribution as rations) were usually fully depleted by the end of the normal campaigning season.

An idea of the general effect on the soldiery of the usual and predictable end-of season shortages can be gained from the day-journal account of Sultan Süleyman's march to and march back from Vienna in 1529. Over the 89-day period between 6 August (1st Zilhicce 935) and 3 November (1st Rebi I 936) grain prices soared to levels 27 times greater than those prevailing during the early phases of the campaign.[49] Even as the army advanced to the battlefront, its progress was slowed by the search for food and fodder, and the details recorded in reliable contemporary accounts suggest that members of the parties sent out to replenish camp stores rarely returned to base unscathed.[50] Conditions of plenty and scarcity in camp form a constant theme of the campaign itinerary logbook entries. The former condition was rare enough to elicit the celebratory expression: "No one paid any mind to [worries about] God's bounty".[51] In spite of all the care and attention lavished by the Ottomans on ensuring the regularity and predictability of the food supply, especially to their elite troops, grain delivery remained an area of uncertainty and inevitable anxiety. Supply disruptions of varying severity and duration were an inescapable part of military campaigning before the transport revolution of the nineteenth century.

Motivational limits

The Ottomans' Western contemporaries were so impressed with the discipline and valour in battle of the sultan's regular army that they were inclined to attribute Ottoman success to the superhuman efforts of Ottoman soldiers driven, or so they believed, by an irrepressible missionary zeal. Such views still have their modern proponents, who are convinced that Ottoman military success can be explained by the extreme mental concentration inherent to soldiers with a "fanatically pursued mission".[52] While devotion to a higher cause cannot be altogether discounted as a contributory factor, the degree to which religious loyalties actually inspired battlefield performance can be questioned. In an army made up of heterogeneous elements – both devshirme recruits hailing for the most part from the European provinces and timariot forces drawn from diverse backgrounds and some of them recent converts – forms of religious expression and practice spanned the whole spectrum of belief from crypto-Christianism to mainstream Sunnism, and from moderate Bektashism to the more extreme forms of heterodox Muslim sectarian practice. Religion remained a highly personal matter in broadly tolerant Muslim Ottoman society and, as a consequence, shared belief was neither expected nor required for the Ottoman army to function as a cohesive whole. In the main it is best to treat both religion and ideology as present but never predominating influences on Ottoman military practice in the sixteenth and seventeenth centuries.[53] The presumption that the Ottoman soldier's performance was guided principally by physical and material concerns implies no denial of the importance to each individual soldier of spiritual values or the strength and sincerity of religious belief. But ascribing to Ottoman soldiers a paramountcy of spiritual over mundane concerns remains a problematic premise, since much of their observable behaviour contradicted this order of priorities.

Troops, no matter what their level of training, professionalism and discipline, have finite endurance thresholds. Pre-modern armies in a pre-mechanized age were totally dependent on animal and human sources of power. When either the men or their mounts were deprived of adequate food or water supply or subjected to extremes of winter cold and summer heat, the whole body of the army rapidly became dysfunctional. In addition to these physical limits there were the psychological and motivational ones. Underpaid, underappreciated soldiers rapidly lost morale, and if conditions were right did not hesitate to rebel against their commanders or withdraw their co-operation in subtler ways. Ottoman soldiers were intrinsically no more dedicated, loyal or obedient than their counterparts in the West; individually each had a limit of stamina and a physical breaking point. Psychologically and collectively, too, they could only perform their duties when they received what, in their view and perception, constituted proper recognition, reward or compensation in some accepted form for their efforts. The expectation of recognition in the form of salary promotions (terakki) and cash bonuses (bahşiş) for members of the regular army, and of booty and spoils (ganimet) for irregular and auxiliary forces was an in-built part of the Ottoman system of incentives for military service. If promises were broken or expectations unmet, troop morale was perceptibly affected. The promising and the awarding of specific rewards for specific services was the most powerful motivating tool any commander possessed. For example, we know that on the eve of the Ottoman assault on the walls of Vienna in 1529 the sultan announced his intention to grant a generous reward to the first soldier to breach the enemy defences and enter within the city walls. If the winner of the challenge was rank-and-file timariot, the sultan offered immediate promotion to *subashi* (Ottoman provincial prefect) and, if the winner already held that rank, his reward was to be promotion to *sanack bey* (commander of forces at the county level). On the other hand if the winner was either a volunteer or an individual without previous service-connected revenue assignment (*dirlik yememiş*), he was to gain instant elevation to the senior ranks of the timariots with a top-grade land assignment (*ziamet*) valued at 30,000 akçes per year.[54]

The offer of extraordinary rewards for services beyond the normal call of duty were a routine part of Ottoman military practice. Motivating the troops was of course never as simple and straightforward a task as offering them bribes and incentives for good behaviour and loyal service but, as part of a comprehensive package made up of a healthy diet and regular pay, these special rewards proved a very effective means of maintaining a high level of interest and personal engagement among the soldiers in the pursuit of their joint enterprise. Even those who failed to win a reward could enjoy a comrade's success vicariously and hope to gain it for themselves in the next phase of battle or in a subsequent campaign.

The effective commander always strove to keep such hopes – even if they were essentially illusory and unrealistic – alive in his subordinates' breasts. As will be explained in greater detail later (see Chapter 7 below), the effective distribution of incentives and rewards formed a vitally important dimension of the Ottoman commander's overall responsibilities.

Concerning the limits of the regular soldiery's toleration for privation, the example of Ottoman efforts at mobilizing a relief force for Buda in 1686 is instructive. Surviving accounts of this campaign show a higher than usual level of failure to comply with mobilization orders.[55] The high level of truancy can be closely linked with the persistence of lower than average harvests over several successive seasons in the years preceding the campaign. This made it a virtual certainty that those who reported for duty would receive short rations and experience unusual privation.[56]

As a general rule the service ethic in the elite units such as the Janissaries was quite strong. Selection for service in permanent standing regiments with high pay and other generous benefits was a privilege, and the risk of dismissal alone acted as sufficient discouragement to slack performance. But maintaining unanimity of purpose and dedication under conditions of severe strain at the front required a careful nurturing of the sense of shared sacrifice and mutual enterprise. Apart from the background tension arising from sometimes intensely-felt, inter-service rivalries, particularly between the two main divisions (Janissary infantry and Sipahi cavalry) of the sultan's standing army, even within ostensibly homogeneous units unresolved grievances had the potential for creating incapacitating divisions with the army ranks as a whole. The theoretical *esprit de corps*, shared naturally by comrades-in-arms under fire where it was well understood that each individual's effort contributed something to mutual salvation, had precise limits when put to the practical test.

Loyalty and collegiality were first and foremost regimental, and communal feelings could only be transferred from cohorts counted in hundreds to legions counted in tens of thousands with considerable loss of intensity. Some army divisions such as the Tatar auxiliaries participated in imperial campaigns more or less on their own terms: obedient to their own most immediate master the Crimean Han, and loyal to their own traditions of service. Both Tatar tactics and military organization were furthermore prone to clash with established Ottoman army custom and procedures.[57]

Apart from issues of incompatibility deriving from fundamental or basic systemic differences between the Ottomans and their allies, it is clear that even on an internal or regimental level the fostering of an abiding *esprit de corps* posed a constant challenge. The example of the 1649 campaign season in Crete serves as a case in point. The commander in the field, Deli Hüseyn Pasha, though second in rank to the grand vezier who presided over him from his comfortable remove in Istanbul, had principal responsibility for the maintaining of troop morale. When confronted with demands by his exhausted troops for a much-deserved period of home leave after two years in the trenches around Candia, he realized that by granting leave to some and denying it others he would achieve nothing but the collective undermining of the soldiers' will to fight. Thus, although he was sympathetic to their demands, he recommended to his superiors in Istanbul the wisdom of a policy of all or none in the granting of leaves, and a deferring of all decisions concerning leave until the end of the campaigning season. The grand vezier, deciding to ignore Hüseyn's sound advice, set about authorizing immediate leaves to a select group of 1,500 Janissaries.[58] This single gesture of inequality and apparent favouritism, even though granted in opposition to the commander's wishes, was enough to lead to a complete collapse of morale among the troops. Those who were forced to remain behind in the trenches laid down their arms, bringing a virtual halt to further fighting for that season.

It is necessary to draw a clear distinction between the motives and motivations of temporary recruits on the one hand, and of army regulars with permanent regimental affiliations on the other. Because of the inherent insecurity of their position, the irregulars had to be particularly fierce in advance negotiations concerning the precise terms of their service. Under conditions that normally applied during the second half of the seventeenth century temporary recruits (called *levend*, pl. *levendat*) were entitled to a monthly wage of two and a half gurush (200 akçes) per man for a guaranteed minimum period of six months' service. This implied a cost to the treasury (excluding separate payments of 10 akçes per man per month as a food and fodder allowance) of 15 gurush (1,200 akçes) per man for a season of campaigning.[59] This pay offer constituted the fixed and non-negotiable terms of service for irregulars. What was, however, negotiable, and fiercely disputed, was the amount of the signing up bonus (*bahşiş*). During the seventeenth century the range of the *bahşiş* varied between five gurush (the equivalent of two months' pay) and twelve gurush.[60] In times of exceptional crisis, however, when reinforcements were needed urgently at the front, the *levends* were in a position to bargain for better terms and were successful, on exceptional occasions, in raising the bonus ante to as much as 50 or even 100 gurush per man.[61] The cost to the treasury under normal circumstances was capped at 27 gurush per man (15 gurush wages plus 12 gurush signing-up bonus), but under pressure it could be forced to yield to demands for 65 or even as much as 115 gurush.[62] The leaders of the irregular troops naturally held out for the best possible terms for their men, but the unfortunate result of prolonged negotiations was delay of action at the front. As an example of the form this bargaining process might take, the context of the Ottomans' exceptional efforts to mobilize a coherent and effective counteroffensive to match the onslaught being mounted by their enemies following the defeat at Vienna is perhaps instructive. Although by the middle of May 1687 a band of some 4,000 Anatolian *levends* under the leadership of Yegen Osman Pasha had congregated in the vicinity of Istanbul ready for dispatch to the Hungarian front, it was not until after the end of June of that year that a much reduced contingent, seemingly no more than 1,500, actually set out for the front.[63]

In terms of regimental identity and loyalty the *levends*, whose unalterable destiny was immediate disbandment at the conclusion of a single season's campaigning, were also different from other recruits. Unlike the Janissaries who received regular pay and served a stable officer corps both in and out of wartime, the *levends* were obliged to maximize their short-term gain and fend for themselves during periods when they were out of active service. Their participation in warfare was neither more nor less materially motivated than other military groups but, influenced by the special circumstances of their recruitment, their performance in battle was shaped by different expectations. They were no different from other troops in that they performed best for the commander who acted most faithfully as their advocate and defended their interests most energetically.

The securing of tolerable conditions of service was of equal importance to generous terms of remuneration in gaining the troops' loyalty and co-operation. Contemporary Western observers of Ottoman military institutions and traditions single out the comfort and security of Ottoman camp life as an important contributory factor to the Ottomans' success against their adversaries in the sixteenth and seventeenth centuries.[64] Ottoman commentators too are very clear in assigning ultimate blame for significant Ottoman military setbacks to selfish or unnecessarily harsh commanders who, by setting a negative example and tone, had an infectious and highly negative influence on their subordinates, fatally undermining their joint resolve and willingness to sacrifice themselves for the common cause.

Limits of state power and coercion

Contemporary Western perceptions of Ottoman authoritarianism have left the misleading impression of a society in which personal desire and individual identity were suppressed so successfully and completely as to allow a fusion of the "oriental" individual's self-identity with state interest.[65] Indeed, many professional historians of our own day still believe in the Ottomans' hegemonic concern with the infinite extension of the Abode of Islam (*Darul Islam*), and are convinced that this imperial mission typifies them and sets them clearly apart from their early-modern European contemporaries. But the notion that adherence of the majority to Muslim custom or acceptance of the tenets of Islam eliminated all social divisions and removed all sources of political dissent rests on a fundamental misunderstanding of the nature of religious influence in Ottoman society.

Narratives of Ottoman campaigns in the sixteenth and seventeenth centuries are riddled with plots and subplots recounting the desperate struggle for power between influential veziers supported by their lobbies and factions. In these stories accounts of the behind-the-scenes wrangling over succession to the grand vezierate sometimes take precedence over the reporting of tactical progress by Ottoman forces at the front. These accounts confirm that in a number of cases the deliberate withholding of strategic supplies or financial support by a jealous deputy grand vezier (*kaim mekam*) in Istanbul could seriously compromise the readiness of commanders at the front to do battle. The struggle for personal influence and the ambition to obtain higher office amongst the highest ranking of the sultan's *kuls*, all of whom were potential candidates for sudden elevation to the grand vezierate, was most pronounced under weak and, especially, underage sultans. But even the celebrated

Süleyman (reigned 1520–66) was not spared the tumultuous effect of vezierial ambition and uncompromising mutual animosity.[66] Even when the succession of a new grand vezier was the result neither of political sabotage nor of a messy power struggle, but was necessitated by the natural death of an incumbent in office, the disruptive effect of a change of leadership on military activity was the same. Damad Ibrahim Pasha's death, which coincided with the spring season of frenetic mobilization activity and preparations for renewed war efforts in Hungary in 1601, resulted in the effective wasting of a whole season of campaigning potential while the details of succession were being worked out.[67] Such intrusions of the leadership question on the conduct of military affairs were by no means unusual.

Leadership disputes assumed particular prominence in the period after Mehmed III's campaign against Egri in 1596. Because of the succession of several minors to the sultanate during the early and middle years of the seventeenth century, it became a rare and exceptional event for the sultan to lead the troops into battle, and both state administration and the waging of war were left to an ever-increasing extent in the hands of the grand vezier. For most of the period between the mid-1650s and late 1670s a single family, the Köprülüs, seized the initiative, monopolizing political as well as military power in the state. But this concentration of power in the hands of the sultan's *kuls* did not go unnoticed in Anatolia, and the resulting rift gave rise to a series of provincial rebellions whose suppression became a major undertaking for the government and seriously distracted it from the pursuit of its expansionist ambitions. Under such conditions of internal instability the effective prosecution of foreign wars was clearly not possible. The combined effect of divisive power struggles in the capital, and the emergence of determined pockets of resistance to state authority in the provinces should not be underestimated as factors affecting the Ottomans' ability to realize their full military potential during the seventeenth century. It is questionable whether, even by the end of the seventeenth century, the Ottoman armed forces had yet been suffi- ciently tamed to become useable as an effective instrument for the execution of the will of the state. The ethnic diversity of the population base from which the Ottoman military was recruited was perhaps one element in its general tendency to resist the state's authority but, whatever the source of its recalci- trance, it never developed into an effective or unequivocal enforcer of state interest.[68]

The relative accessibility of firearms and the wide diffusion of simple (as well as rather inexpensive) technology of the flintlock musket that predomi- nated in the seventeenth century meant that arms could be borne and used as easily *against* as *for* the state.[69] In most periods of Ottoman history, and 1500– 1700 was no exception, a balance of give and take between master (the sultan) and servants (the *kul*) was carefully maintained. When this balance was upset, however, it was usually the *kuls* who, temporarily, dominated while shoring up the rule of a weak or newly-installed sultan or, conversely, by conspiring to depose an incompetent, excessively self-willed or avaricious overlord. The Ottomans unquestionably preceded the Europeans in the development of a high degree of bureaucratic and fiscal centralization that put generous resources (especially tax revenues) at the direct disposal of the sovereign, but in the military sphere these centralizing trends were not so pronounced and, despite some consolidation, the Ottomans in the seventeenth century still relied on fragmentary and not always reliable sources for military support.

The Ottomans' relations with their Tatar allies in particular proved problematic and were often marred by an atmosphere of mutual distrust. As perceived by the Ottomans, the Tatars' natural propensity for insubordination led them to acts which bordered on active disloyalty, both provoking and justifying Ottoman interventions aimed, by the dismissing of the incumbent *han* and installing of a rival candidate, at the "restoration of order". One striking example of the deterioration in relations between the Ottoman and their Tatar allies took place in 1584. At this time the reigning *han* Mehmed Giray II (reigned 1577–84) was accused, according to Ottoman sources, of halfhearted participation in successive Caucasian campaigns led by Lala Mustafa Pasha (in 1579) and Özdemiroghlu Osman Pasha (in 1582–3).[70] Mehmed Giray was forced off his throne, executed and replaced by his brother Islam Giray II (reigned 1584–8) whom the Ottomans hoped might make a more compliant instrument for the execution of their policy of gaining a permanent foothold in the Caucasus. Ten years later in August 1594 the now contrite Tatars reported under their ruler Gazi Giray Han II for the siege of Györ in numbers estimated in contemporary sources at around 100,000 men.[71] However, tensions arising from contradictory styles of combat and conflicting war priorities already apparent at the time of the Györ campaign led to a renewed rupture in relations, and once again the han was deposed.[72]

With each of its allies, vassals and even internal agents such as the semi-independent Kurdish *begs* of Eastern Anatolia the Ottomans had to reach compromises and define mutually-agreed terms for co-operation. The maintaining of good relations required effort, and a good measure of give and take from both sides. Active and effective diplomacy and sharp negotiating skills were as important to success in Ottoman imperial warfare as the quality and quantity of army munitions and supplies. The Ottomans' success in expanding their empire between 1500 and 1700 was only in part due to their command of then current gunpowder and related technologies. It derived also from their skill in the areas of international diplomacy and mastery of the bargaining techniques appropriate to the sphere of internal tribal politics.

The challenges faced by the Ottomans in the diplomatic sphere are nowhere more apparent than in their venture into Caucasian politics in the three and a half decades between 1578 and 1612. Ottoman diplomacy among the various royal houses of tripartite Georgia[73] in this period was both continuous and wide-ranging. As early as 1580 in the early phases of their war with the Safavids the Ottomans had already approached Simon I (restored as ruler of Kartli between 1578 and 1598) with proposals granting Ottoman recognition of the semi-independent status of his kingdom in return for an annual tribute set at 100,000 gold pieces.[74] When these overtures were rebuffed, the Ottomans approached (in 1584) his brother Davud Han (deposed on Simon's restoration to the throne in 1578) and offered, in addition to his appointment as Ottoman governor in Marash (Zulkadriye), to grant him hereditary title over Simon's lands should he succeed in capturing them on the Ottomans' behalf.[75] Simon continued to resist the Ottomans' attempts to win him over until 1599, when he was captured and brought forcibly to Istanbul where he was kept under house arrest.[76] From the historical record it is obvious that the Ottomans exerted a great deal of effort among various factions of the Georgian nobility to win support for their cause, and incurred considerable expense in the undertaking.[77] As a measure of the Ottomans' longer-term success in the diplomatic sphere it is noteworthy that more than a century later in 1698 the Imeretian stronghold of Kutaisi was able to resist a determined assault aimed at incorporating it within the boundaries of a United Kingdom of Georgia, in part because it could still rely on the strength of pro-Ottoman feeling among the local populace.[78] Although the Ottomans were clearly successful in mobilizing support among the Tatars, Georgians and other potential backers of the Ottoman imperial cause, it would be pointless to deny that the structure of Ottoman diplomatic endeavour was not also studded with some casualties. But, whatever their record of win and lose in the diplomatic game, it is important that we never lose sight of the importance of the non-military options pursued by the Ottomans to advance their cause.

With the foregoing brief and highly selective sketch of Ottoman diplomacy we bring to a close our account of the five principal restraining factors that inhibited the scope for the application of overwhelming or decisive force in determining the outcome of war in the early-modern period. From our account it should be apparent that – for this era in warfare – success in battle was contingent, not just on science or even human ingenuity and bravery, but on the coincidence of a set of fortuitous (or at least not easily controllable) circumstances, such as good weather, adequate harvests and the persuasive voice of sound (and psychologically insightful) leadership assisted – in the most dramatically successful instances – by a large measure of plain good luck.

This is not to say that successful armies could dispense with the discipline of careful fiscal and logistical planning and forethought (our subject in Chapters 3, 4 and 5, which follow), but it serves as a useful reminder that even the best-laid plans could (and often did) go awry. In the final analysis it was the uncertainties of war that stubbornly persisted and formed the defining characteristic of its immutable context.

Chapter Three

Military manpower and military spending: an attempt at realistic assessment

Military manpower

In describing Ottoman military strength and capabilities, it is essential that we maintain with as much clarity as possible the essential distinction between resource potentialities, and the extent to which these potential strengths could realistically be activated and deployed. Although tempted by the challenge of providing a fully-comprehensive picture of Ottoman military might including all actives and reserves, we must not suppose that anything like such full capacity could ever be concentrated on a single battlefield. At any given time a large proportion of Ottoman military personnel was either tied up in a defensive posture for the garrisoning and patrolling of its extensive frontiers in Europe and Asia, or already deployed on secondary and tertiary fronts. Furthermore, in actual practice, for combat purposes it was only a fraction of the fraction which had been mobilized for action on a particular front that took any direct part in battle. Bearing these features firmly in mind, it behooves us to maintain a healthy scepticism both about the scale and destructiveness of Ottoman warfare. Our aim in this chapter will be to present and contrast the theory and the reality of Ottoman military capacity and campaign financing.

Until the start of the sixteenth century the Ottoman military establishment was dominated by the freelance light cavalry or *akinci* forces who offered their services to the state in exchange for the lion's share of the disposable war booty. As late as the reign of Mehmed II (1451–81) these cavalry "raiders" numbered as many as 50,000, and it took some time for their numbers to dwindle to the vestigial numbers recorded by Ottoman commentators of the early seventeenth century such as Koçi Bey.[1] During the sixteenth century, however, reflecting in part changes in tactics and armaments, and in part the

35

growing number of state-sponsored and -maintained military forces, military provision became the nearly exclusive preserve of two groups: the seasonally-mobilized, provincial cavalry supported by timar land grants, and the sultan's permanent, standing, cash-paid, armed forces (both infantry and cavalry, but predominantly infantry) called the *kapu kulu* (lit. "servitors of the [palace] gate", or household troops). The absolute number and proportional mix of these two troop categories, the provincial and permanent, actually present in the Ottoman army in particular campaigns fluctuated considerably according to circumstances and tactical needs, but it is important to remember that even in the era of expanding Janissary enrolments with membership peaking at around 40,000 men in the second half of the seventeenth century (see Table 3.5), the proportion of deployed foot to deployed cavalry troops never exceeded one to two and was more usually of the order of one to three. One obvious exception to this rule was the composition of the Ottoman expeditionary forces in Crete between 1645 and 1669 but, in almost any but an insular context, the rapid mobility provided by a predominance of horse served as a key element of Ottoman operational success.

An indication of the usual patterns of deployment is provided in the eye witness account by Zarain Agha, who describes, the Ottoman mobilization for the siege of Baghdad in 1638. According to Zarain, the Ottoman army fielded for this campaign consisted of 108,589 men composed of: "35,000 footmen, in part Janissaries, and 73,589 light horses".[2] Thus, for all practical purposes the Ottoman army, despite the critical importance of specialized technical services provided by the Janissaries during siege, remained an army whose membership and ethos was dominated by the cavalry. It is therefore appropriate that we begin our assessment of potential troop strengths and actual deployment patterns in Ottoman warfare of the sixteenth and seventeenth century with an account of the timariot forces.

The timariot army

The predominance of the light cavalry in the Ottomans' military profile was dictated in part by practical considerations. Their largest source of military manpower was the land revenue assignment or *timar* which was granted in exchange for obligatory military service. Estimates of the potential timariot strength vary greatly between observers.[3] Should the need arise, claimed the Venetian diplomat Alvise Contarini somewhat extravagantly in 1640, the sultan could put into the field an army of 200,000 horsemen without spending a penny of the treasury's money.[4] Even though it proved impossible to achieve anything like the full mobilization potential of the provincial cavalry, it remained a matter of fiscal principle for the Ottomans to maximize their participation in campaigns. Whether we accept the conservative figure of 100,000 or the more generous estimate of 200,000 as best representing the reservoir of potentially mobilizable timariots (together with their retainers), it remains a fact that in any given campaign only a proportion of these needed to be activated and deployed. In real terms this rarely exceeded the 73,000 figure suggested by Zarain Agha (see above), and even this may subsume within it a component of non-timariot skirmishers supplied by the Kurdish and Turkmen chieftains of the regions nearest to the active front. One feature of the *timar* system that actually contributed much to its success was the fact that at any given time (even with fighting on more than one active front) there always remained a large untapped reserve force. Without losing sight of these functional realities, to permit clearer comparisons of the relative position of the timariot army in the two centuries under investigation, we will base our analysis on global figures and registered ranks as opposed to actual deployment numbers.

Figures for the early sixteenth century before the Ottoman conquest of Hungary in 1541 indicate a timariot army with a potential strength of approximately 90,000 men, of whom approximately 60,000 came from core provinces of the interior within easy riding distance from key battlefields along the Danubian frontier.[5] The regional balance of the timariot forces towards the beginning of Süleyman's reign in 1527 is shown in Table 3.1.

The participation of timariot forces on such a scale presented no serious challenges as long as prevailing patterns of warfare allowed for regular, seasonal demobilizations during which the timariots could return to base and manage their estates. In the warfare of the early sixteenth century before the dramatic extension of the empire's borders this was the usual case. Mobilization, march to the front, engagement of the enemy and return to base were then confinable to the normal campaigning season between April and October. In the seventeenth century, when prolonged conflicts and multi-season mobilizations became increasingly common, reliance on seasonally-mobilized timariot forces was less practical. But even with the presumption of declining rates of timariot participation in the seventeenth century, evidence suggests that (partly because new provinces were constantly being created as the empire grew) timariot reserve levels were not just maintained, but even expanded. While the potential timariot force in Süleyman's reign had consisted of 90,000 men, about four-tenths of them concentrated in the European provinces, by the reign of Murad IV (1623–40) the total had risen to approximately 106,000. Despite these changes the proportional representation of the European timariots was still roughly the same.[6] A summary timar

Table 3.1 Potential strength of timariot army circa 1527[1]

Size and Administrative structure of Empire in 1527

Province name	No. of sancaks	
Rumili		27[2]
Anadolu		
Anatolia West		17[3]
Anatolia East		
Karaman	7[4]	
Zulkadriye (Maraş)	2[5]	
Rum (Sivas)	10[6]	
		19
Syria		14[7]
Diyarbekir		11[8]
Total		88[9]

Troop figures based on the above-listed provincial divisions

Provincial name	kiliç timars	cebelu[10] (retainers)	mustahfiz[11] timars	Total potential force
Rumili	10,688	26,720	6,620	44,028
Anatolia (W)	7,536	15,072	1,307[12]	23,915
Anatolia (E)	6,518	13,036	1,307	20,861
Syria	2,275	4,550	419	7,244
Diyarbekir	1,071	2,142	–	3,213
TOTALS	28,088	61,520	9,653	99,261

inspection carried out in 1631 revealed the troop levels shown in Table 3.2.

Additional troops were supplied as part of the personal retinues of the provincial governors, but empire-wide these contributed an increase of only some 3,500 men, not enough to tip the balance of forces significantly in real battle contexts. From their distribution it would appear rather that they were used mostly to supply home defence services to those governors whose provinces were situated in vulnerable frontier zones, especially in the eastern parts of the empire. Table 3.3 shows the regional distribution of these forces according to data supplied in Ayn-i Ali's treatise of 1609.[7]

The complexity and regional specificity of the timar system prevents meaningful generalization, but it would appear (based on the assessment of

Table 3.1 (cont.)

Summary of Statistics on Total Potential Mobilizable Force
(combination of figures columns 1 and 2 above)

		% of Total
Europe	37,408	42
W. Anatolia	22,608	25
E. Anatolia	19,554	22
Syria	6,825	8
Diyarbekir	3,213	3
Total	89,608	100

[1] The information used in this table is taken from a document in the Topkapi Palace, D. 3442. A summary of its contents is given by Barkan in IFM XV (1953–4), p. 255.

[2] See IFM XV: 258 (fn. 13) and the list on 267 (fn. 25).

[3] See the list in IFM XV: 258 (fn. 14).

[4] IFM XV: 261 (fn. 16).

[5] IFM XV: 261 (fn. 17).

[6] IFM XV: 261 (fn. 18).

[7] IFM XV: 263 (fn. 20).

[8] IFM XV: 264 (fn. 22).

[9] 6/10ths as many as in 1631. Compare Table 3.2 below.

[10] Figures for this column are not provided in the data. They are projections calculated from the different multipliers of 2.5 for Rumili, and 2.0 for other parts of the empire based on the assumption that the proportion of holders of larger grants (zaim) to ordinary timariots (sipahi) was higher in Rumili than elsewhere. Nearly contemporary figures (for 940 A.H./AD 1533) show however that of 11,588 kiliç holders (unaccountably, 900 more than in the registration of 1527) only 384 or 3.3% were zaims or holders of land grants yielding them an annual income in excess of 20,000 akçes. In the early sixteenth century it appears that the overwhelming majority of timar grants were small. For the European provinces, an exact idea of income distribution by district is given in IFM XV: 301. Judging by general patterns, our assumption of 2.0 retainers for every timariot is perhaps over-generous and a multiplier of 1.5 more realistic. But assuming a stricter enforcement of timar mobilization quotas in the sixteenth as compared with the seventeenth century, we have elected to err on the side of overcount and allowed for 3 persons per timar (self + 2 retainers) in calculating the figure for TPF (Total Potential Force) for the early sixteenth century. Compare Table 3.2, note 6.

[11] Timar grants for the support of fortress guardians who were not expected to provide any cebelu and who were not themselves mobilizable to any significant extent without making the frontier vulnerable to enemy attack. The figures are included in this table for the sake of completeness, but a realistic assessment of TPMF (Total Potential Mobilizable Force) would have to be based on the addition of figures from columns 1 and 2 only.

[12] The figures for eastern and western Anatolia are given only in aggregate form. We have assumed an even split (1,307 for W and 1,307 for E) to reach the registered total of 2,614. It is likely that the greater proportion was concentrated in the East.

knowledgeable contemporaries such as Koçi Bey) that even for the largest mobilizations the government made use of no more than about seven-tenths of its total potential reserve force. Writing circa 1640, when near contemporary evidence suggests there were approximately 40,000 basic timar

Table 3.2 Potential strength of timariot army circa 1631[1]

European provinces

Province name	sancaks	kiliç ziamet	kiliç timar	total kiliç
Rumili	15[2]	802[3]	6,719	7,521
Özü	6	188	1,186	1,374
Budin	17	278	2,391	2,669
Bosna	7	150	1,793	1,943
Temeşvar	6	59	290	349
Cezayir-i				
Bahr-i Sefid	12	730	2,804	3,534
Total	63	2,207	15,183	17,390

Asian provinces

Anatolia	14	294[4]	4,589	4,883[5]
Karaman	7	68	2,110	2,178
Sivas [Rum]	7	108	2,669	2,777
Maraş [Zulkadr]	4	29+	2,159	2,188
Şam	7	128+	868+	996
Trablus-i Şam	6	63+	571+	634
Haleb	5	99	823	922
Adana	5	42	1,509	1,551
Ruha	4	37+	626	663
Diyarbekir	12	52	688+	740
Erzurum	9	123	5,159+	5,282
Trabzon	2	56	398	454
Total	82	1,099	22,169	23,268

Summary figures

	EUROPE	ASIA	TOTAL
provinces	6	12	18
sancaks	63	82	145
ziamets	2,207	1,099	3,306
timars	15,183	22,169	37,352
kiliç	17,390	23,268	40,658

Table 3.2 (cont.)

	PTS (potential troop strength)		
	EUROPE	ASIA	COMBINED
$2{,}207 \times 4^6$ =	8,828	4,396	13,224
$15{,}183 \times 2.5^7$ =	37,957	55,422	93,379
TOTAL	46,785	59,818	106,603
	(44%)	(56%)	

+ Figure coincides exactly with that given by Ayn-i Ali in his *Risale* of 1609.

[1] Figure taken from TKSA, D. 9665.

[2] Compare Ayn-i Ali's list of 1609 (Barkan, "Timar", IA XII: p. 290) which records 24 sancaks with a total of 9,274 kiliç, and the 1527 figures (Table 3.1) of 10,688 for 27 sancaks.

Due to administrative consolidation over time the average number of timar holders in each administrative unit actually increased from $10{,}688 \div 27 = 396$ per sancak to $7{,}521 \div 15 = 501$ per sancak in the European provinces of the empire. The overall proportion of troops supplied by the European provinces remained almost the same: 42% in 1527 as compared to 44% in 1631.

[3] Proportion holding large grants with revenues in excess of 20,000 akçes, 802/7521 = 10.7%. This represents a significant change to the situation obtaining 100 years earlier. See Table 3.1, note 10 above.

[4] Proportion with large grants, 294/4883 = 6%.

[5] This number, taken in isolation and compared with the figure of 7,311 for 1609 given by Ayn-i Ali, suggests a serious decline in the potential strength of timar forces mobilized from Anatolia, but a closer examination reveals that these losses were compensated for by shifting the burden of providing troops away from the agricultural districts of Western Anatolia on to pastoral zones in Central and Eastern Anatolia.

[6] Assumes average of 3 retainers accompanying each *zaim*, (self + 3 = 4). Since the European *zaims* had, on the average, larger grants (see notes 2 and 3), the troop total for this category could be increased. Such adjustments to the figures would bring the European total to approximately 50,000 as compared with the Asian total of approximately 60,000.

[7] Assumes an average of 1.5 retainers accompanying each timariot (self + 1.5 = 2.5).

assignments supporting an average of 2.65 armed retainers which suggests a cumulative total of 106,000 men (see Table 3.2 above), Koçi Bey gives his own, perhaps more realistic, assessment of potential timariot strength as approximately 70,000. In his opinion the maximum achievable timariot troop levels even for sultan-led campaigns had sunk by his own time to 30,000 for the European provinces, 17,000 for western Anatolia, and an unspecified number (perhaps 23,000) from the empire's easternmost provinces.[8] For smaller-scale campaigns, especially when the sultan was not himself present, mobilization quotas were correspondingly smaller. For example, in the campaign led by the Grand Vezier Kara Mehmed Pasha against Erivan in 1616 an inspection of timariots actually present in the field revealed the presence of just 16,846 timar holders.[9] Even if each timariot had been accompanied in battle by an average of two armed retainers, the total would still only just have reached the level of 50,000 combatants. If we accept 50,000 as the upper limit for lesser campaigns and a generous 80,000 for sultan-led campaigns, we will

Table 3.3[1] Prescribed/putative size of the timariot army in 1609

European provinces

Name of province (eyalet)	Optimal strength (asker)	
Bosna	3,000	
Buda	ND	
Cezayir-i Bahr-i Sefid (Gelibolu)	4,500	
Rumili	33,000	
Temeşvar	ND	
	40,500	
Estimate for ND provinces	10,000	
European Provinces		50,500

Asian provinces

Name of province	Optimal strength	
Anadolu	17,000[2]	
Bağdad	ND	
Çildir	1,800	
Diyarbekir	1,800[3]	
Erzurum	7,800	
Haleb	2,500	
Karaman (Konya)	4,600	
Kars	ND	
Kibris	9,000	
Mosul	ND	
Rakka	1,600	
Rum (Sivas)	9,000	
Şam	2,600	
Trablus-i Şam	1,400	
Trabzon	1,750	
Van	ND	
Zulkadriye (Maraş)	5,500	
	66,350	
Auxiliaries (Turkmen and Kurdish)	33,700	
Estimate for ND provinces	20,000	
Asian Provinces		120,050
GRAND TOTAL		170,550

[1] Table based on data from Ayn-i Ali's treatise of 1609. See *Kavanin-i Al-i Osman Der Hulasa-i Mezamin-i Defter-i Divan* (Istanbul, 1280), pp. 48–61.
[2] The western portions of the province were capable of supplying an additional 26,000 Turkmen troops (the *yaya* and *müsellem*).
[3] The province was capable of supplying a further number of 7,200 Kurdish auxiliaries organized as tribal units.

be much closer to an accurate portrayal of the actual battle strength of the timariot forces than by sticking to any of the theoretical projections offered by the contemporary Venetian diplomatic envoys.[10] Pero Tafur, a traveller from Spain who visited the Ottoman empire in the mid-fifteenth century, is another example of a Western observer whose military assessments are more evocative than real.[11] Of course, with the input from Tatar skirmishers during northern campaigns, and from Kurdish and Turkmen allies in eastern campaigns the cavalry component in the Ottoman army was expandable and could reach a critical mass approaching 100,000 men, especially during the ceremonially significant initial phases of campaign.

The sultan's standing army

Conditions governing recruitment into the sultan's standing regiments barracked in the capital were strict. The need for thorough and unhurried training in the technical aspects of siege warfare, and the practical desire not to waste this training on recruits who had little natural aptitude provided part of the rationale for careful selection, but inevitably also it was a question of limiting expense. The quarterly pay distributions to members of the sultan's standing regiments at the Porte were the single largest item of expenditure supported by the treasury's regular sources of revenue. In origin functioning as an imperial bodyguard and intended for the sultan's exclusive use, from the late sixteenth century onwards they became an indispensable part of the army and attended campaigns even if the sultan was not present. Despite these changes they still regarded themselves as the sultan's personal servitors (hünkâr kulu) and resisted attempts by veziers and other temporary office holders to subject them to a substitute authority.[12] The restriction of their membership to key personnel with specific technical functions thus achieved two purposes: protecting the treasury from waste (a state priority) and preserving the elite status of the corps and its privileged position under the direct patronage of the sultan (a Janissary priority). It was principally the fiscal argument which ensured that retired and deceased Janissaries were replaced only reluctantly and cautiously. Table 3.4 shows the share of annual central treasury disbursements accounted for by salary payments to the Janissaries.

Since indiscriminate recruitment of large numbers of new members was fiscally impossible, the devshirme levies of the seventeenth century tended to be infrequent and carefully controlled events.[13] The number of Janissary cadets or trainees maintained as a source for the replacement of retiring Janissaries typically consisted of between one-fifth and one-third of the total member-

Table 3.4 Annual treasury payments for the salaries of the sultan's standing troops and other (mostly non-military) palace staff

	Janissaries	Alti-Bölük Sipahis	Other (mostly non-military)	Salary payments Annual budget	%
1527–8[1]	15,423,426	30,957,300	19,502,212	65,882,940	44
				150,228,227	
1547–8[2]	19,263,841	21,439,959	25,946,217	76,650,017	39
				198,887,294	
1567–8[3]	34,264,772	65,073,692	27,978,579	127,316,983	37
				348,544,181	
1582–3[4]	30,008,019	49,799,767	ND	ND	–
1613–14[5]	83,883,911	83,765,760	50,658,906	218,305,577	52
				540,659,908	
1623–4[6]	64,426,302	116,313,995	11,822,253	192,562,550	75
				258,412,884	
1627–8[7]	58,606,749	112,584,840	10,070,347	181,261,936	77
				233,468,535	
1628–9[8]	67,845,031	138,410,729	13,371,335	219,627,095	67
				326,322,676	
1630–1[9]	77,194,470	123,690,811	8,017,170	208,902,451	77
				272,350,317	

[1] IFM XV (1953–4): 228 and 360.
[2] IFM XIX (1957–8): 237 and 252.
[3] IFM XIX (1957–8): 298 and 305.
[4] *Belleten* XXXIV/136 (1970): 603.
[5] B.B.A., Maliyeden Müdevver 2275.
[6] B.B.A., Maliyeden Müdevver 744.
[7] B.B.A., Kamil Kepeci 1919.
[8] B.B.A., Kamil Kepeci 1921.
[9] B.B.A., Kamil Kepeci 1927.

ship, but not all of these were destined to complete the rigorous course of training lasting a full seven years. Table 3.5 shows the proportion of cadets in the general membership of the Janissaries at various intervals during the sixteenth and seventeenth centuries.

Apart from the increasing restriction of recruitment quotas there were other changes affecting the Janissary corps in train during the seventeenth century. In an order sent in multiple copies to authorities throughout the

Table 3.5 Size and composition of sultan's standing army (*kapu kulu*) 1527–1670[1]

	1527[2]	1574	1597	1609	1670[3]
I Janissary Corps					
Janissaries	7,886	13,599	35,000	37,627	39,470[4]
Janissary Cadets	3,553	7,495	10,000	9,406	8,742
TOTAL	11,439	21,094	45,000	47,033	48,212
II Six standing cavalry regiments					
1. sipahiyan	1,993	2,210	7,000	7,805	6,615
2. silahdaran	1,593	2,217	5,000	1,683	5,925
3. ulufeciyan-i yemin	589	400	1,800	2,055	467
4. ulufeciyan-i yesar	498	407	1,500	1,423	435
5. gureba-i yemin	211	406	1,000	928	355
6. gureba-i yesar	2,014	407	800	975	273
TOTAL	5,088	5,957	17,000	20,869	14,070
III Artillery corps					
1. cebeciyan	524	625	ND	5,730	4,789
2. topcuyan	695	1,099	ND	1,552	2,793
3. arabaciyan-i top	943	400	ND	684	432
TOTAL	2,162	2,124	ND	7,966	8,014
GRAND TOTAL	18,689	29,175	?	75,868	70,296[5]

[1] Except where otherwise indicated figures are based on the table in R. Murphey (ed.), *Aziz Efendi, Kanunname-i Sultani* (Cambridge, MA, 1985), pp. 45–6.
[2] Figures for 1527 from budget published by Barkan; see IFM XV (1953–4): 300.
[3] Figures for 1670 from budget published by Barkan; see IFM XVII (1955–6): 314.
[4] The figure excludes 14,379 Janissaries assigned to provincial garrison duty. Compare Barkan, IFM XVII (1955–6): p. 263. The total membership in 1670 with the Janissaries on garrison duty was 53,849 men. The comparable figure in 1660 was 54,222 men in total, of whom 21,428 were assigned to provincial garrison duty; cf., Barkan in IFM XVII: p. 310. For the year 1653 the global Janissary enrolment figure was 51,047 men; see the Tarhoncu 'budget' in A. Feridun, *Münşeat II:* p. 305.
[5] The significant decline in the size of cavalry regiments between 1609 and 1670 amounting to a net loss of more than 6,000 men was offset in part by significant gains in other regiments. See, for example, the jump of 80% (from 1,552 to 2,793) in the number of gunners.

European provinces in 1666 a devshirme recruitment target of between 300 and 320 was set for an area covering the whole of the central and western Balkans.[14] It seems clear that by this time (mid-seventeenth century) the perception as well perhaps as the reality of the Janissary institution was that the expense of maintaining it was no longer justified by the battle achievements of its members.

From the mid-seventeenth century the Ottomans experimented with alternative forms of military recruitment, including the temporary employment on a contract basis of irregulars, called pejoratively "overnight soldiers" (*türedi asker*) in the sources. As these largely untrained and inexperienced last-minute recruits from the peasantry came into prominent use towards the end of the seventeenth century, they gradually became the preferred and cheaper option to replacing Janissaries as they retired. Here too the operation of the fiscal imperative is all too apparent. As a further indication of the consistency of these trends the graduation (*chikma*) of the trainees in various branches of the palace services in 1687 is noteworthy. On this occasion, marking the accession of Sultân Süleyman II, the graduation added only 130 "white caps" (i.e. Janissary inductees) to the Janissary ranks.[15] Slowing the pace of new Janissary recruitment had, even in the midst of the military crisis after the fall of Buda in 1686, become a fiscal necessity for the Ottomans.

The Janissaries and members of the six standing cavalry regiments at the Porte (*alti bölük*) were paid in regular quarterly pay instalments called *mevacib* ("necessities") or *ulufe* ("fodder money"). Because of the unusual accounting system employed according to which each wage period was held to consist of a fixed number of 85 "working" days, it is relatively easy, using muster rolls and tallies compiled in both peacetime and during wartime mobilizations, to calculate not just global figures for Janissary and other troop enrolments but, more important, to reconstruct the full detail of how they were used and deployed by the Ottomans. At pay distributions during the course of campaigns care was taken to distinguish between members of the corps actually present in the ranks and those on special assignment elsewhere or confined to barracks in Istanbul. The "actives", "actuals", and "effectives" present at the front at any given time naturally only represented a proportion of the total ranks. Documentation from the 1620s and 1630s recording troop mobilization levels for two middle-sized campaigns (see Table 3.6 below) suggests that at a time when full Janissary membership in the Istanbul barracks amounted to some 30,000 men[16] those actually deployed at the front ranged between 20,000 and 25,000. Information from the mid-sixteenth century indicates that, for that period, even the lower figures may exaggerate the actual deployed troop strength of Ottoman armies of conquest. A roll call held in Hungary in 1541, reflecting the actual deployed strength of the Ottoman regular army forces participating in campaign, registered 15,612 men as present. Of these approximately 6,350 were Janissaries, 3,700 were Sipahis and another 1,650 were members of the artillery corps. The remaining one-quarter (roughly 4,100 men) were mostly non-combatants.[17]

Information for the year 1660 when the only active front was in Moldavia (siege of Varad/Oradea in July-August) indicates 18,013 "actives" (*ehl-i sefer*)

Table 3.6[1] Figures contrasting total potential Janissary strength with numbers actually deployed in battle

	1029/1602	1033/1624	1035/1616	1038/1628	1044/1634
Regs 1–61 (Ağa)	13,518	16,076[2]	11,338	ND	11,110
Regs 1–59 (piyadegan)	8,819	11,118	5,927	ND	7,100
Regs 60–101 (piyadegan)	7,082	8,277	4,585	ND	6,946
1–34 (sekban)	1,755	2,338	–[3]	ND	–[4]
TOTAL (for 196 Jan. Regs)	31,174	37,809		31,794	
Present at roll call on campaign			21,850		25,156
Present at ordinary roll call		26,041[5]			
Difference		11,768[6]			

[1] Sources for this table are: for 1620, B.B.A., Maliyeden Müdevver 7245; for 1624, Ahmed Cevad, *Tarih-i Askeri-i Osmani* (Istanbul, 1299), pp. 81–91; for 1626, B.B.A., Maliyeden Müdevver 6554; for 1628, B.B.A., Maliyeden Müdevver 7167 and for 1634, B.B.A., Maliyeden Mudevver 3565.

[2] This figure includes only active members of the corps, 12,768 of whom were present for roll call and the remainder (3,308) not present. With the retired members (2,396), and trainees (828) included, the registered total for these 61 regiments was 19,300 men.

[3] The sekban companies remained behind in Istanbul on guard duty on occasions when the bulk of the corps was absent on campaign. All sekbans would thus be counted "not present" (*gayr mevcud*) when the roll call was taken in the field.

[4] See previous note.

[5] The breakdown by regiment of those counted present was: Reg. 1-61 (Ağa), 12,768; regs. 1–59 (Piyade), 7,380; regs., 60–101 (Piyade), 5,826 and regs. 1–34 (sekbans), 67. At the time of this roll call most of the sekbans were on assignment in the provinces. Conversely, when the army was on campaign, the sekbans remained in Istanbul on guard duty. See above notes 3 and 4.

[6] The proportion of the corps assigned elsewhere or counted absent on this occasion was roughly one-third (actually 31%) of the total membership.

out of a total Janissary enrolment of 32,794.[18] It does not follow from the fact that 18,000 Janissaries were present for salary distributions in the field that even they took a very active role in the fighting. An example from the early eighteenth century showing the dispersed character of Janissary deployment at the front exemplifies what was undoubtedly a very common phenomenon in seventeenth-century Ottoman warfare too. A campaign journal recounting

Ali Pasha's confrontation with the Venetian forces occupying the Morea in 1715 records that of 67,000 Janissaries called up for service in the early summer,[19] only about one-seventh of their number were found to be present at the main army camp on the plain near Modon in August 1715.[20]

The general pattern of evidence, both anecdotal and documentary, suggests that Janissary enrolment continued to expand through the seventeenth century, reaching a peak of roughly 40,000. This figure implies an average full membership of just over 200 men for each of the 196 companies with barracks in the capital (see Table 3.6 above). But, apart from a few highly exceptional occasions, such as the reconquest of Baghdad by Murad IV in 1638 and Kara Mustafa Pasha's ill-fated attack on Vienna in 1683, Janissary deployments rarely rose above 25,000, while Janissary "effectives" who actually served in the trenches and confronted the enemy in combat represented a still smaller proportion, perhaps 50 full-strength companies, or 10,000 men.[21]

In the above discussion we have focused attention on the problem of *overcounting* and *overestimation* of Ottoman military strength by noting the importance of drawing careful distinctions between paper strength on the one hand, and actual participation by "effectives" on the other. The ability of active combatants to function effectively of course depended on the support services provided by non-combatants. Because many of the groups who contributed most to Ottoman success in siege were unregistered, their input is easily overlooked. Unlike the Janissaries who appear on the regular payroll muster lists or the timariot forces whose land grants were inscribed in centrally maintained land registers, grain transporters, army provisioners, kitchen staff, sutlers, merchants and others who swelled the army ranks during campaign make only a shadowy presence in official campaign records. All told, the combatants, army support staff and camp followers did constitute a mass of humanity comparable in size to a large metropolis of the period.[22] Yet, for reasons already discussed,[23] it is wise to be wary of accounts which grossly inflate Ottoman troop strength. If, as authoritative contemporary accounts recommended, the optimal suggested troop strength for Habsburg armies in the late sixteenth century was 50,000 men,[24] it seems hardly credible to suppose that the Ottomans could have enjoyed as much as a two to one numerical advantage over their adversaries in a period when, with a few exceptions such as the battle of Egri in 1596, decisive victory seemed to elude them. The prolongation of conflict with the Habsburgs during the turn-of-the century "Long Wars" (1593–1606) suggests opponents whose resource bases were stretched close to the limit. The situation from the standpoint of deployable troop strength changed very little in the 60 to 70 years which followed. At the battle of St Gotthard in August 1664 Raimondo Montecuccoli, supreme commander of a Habsburg force significantly strengthened by units both from France and the Rhine confederates, still only managed to field an army of some 40,000 men.[25]

Realistic assessment of the actual battle strength of Ottoman armies, even in the last quarter of the seventeenth century which witnessed a dramatic increase in mobilization levels spurred by the challenge from the *Sacra Ligua*, points to a maximum figure in the neighborhood of 65,000–70,000 men. A typical Ottoman army in the seventeenth century might be composed, supposing a relatively high rate of compliance with mobilization orders, of roughly 50 per cent of the total potential timariot troop strength (see Table 3.2) or 50,000 timariots and up to 20,000 from the sultan's permanent standing regiments (see Tables 3.5 and 3.6).

The conclusion that may be drawn from the above discussion is that despite its reputation as a "gunpowder empire" *par excellence,* the Ottoman state was far from being an armed camp. The Ottoman empire was exceptionally early in its development of an institutional framework for the military, as the creation of the Janissary corps in the late fourteenth century testifies. But it cannot be said of any period of its history that military institutions dominated civil society. Judged by the yardstick of the empire's wide territorial scope, it might even be said that the military forces played a minimal role in the state's survival. The number of dedicated military personnel (in this calculation the timariots should be excluded since their performance of off-season administrative duties was of equal importance to their military function) even with the inclusion of provincial garrison forces (see Table 3.5, notes 3 and 4) was modest for an empire whose population probably exceeded 20 million by the end of the sixteenth century.[26] As we hope to illustrate more fully later (see Chapter 5: Army Provisioning) it was not so much by the numerical predominance of its military forces that the Ottomans were distinguished from their contemporaries in the West as by the thoroughness of the administrative backup and general support that maintained them in the field. The oft-repeated attributions of Ottoman military success to their alleged ability to fight more ferociously than their opponents, and assertions that they seriously outmanned them are not supported by the facts.

Military spending

As part of our effort to determine the true scale of the Ottoman military enterprise, we turn next to the evidence relating to campaign finance. Our treatment of the subject falls under three headings: general finance, defence expenditure and campaign costs. Only by such division can we hope to isolate the full range of direct and indirect costs associated with Ottoman warfare. Whatever approach is used, however, it must be acknowledged that full assessment of state expenditure for military purposes is complicated by the fact that many expenses were incurred "off-budget" and are therefore difficult to trace. The best we can hope for here is to present a summary of a few of the most comprehensive accounts and offer some suggestions for their interpretation. Sifting through the mass of material relating to campaign finance and expenditure has been attempted for single campaigns, but in spite of the most thoroughgoing research it cannot be said that our knowledge is yet anything but fragmentary.[27]

It has often been observed as a general point that the principal contrast between the sixteenth and seventeenth century fiscal eras in the Ottoman empire is that the former was an era of budget surpluses and the latter of budget deficits. Upon closer examination, however, it becomes readily apparent that sixteenth-century budget surplus was not as universal a phenomenon as is sometimes supposed. Interpreted as an isolated figure, the general balance recorded in the budget of 1527 of 91.6 million akçes, based on income of 277.2 and expenditure of 185.6 millions, seems to represent an unspent treasury surplus of fully one-third of the treasury's regular revenues for a year.[28] But when Egypt and its revenues are removed from the equation, the apparent revenue excess is reduced to near-insignificance. In the seventeenth century the source of budget balancing was precisely the same: transfers of surplus revenue from the sultan's Inner Treasury, a reserve fund made up in very large part by remittances from Egypt and other revenue-surplus provinces, to the Outer Treasury which oversaw current expenditure.[29]

The amount of the remittance from Egypt varied in the late sixteenth to early seventeenth century between 560,000 and 610,000 gold pieces.[30] Effectively speaking, therefore, the treasury, assuming a steady rate of remittance of 600,000 gold pieces and fixed exchange rate of 120 akçes per gold ducat, could rely on a cushion of at least 72 million akçes against the threat of rising levels of either regular or extraordinary expenditure. While it is true that treasury reserves might dwindle during prolonged periods of extraordinary expenditure (especially during wartime), net balances remained positive.[31] From the early 1600s the Outer Treasury typically received infusions from the Inner Treasury of between 20 and 30 million akçes to balance its books.[32] Despite some superficial differences connected mostly with the effect of the dramatic devaluation of the silver akçe in the mid-1580s, in terms of actual fiscal practice there was a considerable degree of continuity between the sixteenth and seventeenth centuries.[33]

As levels of akçe-denominated expenditure rose in the seventeenth century, a further means employed by the state to offset the effect of cash-flow shortages was to increase its reliance on tax surcharges for military provisioning called the *bedel-i nüzul*. Military surtaxes of this kind were a common means of revenue-raising practised by all cash-strapped states in the early-modern era. France in particular seems to have perfected a means for maximizing revenues from extraordinary levies of this kind.[34] Information provided in the Tarhoncu budget of 1653 suggests this source contributed 48.1 million out of revenues of 580 million akçes, equivalent to 8.3 per cent.[35] While not insignificant as a source of campaign financing, the *bedel-i nüzul* should not be regarded as a crippling extra burden on the peasantry. In partial compensation for its requisitioning of grain or the cash equivalent the state made supplementary purchases of grain at current market prices from villages along the army's route of march. Judging from the example given in the 1653 "budget", a year which ended with a deficit of 13 per cent with expenditures of 656 million akçes against revenues of 580 millions, the state preferred to accumulate short-term debt as an alternative to the maximizing of current revenues for the financing of wars.[36] Another example from a budget covering a 12-month period between June 1630 and June 1631, during which time the Ottoman army was on the march in eastern Anatolia and Iraq, shows income assigned to the grand vezier's war treasury of 271.6 million akçes of which roughly one-fifth (55.5 million) derived from a cash contribution from Egypt, another quantity amounting to slightly less than one-fifth (50.6 million) from other transfers from the central treasury and the remaining three-fifths (165.5 million) from attribution of revenues.[37] The latter category of revenue was made up as follows: two-fifths general revenue and one-fifth special levies. The bulk of the special levies amounting to 51.1 million akçes (18.8 per cent of the revenues of 271.6 million) came from the grain provision tax (*bedel-i nüzul*).[38]

Another issue relating to the question of the burden placed by war-related expenditure on general finance concerns the seemingly inexorable rise of treasury outlays for wage payments to members of the sultan's standing regiments, the *kapu kulu*. The issue of greatest relevance here is not so much overall troop levels *per se*, as the cost to the treasury of maintaining them. New recruits and the Janissary infantry forces cost the treasury less than senior officers and, as a class, the cavalry troops (Sipahis). Though substantially fewer in number, the Sipahis cost the most to maintain (see Table 3.4 above). Thus even relatively small reductions in the numbers of the Sipahis resulted in significant savings (see Table 3.4 above).[39] The fact that Janissary enrolments continued to increase over the course of the seventeenth century is not, from a fiscal point of view, as significant as the government's success in achieving a steady reduction in Sipahi enrolments.[40] Increased costs to meet the steadily expanding payrolls of the infantry and artillerymen were more than offset by

Table 3.7 Treasury savings from reductions in the ranks of the permanent standing cavalry regiments 1609–92[1] (figures in akçes)

Regiment	1609[2]	1628[3]	1631[4]	1660[5]	1670[6]	1692[7]
1	58,267,588	38,039,313	42,445,383	43,431,196	33,782,216	33,323,436
2	47,863,132	32,753,539	37,377,184	31,912,036	29,311,552	27,551,980
3	9,545,072	4,656,361	4,567,361	2,171,432	1,840,796	1,803,980*
4	6,081,548	3,541,800	3,914,601	1,936,012	1,653,532	1,620,461*
5	4,490,584	3,168,752	3,335,232	1,967,176	1,662,380	1,629,132*
6	4,409,772	2,885,250	2,956,550	1,414,584	1,206,076	1,181,954*
7[8]		53,365,714	29,094,500			
Total	130,657,696	138,410,729	123,690,811	82,832,436	69,456,552	67,110,943

* Estimated amounts assuming a (modest) reduction of 2% over pay levels recorded for 1670.
[1] For troop numbers in these years see Table 3.5 above. For a comparative idea of treasury outlays for the salaries of standing cavalry regiments in the sixteenth century when they numbered 5,088 and their annual salary payments amounted to 30,957,300 akçes, see the 1527 budget published by Barkan in IFM XV (1953–4): p. 300.
[2] Annual figures based on quarterly pay statistics given by Ayn-i Ali; Risale, p. 91.
[3] B.B.A., Kamil Kepeci 1921.
[4] B.B.A., Kamil Kepeci 1927.
[5] IFM XVII (1955–56): 314 (based on six regiment membership of 15,248 men).
[6] IFM XVII (1955–56): 314 (based on six regiment membership of 14,070); cf. IFM XVII (1955–6): 228–9.
[7] H. Sahillioğlu, "1683–1740 yıllarında Osmanlı Imparatorluğunda hazine gelir ve gideri", VIII. Turk Tarih Kongresi Bildirileri Vol. 2 (Ankara, 1981), p. 1404 (Table 3).
[8] Rows 1–6 apply to the cavalry regiments in their usual order: sipahiyan, silahdaran, ulufeciyan-i yemin, ulufeciyan-i yesar, gureba-i yemin and gureba-i yesar. Row 7 records collective payments to all six regiments made by the treasury at various times outside the regular quarterly salary distributions. It cannot be determined from these records what proportion of the payments is accounted for by current-year salary arrears as opposed to unpaid balances carried over from previous years.

the dramatic savings in salary payments to the standing cavalry regiments. As shown in Table 3.7, by the end of the seventeenth century the annual cost to the treasury for salary payments to the Sipahis had shrunk to about half its budget-breaking levels of the early decades of the century. The fact that selective increases in some troop categories were balanced by impressive savings from reductions in others places a whole new complexion on standard views about upward spiralling military costs in the late-seventeenth-century Ottoman empire, and assumptions about the disruptive economic impact of increased resource commitments to the military sphere. It seems that, without pursuing confrontational or socially divisive strategies and without imposing high-profile cuts aimed at particular groups, the Ottomans were able to achieve their objective of cost containment through modest reductions and reallocation of available resources. The views of the Ottoman historian Katib Çelebi on the undesirability of sudden troop reductions were, with the notable exception of savage cuts imposed during the years of the vezierate of Mehmed Köprülü between 1656 and 1661, consistently followed. Katib Çelebi, although writing in an era of severe fiscal crisis around the time of the Tarhoncu budget of 1653, had insisted that if the price of achieving peace between rival services and harmony among the sultan's *kuls* was a little added treasury expense, this was a price well worth paying.[41] As a payroll reduction technique, trimming the ranks of the senior officers and of the two upper regiments of the top salaried Sipahis and Silahdars (literally, horsemen and swordsmen) was far more effective and sustainable than deep cuts that were inevitably reversed at the next military emergency.

Apart from the general effect of inflation which was unavoidably transferred to the military sphere, there is no convincing evidence to suggest that mounting military costs in the late seventeenth century were serious enough to engender a resource-related crisis affecting the Ottomans' ability to wage war.[42] At the close of the seventeenth century, the empire's position as a universally-acknowledged European "superpower" was still largely intact. Although its military reputation was left tarnished by the defeats suffered during the pan-European counteroffensives of the late 1680s and 1690s, it was not long before former members of the League, as they were confronted singly, had to acknowledge the still-impressive strength of the Ottoman military machine. Russia (after Pruth in 1711), Venice (after the Ottoman counteroffensive in the Morea in 1715) and Austria (following the Ottoman campaigns in Serbia during 1737–9) were each in their turn forced to return significant amounts of territory ceded by earlier treaties.[43] Until the mid-eighteenth century the Ottoman empire was still regarded in Europe with considerable awe, and Voltaire and his contemporaries still marvelled at the vastness and seeming inexhaustibility of its resources. When Voltaire wrote his *Siècle de Louis XIV* in 1751, the resilience, wealth and military proficiency as well as self-sufficiency of the Ottoman empire were still the principal terms of reference used by historians and commentators on the contemporary scene in Europe.[44]

Expenditure for defence

Another area of state military expenditure that requires attention is outlays for fortress construction and maintenance. Because expenses for construction and repair of fortresses were registered in self-standing reports, and not usually incorporated in central treasury accounts, their contribution to overall military costs is all too easily overlooked. Especially in the immediate aftermath of campaign, large sums were devoted to repair walls damaged during siege and for the extension and improvement of substandard or vulnerable fortifications.[45] In addition to allocating cash resources and raw materials the army invested considerable amounts of time and labour. Since we have already touched briefly in a previous section (see above, Chapter 2: Cost Constraints) on the scale and expense of military construction, our discussion here will focus primarily on fortress maintenance and garrisoning costs. From information supplied in Mustafa Ali's history we learn that during the Ottoman expansion into southern Georgia during the Caucasian wars of 1578–1590 the annual cost of garrisoning just three newly-occupied fortresses situated in the 80-mile corridor between Erivan and Domanisi came to 48 million akçes for wages alone. The distribution of the more than 10,000 garrison troops between the three fortresses is shown in Table 3.8 below.[46] By allowing an extra margin of expense of just one-eighth for grain supplies we can compute the cost to the Ottomans for garrisoning this newly acquired province at around 54 million akçes – a not inconsiderable sum when juxtaposed with figures for regular state treasury revenues in the mid-to early-seventeenth century which typically ranged between 400 up to a maximum of 600 million akçes.[47] In reality, the six million akçes allowed in the foregoing calculation for the cost of grain supplies to 10,000 garrison soldiers represents a serious underestimation. Allowing a grain ration of one *kile* per man per month, 10,548 men would have consumed 126,576 *kiles* of grain in a year. Even assuming a low and stable base price of 40 akçes per *kile*, the purchase price of

Table 3.8 Costs for garrisoning fortresses in newly-conquered Ottoman provinces in the Caucasus circa 1585

	Men	Annual wages
Beylerbeylik of Revan (Erivan) and five smaller forts around its perimeter		
Erivan	5,601	25,035,072
Five smaller forts	673	1,852,036
	6,274	26,887,108
Beylerbeyliks of Lori and Domanisi (i.e., Southern Georgia)		
Beylerbeylik of Lori	1,897	8,130,303
Beylerbeylik of Domanisi	2,377	12,915,104
	4,274	21,045,407
TOTAL FOR ALL THREE BEYLERBEYLIKS	10,548[1]	47,932,515

[1] Mustafa Ali, *Kunh ül Ahbar* (Nuruosmaniye Library Ms 3409), f. 361a. Some of the 10,000 garrison troops were men transferred from nearby fortresses such as Erzurum and Kars, but fully 82 per cent of the men (8,650) and 40 million akçes of the total wage bill were new recruits whose costs could be met only by the allocation of new resources or the reallocation of existing ones.

the wheat itself would come to more than five million akçes, leaving only one million (estimated at the unrealistically low rate of 8 akçes per *kile*) for overland transport to a remote frontier location. The implausibility of such low transport costs can be seen by comparing known data about the hiring of pack animals for grain transport over comparable terrain between Erzurum and Diyarbekir, which cost the treasury an average not of 8 but 88 akçes per *kile*.[48] Even allowing for the effect of seventeenth-century inflation and of the akçe's devaluation after 1584 reflected in comparable figures for the seventeenth century, it can be readily seen that keeping the food and transport bill to sustain 10,000 garrison troops for a whole year to under six million akçes would have presented a real challenge in Ali's time as well. If we were to interpret Ali's data for the late sixteenth century in the light of known information for grain prices in the mid-to-late seventeenth century, the above mentioned 40 akçes per *kile* price for wheat would have to be replaced with a price ranging between 55 and 80 akçes per *kile*.[49]

It is possible to extrapolate from data of the late seventeenth century for the provisioning of the garrison of Azak (Azov) on the empire's remote northern frontier with Russia what general costs for fortress maintenance in other areas might have been. Information provided in Mevkufati's history for the year 1693 suggests that the Azov Janissary complement consisted of 2,272 men provided with an annual grain allowance of 27,264 *kiles* of grain.[50] Divided into 12 equal rations, this quantity was precisely enough for one *kile* per man per month. By the 1690s the average price of a *kile* of wheat (at state-controlled prices) had risen to 80 akçes per *kile*, bringing the food bill for the 3,656-man garrison staff of Janissaries, artillerymen and others to 3.5 million with an additional 600,000 akçes for grain transport by ship.[51] A monthly allowance of a *kile* of wheat (20 okkas) per man suggests a daily rate of consumption of two-thirds of an okka per man per day, equivalent to approximately 855 grams or 1.9 pounds. This compares with the 0.55 okka daily grain allowance allocated to troops during march when minimizing of baggage and animal loads was a pressing concern. According to information found in a register book of imperial writs belonging to the reign of Murad IV (r. 1623–40) military planners reckoned that allowing a minimal daily allowance of 1.25 lodras (220 dirhems or 0.55 okkas) of dry biscuit per man meant that an army of 80,000 men on the march needed 100,000 lodras (1,000 kantars) of provisions per day.[52] It has to be remembered, however, that these were minimal rations designed for easy transportability and did not represent optimal caloric value or ideal dietary intake. When we take into account the pressure exerted by real market prices and the average dietary requirements of soldiers over winter months when supplements to and substitutes for minimal grain rations were less readily available, then Mustafa Ali's estimate of 54 million akçes for the cost of paying and provisioning 10,000 garrison troops seems modest enough.

By multiplying the garrisoning costs illustrated in Ali's figures for 10,000 men in a single sector of the frontier to several tens of thousands assigned to fortresses scattered across the empire's wider borders, it is easy to see how defence expenditures alone accounted for a very significant proportion of Ottoman resource commitments for military purposes. The defence of the empire's borders across the extent they had come to assume by 1590 – not allowing extraordinary expenditures for new fortress construction which would tip the balance to still higher levels of outlay – implied (based on Ali's 50 million-plus akçes for 10,000-plus men) an annual outlay of at least 150 to 200 million akçes. In the seventeenth century some of the expenses for border defence were met by cash transfers from contiguous regions, but even with such cost-sharing arrangements the cost to the central fisc remained high.[53]

Let us now take a closer look at the defence requirements of the empire at successive points in its history, starting with the Ottoman establishment in Hungary after 1541 and ending with the final offensive in Crete during the 1660s. Estimations of the number of garrison troops stationed in Hungary vary, but according to one assessment their total number during the peak period of Ottoman involvement in the mid-sixteenth century rose to between 20,000 and 22,000 men.[54] As a force of occupation for a country the size of Hungary, even confined to the central portions which made up the Ottoman province, this implies a rather low-profile military presence in much of the country. We know that in fact a relatively large proportion of the total force was concentrated in a few key fortresses.[55] Troop commitments at even these relatively modest levels were themselves only required when there was active or continuous fighting along the province's borders. In the 1640s, when the Hungarian front remained relatively quiet as the Ottomans were winding down the Iranian wars and about to fully engage in the Cretan wars, a centrally-supplied force of some 8,000 Janissaries (supported by an undocumented number of local recruits) was sufficient to garrison the whole of the *eyalet-i Budin*, the most strategically situated of the four provinces which made up Ottoman Hungary.[56] The available evidence strongly suggests that, far from being content with maintaining expensive and unnecessary troop commitments in relatively inactive military zones, the Ottoman state bureaucracy was adept at identifying the areas where current military needs were greatest, and reallocating underutilized spare resources to those areas.[57]

Since the Janissary contingent was always the predominant group in the most important provincial garrisons, their numbers may be used as the most appropriate and consistent unit of comparison for measuring the scale of

Ottoman defence requirements. In the era of expansion during the sixteenth century records indicate a total Janissary strength of 13,661 of whom 11,535 were Istanbul-based, and only 2,126 (15.6 per cent) assigned to provincial garrison duty.[58] Information on Janissary strength in the mid-seventeenth century shows that, while enrolment in the Istanbul regiments had tripled, the increase in their provincial presence was even more dramatic. Global figures for Janissary membership in the period 1653–1670 indicate a Janissary membership of between 51,000 and 54,000 men, of whom a peacetime minimum of 27 per cent was assigned to provincial garrison duty.[59] In wartime the proportion concentrated in the border zone rose to 40 per cent. For example, in 1660 when the Ottomans were engaged on two fronts in Moldavia (Varad/ Oradea) and in Crete, the global enrolment of the corps rose to 54,222, of whom 32,821 (60 per cent) were barracked in Istanbul and the remaining 21,401 on prolonged assignment to the provinces.[60] The global enrolment figure for 1670 after the conclusion of the war in Crete, but too soon to reflect any large-scale demobilization, was 53,849 men, only imperceptibly smaller than the figure recorded for 1660. But while the number registered as present in the Istanbul barracks rose from 60 to 73 per cent of the total, this still left a very substantial number, 14,379 men, on assignment in provincial garrisons.

Both numerically and proportionally the balance of forces stationed in the provinces represented a significant change from the situation of the sixteenth century. Although some frontiers, such as the Georgian-Azerbaijani sector of the eastern borders of the empire, were no longer as active or heavily defended as they had been in the time of Mustafa Ali, when 10,000 men were required to man a number of newly-acquired key strategic fortresses, the residual defence requirements of the empire in its maturity were much heavier than envisaged by empire builders such as Sultan Süleyman I. The maintenance of the *status quo* in the seventeenth century, even without the opening of new fronts as, for example, in Crete, required the Ottomans to set aside a growing proportion of their military resources for defence.

In the seventeenth century the Ottomans experimented with new ways of financing military campaigns through short-term debt, borrowing against future revenues and a variety of treasury manipulations including profit from exchange rate fluctuations. Such means were adequate to meet one-off costs for the launching of campaigns, but the demands of defence were relentless and required more permanent solutions. In general, the Ottomans tried to avoid raising levels of revenue extraction to new heights to meet purely military needs. Seemingly, they preferred − in a manner reminiscent of robbing Peter to pay Paul − the redeployment of existing wealth and resources to making new demands for sacrifice on the part of taxpayers.[61]

In gauging the impact of rising military expenditure on provincial society, it is not so much the absolute sums involved as the apportionment of defence costs that merits our closest attention. Both the benefits and the burdens of waging war fell differently on different regions, and, paradoxically, state investment for infrastructure improvements and increased circulation of cash in support of the army's massively proportioned need for provisions and materials provided greatest benefit to the economies of the regions situated nearest to the active front of the moment. From the standpoint of burden-sharing, too, it was the most exposed areas which made up the front line defence system of the empire that were most heavily subsidized by revenue transfers from inland regions. We see this pattern of inward investment most clearly in the case of Hungary, where Ottoman military commitment and imperial priority were consistently maintained over one-and-a-half centuries. Hungary's case was exceptional in that, unlike the Ottomans' Eastern policy, to which priority was only sporadically assigned, or its mid-Mediterranean ventures which claimed priority only during the middle decades of the seventeenth century,[62] this province retained its status as the jewel in the crown of the Ottomans' European possessions. A very large proportion of the ongoing costs of imperial administration in Hungary was subsidized by treasury grants and cash transfers from the surplus revenues of Egypt.[63] But the very magnitude of the outside help for defence (amounting to roughly one-half of Egypt's yearly remittance to the central treasury) suggests an expense that in peak years at least took a separate toll on populations inhabiting the border regions as well.

In the case of defence expenditure we confront the opposite problem to that noted in the first part of this chapter where the tendency to overestimate Ottoman troop strength was noted. Because of the difficulty of calculating the many hidden costs, particularly for fortress maintenance and repair, and the near-impossibility of estimating local labour input, much of which was unregistered, we can only offer a sketchy account of the means by which the Ottomans managed to keep the system in balance. It is difficult to say how serious our underestimation of real defence costs might be, and how these real burdens were shared is even less well-studied or understood. This is an area of study on Ottoman military organizational affairs that deserves much more thorough investigation. What can be said with a fair degree of certainty, however, is that, by comparison with their contemporaries, the Ottomans maintained a careful and very clear distinction between military and civilian status groups. Members of the tax-exempt *askeri* class jealously guarded their particular identity and regarded the fulfilment of their assigned duties by civilians as an encroachment on their position and a threat to their privileges. They naturally regarded any such encroachments with suspicion, which meant that the taxpayers (civilians) in Ottoman society were excluded from, but at the same time also protected from demands for their labour in military-related tasks. Unless explicitly assigned a tax-exempt status and a military or semi-military function as guardians of the passes (*derbendci*), bridge repairers (*köprücu*) and the like, the exploitation of civilian labour for military purposes was in general avoided by the Ottomans. In the chapter's final section we turn our attention to the better-documented and more visible, but in some ways no less problematic area of military finance: the funding of Ottoman campaign costs.

Costs of launching campaigns

Consideration was given above to the fixed costs, such as the Janissaries' wages, connected with the Ottoman military enterprise. Tracking these costs that were both recurring and emanating from a central source is relatively easy. However, calculating expenditures connected with actual campaign operations is not so straightforward. Expenses for operations in the field were typically met from disparate sources. A principal source was cash transfusions from the Inner Treasury called *sefer filorisi*. These disbursements were irregular and made entirely at the sultan's discretion. They began in the winter months before the army had set out and gathered pace as the date of departure for the front approached. The bulk of these funds was set aside to meet the cost of purchases of equipment and provisions for the sultan's household troops, the *kapu kulu*. Since the figures do not reflect provisioning costs for army irregulars and timariots who made their own equipment purchases, they can only be regarded as a partial accounting. An example from 1541, solidly in the period before the drastic devaluation of the silver akçe, documents the disbursement of 38 million akçes from the Inner Treasury as an advance to meet the cost of campaign preparations.[64] The seventeenth century was no different, except that the street value of the sultan's largesse steadily increased when calculated in terms of the post-devaluation akçe. Thus, for instance, Osman II's campaign fund as he set out for Poland in 1621 was composed, in addition to the 50.4 million akçes provided from his own Inner Treasury, of substantial amounts in gold belonging to Egypt's treasury remittance arrears from immediately preceding years. The latter sums consisted of 190,000 gold pieces for 1617 and 580,000 (the entire annual remittance) for 1619 and a further 120 purses of gurush (equivalent to 60,000 big silver or 40,000 gold pieces) from the Yemen Treasury. The combined value of these campaign contributions was no less than 150 million akçes: considerably more if converted at open market rates of exchange.[65]

The timing of these distributions and the sources from which they were drawn indicates that they were used by the sultan as a means of jump-starting the campaign, ensuring the co-operation of his *kuls* by generous advances both in the form of equipment allowances and other cash bonuses paid out before the army's departure for the front. This pattern is apparent from another register which records disbursements made from the Inner Treasury by Murad IV during January, February and early March of 1635, which were designed to ensure that all would be in readiness for his departure to the Erivan campaign planned for that Spring. Starting at a slower pace over the winter months, by the end of February the cumulative sum disbursed amounted to 220,000 gold pieces but, with a final burst of generosity during the final week of preparation for departure, a further 157,150 gold pieces were distributed bringing the pre-campaign total to 377,150 gold pieces.[66]

Record-keeping covering the preparatory phases for battle was quite systematic and is relatively easy to trace,[67] but calculating the more haphazard disbursements made during the actual course of a campaign poses a real challenge. Consolidated reporting on military costs for specific Ottoman land campaigns is a relative rarity, and no example relating to major campaigns seems to have survived. We are fortunate, however, that a detailed account covering a minor campaign in the Yemen during 1629 has been preserved.[68] Though the scale of mobilization for this campaign was small by comparison with full-blown imperial campaigns led by the sultan or his deputy the grand vezier, the comprehensive account of expenses kept by Governor of Egypt Tabani-yassi Mehmed Pasha on this occasion serves as a uniquely detailed guide, if not to the true scale, then at least to the relevant categories of expenditure.[69]

The money of account used in this register was the Egyptian silver coin, the *para*, whose market value in this period had risen to between two and three akçes, while rates for official currency conversions remained fixed at the two-akçe level.[70] On this basis, the recorded disbursements of 14,476,080 paras for the soldiers' wages and 13,420,604 paras for equipment for a cumulative total approaching 28 million paras represented an akçe expenditure in the order of 56 million. These sums take on greater significance when it is recalled that relatively few troops were deployed from the centre for this campaign. The imperial army had only recently returned (in the winter of 1628–9) from a prolonged period of absence stretching over the better part of four years. During this period the army had been engaged in a failed attempt to recapture Baghdad from the Safavids and a series of campaigns aimed at the suppression of Abaza Mehmed Pasha, the rebel governor of Erzurum. By the Autumn of 1628 the troops were determined to resist any plans to remobilize for campaign in spring 1629.[71] These war preparations reflect, in effect, the mobilization of local resources under the initiative of the Governor of Egypt without significant help in terms of men, money or materials from the centre. In the event, the planned mobilization was delayed until January 1630, in part because of the difficulties encountered in readying supplies in the absence of significant help from outside the province.[72] The accounts for purchases of equipment intended for use in the Yemen expedition were submitted separately by imperial commissioners (emin) each of whom had his own particular area of responsibility to prepare the army for campaign. The six principal accounts were:

Purpose of expenditure	Cost in Egyptian *para*
I Supplies for 4,436 bread ovens to be constructed in the field	421,046
II Supplies for fleet preparations	3,897,934
III Supplies for use of imperial treasury staff	75,481
IV Supplies for army commissary	589,983
V Purchases for army ordnance	171,030
VI Miscellaneous purchases and army transport costs	8,265,130
TOTAL ALLOCATION	13,420,604

In order to gain a more textured appreciation of the principal areas and proportional weight of expenditure for specific campaign-related purposes, it will be helpful, in addition to the obvious observation concerning the heavy costs associated with various forms of transport from ship repair to camel hire and purchase (see items listed in Accounts no. II and VI below), if we provide a further breakdown of expenses under the purview of each of the six commissioners.

No. I: Account of Omer Agha, Imperial Commissioner in Charge of Household Disbursements (421,046 paras)

Building materials for the construction of 4,436 bake ovens	255,755
Flour sacks	104,656
Lumber and miscellaneous supplies for the confectionery cooks	60,635
	421,046

No. II: Account of Yusuf Agha, Imperial Commissioner in Charge of the Bulak (Cairo) Shipyards

Timber for repair of galleons and galleys	1,015,162
Miscellaneous building supplies	913,596
568 pieces of timber for ship construction	31,220
Ship's stores and provisions	1,937,956
	3,897,934

No. III: Purchase of supplies (timber, iron, etc.) for wagons to be used by the staff of the imperial treasury

	75,481

No. IV: Account of Mehmed Agha, Comptroller of Market Dues and Internal Revenue for Egypt (supplies for the imperial kitchens)

380 kantars of honey	44,900
100 kantars of clarified butter	25,650
25 kantars of lemons	5,000
400 okkas of vinegar	2,400
51 kantars of cotton-seed oil	5,100
Grain supplies	15,028
Dry biscuit and grain supplies	14,693
Miscellaneous food purchases	477,212
	589,983

No. V: Account of Osman Agha, gunner attached to the Cairo garrison (materials to make 30 bombs [humabara])

133 kantars of copper	79,200
14 kanars of tin	19,040
Miscellaneous materials	72,790
	171,030

No. VI: Miscellaneous accounts covering grain, gunpowder, transport animals, etc.

Wood for cooking while on desert campaign	326,000
Tents	225,000
Grain purchases	2,558,500
Three camel-hire transactions	2,750,000[73]

505 kantars of gunpowder	505,000[74]
500 kantars of lead	150,000
Miscellaneous purchases of equipment	1,750,630
	8,265,130

As can be deduced from the foregoing account of expenses for standard equipment purchases, standard wage payments, and special grants allowances and campaign bonuses relating to a military action carried out against an ill-equipped rebel governor in the Yemen, the decision to mobilize for campaign (whether major or minor of short or long duration) was not undertaken lightly. Whatever course the campaign might ultimately take, or even if the campaign was prematurely abandoned before any real engagement of the enemy had taken place, a very heavy burden of expense was incurred simply in order to get the campaign launched. The opportunity which such detailed documentary evidence provides to observe Ottoman military planning at the micro level also helps us better to appreciate the important contribution made by the invisible organizational structure which underpinned all Ottoman campaigns. Although, for reasons already discussed, there were no guarantees of triumph in the operational sphere, the fact that such detailed contingency planning had taken place in government bureaux in the capital played its own role in at least averting some of the more obvious potential problems in the field. Whatever the outcome of battle and even in the absence of a decisive engagement of any sort, Ottoman field manoeuvres were invariably a *tour de force* of administrative precision and finesse.

In the two next chapters we will focus in some detail on the mechanics of troop movement and supply in order to complete our picture of the physical realities connected with Ottoman warfare. Only by immersing ourselves in the minute detail of the Ottomans' organization of the "smaller tasks" associated with the military enterprise can the daunting scale of the physical and material challenges that faced them be appreciated fully. No other variables had so pronounced an effect on the outcome of warfare in pre-modern times as the linked concerns of army transport and logistics. Ottoman success in warfare was closely linked with their ability to mobilize both men and material on an impressive scale. Without the administrative and procedural expertise supplied by the Ottoman central bureaucracy it is hard to imagine how the supposed ferocity and battle dedication of the Ottoman warrior alone could have carried the day.

Chapter Four

Troop movement and army transport

Getting the troops to the appropriate field of action was expensive by sea,[1] difficult by land and a major preoccupation either way. Over established itineraries within normal seasonal boundaries and fully supported by the network of imperial supply depots, the army was able to maintain its measured pace of advance or retreat. But even under these optimal conditions, army movement was never rapid. To avoid advancing too far ahead of its baggage trains, a normal day would see the army on the move for no more than about four to four-and-a-half hours. Proceeding at a relaxed walking pace for horses of three miles per hour and assuming no prolonged stops, this would allow the vanguard of the army to advance approximately 13.5 miles (22 km) in a day's march. The rear guard and baggage trains proceeding at a slower pace (perhaps 2 mph) would need the better part of six hours to reach the advance camp. Speculation about average travel times that might have applied to movement overland in the pre-steam, pre-electric transport era – even when details of the terrain can be factored in – is futile, since road and weather conditions were rarely consistent or predictable enough to allow even individuals, let alone legions travelling together, to think in terms of "on-schedule" arrival. Still, it will be useful if we can identify maximum rates of advance achievable under optimal conditions to serve as a point of reference. One researcher, referring to the standard Istanbul to Belgrade itinerary that represented a round-figure distance of 1,000 km (621 statute miles) over good roads, assumed a travel time of 77 days. This estimate allows 20 days (roughly a quarter of the total travel time) during which there was absence of movement, used partly for rest and partly for river crossings. On the 57 days during which some movement was logged the same researcher suggests an average rate of advance of 17.5 km (11 miles) per day. The average rate of advance over the whole period with the rest days included was thus only 13 km per day.[2] Examples from a variety of different terrains suggest Ottoman armies operated under similar restrictions on the scope of their movement. An army that managed to be on the move for more than 70 per cent of the time as allowed for in the calculations by Perjés was achieving something exceptional by the standards of the time. Two examples, one each from the European and Asian spheres of operation, amply demonstrate the point.

Apart from the effect of weather, terrain and road conditions the army's pace of march and rate of advance bore an inverse relation to the quantity of provisions and equipment it had to carry with it. In most cases the return journey from the front after battle when the equipment consumables (ammunition, etc.) and most of the provisions had been used up was considerably quicker. Figures on the march to and return from Baghdad in 1638–9 confirm this pattern. The outward march took 544 hours, spread over 197 days, of which 121 (61.5 per cent) were spent in march and 76 (38.5 per cent) at rest. By comparison, the return journey was accomplished in 393 hours of active march. On the return journey, though, despite the fact that the army was able to remain on the move for an average of six hours per day during the 65 days on which some movement was actually logged, advance to the final destination was significantly delayed by the much higher proportion of total travel time devoted to layover days. On the return march from victory in Baghdad in 1639 the army spent 81 days (55 per cent) of the 146 days needed to complete the journey at rest.[3] Whether encumbered by its pre-battle baggage or relaxed by post-victory elation among the soldiers, the army's movement was always deliberate.

Another seventeenth-century example, taken this time from the European sphere, concerns the march of the Grand Vezier Köprülü-zade Fazil Ahmed Pasha's army *en route* to Uyvar in the Spring of 1663. Although the commander managed a timely departure from Edirne on the 14th of March 1663, a 16-day layover at Sofya to pasture the horses and to allow for the gathering of timariot troops reporting for duty from distant provinces, together with an 11-day halt at Belgrade to complete the army's provisions and equipment, meant that the assembly of a fully-battle-ready force at the ford over the Drava River at Ösek was accomplished only 74 days after the grand vezier's departure from Edirne. Having arrived at Ösek, the army's progress was delayed a further eight days while the bridges were made ready for the assembled troops to make their crossing. In total the travel time from Edirne to the Drava crossing was 85 days. The journey was made up of 181 hours of march completed in 39 days at an average pace of 4.64 hrs. per day, and 46 days (54 per cent of total elapsed time [t.e.t.]) for rest.[4] The high proportion of the total elapsed time devoted to rest even as the army advanced towards its military objective is suggestive of the special challenges (frequent river crossings, etc.)

encountered by the army when operating in the European theatre.[5] The remainder of Fazil Ahmed Pasha's 1663 itinerary between the Drava crossing and Esztergom was accomplished in 34 days, divided into 13 days of march (38 per cent t.e.t.) and 21 days of rest (62 per cent t.e.t.). In the 13 days of movement undertaken at a stage when the army had reached a level of full mobilization, the army logged only 50 hours of active march, an average of only 3.85 hours per day.[6] The wide range of practice which characterized the army's pattern of movement meant that it marched only two hours on some days, while on others as much as seven.

The wide divergence in patterns of army march was made necessary by a number of factors. One of the factors which restricted movement most was the availability of a plentiful supply of pure drinking water for both men and animals in the near vicinity of the chosen halting place. In Ottoman campaign journals careful note is always made of streams (chay), rivers (nehir) and irrigation canals (hark) situated near the army's route of advance. In the case of the siege planned by the Ottomans for the 1663 campaign season, from the setting out of the first units from Edirne to the positioning of a fully-manned and fully-equipped military force at Esztergom ready to make the final river crossing and proceed against Uyvar 119 days had passed. It is worthy of note that this rate of advance was realized at a time when (during the normally dry summer months) road conditions were near ideal.[7]

An example of how unscheduled stops necessitated by unseasonable weather patterns might further delay the army's already naturally halting pace of advance is provided in a diary relating to the campaign against Erivan in 1635. When the army's march to the eastern front was only at about the mid-point, the diary records the collapse of the bridge over the Kizilirmak on the western approaches to Sivas that necessitated an unscheduled halt of 16 days to allow time for emergency repairs. After the army had arrived at Sivas in the last week of May, its forward progress was further delayed by the onset of a freak storm which brought unremitting high winds, heavy rain and hail lasting 11 days.[8] As a result of the chance coincidence of two operational setbacks both connected with unforeseen environmental and climatic obstacles the army was not ready to continue its march to the final destination of Erivan until 6 June 1635, almost a month "behind schedule".

In view of all the uncertainties associated with the army's movement, the importance of the scouting and reconnaissance function provided by Ottoman auxiliary forces can be readily seen. In the European theatre of operations it was Tatar scouts and foragers advancing at rates unsustainable by the more heavily-armed main army units who gathered vital information about general conditions beyond the army's immediate perimeters. This information gathered by Tatar forces, who positioned themselves at a distance of one or two days' march ahead of the main body of the army, was important not so much for tactical as for general operational purposes. These forces in the vanguard acted as the eyes and ears that guided and, in a pre-electronic age of communications, also the voice that directed army movement. To perform this function effectively and to ensure their ability to cover large distances quickly, it was standard procedure for Tatar contingents to report for battle with several spare mounts (*chatal ati*) in tow. Reliable evidence suggests the Tatar forces were capable of sustaining up to 13 hours of continuous march.[9] In emergency situations the pool of spare mounts could also be used to assist in the extraction of trapped infantry forces from exposed forward positions. This capability was tested for example in the aftermath of the defeat at St Gotthard in August 1664 when the collapse of makeshift bridges thrown up over the Raba necessitated the immediate abandonment of Ottoman bridgehead positions established on the far bank of the river.[10]

Another function assigned to the Tatar, or other auxiliary, mostly light cavalry, forces was the opening up of diversionary fronts. Using the methods typically associated with steppe warfare, which were characterized by rapid advance, sudden attack and rapid return to base, the light cavalry were generally deployed in small concentrations over a wide territory, encircling the enemy and sending intentionally confusing multiple signals about the planned direction of attack. The result of these operations, when successfully executed, was a scattered and disoriented opponent left to face the main Ottoman army as it advanced to join the vanguard. But one must not be misled by the dazzling performance of its modestly proportioned vanguard forces, who shielded and obscured the more ponderous movements of the main army camp, into supposing that the Ottomans were ever capable of achieving anything like agility, speed or, least of all, surprise when besieging fixed enemy defences. Moving large concentrations of troops, accompanied by their heavy siege guns and light field artillery, into place for siege was by definition a slow process for all pre-modern armies. The risk of failure due to the late or non-arrival of essential equipment was always present even in the best-managed campaigns.

The next feature of army movement and troop mobility that requires our attention is the element of timing and normal seasonal limitations, especially end-of-season limits, associated with Ottoman troop mobilization and demobilizations. Precision timing had a particular importance in the European theatre where the onset of winter could be both sudden and severe. One of the few examples where Süleyman I's military record was marked with only qualified success was the 1529 campaign, when his decision to extend the normal close of the campaigning season by a margin of just two weeks was sufficient to put the whole army at risk. On this occasion the army's delayed retreat from the abandoned siege of Vienna in mid-October took an exceptionally high toll in lost men, animals and equipment. During the crossing of the swollen Leitha river at Brück on the 19th and 20th of October the pack horses became mired in the marshy ground and a large part of the baggage (including the tents crucial to the troops' safety and comfort during the remainder of the retreat) had to be abandoned.[11] Because of the late-season delay in the start of the retreat, the army suffered unusual privation throughout the march back via central Hungary to Belgrade. At one stage *en route* to a makeshift camp set up in the vicinity of Petrovaradin on the 6th of November, the army remained on the move from daybreak to nightfall for 15 hours of continuous march, leaving a litter of pack animals and exhausted troops in its wake struggling to keep up.[12] The fact that the Hungarian theatre was criss-crossed with major rivers and their tributary systems is a material reality of the military context within which Ottoman armies in Europe were called to perform that is all too often overlooked. See map no. 5, p. xv.

The danger of the army's preferred path of retreat being cut off by rivers swollen by autumn rains was by no means confined to the 1529 campaign or the landscape of western Hungary. In a directive sent in early September 1663 by the sultan to the grand vezier in charge of the siege of Uyvar, in which he commented on the military situation as of the 10th day of the siege, he warned the field commander against prolonging the operation in enemy territory for any longer than 50 days (until mid-October at the latest), so as to avoid placing the army at risk from entrapment by steadily rising water levels in nearby streams and rivers.[13]

Late season offensives, when attempted, were always undertaken as a calculated risk in full knowledge of the likelihood that basic tasks, such as the manoeuvring of guns into position for bombarding enemy defences, would take twice as long to achieve as in early summer when the ground was hard. An example from the Ottomans' military operations north of the Danube bend in 1663 illustrates the difficulties the army might face. On this occasion the commander Fazil Ahmed Pasha − not content with his notable success in subduing the stronghold of Uyvar which fell on the 25th of September − decided to advance still further, beyond the banks of the Nitra river, for another offensive. However, because of the onset of the muddy season, the animals charged with dragging the guns to the new forward positions needed two days to deliver their loads instead of the two hours it had taken the troops to advance and take up their offensive positions.[14]

As can be seen from the examples given above, the necessity of bringing the campaigning season to a close by the mid-to-late October cut-off point was dictated, not just by long-established military custom or acquiescence to troops' demands for winter leaves, but above all by practical necessity. Aware of Ottoman military habits, the enemy sometimes launched winter offensives timed to coincide with predictable patterns of Ottoman demobilization. Although such attacks prompted a swift Ottoman response, they rarely lasted long enough to require a full remobilization of forces and, for their part, the Ottomans rarely initiated out-of-season attacks, having learned from past experience that the hardship and expense which such operations entailed was not justified by the results achieved. To reach a better understanding of the scale of the material challenges faced by Ottoman armies on the move and the interplay of factors such as distance, terrain and climate, we must now take a closer look at some details of the transport conditions that prevailed during particular Ottoman campaigns.

Ottoman army transport: the scale of the challenge

In the preceding section the broader context of troop movements and general army mobility was considered. To complete this general picture, we will now focus our attention on the specifics of how large bodies of men and animals mobilized for military action were sustained in the field. The delivery of adequate grain supplies to the army posed the most serious transport challenge. Although the Ottomans were exceptional among their European contemporaries in their early development of a comprehensive system of grain-storage depots strategically placed along the central highway system linking the full extent of their Asian and European provinces, there were occasions when they were required to operate for prolonged periods outside easy reach of the *menzil-hane* network. This network did not fully encompass border regions, and it was still further removed from access as the army operated in the enemy's interior. During periods of detachment from the reach of its own supply bases, the Ottoman army had to be accompanied by massive numbers of transport animals (especially camels) charged with the delivery of food and fodder for the army. A large army, such as that mobilized for the reconquest of Baghdad in 1638, required a quantity of 5,000 *kiles* of barley (roughly 141 short tons) a day for distribution as animal feed just for the use of the sultan's own retinue and for members of his own household regiments.[15] Assuming a full barley ration of ten pounds per day per horse designed for horses on the march who were customarily fed a calorie-rich diet consisting mostly of dry fodder,[16] this allowance was only enough to support a relatively small proportion (fewer than 30,000) of the army's mounts.[17]

Evidence is lacking on the details of Ottoman practices for the care of army animals during campaign but, by extrapolating from what we do know of feeding practices during the stabling of the imperial herds over the winter months when the animals were at rest, it is possible to gain some idea of general principles. The evidence suggests that during the winter months the nutritional requirements of the camels were met with a daily ration of four okkas of barley feed and 8.8 okkas of straw. This proportion of 11 pounds of grain to 25 pounds of straw (a ratio of 1:2.2) used for the winter feeding of camels is documented in a number of sources.[18] The transport of the grain rations for the mounts of the household troops alone, leaving aside for the moment any supplementary amounts provided in the form of hay or straw and not including the nutritional needs of the camels used to transport the grain itself, required the animal power provided by upwards of 500 camels each carrying a "standard load" of between 9 and 10 *kiles*.[19] The longer the army remained in the field, the greater the number of animals required for grain transport. If we assume a daily minimum of 500 camel loads of grain to represent the average consumption of the mounts of that part of the army entitled to a supply from central stores, the carrying of provisions sufficient to last two to three months in the field implied the transport services of no fewer than 30,000 – perhaps as many as 50,000 – camels just to transport barley rations. The troops' own daily dietary requirements consisting of a hypothetical but realistic ration of an okka's worth of baked goods (one-half okka of bread plus one-half okka of dry biscuit per man per day)[20] would add a quantity of 20,000 okkas (105 camel loads) for a force of 20,000 Janissary and Sipahi actives.[21] For each 30-day period in the field this force would require 600,000 okkas of supplies borne on the backs of 3,150 camels, carrying an average burden of 190 okkas (9.5 *kiles*). In two to three months of campaigning the transport of the barley (animal) and wheat (human) requirements of only a fraction of the army, consisting of its most privileged units, required the transport equivalent of between 35,000 and 55,000 camels.[22]

For the first part of the army's outward itinerary substantial amounts of grain were stored in advance at each of the *menzil-hane* stations along the army's route of march, but long periods during the last phases of campaign were spent well beyond the reach of government supply depots. During operations in some sectors, the army could depend on the assistance of friendly tribes. For example, during the third week of the Baghdad siege in 1638 the arrival of the Arab chieftain Tarpush with 12,000 camel loads of grain (a month's supply for the men) was celebrated in the Ottoman camp with ceremonial feasts.[23] For operations conducted north of the Danube, however, Ottoman armies had to carry virtually all their basic requirements with them. In his comments on the military disaster at Szenta in 1697 the Ottoman historian Rashid stressed the army's vulnerability, which in his opinion derived not so much from general lack of supplies or grain shortages *per se*[24] as its incapacity, using existing transport facilities, to bring sufficient quantities forward with it into enemy territory to sustain more than 15 or, at the outside, 20 days of military operations.[25]

Safe delivery of grain represented only a part of the army's overall transport needs. Information on the length of typical Ottoman army baggage trains is supplied in a variety of sources. Hüseyn Hezarfen, writing circa 1660, suggests a minimum provision of 11,500 camels for the sultan's use on campaign to be allocated as follows: 4,000 for transport of the army arsenal; 5,000 for the sultan's larder (presumably including its grain supplies)[26] and for the Treasury; 500 for the sultan's tents; and 2,000 to be used for transporting the provisions and equipment of the Janissaries.[27] By contrast, more detailed registers from the sixteenth century suggest that the sultan's pantry staff were allocated no more than 800 to 900 camels. These latter figures, however, reflect the Ottoman army circa 1550 at a time when the standing regiments at the Porte entitled to rations from central stores represented a much smaller proportion of the army ranks than in 1660.[28] The figure suggested by Koçi Bey, writing circa 1640, of 1,000 *kitar* or 5,000 camels may be considered as representing the actual length of the Ottoman army's baggage trains while on campaign, whereas Hezarfen's figures may accurately reflect the army's overall transport requirements including advance deliveries to forward supply depots.[29]

The delivery of cannon and armaments represented another critical dimension of army transport. Because of the difficulties involved in moving arsenals even the relatively short distance between a regional storage depot such as Belgrade and a nearby site such as Szenta, accessible both by river via the Danube and Tisa and on overland routes, commanders often opted to leave a proportion (sometimes the bulk) of their heavy artillery in reserve at a convenient location behind the front. This allowed them greater flexibility of movement and the ability to advance quickly to engage the enemy when sudden opportunities presented themselves. Undertaking to carry more than a minimal supply of basic armaments was too costly in time, and time was the commodity which commanders of the period could least afford to squander. With the potentially crippling effect of his transport difficulties firmly in mind, it is not at all surprising that, when Mustafa II set out from Belgrade on the 18th of August 1697 to meet the enemy at Szenta, he took with him only a very careful selection of the most essential munitions and supplies arrayed for his choice in the Belgrade arsenal. For this encounter the mobile artillery units took with them only 17 culverins, 7 mortars and 85 light field pieces (zarbzens).[30] In the event, even after every attempt had been made to stream-

72

line the army and its supply trains, the encumbrance resulting from an oversupply (or unnecessary duplication) in both men and equipment seems to have played a critical role in the Ottoman defeat in this battle. As far as the context of seventeenth-century combat was concerned, more was hardly ever likely to be better.

From the above examples it can readily be seen that, while the availability through advance preparation of essential supplies was of considerable military importance, it was the issue of their deliverability that carried perhaps the greater practical significance. Overcoming operational obstacles, whether posed by intricate river systems requiring multiple crossings as in the European sphere, or by the combined effect of longer distances and more rugged terrain as confronted on campaigns to the east, posed a formidable challenge to Ottoman military planners. In the end, even with the most thorough fore-thought, the risk of things going awry could never be eliminated entirely. It is beyond question that for the Ottomans – as for all pre-modern armies – primitive transport was the weakest link in the military system. The reasons for this will be outlined in the remainder of this chapter, which focuses on details such as standard load factors, transport costs and the effect of distance on the Ottomans' ability to wage war – or for that matter to effectively monitor the peace – in particular sectors of their empire.

Since in this part of the chapter we will be placing particular emphasis on the role played by distance in determining and proscribing Ottoman military activity, most of our examples will be taken from the eastern sphere of operations.[31] It is in this part of the empire, where absolute distances were greatest and relative remoteness of supply bases to army forces operating in the field most pronounced, that we can best observe the scale of the transport problems faced by the Ottomans and judge the adequacy of their solutions to these problems.

Transport and transport costs in Ottoman land warfare

Ottoman overland transport systems relied on animal power, in part state-owned and controlled and in part leased for particular purposes related to the general context of military campaigns. Because of the variety of the types of animal used and the sources from which they were drawn, organization of transport had a natural complexity which makes it difficult to summarize adequately in a few pages. Much of the relevant detail can, however, be documented authentically and retrieved from contemporary sources. We cannot undertake here a fully comprehensive summary, but by drawing on specific examples we should at least be able to convey a sense of the magnitude of the undertaking. The Ottoman empire was land-based and held together from the earliest phases of its history by overland road systems inherited from both its imperial predecessors the Romans (in the Balkans) and the Seljukids (in Asia Minor). Building on this impressive heritage, the Ottomans developed considerable experiential expertise in their own right in overland transport. The state of our knowledge on this important topic is best presented under three separate headings: (1) information on transport prices: the purchase/hire option in military applications; (2) information on standard load factors appropriate to the alternative kinds of animals used in military applications; and (3) distances on standard itineraries and an assessment of per kg/km costs associated with different kinds of animal transport.

Prices

In deciding between the options of hire and purchase to meet its overland transport needs, the state had to reach a balance between cost and convenience, taking into consideration in its calculations both fairness and fiscal reality. The purchase or ownership option was attractive especially from a cost perspective. The camel, excepting the water buffalo, was the heaviest load-bearing animal, and it had the further advantage of being able to sustain a relatively quick gait even when fully loaded. If camels could be purchased by the government at controlled prices, a standard value for the seventeenth century being roughly 8,500 akçes,[32] and used for multiple purposes throughout the course of a campaign from its preparatory to its final stages, the per diem costs spread over a period of five months or longer was actually quite modest. The principal fiscal disadvantage of this method of organizing transport was that the feeding, grooming and general care of the animals became the responsibility of the owners. From the standpoint of strategy, the gain in flexibility obtained by the ability to hire animals when and where they were most needed, and the consequent relief from the burden of their care and pasturing during the interims when they were not being actively used had considerable practical advantages. Carefully weighing the advantages and disadvantages of the different options available to it, the state opted for a mixed transport system that minimized the burdens as well as expense of underexploited transport capacity on the one hand, and sought to contain costs on the other.

By good fortune a detailed register dated 1635, illustrating which sources the government relied on most heavily to meet its transport needs, has been preserved. This register, drawn up during the period of preparations between late December 1634 and mid-June 1635 for the campaign against Erivan planned for early summer, records expenditures of more than 11 million akçes for the acquisition of some 1300 camels.[33] For the enumeration of camels Ottoman sources make use of the term *kitar*, meaning a string of camels. Most commonly the term is used to refer to units of five camels, but for the purposes of accounting in this particular register an alternative value of six camels for each *kitar* is used. This may reflect the need on campaigns of longer distance and duration to keep a larger margin of unused spare capacity. On longer journeys the spare pack animals were used to allow periodic rests for the most heavily-burdened animals. In other sources clear reference is made to a practice of rotating loads and generous provision of spare camels amount-ing, in an example from the European sphere where distances were shorter and conditions more moderate, to one in seven.[34] The information on state purchase and requisition of camels based on the example from 1635 is summarized in Table 4.1.

Load factors

The record reflects a wide divergence in actual practices employed by the Ottomans to adjust to particular circumstances. This seeming inconsistency, which began with variations in the size of the standard load already referred to,[35] was in fact deliberately introduced by the Ottomans with the obvious intention of achieving optimal efficiency. The decision about how heavily to load an animal rested on factors such as the availability of spare mounts, an assessment of the fragility or (conversely) the density of the load, and a consideration of general terrain as well as climatic conditions. In view of such purposeful divergence it is perhaps hazardous for us to offer too much in the way of generalization, or to attach too much significance to averages resulting from our calculations. Our aim in presenting some of the more fully-documented examples is not to identify fixed rules and procedures, but rather to convey a clearer sense of the logic which animated Ottoman transport practices.

Evidence on the range of recorded load factors used for pack horses shows less variation than that found for camels. Two examples from a register dated 1635 show a close convergence in the narrow range between 107 and 109 okkas, the equivalent of 302.5 to 308 pounds.[36] In common practice, a maximum load factor for pack horses seems to have been 2.5 kantars, the equivalent of 5.5 *kiles* or 110 okkas.[37] Information from the same register of

Table 4.1 Requisition and purchase of camels for army transport at the time of the Erivan campaign of 1635

	No. of Camels	Cost p. camel	gurush	akçes
	303	80	24,240	2,424,000
	639	100	63,900	6,390,000[1]
	143	35	5,005	500,500
	66	miscellaneous	–	553,900[2]
	180	80	14,400	1,440,000
Totals	1,331			11,308,400

Equipment for 180 camels
(30 kitar) @ 20 gurush
per kitar   600   60,000

Grand Total Spent   11,368,400

	kitar (×6)	mahar (×1)	total	%
Purchases	221	5	1,331	28
Camels supplied from the provinces	559	5	3,359	72
			4,690[3]	100

[1] The price paid for roughly half of the camels (48%) acquired by purchase was 10,000 akçes per head.
[2] The average price paid for each camel in this group was about 8,400 akçes (553,900/66 = 8,392). With this group included, roughly four-tenths of the camels purchased (303 + 180 + 66 = 549 out of a total of 1331) were acquired for an average price of approximately 8,000 akçes.
[3] The total number provided (4,690) is very close to the number considered by Koçi Bey as sufficient to carry the baggage of the imperial household on campaign. See Chapter 4, fn. 29.

1635 suggests a usual camel load should be approximately 70 per cent greater than that carried by the average pack horse, amounting in many cases to about 9.5 *kiles* or 190 okkas.[38] The 190-okka upper limit for camels could be stretched to 200 okkas for shorter distances over easy roads, or in cases where substantial numbers of spare camels were available to rotate into the transport pool. Evidence from contemporary sources strongly suggests that load factors greater than 200 okkas were regarded as insupportable over longer distances, and at the same time as a threat to the health of the animals.[39]

In seventeenth-century practice, especially for long distance travel, the preponderance of the evidence suggests that standard loading practices were deliberately maintained at levels significantly below the theoretical maximum bearable burdens. Thus, for example, general practice observed at the time of the Baghdad campaign in 1638 shows that, when confronted with the challenge of delivering 542,113 *kiles* (about 14,000 metric tons) of grain for the army's use on campaign, rather than overloading the animals belonging to the imperial herd, the government opted to hire more animals, significantly reducing the average burden distributed to each individual animal. The 542,113 *kiles* of grain (mostly barley for use by army mounts) was distributed into 154,888 sacks, each containing a load weighing 3.5 *kiles*. The grain was then transported, using 77,444 camels each carrying two sacks. Each camel's load factor was thus a relatively modest 140 okkas, or about 396 pounds.[40] The government was under obligation to return borrowed or hired animals in good condition to their owners after the conclusion of a campaign or face the risk of paying compensation, so there was no advantage to be gained from seriously overworking the hired animals.[41]

To determine standard load factors for oxen and water buffalo we have relatively fewer sources to rely on. But the phenomenally high replacement cost for water buffalo, used where environmentally appropriate for the most physically demanding tasks such as dragging of the heavy siege cannons overland, is hinted at in contemporary narrative sources.[42] A chronicle of the late seventeenth century provides evidence that for campaigns in some sectors, where road conditions permitted, ox-drawn carts were used to transport campaign provisions. From the example provided by the historian Mevkufatî, relating to Chalik Ali Pasha's efforts to organize a relief force for Varad (Oradea) in 1692, it appears that the standard load factor for a single ox was approximately 18 *kiles* or 360 okkas, equivalent to slightly more than 1,000 pounds. A pair of oxen harnessed together would thus have been capable of pulling a cart loaded with a short ton of goods. Table 4.2 provides details of the manner in which 17,000 *kiles* (480.75 short tons or 436 metric tons) of barley and wheat were transported to the Danubian front from inland regions of the Balkans.

Transportation by sea to the mouth of the Danube and thence by river to Belgrade, where the supplies were in this instance urgently required, was clearly the cheaper option. But, with perishable cargo such as flour, the state willingly underwrote the cost of overland transport in covered ox carts to avoid the risk of spoilage. Thus, of the 22,000 *kiles* of flour requisitioned from various inland regions of the Balkans for use at the front in 1692, fully one-half (11,302 *kiles*) was transported using this costly and time-consuming method.[43] Apart from the consideration it gave to the transport method that minimized the cost while maximizing the speed of delivery, the state also had to factor into its calculations an assessment of the safest and most secure method of delivery for each kind of cargo.

Table 4.2[1] Data on grain transport by ox cart showing the typical load factor for oxen

Departure point	Barley[2]	Wheat flour	Total weight	No. of animals	Load factor
Edirne	2,311	4,622	6,933	383.5[3]	18.078
Delvina	1,931	3,862	5,793	321	18.047
Elbasan	1,410	2,818	4,228	235	17.99
TOTALS	5,652	11,302	16,954	939.5[4]	

[1] Information taken from Mevkufatî, *Vakiat-i Ruz-merre* Vol. IV (Esad Efendi Lib Ms 2437), f. 116b dated 1104/1692–3.
[2] Figures are in kiles of 20 okkas, the equivalent of 25.656 kg.
[3] Oxen were requisitioned at the rate of one animal for every three taxpayer households. The requisition for the 1,156.5 registered households of the central district of Edirne and its environs (Liva-i Paşa) was thus 383.5 animals. See the *Vakiat-I Ruz-merre* Vol. IV, f. 115b.
[4] The average load factor of approximately 18 kiles (461.808 kg) per animal would mean that a pair of oxen hitched together could pull 923.6 kg, or just over a short ton in weight.

Although overland transport costs always constituted one of the most substantial hidden dimensions of military expenditure in the seventeenth century, they could, as documented in the preceding example from a Balkan context, be held to a supportable level in those parts of the empire where the roads were relatively well-maintained, and in the core provinces which possessed a developed administrative structure to support the requisitioning of animals for state use.[44] At 20 akçes per *kile*, the per *kile* per kilometer transport cost to the treasury to cover the 705 kilometers between Edirne and Belgrade, even expressed in the high akçe prices endemic during the war-induced inflation of the 1690s, was just 0.0284 akçes. The information displayed in Table 4.3 (see below) shows how transport costs for much shorter excursions in the remoter parts of eastern Anatolia might, in exceptional circumstances, soar to levels twenty or even thirty times greater than this.[45]

Inland transport over specified itineraries using various animal-hire options

The information summarized in the preceding two sections (on prices and load factors) can be combined with documentary evidence on movement of specific consignments of goods over known itineraries to gain a more textured appreciation, not just of operational realities connected with Ottoman campaigns, but also of the manner in which both the benefits and the burdens of providing transport services were apportioned. How resources (including animal power) were activated in the regions surrounding a prospective front in the months preceding a major Ottoman campaign can perhaps best be observed by focusing on a region outside the core administrative areas of the empire in Europe and the western districts of Asia Minor. Since these core areas were better integrated into the imperial economy, it can be difficult to identify and, still more, to separate both war-related extraction of resources (through taxation and contributions in kind) and exceptional economic opportunities connected with mobilization for war. In the core areas of the empire basic services and infrastructure maintenance were often the responsibility of officially registered, tax-exempt service groups, many of whom served explicitly military functions such as road repair, security patrol services and the like.

Outside the core areas the state was far more likely to contract for services on a cash-and-carry basis. Such arrangements were, typically, accompanied by their own record-keeping procedures, making them more transparent to the gaze of modern investigators. For the core provinces, where direct taxation applied most fully the offer of tax exemptions for crucial services including both the provision and the transport of grain, the basis of the relationship between taxpayer and state as provider on the one hand and extractor on the other was more clear-cut. For the populations in the border regions, who by virtue of their geographic locations bore the brunt of the disruptive impact of war, the relationship was less determinate. In exchange for co-operation with its aims (whether in war or peace) the state was obliged to offer (to tribal groups and others who had resources – for instance, animal power – under their direct control) some form of tangible reward. In the case of border regions the size of the reward was linked in some fashion to the extent of the co-operation that was forthcoming. By focusing on the Ottoman organization of transport services we will seek to show how this relationship worked in a key area of mutual interest as well as interdependence.

Because it was impossible for the state either to anticipate fully or to fulfil its transport needs using only animals belonging to the imperial herds, it placed a heavy reliance on supplementary services provided by private interests. While a portion of its transport needs was met as part of the *avariz* contributions of taxpayers,[46] such arrangements fell far short of meeting all its needs. In actual operational contexts it contracted for transport services with individual owners of animals at rates that conformed closely to fair market rates of the time, and for special services, or express delivery it was obliged to offer a premium over average open market rates.[47] The very fact that prices for transport services might range from as little as two-tenths of an akçe per *kile* per kilometer to nearly nine-tenths of an akçe p. *kile*/km itself suggests the state's inability to determine and impose a flat rate of its own choosing. The arena of transport was clearly an area of economic activity in which the state had to bend to market forces and conform to the dictates of local custom. Local practice was, in turn, itself determined by the geography and other peculiarities relating to each specific place. Table 4.3 shows the wide diversity of Ottoman practice in transport that could exist even within a relatively confined geographical space.

The price of 0.54 akçes p. *kile*/km shown in the first row of Table 4.3 was seemingly calculated to reflect the long duration of the journey rather than the arduousness of the route travelled. The long delay in the return of the animals to their rightful owners because of the equally long return journey is also implicitly acknowledged in the price. In this example the owner of a camel burdened with the designated 7-*kile* load would have received remuneration of 5,600 akçes (800 × 7). Interpreted in the light of current prices for purchase of camels, commonly in the range of 6,000–8,500 akçes (see Table 4.1 above), this level of remuneration seems generous enough. The state as hirers showed the further consideration in this instance of keeping average load factors at a deliberately restrained level.

At the upper end of the scale among the examples shown in Table 4.3 we find the state contracting for transport services at the rate of 0.866 akçes p. *kile*/km. This price seems to reflect an opportunistic rate charged by animal owners in a borderland region of the empire for the urgent delivery of war-related supplies (in this case empty sacks for the packaging and transport of other strategic materials) from their production site at Gaziantep to the army's off-season base of operations at Koç Hisar near Mardin. The order to expedite delivery of the sacks was sent at a time (in late August 1631) when other essential materials including the siege guns were already being sent to the army's forward base of operations at Mosul in preparation for an autumn/winter siege of Baghdad.[48] At this level of detailed record-keeping we are able to observe at first hand the way that Ottoman commanders and other imperial commissioners, charged with specific aspects of campaign preparations, acted to prioritize particular transport operations by offering exceptional incentives and rewards. Examples of this kind showing a multitiered pricing structure based partly on transport conditions and partly on urgency of need could be multiplied at will. Our purpose in citing such examples of exceptional, seemingly anomalous, generosity by the state is to show how even in its most hegemonic poses as initiators and pursuers of expansionist or imperialistic wars, the state on closer examination revealed its position as a hostage of

Table 4.3 Per kile/per kilometre transport costs (in akçes) using various modes of transport

Mode of transport	Transport cost per kile	Load factor	Distance travelled (in kilometres)	Cost per kile/kg
Camel	800[1]	7 kiles	1490 (Manisa to Diyarbekir)[2]	0.5369
Pack horse	100[3]	5.5 kiles	488 (Diyarbekir to Erzurum)	0.2254
Pack horse	73[4]	5.5 kiles	125 (Bayburd to Erzurum)	0.5840
Pack horse	109[5]	5.5 kiles	325 (Trabzon to Erzurum)	0.3354
Camel	50[6]	9.5 kiles[7]	253 (Diyarbekir to Mosul)	0.1976
ND	291[8]	ND	336 (Gaziantep to Mardin)	0.866
Camel	42[9]	9.5 kiles[10]	157 (Mardin to Mosul)	0.2682

[1] Data from B.B.A., Maliyeden Mudevver 4374 covering 1047–49/1637–39 cited in Güçer, *Hububat Meselesi*, p. 138. Convoy of 82 camels carrying 574 kiles of grain (7 per head) was paid a total of 459,200 akçes or 800 akçes per camel.

[2] Travelling via the following route: Manisa to Afyon (307 km), Afyon to Konya (232 km), Konya to Kayseri (331 km), Kayseri to Diyarbekir (620 km); date same as in fn.1.

[3] B.B.A, Maliyeden Müdevver 18,708, p. 2 documenting the payment of 351 gurush (35,100 akçes) for the use of 58 pack horses to transport 319 kiles of rice; dates from Şevval 1044 to Cemazi I 1045/late March to early November 1635.

[4] *ibid.*, 7,000 kantars (15,400 kiles) of hardtack divided into 2,800 pack horse loads each reimbursed at the rate of 4 gurush (400 akçes). The cost for transporting each kile was thus 72.72 akçes; date same as in fn. 3.

[5] *ibid.*, 1,500 pack horse loads at the rate of 6 gurush (600 akçes) per load, or 109.9 akçes per kile.

[6] B.B.A., Maliyeden Müdevver 5853 (dated 1041/1631) documents the hiring of 6 camels at a rate of 6 gurush per camel for the transport of the Janissaries' wages paid in coin. If we assume a load factor of 9.5 kiles (see notes 7 & 10 below), the per kile transport cost is 50.526 akçes.

[7] The average load factor of 9.5 kiles per camel is an estimate. The document unfortunately provides no more detailed information on this point; source and date same as in fn. 6.

[8] B.B.A., Maliyeden Müdevver 8475, p. 114 a document dated 1041/1631 requesting transport by unspecified means for 16 kantars (35.2 kiles) of empty sacks at a total cost of 128 gurush. The per kile cost was thus 10,240 ÷ 35.2 or 290.9 akçes. Unless specified otherwise, it is assumed that the official exchange rate of 80 akçes per gurush applied.

[9] B.B.A., Kamil Kepeci 1927, mukerrer, f. 51a dated 1040/1630 which documents the payment of 5 gurush per camel for a convoy of 220 camels travelling between Mardin and Mosul. Assuming a load factor of 9.5 kiles, the transport cost per kile was 42.105 akçes.

[10] See n. 7.

circumstances.[49] To achieve its aims without compromise or sacrifice on its own part proved impossible and, in many cases, including the one just cited connected with Hüsrev Pasha's prematurely aborted siege of Baghdad in 1630, such sacrifice was made in vain.

Mobilization for war including advance planning for provision of basic supplies conformed for the most part to predictable patterns, norms and expectations but, under more fluid operational conditions when an army was actually on the march, the state frequently found itself compelled to delve deep into its pockets to meet unforeseen expenses or counteract an unexpected setback. At such times of vulnerability the service sector in the regional economies of areas in the immediate hinterland of active military fronts were presented with repeated opportunities for sudden windfall profits arising from the mere presence of the Ottoman army (a captive market consisting of as many as 70,000 men and 100,000 animals) in their midst. Unless it failed to pay, or underpaid for what it received in the way of material assistance from the region's inhabitants, the fulfilling of the army's needs gave a welcome boost to the local economy.

During most of the period 1500–1700, with the possible exception of the brief depredations of the Celali deserters in their flight from the eastern front in the years (especially between 1603 and 1612) when the Ottomans renewed their conflict with the Safavids, an orderly relationship between suppliers (provincial residents) and requisitioners of supplies (the state as represented by its armed forces) was maintained. Horseshoers, saddlers, carters, and drovers and a range of other specialist craftsmen related to the transport sector were among the principal beneficiaries of Ottoman mobilization for war. An example from one of Murad IV's campaigns against Baghdad records that, when the government put out an offer of 2.5 gurush (200 akçes) per kantar (about 125 pounds or less than half the average pack horse load) for the transport of 3,181 kantars of armour and ammunition from the Mediterranean seaport of Iskenderun to the riverine launching pad of Birecik on the upper Euphrates, approximately one-third (1,000 out of 3,181 "loads") were claimed by a consortium of the professional muleteer drovers from Aleppo (mükâriyan-i Haleb), and a substantial proportion of the remainder by other private sources including the principal Arab tribes of the region. Only a modest proportion was requisitioned as "contributions" from local counties and townships.[50]

The mobilization of resources for war was by no measure or means a simple one-way transaction confined to the state's extraction of wealth from a region's economy. The challenge (and stimulus) presented by the fulfilment of the army's needs had a ripple effect, not just on the economies of the border regions, but also on war-related industries in provinces of the interior. In the next chapter on army provisioning we will explore the Ottomans' particular approach to military supply designed to maximize participation and ensure compliance with state demands by a careful balance of expected sacrifice and proffered reward. The methods used by the Ottomans to organize those critical dimensions of the military enterprise relating to transport and supply reveal the true character of Ottoman imperial rule, which relied to a far greater extent than is commonly recognized on governance by negotiation, compromise and shared interest as opposed to compulsion and imposed solutions.[51]

Chapter Five

Provisioning the army

We have already dealt in some detail in the preceding chapter with those aspects of food provision connected with the calculation and delivery of the troops' and animals' daily grain rations while on campaign. In this chapter we focus on the scale and quality of provisions for the soldiers' consumption, and give some examples of the burdens and benefits associated with army supply. From the standpoint of his basic daily diet the Ottoman soldier, especially if he was a member of one of the elite regiments such as the Janissaries, was the envy of his European contemporaries. Before setting out for the front, members of the sultan's standing regiments received generous supplementary allowances to complete their outfitting for campaign. In addition to their regular salaries, the Janissaries were also provided a yearly clothing allowance.[1] A special cash fund (*vakf -i nukud*) was set up to subsidize the Janissary companies' purchases of staple commodities under the names *zarar -i nan* (price supports for bread) and *zarar -i lahm* (price supports for meat).[2] Even though everyday needs were provided for,[3] in campaign years exceptional allowances were handed out to the troops to defray their additional equipment expenses.[4] The individual Janissary companies also themselves took up special collections to use as a reserve fund for the communal mess during campaign. Each member contributed two gold pieces to the common provisions fund (*kumanya*).[5] These allowances and cash bonuses distributed to Janissaries and others as they set out on campaign also served to cushion the effect of price surges, especially for basic foodstuffs, that unavoidably took effect in the last weeks of the season's campaigning when supplies dwindled to dangerously low levels. Because they were foreseeable such endemic shortages could usually be compensated for, but in years of extraordinary crop shortages price fluctuations for basic army supplies reached unmanageable proportions. During the famine of 1625, which coincided with a nine-month siege of Baghdad by the Grand Vezier Hafiz Ahmed Pasha in 1625–6, Ottoman military reports testify to the seriousness of the problem, noting the rise of the price of dry biscuit to 5 gurush (500 akçes) per okka, and of barley to 10 gold pieces (1,200 akçes) per *kile*.[6] Local sources from Baghdad indicate that the situation for the civilian population of the besieged city was, if anything, worse. One observer recorded that the price of a *ratl* (approximately a third of an okka) of wheat rose to seven silver dirhems.[7] While the examples given here may be extreme, they accurately reflect a phenomenon that itself was all too common. While price rises were clearly connected with the presence of the army and increased demand on local grain supplies, the underlying problem of crop shortages was a cyclically repeating phenomenon which sometimes coincided with war, but was not demonstrably causally connected with it.

Army victualling was carefully organized by the Ottomans with the clear objective of preventing all avoidable disruptions to normal civilian and agrarian life. The Ottoman army brought with it what it could (see Chapter 4 above), and what it was unable to bring with it or have brought to it from the empire's extensive hinterlands it acquired from local suppliers, not by forced requisitions or by authorizing soldiers to raid civilian sources of grain, but through orderly purchases which were often prearranged with the residents of provinces closest to the prospective war zone. In a published example relating to Murad IV's preparations for the siege of Baghdad in 1638 it has been estimated that 67 per cent of the barley, 27 per cent of the wheat for bread, and 22 per cent of the flour consumed during the campaign were acquired by means of cash purchases (*ishtira*) made on the spot. It is significant that the army relied most heavily on local sources, not for the supply of the men's provisions (wheat and flour), but for the replenishment of the transport animals' rations (barley). Further amounts of grain that were categorized as contributions in kind to be levied on the provinces (*sürsat*) were also paid for with treasury funds, with the difference that responsibility for the transport of the grain to the army was assigned to the provincial taxpayers who supplied it.[8] An order from Sultan Murad to the grand vezier during the winter of 1637 praised him for his just treatment of the provincial populace (*reaya*), by having provided for the Janissaries' grain supplies out of treasury (*miri*) funds without having resort to any forced contributions.[9] The army's large-scale purchases of grain and other military supplies were a boon to regional economies in Anatolia, as long as harvests were abundant enough to satisfy both local demand and the needs of the army.

By comparison with European foot soldiers of the day, the Ottoman Janissaries were regarded as being singularly well-provided for in all respects.[10] The remarks of the French traveller Jean de Thévenot are indicative of the positive impression formed by contemporary European observers concerning the Ottomans' organization of their commissary service. Thévenot observed:

> Their armies never perish with hunger, victuals being brought them in sufficient quantity from all lands, for seeing they punctually pay for what they have, commit no disorder, – all things are brought to the camp, as to a common market.[11]

Since the Ottomans were exceptional in the precision and care which they lavished on the planning of army provisioning, it is perhaps appropriate that we focus here on the organizational aspects of the task. Much of the rest of Ottoman military enterprise, from the weather to the attitude of the soldiers and even the reliability of the arms and equipment issued to them, was subject to chance, subjective mood or, especially in the case of technical performance, somehow managing to beat the odds. Because of these general uncertainties, the Ottomans showed themselves the more determined to ensure that in the administrative realm where they could exercise some control nothing was left to chance. Evidence of the Ottomans' bureaucratic sophistication and how it was marshalled to ensure the adequacy of food supply during military campaigns is found in a range of documentary and narrative sources.

In the European theatre the Ottomans were favoured by geography, since it was possible to make grain deliveries via the Danube waterway to within a few days' march of any prospective front.[12] Each area of the empire presented its own environmentally-specific challenges. Writing to the grand vezier during the winter of 1637 on the subject of troop rations, the sultan reckoned a quantity of 80,000 kantars of hardtack was required to sustain an army in the field for a period of 80 days.[13] We know from contemporary documentary evidence that a quantity of nearly 83,000 kantars of hardtack was, in fact, deposited in a series of fortified places and major river crossings along the army's route of march to the proposed front in Iraq. The contribution from each location was predetermined on the basis of a careful calculation of its ability, not just to supply, but also to store the quantities requested adequately. By careful allocation of a supply quota to regional collection points near the front, Diyarbekir for southern districts and Erzurum for the north (each supplying approximately 15 per cent of the total needed), and a larger quantity (approximately 25 per cent of the total) to the river port of Birecik from where it could be moved with relative speed and ease to the locations nearest to the points where the heaviest troop concentrations were anticipated, the Ottomans were able to maximize efficiency, while at the same time ensuring fairness. By organizing the troops' food supply in this fashion less than half (more precisely 45 per cent) of the total quantity needed was left to be requisitioned locally from places in the immediate hinterland of the front. The filling of this residual quota was, in turn, shared between eight different locations scattered around the military perimeter close to the active front. A part of the quota (10,300 kantars or 12 per cent of the total amount needed) came from stores held over in Mardin from a previous season's campaigning. These surplus stocks were retained in anticipation of the surge in local demand that would result from the imminent arrival of the army.[14] Such evidence, pointing to the availability of substantial unused surpluses from previous campaigns, demonstrates the Ottomans' effective use of advance planning to avert local supply shortages. Such measures neutralized at least one element of uncertainty among the complex set of variables that affected the outcome of campaigns. At the same time, such foresight went a long way towards cushioning local markets from the major disruptive effects of last-minute supply requests on a massive scale. The method used by the Ottomans for disposing of grain surpluses remaining at the conclusion of major campaigns also shows how they fostered a willingness among taxpayers to co–operate with the supply demands. One gesture of goodwill that was frequently employed was the recycling of grain to those who had first supplied it, not at speculative, shortage-driven or extra-market winter prices, but at the same state-controlled, fixed prices that had applied when it was first requisitioned.[15] The Ottomans seemingly put equal care into the administrative detail of organizing pre-campaign supply requests and making suitable arrangements for disposing of surpluses after campaigns.

The Ottomans fully appreciated that at an operational level ensuring the soldiers' minimal daily dietary and nutritional needs had a direct bearing on troop discipline and morale. If a soldier's basic diet had consisted solely of a daily ration of 1,200 grams (2.6 pounds) of bread, its caloric value would suffice to sustain a fairly brisk pace of physical activity. By applying the modern equivalent (based on the vitamin–rich bread of the present day) of 270 calories for each 100 grams of bread,[16] the relevant energy transfer would amount to 3,240 calories. According to modern scientific calculations the average energy needs of healthy males aged between 17 and 22 amount to 2,900 calories.[17] However, during periods of exceptional physical activity their daily (24-hour) energy requirement can easily rise to levels between 3,100 and 4,000 calories.[18] From a variety of different sources it appears that the Ottomans were successful, not just in meeting such basic dietary require-ments, but also in providing their soldiers with a more varied, protein-rich diet. They enjoyed the best diet when under controlled conditions resting in barracks, but even on campaign the army was accompanied by flocks of sheep which acted as a kind of travelling larder and an important supplementary source to their regular diet which was composed of the daily bread ration. Marsigli, a close observer of Ottoman military affairs in the seventeenth century, gave a detailed account of the daily allotment assigned to Ottoman soldiers during periods of rest in barracks.[19] The diet he described would have provided each man with roughly 3,000 calories, calculated as follows:

Description of ration	Gram equivalent	Caloric value
100 dirhems of bread	320	
50 dirhems of hardtack	160	
50 dirhems of rice	160	
Cereals Total[20]	640	1,728[21]
60 dirhems of mutton	192	683
25 dirhems of clarified butter	80	571
	Total Caloric Value	2,982[22]

The Janissaries were also protected from the worst effects of speculative prices for foodstuffs during campaigns both by subsidies and by the provision of guaranteed source of supply for certain basic components of their diet. According to a source from the early seventeenth century, a quantity of 300,000 sheep was set side each year from the Rumelian provinces for the use of the palace kitchens, and a significant proportion of this was in turn assigned for the exclusive use of the Janissary messes.[23] In a more detailed source it is documented that during the 21 months of the army's march from the capital to Baghdad and back to base in the period between March 1638 and January 1640, the members of the sultan's standing regiments consumed 217,279 sheep. Of these 128,242 head (60 per cent) were purchased on the spot (ishtira) at a cost to the treasury of 220,418 gurush or 17.6 million akçes. The remaining 88,437 sheep (40 per cent) were acquired as purchases along the way to the front, or as contributions credited against provincial tax obligations (sürsat). With the average sheep supplying 12 okkas of meat, this provided the army with a quantity of more than two and a half million okkas of mutton. The precise amount (2,576,515 okkas) was sufficient (using the standard ration of 60 dirhems = 0.15 okka) to cover distribution of 17 million meat rations to the troops.[24] The historian Mevkufatî recorded that the daily mutton requirements of the Janissary corps in the 1690s amounted to 1825 okkas (2.34 metric tons). On this basis, in an average 365-day period, not including special rations and allowances on feast days, the Janissaries alone accounted for 666,125 okkas, the equivalent of 4.44 million individual rations.[25]

Because of the transport difficulties typically encountered by the army (see Chapter 4 above), the mutton component of the soldier's daily diet, beyond its nutritional significance, represented added value by reducing both the scale and expense of systems required for the delivery of alternative foods. The availability of generous supplies of meat might make the small but critical margin of difference between otherwise equal opponents, and the Ottomans had early on developed a centralized system for meat provision which provided adequate spare capacity for both civilian and military use.[26]

During campaigns led by the sultan the imperial kitchen was able to supply from its own resources a large proportion of the meat consumed by the household troops. During the course of the campaign for the retaking of Baghdad in 1638–9, for example, the treasury disbursed 220,418 gurush just to meet the cost of purchasing sheep to feed the imperial entourage.[27] From examples of this kind it can be seen that the level of comfort provided (at least in the case of the better-cared-for elite troops) for soldiers on campaign was not substantially different from that offered to troops barracked at Istanbul during the off-season. The example cited above of meat supply during the Baghdad campaign indicates that after a period of nearly two years of continuous service in the field there still remained a sufficient reserve supply of mutton for the sultan to distribute celebratory benefactions both to the Janissaries and the Tatar auxiliaries with enough left over to allow the sultan to host victory banquets upon his return to the capital.[28]

The sure knowledge that such food reserves remained secure throughout the campaign acted as an important source of psychological comfort to the soldiers. It is beyond question that persistent worries about the adequacy of food supply for themselves or for their mounts had a potentially corrosive effect on the fighting spirit of the troops. It is no accident that food, feasting and the imagery of plenty played such a prominent role, especially in the initial phases of a campaign, in army camp routine and ritual practice. Achieving the levels of comfort and margins of plenty depicted in such images was never accidental. It required considerable care both in planning and execution. As part of the ceremonies for seeing the army off on campaign, whether in the provinces from winter quarters to a place designated as the pre-battle assembly point, or from the capital, banquets were held and food distributed to all members of the sultan's standing regiments. An example from the Erivan campaign of 1635 documents the allocation of a thousand okkas each of honey and butter for the preparation of baked sweets to serve at the pre-departure banquet for the troops.[29] On another occasion the arrival in camp of the new commander Bayram Pasha in July 1637, following the sudden dismissal in February 1637 of the commander Tabani-yassi Mehmed Pasha during a critical phase of preparations for the planned assault on Baghdad, was marked by the distribution of a sum of 40,000 akçes. This money was to be spent to buy supplies for a festive meal to mark the transfer of command (and the accompanying duties of benefaction and patronage) to the new commander. By their participation in a communal meal, the troops symbolically underlined their personal loyalty to their new master and a collective acceptance of the transfer of power to him.[30]

One of the organizational means by which supply of basic necessities to the troops in the field was achieved was the registering and efficient mobilization of representatives of essential trades and crafts who were required to accompany the army physically throughout the course of a campaign. A particularly well-documented example of how the system worked is provided for the eastern campaign planned for the year 1730, but abandoned in September before the army had yet left the capital. This example records the presence and planned participation of 28 different crafts (hirfet) housed in single or, for the essential crafts, multiple tents and comprising the army's mobile commissariat called the ordu bazar. In the example from 1730 the army market was composed of 85 separate tents.[31] The most represented craft whose members occupied eight tents with a working capital of 129,600 akçes were the bootmakers (hiffafan). The most heavily invested group was the grocers (bakkalan) who occupied four tents with a working capital of 1.4 million akçes. While providers and repairers of essential military equipment were naturally among the groups represented, it is noteworthy that concerns of basic hygiene and soldierly comfort were not neglected. Six of the 85 tents were taken up by barbers who, apart from personal grooming, played a secondary role in the dressing of wounds.[32]

We know from a post-bellum account of the Cyprus campaign of 1570–1 that higher-ranking officers went into battle (and left behind them for probate assessors' inventorying) significant quantities of material goods and other seeming impedimenta. These were used, it may be assumed, to recreate the illusion of the comforts of home while away on campaign.[33] The Cyprus example records that a grocer (bakkal) and a surgeon (cerrah) were among those who left fortunes of between 4,000 and 7,000 akçes, and two merchants (one from Basra and the other from Tunis) both left estates valued in excess of 10,000 akçes in tangible assets that were readily capable of being assessed and registered on the battlefield.[34]

Some researchers, particularly those working on the economic impact of Ottoman war in the eighteenth century, have suggested that the burden of repeated demands on the merchant community for such rotational fulfilment of campaign services became oppressive. The burden, it is argued, was felt not just by the participants, but began also to have a generally depressive effect on the Ottoman manufacturing sector as a whole. The basis of such arguments is the assumption that, through the removing of basic raw materials from general circulation and their reserving for "strategic" military use, the domestic economy was deprived of goods essential to its own growth and

1. Army market place, *ordu bazar*. *Source*: Hazine 1365, folio 93a.

development.[35] There is, however, considerable doubt about whether the scale of military demand present in Ottoman warfare of the sixteenth and seventeenth centuries ever assumed sufficient proportions to cause either significant denial of goods to, or major disruption of production within, the non-military sectors of the economy.[36] On the contrary, there is plenty of evidence to suggest that the merchant community regarded its participation in military supply contracts as an opportunity for exceptional gain. When circumstances prevented merchants' expectations from being met, they openly expressed their discontent. The author of the account on commercial participation in the 1730 campaign even goes so far as to suggest that the merchants' dissatisfaction with the government's inability to protect their capital investments mobilized during July of 1730 in preparation for the campaign played a significant role in the emergence of a consensus favouring first a change of government and, ultimately, in early October, the deposing of Ahmed III.[37] Careful analysis of these events strongly suggests that the merchant community's protests and sense of grievance stemmed not so much from the fact of their compulsory participation in the campaign, as their disappointment at the squandering of economic opportunity through government indecision and mismanagement.

Grain provision

The mobilization of grain resources for use in Ottoman campaigns was a multi-stage process which required active input from all levels of the state bureaucracy many months in advance of the campaign. No single concern was more critical to the troops' performance in battle than the adequacy of food supply for themselves and their mounts. The elaborateness (as well as generosity) of Ottoman arrangements for grain provision shows their appreciation of the fact that in warfare of the pre-modern era logistics played a more decisive role than tactics. Any disruption of regular supplies organized through central planning and distribution put immediate and severe restraints on the scope and reach of army operations in the field. The critical importance of the bureaucratic structure which intervened to meet supply demands even before they were yet sensed or even foreseen by forces in the field was critical to the success of the Ottoman military enterprise. Military administration and general bureaucratic skills form the most hidden (and therefore underrated) dimension of Ottoman military strength.

The constraints placed on the conduct of warfare by the absence of a well-organized system providing backup support and supply is obvious from the known (but for the Ottomans exceptional) cases where it was lacking. One such case was the 11-month Ottoman defence of Tabriz against a determined counterattack by the Safavids, beginning soon after its capture by Özdemiroglu Osman Pasha in September 1585. During the 11-month Safavid countersiege the Ottomans had no external source of logistical support and were forced to meet the supply needs of the Tabriz garrison by launching an almost continuous series of small raiding parties whose remit was not offensive action, but the scouring of the countryside surrounding the garrison for foodstuffs in easily transportable forms and quantities. It is recorded in contemporary Ottoman sources that these small raiding parties, composed of between 500 and 1,000 men, were sent out to seek supplies on 170 separate occasions during the enemy offensive, an average of every other day during the siege lasting 330 days. In total the members of such raiding parties were, typically, capable of carrying back with them only some 300 packloads of supplies, mostly grain, sufficient to support the combined garrison staff for a few days.[38] The sustained intensity of effort required to mount these foraging expeditions during the defence of Tabriz seriously hampered the Ottomans and prevented them from pursuing other military objectives. Because of the Ottomans' supply vulnerability, the smaller Safavid force consisting of some 30,000 warriors from diverse tribal origins were able to keep an Ottoman army of 80,000 men, organized in permanent regiments and provincial contingents of timariot troops, effectively immobilized over the full extent of the spring-summer campaigning season of 1586.[39]

It is estimated in one contemporary source that only a small percentage of directly campaign-related expenditure was accounted for by grain purchases. In describing the preparations for Koca Sinan Pasha's campaign against Györ in 1594, Hüseyn Hezarfen estimated that in addition to the 100 million akçes set side from the privy purse for general campaign preparations, an extra 40,000 gold pieces (4.8 million akçes) were allotted to the grain commissioner Gezdehem Ali Chavush for the purchase of necessary provisions.[40] However, contradictory evidence suggests that, when advance purchases and supplies are taken into account, the army's food bill assumed truly impressive proportions. In one sultan's estimation, the amount of barley required to meet the animals' fodder rations during a single campaign amounted to three to four times the amount consumed by the Imperial Stables during the course of a whole year.[41] During the Baghdad campaign of 1637–8 a quantity of more than a million and half *kiles* of barley was made available for the army's use which (even using a reduced market rate of 16 akçes for each *kile* of grain) represents an economic value of the order of 24 million akçes.[42] Outlays on this scale dwarfed those for equipment in the Ottoman army by a very substantial margin. The same was characteristic for all armies of the period. The general scale of army provisioning needs is confirmed by some details included in the budget for 1669, the final year of the war in Crete. This budget shows line item allocations for military provisions (including grain purchases) as follows:

Recipient and purpose	Amount (millions of akçe)
To the barley commissioner for expenses	21.3
To the secretary of the bread rations for the Janissaries' loaves	1.6
To the hardtack commissioner	5.2
Wheat and meat subsidies for Janissaries and others assigned to provincial garrison duty	11.4
Mutton subsidy for Janissaries stationed at the Porte	8.2
Total of Disbursements	47.7[43]

Because such a large proportion of Ottoman army forces was excluded from commissariat privileges, it is difficult to determine precisely what proportion of army provisioning costs was assumed by the treasury. But, as the evidence for 1669 shows, even partial provision represented an undertaking of massive proportions and economic import. The government had a vested interest in rising to the challenge, since failure to provide adequately for its troops led to pressures for early demobilization that it was powerless to resist. In extreme cases supply failures led to rising levels of army desertion or even permanent abandonment of key Ottoman defensive positions.

The extreme difficulty of the terrain on the Caucasus front, where the Ottomans were particularly active between 1578 and 1590, made it more prone to supply shortages than most other areas. The general reluctance of Ottoman soldiers to participate in eastern campaigns came in part from their anticipation of the exceptional hardships campaigns in this sector inevitably entailed. An example taken at random from Mustafa Ali's eulogistic account of his patron Lala Mustafa Pasha's exploits during the Shirvan campaign of 1578, with some allowance for Ali's natural penchant for rhetorical excess, accurately expresses the plight of the common soldier. Ali states that in this campaign the price of a *kile* of barley soared to six gold pieces,[44] white flour changed hands for 11 gold pieces per *kile* (the equivalent of 66 akçes per okka at post-devaluation rates), while bread sold for 40 gold pieces per *kile*, the equivalent of two gold pieces for a daily ration amounting to one okka.[45] Since the average garrison soldier's daily wage was fixed at five akçes, the effect of such price inflation was to transform the purchase price of the average soldier's daily bread ration into the equivalent of a month and half's wages.

Although the period between 1590 and 1603 witnessed a temporary lull in the Ottoman-Safavid wars, the expense of continuing Ottoman presence and involvement in the Caucasus had to be shouldered under mounting fiscal pressures, the effect of which was intensified by a period of extreme monetary instability at the close of the sixteenth century. The akçe was drastically and suddenly devalued in 1586, but even such radical measures proved no panacea.[46] The effects of monetary instability were greatest in the border areas, and difficulties for the soldiers were compounded by the exercises in "creative financing" which the commanders, provincial governors and garrison chiefs under whom they served had to resort to in order balance their own books. As an isolated example, the case of Cafer Pasha, Ottoman governor in Tabriz from the time of its successful defence against Safavid counterattack in 1586, is illustrative. His decision to pay the Tabriz garrison with the half sequin *nisfiye* coin that was common in Iran and in the Ottoman zone of occupation in Azerbaijan, but had limited circulation and acceptance in the rest of the Ottoman lands caused an irreversible rupture in relations with his troops. More significantly, the cumulative reverberations from actions taken by garrison commanders under similar fiscal pressures throughout the emerging new frontier's extent were felt far beyond the war zone with the Safavids. Even locally, the intrinsic value of the *nisfiye* rapidly sank to about six-tenths of its value prior to the Ottoman devaluation of 1586. The dramatically declining purchasing power of their wages represented an intolerable hardship, especially for garrison troops stationed in remote areas where the general scarcity of goods was already reflected in higher prices for basic supplies in local markets. From such evidence it would appear that the price of keeping the peace represented as great a sacrifice to the troops assigned to frontier garrison duty as facing the dangers and rigours of war itself.[47]

When conditions such as those described above relating to the context of the Caucasus front prevailed more generally, even contemporary Ottoman thinkers and political observers, naturally disposed to recoil at the very thought of insubordination by the sovereign's *kuls*, expressed an understanding of the soldiers' plight. When commenting on the sources of discontent among the sultan's fighting forces these thinkers were often disposed to lay the blame on the cupidity of the commanding officers rather than an inherent lack of discipline among the rank and file. Shortages of specie and the use of debased coin for the payment of the Janissaries' wages was by no means a new phenomenon in the seventeenth century. It had been known since the time of the 1446 Buçuk Tepe rebellion of the Janissaries when the empire was still capitaled at Edirne. But the dramatic growth in the size of the corps (see Chapter 3 above, especially Tables 3.4 and 3.5) greatly magnified the scale and intensity of such problems.

The government was not unaware that monetary instability, coupled with natural price rises resulting from supply shortages and intensified by speculation in basic commodities, posed a serious threat to the army's operational effectiveness. Their disciplined interventionist approach to the question of securing the army's food supply was founded on an appreciation of its central importance to the success of their military ventures. Especially in campaigns carried out on the eastern front, when the army was called upon to operate for extended periods beyond the usual reach of the supply system based on the *menzil-hane* network, the Ottomans placed a very high priority on ensuring the adequacy and efficient delivery of the army's grain supply, regardless of cost. Fiscal concerns came second, and the accumulation of short-term debt and authorization of budget overruns by transfers from the inner treasury (see Chapter 3 above) was considered a small price to pay for the orderly preparation for battle through advance stockpiling of necessary supplies, especially grain.

Ensuring that adequate grain supplies were made available for use during military campaigns required considerable forethought and market control. Ottoman merchants and interlopers were naturally tempted by a desire to profit from high prices offered for grain in Western countries. In some years, especially during years of exceptional demand linked with preparation for war, export of wheat was forbidden.[48] But the assumption that domestic shortages were always or only connected with the rise and fall of military demand rests on a still (at least for the Ottoman empire of the sixteenth and seventeenth centuries) untested hypothesis. Grain surpluses were seemingly adequate to support dramatic urban and general demographic growth in the sixteenth century, and the seriousness and permanency of the slowing of this pace of growth in the seventeenth century is now being questioned.[49]

As a precautionary measure to avert the danger posed by unanticipated shortages, the amount of grain locally purchased and collected for military use was sometimes well in excess of what was likely to be needed during the army's brief sojourn in a particular region during its march. Following the campaign, when the need for maintaining an emergency surplus supply had passed, the grain could be recirculated to the populace at current market prices.[50] Redistribution of the excess in the aftermath of battle was a far easier matter than attempting to make up supply shortfalls at short notice in the general confusion leading up to battle. In calculating the army's food supply, the Ottomans chose the safer option which was to err on the side of temporary oversupply. Underestimation of military need for grain was a risk they were not prepared to take when there were so many other military uncertainties (weather, conditions of transport, etc.) whose effects they were powerless to counteract.

Concern for social justice and the protection of the *reaya* was also an underlying concern governing the Ottomans' organization of food supply for the army. Disorderly, last-minute emergency requisitions on the spot were far more likely to cause hardship for the taxpayers than supplies acquired through careful prearrangement, under strict government supervision and backed by central financing. By extracting resources in the way it did, the government was not just protecting its own interests, it sought also to maintain a balance between the public interest and legitimate private gain from the massive trans-societal undertaking of producing, supplying and delivering goods for consumption in war.

The imperial *menzil-hane* network operated by the Ottomans was, both in its scale and comprehensiveness, quite advanced for its time. The Ottomans' European contemporaries lacked similar facilities for their armies until the time of Louis XIV's wars against the League of Augsburg after 1688. The organizational revolution which transformed European military practice and allowed for the sustaining of armies of mass mobilization for the first time came to realization only in the closing decades of the seventeenth century. This revolution in practice was initially driven by necessity rather than invention, and results were at first mostly limited to France.[51] At the close of the seventeenth century the Ottomans were still leagues ahead of their European contemporaries in the development of centralized modes for resource extraction and allocation for use in war. As late as the failed siege of Vienna in 1683 European observers continued to marvel at the Ottomans' organizational skills and their ability not just to mobilize but to support and supply large armies in the field. Part of the orderliness and discipline which characterized the Ottoman army in the eyes of contemporary Western observers is attributable to the reliability and consistency they achieved in the delivery of food to their troops. Paul Rycaut who accompanied an Ottoman army bound for Transylvania in 1665 was particularly impressed by this aspect of Ottoman army camp life. He notes that:

> In the Turkish camp no brauls, quarrels or clamours are heard; no abuses are committed on the people in the march of their army; all is bought and paid with money, as by travellers that are guests at an inn.[52]

Opinions vary on the pace and significance of late seventeenth-century European military reforms aimed at regularizing procedures for army supply, but it is clear that the organization of a system of storage depots (*étapes*) began relatively late in Europe compared to the Ottoman Empire. In the opinion of one specialist, the reforms of Louis XIV's ministers Le Tellier and Louvois promised much more than they were, at least initially, capable of delivering.[53] A fully co-ordinated supply system required not just the building of storage depots, but the devising of a centralized system for requisitioning supplies to fill them.[54] The inadequacy of previous *ad hoc* systems for supplying European armies was brought forcefully home by the French experience in the invasion of Germany during the late 1680s, and it was this experience that acted as the catalyst for dramatic change.[55]

The greatest strides in the institutionalization of warfare in Europe were taken not in the seventeenth century, but during the eighteenth. By comparison, Ottoman use of mechanisms for the levying of campaign provisions and advance requisitioning of grain through the *avariz* and *bedel-i nüzul* tax categories had advanced by the mid-sixteenth century well beyond the prototype stage and already assumed the character of well-established practice. That such procedures had already been substantially routinized by the reign of Süleyman I is indicated in a law code of 1545 governing the Ottoman subprovince (*sancak*) of Pozega in eastern Croatia. This code stipulates that the taxpayers' obligation to pay supplementary taxes for campaign provisions (*sefer harcı*) was based on what it terms "established practice".[56] Although the supply of armies in the field (especially when they stayed in the field over the winter months, as happened with increasing regularity after the mid-sixteenth century) was still the Achilles heel of all pre-modern armies,[57] Ottoman capabilities in the area of "*logistikos*" (calculation) were immensely enhanced by the record-keeping revolution and general regularization of bureaucratic procedures associated with the reign of Süleyman I and by their possession of a centralized land tenure system (the *mirî* land regime). To a far greater extent than was possible in any contemporary state of the sixteenth century, the Ottomans were capable of judging, predicting and extracting both the productive capacity and the revenue potential of the lands they administered.

The tactical sphere was naturally and appropriately left to the discretion of the commanders in the field. The areas of army logistics and supply on the other hand were too important to be left to chance or entrusted to the organizational skills, but doubtful mercy, of grain merchants. It was the efficient central requisitioning and distribution of military supplies in the period 1500–1700 that most set the Ottomans apart from their European adversaries. The rapid development of commissariat services in European armies during the first half of the eighteenth century eventually closed the developmental gap that had long existed between the Ottomans and the West, but it is worth remembering that in the fields of transport and logistics it was the Ottomans who were the trend-setters and models of perfection whom the others strove to emulate.

Because worries and distractions connected with supply had been eliminated to the degree possible through detailed foreplanning, Ottoman soldiers were left free to focus their minds on the conduct of battle itself which began to take on an increasingly technical aspect. The rapid evolution of siegecraft after the mid-sixteenth century required the timely performance of a range of highly specialized tasks. The historian Pechevi notes with obvious scorn and disapproval the ill-judged participation of members of regular cavalry regiments in an apple-picking expedition which left the Ottoman garrison of Valpolata in Hungary temporarily undefended. During their unauthorized (in Pechevi's view indefensible) absence the garrison was attacked and forced to surrender in October 1593 after a resistance lasting only two days.[58] The clear message being conveyed by the historian was that the organization of food supply was a matter for administrators and bureaucrats and not for soldiers. Foraging might properly become the business of army irregulars assigned specific roles for collection and transport of food supplies from local sources, but never of the regular soldiery. Such division of function was by no means as clear in European armies of the period.

The lifeline to the Ottoman armies countering the onslaught of the *Sacra Ligua* in southern Hungary during the 1690s was kept open by the river fleet whose navigation of the Danube as far as Nicopolis, Ruse and Silistre was for the time being unimpeded.[59] As long as they maintained their control of strategic fortresses such as Titel, guarding the junction of the Tisa and Danube rivers, and Ösek, protecting the approaches to the crucial transport nexus of the Drava-Danube confluence, the Ottomans were capable of maintaining quite large armies for prolonged periods in the field by relying on such well-stocked and centrally situated supply bases as Belgrade. The map insert (see Map 5, p. xv above) shows the extreme strategic importance of river navigation to the conduct of war in the Hungarian theatre where the Ottomans were critically involved throughout the period 1541–1699.

In Hungary, once the riverine links with supply bases behind the front were severed, the Ottomans were reduced to an equal footing with the armies of their opponents, who had to place almost exclusive reliance on slow and unreliable overland methods and routes for transport of crucial military supplies.[60] The magnitude of the transport and supply challenges facing relatively small armies such as the Habsburg forces in seventeenth-century Hungary has been fully revealed in work by Perjés and others.[61] According to calculations made by Perjés based on the ox-drawn cartload, the provision for 30 days to an army of 90,000 men and 40,000 horses required 11,000 cartloads of food and fodder.[62] Significantly, his figures reflect the larger appetites of animals as compared to men, as he notes that seven-tenths of the total was accounted for by the 7,600 cartloads required for the transport of the wet and dry rations of the army's mounts and the general fodder rations of the draught animals.[63] If we translate these quantities into terms more applicable to the Ottomans' transport methods, the conveyance of a 30-day supply of the animal rations alone (7,600,000 kg) represented at least 30,000 camel loads.[64] Unsupported by river transport, the projection of Ottoman military power beyond the Danube became not just impracticable but, given the size of Ottoman armies, impossible.

The magnitude of the Ottoman army's food and fodder requirements, taken together with the often barren and provisionless nature of the terrain in which it had to operate once it left the main highway and began its manoeuvring for position prior to confronting the enemy, gave added importance to the kind of support it received during its progress towards the final battlefield. The army whose troops were least supported through the rigours of march to the front was the one most likely to crumble under the strain both faced when the two opposing forces finally converged. As an illustration of these operational realities, the dispatches of Sir Robert Sutton, Britain's ambassador to Istanbul in the years 1710–1714, are particularly apt. Sutton's assessment of the 1711 campaign in which the Ottomans routed Peter the Great's army on the banks of the Prut ignores traditional concerns such as battlefield position, skilful tactics and great generalship in favour of more mundane (but no less decisive) considerations of the relative health, diet and general spirits of rank and file troops in the opposing armies. Sutton introduces his remarks on the battle of Pruth with the following observation:

> After the Turks passed the Pruth they and the Tatars surrounded them [the Muscovites, i.e the army of Peter the Great] in such a manner that they must have surrendered themselves for want of victuals and water, without necessity of attacking them.[65]

On the critical role played by supply in this campaign Sutton observes:

> Before the Ottoman army came up to them some say they had lost 5,000 men, some say more, from hunger and sicknesse and a great number of horses from want of forage or taken by the Tatars, who hovered about them and continually surprized and attacked their foragers.[66]

In a third passage Sutton stressed the minimal importance of the few head–on clashes in determining the overall outcome of the campaign by noting:

> It is said the Muscovites did not lose above 800 men in the attacks, but the sicknesse was so great among them that there died 300 or 400 men daily.[67]

In the attention they paid to advance planning relating to all aspects of the requisitioning and delivery of supplies, the Ottomans had identified that area of pre-modern warfare most susceptible to breakdowns, and the area of operations that lay at the root of the most spectacular and memorable military disasters of the epoch. During the period 1500–1700 the Ottomans were not themselves immune from the effects of supply failures that sometimes resulted from an overhasty commitment to war without thorough advance preparation. This happened most dramatically during the anti-Ottoman European counteroffensive of the years 1684–8 when the initiative was wrested from them after the failure at Vienna in 1683 and, most disastrously, when the Western alliance redoubled its military efforts after 1695. During these particular phases in its centuries-long confrontation with the military might of Europe, the Ottomans were uncharacteristically placed on a defensive footing and lost the ability to decide independently when and where they could strike with greatest effect. At other times, however, when their hand had not been forced by overwhelming circumstances and a pressing need to strike back regardless of their own level of readiness or the likelihood of success, the Ottomans had earned and still retained an unsurpassed reputation for their logistical expertise. Voltaire writing a half century after the Ottomans' retreat from Hungary was still disinclined to underestimate the organizational capabilities of the Ottomans. In his account of the Ottoman military, he placed particular emphasis on the abundance of their resources and, by implication, their capacity for mobilizing them.[68]

Relying as our sole source of information on Ottoman archival documentation, we are no doubt inclined to form an unrealistically optimistic impression of Ottoman military efficiency. Certainly the system was subject to breakdowns other than those precipitated by weather and other natural disasters. The role played by official corruption and the frequency of incidents of deliberate misallocation of strategic supplies for personal gain cannot be easily identified, much less quantified.[69] It is, however, certain that speculation on and profiteering from the rise in prices for basic commodities during wartime resulted in deliberate withholding of supplies by taxpayers,[70] and to misdirection of supplies earmarked for military use by dishonest officers.[71] The danger exists that we may present too rosy a picture of Ottoman bureaucratic efficiency by exaggeration or idealization of the Ottoman ethos of communal effort, while paying insufficient attention to non-compliance with state wishes, and yet it is noteworthy that seemingly impartial and not always very sympathetic accounts of Ottoman military might by contemporary Western observers confirm these impressions. These contemporary accounts consistently refer to two elements which in their view explained Ottoman success in the military sphere: the first was the size of the Ottomans' resource base; but secondly, and no less important, was Ottoman military efficiency which they ascribed to the Ottomans' emphasis on discipline. Ottoman military discipline extended not just to proscriptions against raiding and looting, but also covered the proper allocation and use of army resources. Western observers of the period all formed an impression of a well-equipped, well-fed and essentially content (i. e. for the most part regularly paid and rewarded) Ottoman soldiery. Although such observations are not proof of Ottoman military efficiency, they do seem to indicate that, even after factoring in losses arising from civilian non-compliance in supply matters and official corruption, Ottoman armies were still better equipped and supplied than most. Accounts which put too much emphasis on the effect of political turmoil and the seeming instability of the empire (or the weakness and incompetence of its rulers) in the mid-seventeenth century miss the essential point that, in general, it was precisely because it possessed such an efficient bureaucracy that the empire was capable of weathering the storms of dynastic crisis and "harem politics".[72]

Chapter Six

Ottoman methods of warfare: experience, competence and adherence to standard norms of contemporary military practice

In a previous chapter[1] we touched on some of the uncertainties associated with the technical side of warfare in the early modern period and concluded that available technology lacked sufficient power and consistency to allow it to act as a principal determinant factor in warfare. There is, however, a persistent view that Ottoman deficiencies in the development and use of weaponry influenced their ability, especially in the second half of the seventeenth century, to confront the West successfully. It will therefore not be amiss if we scrutinize in greater detail in this chapter some of the main elements of the argument that posits the emergence of a technological gap between Europe and the Ottomans towards the end of our period of analysis. The first matter to be confronted is the issue of the pace of technological change and the likelihood, in abstract terms, that significant technological lag should develop. In twentieth century warfare the gap between the nuclear and non-nuclear powers, already broad in itself, is constantly widening as new discoveries are made and old weapons systems replaced. The time span between scientific discovery and implementation has also been dramatically shortened in modern warfare. The assumption that such rapidity either of change or implementation should apply to the seventeenth century is clearly anachronistic. Neither the Ottomans nor their competitors in the seventeenth century produced weapons under conditions of strict quality control. Standardization of weaponry without centralized production was clearly impossible. The quality of the siege guns produced at the central foundries of Istanbul attached to the Imperial Arsenal (*Tophane-i Amire*) were not noticeably different from guns produced elsewhere. All guns were produced using the prevailing technology of the day that was itself far from infallible. The view that the Ottomans' adoption of technology or indeed their general competence in the military sphere, including the sphere of siege warfare, differed significantly – as the result of cultural, religious or other influences (e.g. general "backwardness") – from that found in other parts of the world, especially the Mediterranean world, is not supported by the evidence. Ideas, techniques and, most importantly, the technicians who implemented them travelled with relative ease and rapidity from one end of the Mediterranean to the other. As for religion, the multiplicity of faiths and general tolerance for religious non-conformity found in the Ottoman empire meant that economic migrants, especially those with artisan skills, who came from other regions representing the heartlands of other religions could be unobtrusively absorbed into Ottoman society. In the sixteenth and seventeenth centuries the Ottoman labour market also offered favorable terms of employment by comparison with some other parts of the Mediterranean. From the standpoint of technology transfer, therefore, the Ottoman Empire, far from putting up barriers to change, represented one of the most porous and receptive environments for the introduction of new ideas.[2]

Debate on the question of the Ottomans' technological competence has been dominated by historians who have offered definitive judgements based on highly selective evidence. The legacy of confusion stemming from subjective appraisals of the narrative evidence representing only one side in multiparty conflicts has a long and historiographically interesting history of its own dating back to the mid-nineteenth century, when the Ottoman state was still a largely intact imperial entity with a prominent place at the centre of European politics. Occasionally, the correction of biased views took place at the time in immediately post-publication reviews, but, more typically, negative Eurocentric assessments of the Ottoman "foe" have been accepted more or less at face value. One exception was Wilhelm Nottebohm's objective appraisal and correction of the views of his predecessor Von Kausler on the source of Ottoman military (in von Kausler's view principally tactical) failures at the battle of St Gotthard in 1664. By carrying out an exhaustive multi-lingual comparative analysis of existing accounts of the battle, including those by contemporary Ottoman historians, Nottebohm was able to dismiss Von Kausler's excessively adulatory account of Montecuccoli's generalship as the decisive factor in the victory by the Christian forces, while at the same time giving emphasis to some of the exceptional operational difficulties under which the Ottoman forces performed as the battle unfolded.[3]

The assessment of Ottoman technological as well as tactical competence has mostly rested either on subjective or one-sided accounts such as Von

Kausler's, or on the theoretical capabilities of the standard weapons found in arsenal inventories of the period divorced from considerations of how they were used and, most importantly, how they were deployed. The applicability of prevailing technology and the deployability of standard weaponry in real battlefield situations are two important dimensions of study that have been largely overlooked in the debate on Ottoman military technique.[4] In the latter part of this chapter we will attempt a small corrective to this tendency in current research by presenting an analysis of some Ottoman narrative accounts revealing of actual practice (i.e. how the technology was applied)[5] in the besieging both of heavily fortified and less elaborately constructed defence works.

The Ottomans and current military practice

In the two centuries that preceded the rise of the Ottoman state circa 1300 East and West had already undergone an extended period of mutual exposure, formed by the context of their prolonged struggle to carve out zones of influence in the Near East and the Levant. The extension and permanent transfer of the zone of competition into the Balkans after the fall of Gallipoli in 1354 brought the two sides even closer, not only in terms of geographical proximity, but also in the comparability and compatibility of the styles of fighting adopted by both sides.[6] As far as the sphere of artillery techniques and pyrotechnics is concerned there is no question that the Ottomans were not just aware of and exposed to, but actively and successfully applying, existing knowledge from the late fourteenth century onwards.[7] Although debate still continues concerning the provenance and antiquity of primitive pyrotechnic techniques, it seems well-established that a further breakthrough was accomplished by the introduction of methods for the graining of powder, perfected around 1420 and then rapidly disseminated throughout Europe and beyond during the 1420s and 1430s.[8] The Ottomans' early mastery of these significant improvements in the technique for producing gunpowder is demonstrated in their success in demolishing by concentrated cannon fire the six-mile defensive walls of Hexamilion on the Isthmus of Corinth in 1446.[9]

The "military revolution" of the 1430s and 1440s which the discovery of methods for the corning of powder engendered is of such a scale and importance as to dwarf all subsequent "revolutions" in military practice during the two and a half centuries which followed. Changes post-1450 in combat methods, defensive postures and weapons development can be seen as no more than a series of adjustments to and refinements of the new standard set in the 1430s, as opposed to innovations that set a new standard in their own right. Viewed in this way we see epoch-making technological change in the military sphere circa 1420 followed by a short period of rapid dissemination of new ideas lasting roughly two decades to about 1440, followed by an extended period lasting nearly 300 years during which this new standard was never seriously challenged. Compared with the advances achieved circa 1420 in the sphere of gunpowder preparation, later experimentation with firing mechanisms was both inconclusive and, in relative terms, insignificant.[10]

That the pace of technological advance (and therefore also of technology transfer) slowed during the sixteenth and seventeenth centuries is accepted by most specialists on European military matters. It was effectively only from the time of the Ottomans' more pronounced isolation and withdrawal from their long-standing sphere of conflict in Central Europe after 1739 that one can speak of successful exclusion of the Ottomans from the developing military technology of Europe. In fact, the resumption of conflict between Austria and the Ottomans between 1737 and 1739 may have served to refamiliarize the Ottomans with current military practice in the West. In view of such considerations it seems reasonable also to question the validity of assumptions about a gap in technology between advanced and less advanced regions in Europe prior to the mid-eighteenth century.

If we posit the existence of a universal standard and argue for general parity and relative stasis,[11] both in the development of weaponry and in the level of military advancement throughout the Mediterranean lands, the Ottomans in the early modern era may be more accurately and appropriately regarded as active participants in a shared technology rather than as passive recipients of borrowed means and methods. This assessment becomes the more apt when one stops to recall that the Ottomans made use of the same limited pool of technical experts (often the self-same technicians) as their European counterparts.[12] During the sixteenth and seventeenth centuries most of Europe, including its southern flank, made up a single zone in which similar or convergent technologies prevailed. Techniques developed in one area spread rapidly throughout the Europo-Mediterranean region.[13] After the close of the seventeenth century Russia too joined the exclusive circle. With the possible exception of pre-Petrine Russia it is historically inaccurate to speak of a distinction between the "advanced" and "backward" or developed and undeveloped parts of Europe and its terrestrial extensions in the Ottoman lands. Prior to the industrial revolution which affected only a small part of northernmost Europe, such divisions have no place, and such transfer of ideas as did take place was multi-directional as opposed to exclusively West to East or North to South.[14]

Deployment of Ottoman ordnance and its use in the field

The truism that there is a proper tool for every job applies with particular force to the field of Ottoman artillery practice in seventeenth-century warfare. The transportation of unnecessary (both heavy and unwieldy) equipment to a distant front, particularly when it involved the use of difficult overland routes, was more likely to represent a liability than an asset in the Ottomans' pursuit of victory. It was a recognized fact among the most astute military observers of the time that the lack of manoeuvrability and encumbrance resulting from long baggage trains far outweighed the potential advantages associated with superior fire power.[15] On campaign the Ottoman regular army and timariot forces were always accompanied by large contingents of lightly armed, highly mobile scouting and skirmishing forces. These forces played a vital reconnaissance role, probing enemy territory lying ahead of the main Ottoman army and supplying army command with a continuous stream of information on the most vulnerable targets for attack. This information provided an informed basis for decisions about the optimal mix of cannons and other siege equipment to achieve Ottoman military objectives. In many situations the heaviest guns were of doubtful efficacy or usefulness and, except when they were needed at a predetermined spot for a preplanned siege, they were generally kept in reserve and brought forward for use only as a final recourse when the inadequacy of the lighter equipment had been decisively demonstrated. Delaying the final decision about the commitment of men and material to a particular field position in this way gave the Ottomans an important tactical advantage. To gain maximum benefit from this advantage, the Ottomans possessed both the mineral resources and the technical capability to cast guns of intermediate size either at the final front itself or at nearby regional ateliers. During the 1638 Baghdad campaign, for example, the Ottomans were able to significantly enhance their provision of ordnance by drawing on local resources as a supplement to the hardware shipped to the army from the Istanbul arsenal. Five medium-sized siege guns using 25 okka shot (70 pounders) and three using 18 okka shot (50 pounders) were cast at Birecik on the Upper Euphrates from where they were taken by raft to a location close to the site of the planned siege at Baghdad.[16]

It appears that from the mid-sixteenth century when artillery was becoming a compulsory and steadily growing part of military provision, the 11–22 okka range (30–60 pound shot) was a category commonly required for Ottoman deployments in Hungary.[17] By the mid-seventeenth century these standards had seemingly changed, and evidence suggests that, to have much effect for use in wall-battering by the new standards, shot in the 16–30 okka range (45–85 pounds) was required.[18] But a perfect match between available ordnance and supplies of the appropriate sized balls at a given battle site was rarely achieved or even expected. The best that could be hoped for was a generous advance supply of the most commonly used varieties. Although every effort was made to provide a ready supply of the appropriate quantities of the types of ammunition most needed for both offensive and defensive purposes, evidence suggests that last-minute adjustments were frequently needed. This could lead to the countermanding of previous orders sent to regional supply depots in the months leading up to campaign.[19] Another alternative that allowed even greater flexibility in military planning and required even less advance notice was to cast new gun barrels on the spot to fit the size of the balls in most plentiful supply locally.[20] Evidence from arsenal inventories of fortresses representing all parts of the empire suggests that the 30-pounders (11 okka shot) were not just omnipresent, but in particularly high demand for defensive purposes.[21]

The weapon in most common use by the Ottoman field artillery called the *zarbzen* (also *shahi zarbzen*) weighed only 125 pounds (one *kantar*) which meant that a pair of barrels could be loaded on a packhorse and easily carried in whatever direction the army might decide to take.[22] Moving the larger guns required precise knowledge and decisions taken weeks in advance about where the army actually intended to be. This not only reduced the army's mobility and flexibility of movement, it also sent unmistakable signals to its opponents about its offensive plans and intentions. Strategic thinkers (as we shall see in the analysis of actual Ottoman deployments later in this chapter) were acutely aware that the trading of diminished firepower for greater manoeuvrability was in most situations a wholly advantageous exchange. Commanders had to give consideration above all else to the portability as well as transportability of the weaponry they selected to accompany them into battle.

The large guns were used as a complementary rather than exclusive tool in demolishing enemy defences, and they had their fullest effect only in partnership with skilled miners and sappers. It is significant that, as late as 1663, Uyvar, from the standpoint of its military architecture the most formidable obstacle yet encountered by the Ottomans in Europe, was reduced by the Ottomans using fewer than two dozen wall-battering guns.[23] Much of the preparatory work that made the use of cannon effective had already been achieved by legions of sappers who were assigned in teams of five each to every cubit of the outer perimeter of the defensive walls.[24]

In the main Ottoman military planners were disposed to rely on detailed intelligence reports based on information gathered in the field, often recruiting into their service renegades who had the most detailed and accurate local knowledge about the strength of enemy fortifications and defences. This enabled them to commit to particular operations, sometimes pursued in parallel fashion over a relatively wide swath of territory, only what, after careful calculation, was deemed necessary for the accomplishment of specific military objectives. The suggestion that the Ottomans carried superfluous or inappropriate baggage or equipment into battle with them, which is based on the superficial assessment of the exceptional mobilization and exposure of the Ottomans' forces at Vienna in 1683, is not borne out in the detail found in the numerous Ottoman campaign narratives at our disposal.[25] The typical organization of the Ottoman camp, so far as it can be reconstructed from both visual and narrative sources, suggests the Ottomans conformed closely to the principle: "a place for everything and everything in its place".

In general terms Ottoman artillery practice in the seventeenth century coincided with European practice. As for the standards of production and general capabilities of the Ottoman weapons, it seems they were also broadly comparable with those commonly found in Europe at the time. Around the time of the Thirty Years War European muskets using bullets weighing approximately one and a third ounces (12 dirhems or about 38.5 grams) had an effective range of 220–70 yards (approximately 201–47 metres).[26] By comparison, the range of the muskets in use by the Ottomans about the time of the siege of Vienna was approximately a fifth greater, capable of delivering their loads, according to Western military observers, a distance of up to 300 metres.[27] As in all matters military in the seventeenth century, however, what mattered most was not the technical specifications of or the theoretical capabilities of the standard issue weaponry, but the manner as well as conditions of their use in actual combat situations.

Military architecture and the cost of modernization

The introduction of the bastioned fortress in the sixteenth century and its spread in the seventeenth century represents a development of supreme importance to military history. In practical terms, however, the cost of fully modernizing defensive works on an extended military front was prohibitive. Most states had to content themselves with producing isolated examples of the "new style" architecture in a few strategically important sectors of the wider frontier. In the Habsburg case, two sites, Györ (Yanik Kale) in western Hungary and Nové Zamky (Uyvar) in Slovakia were chosen for extensive renovations and improvements.[28] In the South, on a much reduced scale, a new-style fort was constructed (under local initiative and using mostly local financial resources) at Zrinvár (Yeni Kale) in the Slovenian–Croatian

2. Men pulling field cannon. *Source*: Bağdad Köşkü 200, folio 100a.

borderland. In the case of Nové Zamky, the loss of many years of investment for the improvement of the fortress's defences in the years between 1605 and the early 1660s was compounded by the necessity which its ultimate loss to the Ottomans in September 1663 engendered of constructing a new line of defence along the Vah river dominated by the newly erected fort of Leopoldov.[29] Furthermore, concentration of effort on a small number of strongholds inevitably left the rest of the frontier exposed and vulnerable to attack using conventional means.

Subduing the omnipresent standard fort of the (*palanka*) type, defended only by a rough wooden palisade thrown up around its perimeter, was as easy in many cases as setting torches to a few of the stakes and watching the blaze spread. Even where extensive improvements had been carried out, resources were rarely sufficient to attempt a wholesale rebuilding. More often than not, what emerged from these modernization attempts, whose end-product reflected a convoluted and sometimes very protracted process of need assessment tempered by fiscal compromise, were structures of curiously indeterminate character.[30] The "improvements" consisted in many cases of little more than the addition of a few secure bastions to a wall which was otherwise riddled with weak spots that virtually invited enemy attack. Relatively few of the 85–90 fortresses scattered along the military frontier separating Ottoman and Habsburg Hungary in the seventeenth century were either constructed elaborately enough or sufficiently well-garrisoned to withstand even the haphazard attacks of Hungarian insurgents, let alone more determined assault by fully-equipped and well-trained Ottoman armies.[31] Independent accounts of the Ottoman siege of the Ukranian fortress of Chigirin (Çehrin) in 1678 emphasize the fact that the wooden-framed walls stuffed with earth (*dolma duvari*) provided only partial protection from the Ottoman guns.[32] Çehrin's most secure defence was provided by the natural setting of the fortress whose foundations were set on sandy soil. Because of the soil's inherent instability, the progress of the miners and sappers was slow, and the advance of the trenches to the final wall delayed until the 33rd day of the siege.[33]

Man-made devices and engineering skills were largely applied only as backup measures in case such protections as were offered by the natural surroundings of a fortress should fail. Choosing the site for a fortress nestled between the prongs formed by the bifurcation or confluence of rivers, or in floodplains, marshes and bogs where it was most protected from a terrestrial army's approach was given equal consideration to the scale and architectural ingenuity of the fortifications themselves. One construction technique that was effectively applied both by the Ottomans and their adversaries was called by the Ottomans the "*Horasani*" technique in reference to the rose-colored hues of the chalky soil of eastern Iran. When thoroughly applied, it rendered walls nearly cannon-proof. The technique involved the use of a compound of sifted brick dust and lime in place of sand when preparing the mortar for the main pillars lending support to the walls of a fortress. Only fire at very close range was capable of penetrating walls constructed using this technique.[34] But still more effective than the application of such human artifice, once a close encounter was no longer avoidable, was to rely on natural features to prevent the assailant approaching at all.

For the Ottomans mastery of the art of siegecraft was a cumulative process. Each successive stage was informed by the experiences and discoveries that preceded it. The nature of this evolutionary process, based on applied knowledge and past experience, is made explicit in the Ottoman sources. For example, technicians and engineers active in the first phases of the siege of Candia during 1648 were individuals who had gained combat experience in the Safavid–Ottoman wars of the 1630s.[35] Similarly, during the investment of Çehrin in 1678, Ahmed Pasha, by then elevated to the position of governor of Bosnia, was able to draw on his experience during the final assault on Candia in 1668–9 to advise his troops on the most effective means of attack in the context of the current campaign.[36]

Even the most ingenious and comprehensively applied design improvements using the best construction materials and techniques were not proof against the counterpoised skills of experienced miners and sappers. Ottoman sources describing the state of Uyvar's transformed defences in 1663, equipped with ten-foot thick brick outer walls and high earthen ramparts that towered 18 feet above the highest point of the walls, agree that the enemy's efforts over a number of years had resulted in the creation of a fully cannon-proof structure.[37] But in the end even "Europe's bulwark" proved incapable of resisting the patient and methodical attack directed more at its underground foundations than its above-ground fortifications.[38]

A major hurdle in the Ottomans' path to mastering the technical side of siegecraft had already been confronted and overcome earlier in the century during the 1620s and 1630s when the Ottomans besieged Baghdad on three separate occasions. But, in many ways, the finer points of the art learned in confronting such engineering marvels as Baghdad were largely irrelevant to the everyday practice of siegecraft in the period. To gain a balanced sense of standard Ottoman operating procedure for sieges, we must look beyond the dramatic outcome of the best-documented "major" confrontations and the temptingly straightforward assessment of Ottoman successes in subduing such exceptionally well-designed and defended fortresses as Uyvar and Baghdad. The fuller picture can only emerge if we take a closer look at the lower level of force needed and the simpler methods appropriate to the reducing of enemy fortifications forming the second and third tier of frontier defences. With this objective in mind, we will examine Ottoman methods of war in the remaining part of this chapter by assessing Ottoman battle narratives representing two distinct groups. In the first part we will concentrate on sources relating to major sieges with the subduing of the state-of-the-art fortress of Baghdad as the principal focus of analysis. The second part will be devoted, with lessons of far wider application, to an assessment of the experience and methods of Ottoman warfare, including siege, in the context of lesser campaigns. Forming an opinion about what the Ottoman army was capable of achieving under extreme conditions or in exceptional circumstances has perhaps less relevance and importance for our assessment of general Ottoman military performance than an ability – reached through a realistic assessment of its everyday, oftentimes rather plodding, pace and progress during the course of normal operations in the field – to observe its more usual behaviour. Judged by the yardstick of the unwritten everyday rules of engagement as revealed in the narrative record of actual mobilizations, we will be better able to put the whole question of Ottoman competence in the technical sphere and its applicability to the conduct of battle in its proper perspective.

Ottoman combat (Part One): the major siege as exemplified by the investment of Baghdad in 1638

The case of Baghdad is well-suited to serve as an example of the methods used by the Ottomans for besieging major fortified places, since it twice successfully resisted attack: first a seven-month siege in 1625–6, then a short offensive in October and November 1630, before finally yielding in 1638 to a full-scale Ottoman attack lasting 39 days. Because of the massiveness of its fortifications, Baghdad drew the attention of a wide variety of contemporary observers.[39] The most detailed description of the condition of the walls of Baghdad at the time of the Ottoman siege in 1638 is given by Ziyaeddin Ibrahim Nuri, who was himself present in the Ottoman army as he composed his history of the campaign. Nuri counted 114 towers (kule) along the walls, stretching on three sides from the North Gate (Imam -i Azam) near the Tigris, along the east wall, around to the South Gate (Karanlik Kapu) on the Tigris. An additional 97 towers along the west wall parallel to the Tigris brought the total to 211 towers. In the space between each pair of towers, 52 crenels (beden) were inserted. The entire circumference of the walls was paced off and determined to be 27,309 paces. Thus, assuming a distance between each tower of roughly 130 paces, a crenel was to be found at each interval of two and a half paces throughout the walls' extent.[40] Since each of the over 10,000 embrasures was ideally to be defended by five men, two musketeers, one bowman, and two assistants, the defence of the city walls alone required a small army. The height of the wall was 50 cubits (25 metres) and its width ranged from 32 feet at the base of the moat[41] to 10 to 15 cubits (7 metres) along the top between the turrets.[42] Because Baghdad's walls were constructed of shock-absorbent brick rather than brittle stone, and reinforced throughout much of their length by earthen ramparts,[43] they were able to withstand a heavy bombardment without suffering very great damage.[44]

The approaches to the walls were guarded by extensive outworks, including three parallel ditches.[45] The first ditch was a pike's length deep and broad, while the second ditch in the green between the walls and the outer ditch was half the width of the first.[46] The main moat surrounding the city walls on three sides was at least three to four pikes' length in breadth, but its depth varied, so that in some places it was half filled with water and in others hardly ankle-deep.[47] The main moat was at its widest and deepest along the east wall facing the White Gate (*Ak Kapu*).[48] Following Hafiz Ahmed's siege in 1626 concentrated along the southern wall in the vicinity of the Gate of Shadows (Karanlik Kapu), and Hüsrev Pasha's siege in 1630 concentrated along the northern walls in the vicinity of the gate of Imam-i Azam, the Safavid garrison commander Bektash Khan carried out extensive repairs on these sections of the walls.[49] Ramparts were built behind the main wall of the fortress all along the north and south faces, and an additional ditch was dug and filled with water as a fallback in case the first defences were breached. After these improvements the east wall, surrounded by its extensive outer moat, was the only remaining part of the city's defences protected by a single barrier wall.[50]

In overcoming Baghdad's imposing defences, the Ottoman army was assisted by a large force of trench diggers (*beldar*) and a specially trained corps of army engineers called *lağımcı*, that is, miners and sappers. When the army arrived at its destination, its first task was to establish itself in trenches around the city's defences. With a few exceptions[51] all the infantry troops were assigned to the trenches, while the cavalry were posted behind the trenches to guard against attack.[52] Since many of the 24,000 *beldar* recruited at the rate of one per twenty households from Anatolia,[53] and the 7,000–8,000 *lağımcı* ordered to report for duty by Murad[54] were assigned to other duties, it was a relatively small group of experienced engineers who joined the troops in the trenches. A register made of those actually present in the trenches during the 1638 campaign shows that, since 680 *beldar* had been diverted to duties as oxen drivers (*sürücü*), 91 as construction workers repairing fortresses, and another 1,000 assigned to the shipyards at Birecik, only 1,500 men were counted present in the trenches.[55] The process of sapping or creating a zigzag trench (*siçan yolu*) to the edge of the moat was slow.[56] The average sap proceeded at a rate of no more than fifty yards a day.[57] The reason for the slowness was that, although the first trenches were dug at a distance of one mile from the outer moat, because of twistings and turnings they were five miles long by the time they reached the outer moat, and they had to be wide enough to accommodate the gun carriages to bring the siege guns into close range of the city's walls.[58] In order to protect the front edge of these trenches from enemy fire, as well as to adjust the elevation of the besiegers' gun batteries, extensive use was made of gabions woven out of twigs and boughs (*chit*). Because Baghdad's sparse vegetation fell short of providing the necessary materials, care had been taken to collect sufficient quantities of boughs and twigs during a lay-over day near Kerkuk on the march to Baghdad.[59] A passage translated from Nuri's account of the siege describes how these gabions were put to use during the siege.[60]

When it came to be the time for transferring the cannon to the entrenched positions, boughs of twigs were distributed to the troops and twenty sticks were given out for every thousand men of the provincial cavalry for fashioning into gabions. Once completed, the gabions were placed in front of the cannons and filled with earth. They stood up like towers and by distributing the gabions equally on all sides, a fence-like structure was created, the gaps of which were filled by the cannon. In order that each cannon might be fitted into its proper place along the gabion fence, it had to be adjusted according to the elevation of the castle walls at that part of the trench. If the walls were low, the cannon could remain at the same level, but if they were high, the elevation of the barrel could be altered by stacking one or two more layers of gabions on top of each other.

In the case of Baghdad the walls started from low foundations and rose to a great height, the rise often accentuated by the enemy's own excavations of earth which they piled up on the far side of the moat. As a result, it became necessary to elevate the cannon throughout the length of the gabion fence. We thereupon dug out ramparts of earth at the edge of the moat, taking care to leave aside the earth which had been thrown there by the enemy so that when the base of the walls was exposed to view, by adding five to six layers of gabions, the elevation of the cannons was raised to the required level. Afterwards the gabions were covered over with earth and made level and, when a cover of boards had been laid on top, the timariots were ordered to lend a hand in hauling the cannons into place with hawsers. It was remembered that at the time of the late Hüsrev Pasha's siege in 1630 seven layers of gabions had been

117

placed on top of one another to prepare the gun nests. In short, once the gabions had been constructed, set in place and covered with earth, the cannon were hauled up to the front line for final positioning.

While the army was thus occupied the enemy began to excavate earth from the foundations of the walls starting first at the "Flat Tower" on the north wall near the Imam-i Azam Gate and continuing along the whole extent of the walls all the way to the "Persian Tower" on the south wall. When the experts were consulted about the reason for their digging of this inner trench at the base of the walls they agreed that the enemy's motive was to prevent the laying of mines from our side of the moat. Indeed later on when we reached the moat and attempted to lay our mines they were able, by using this inner trench, to frustrate all our attempts to lay mines through the holes they had opened facing us from behind the walls. However, for the present, we continued our progress with the trenches, moving forward pace by pace each day until we reached within thirty-seven paces of the front edge of the moat. (Translation of an excerpt from Nuri's description of the Ottoman siege of Baghdad in 1638)

Once the painstaking preparatory work described by Nuri in the foregoing passage had been completed, the cannon could begin to train their fire against the city from the first line of trenches. But it was not until the besiegers had overcome the obstacle of the outer moat and the guns could be moved forward to a range dominating both the walls and the enemy movement behind the walls within the city that any real advantage was to be gained from artillery fire.[61] Once the attackers had taken complete control of the moat and could construct high ramparts on top of which their gun emplacements could be erected, the defenders could no longer maintain much hope of holding out. Because its preservation was so critical to the defenders, it was only after a hard fight that the control of the moat was relinquished. The defenders could resort to a number of countermeasures to retard the forward progress of the besiegers' trenches.[62] While the besiegers poured earth into the moat from above, seeking to close it off and erect their ramparts above it for their guns, the defenders excavated pockets from beneath the walls and by means of long-handled shovels removed the earth as soon as it was thrown into the moat.[63] The 1630 siege of Baghdad by Hüsrev Pasha, despite thorough Ottoman preparations including 2,000 camel loads each consisting of two ten-foot bales of cotton to be used in filling in the moat, had been frustrated by similar defensive countermeasures. In 1630, the Safavid defenders built a trap in an area which they had undermined and later covered with grass. This trap collapsed under the weight of the advancing Ottoman attackers and the siege had to be abandoned.[64] From such examples it can be seen how essential it was for the attackers to seize control of the whole extent of the moat before any thought of a final assault on the walls could be considered.

The fight over earth in the moat, like the establishment of the first line of trenches, involved little direct contact between the two contesting armies. In the next phase, high earthen ramparts (*tabiya*) were constructed level with the city walls on the far side of the moat. The cannon were hauled up to the top of these ramparts from where they dominated the so-called "covered way" between the edge of the moat and the walls. To protect the gunners on top of the ramparts, calatrop shields resembling the bristly hairs on the back of a wild boar (*doñuz dami*) were erected.[65] A miniature from the early seventeenth century shows clearly the form which the gun emplacements took (see p. 120).[66]

The prickly calatrop shields protecting the forward positions on a level with the castle walls are visible in the upper part of the composition, while two pairs of siege guns are shown in the background protruding from openings in a fence-like structure constructed of upright gabions (*chit*) filled with earth to give them stability. The forward gun emplacements were manned on a revolving duty basis by companies of 20–30 Janissaries, who from their high vantage point could survey enemy activity within the walls, and protect the artillerymen who continued the business of bombarding the walls undisturbed.[67] Furthermore, the control of the moat area by the attackers meant that the miners could go about their work protected by the calatrop shield erected above them. It was because of incomplete control over the full length of the moat during the 1630 campaign that the miners' efforts produced a breach of only 40–50 cubits.[68] In the 1638 campaign, on the other hand, the miners were successful in opening a breach 858 cubits (*zira*) in length.[69] By installing a handrail (*tarabizan*)[70] on either edge of the flattened top of the ramparts, the combat troops had direct access to the walls. Under the shelter of the Janissary gun outposts, they could now attach their ladders and scale the walls with ease.

Once the attackers had established themselves at the wall, the outcome of the siege was a foregone conclusion. In the hand-to-hand fighting which followed heroic deeds might delay or accelerate the capture of the fortress, but could rarely change the course of events. The investment of Baghdad in 1638 followed the general rule for sieges that the two most critical phases were the preparation of siege works and the capture of the moat. The moving of earth (by both defenders and attackers) was without doubt the chief occupation of the greatest number of men for the longest period of time in most sieges. Far more man-hours were spent in getting ready for the final assault than in direct contact or combat of any description. An indication of the division of labour

3. Besieging a fortress in the Yemen. *Source*: Hazine 889, folio 14a.

present in most sieges is given if we examine the standard equipment listed in arsenal inventories of the period. In an eighteenth-century inventory of the mid-Danubian fortress of Ada Kale sapping tools, including 6,531 shovels, occupied more shelf space than any other category of military equipment.[71] An inventory of the Diyarbekir arsenal for 1636 gives similar prominence to digging tools, and includes 3,600 shovels and picks as well as a supply of 1,900 spare, wooden, shovel handles.[72] Supplies sent to mobile units were of a similar order. We know, for example, that a quantity of 4,000 iron shovel blades and 4,000 pick-heads were issued from central stores as part of the equipment set aside for an army setting out for the eastern front in the 1630s.[73]

Advanced weaponry, whether for use in major conflicts or in the context of small skirmishes, played a mostly non-critical role in determining the outcome of battle. A hint about the undiminished importance of "conventional" weapons such as arrows and sabres during the concluding phase of siege when hand-to-hand fighting broke out is provided in a passage from Silahdar's account of the investment of Çehrin in 1678. According to Silahdar, in the final phases of battle the handguns, issued as a matter of course to the Janissaries, had a rather restricted application. It seems they were used more to provide safe cover for the troops as they rushed forward from their trenches to scale the walls than as offensive weapons in their own right. A final volley fired in unison was more often than not used merely as the preliminary to a clash of swords, hatchets and halberds or the launching of spears which typified the fighting in close quarters. Under conditions of close combat, the resumption, still more the sustaining, of musket fire was too risky, since each halt for the reloading of their weapons placed the advancing soldiers in a fatally vulnerable position.[74] Its supposed status as an "outmoded" weapon did not alter the fact that, for purposes of the final mêlée which inevitably ensued as part of the closing (and therefore determining) phase of battle, the sabre proved the more useful (and therefore lethal) tool of the trade.

The musket, as the more advanced and technically superior, but in the seventeenth century by no means yet perfected, weapon, in fact offered little tactical advantage and its temperamental performance made it not just useless, but a positive liability in situations where rapid reaction and decisive action were required. In close quarters, missing the target on the first shot, or even failing to inflict sufficiently serious wounds, could have fatal results for the musketeer unless he had his more "primitive" fallback weapons (daggers, swords, etc.) ready to hand. The continuing reliance on relatively "primitive" or non-technical solutions to combat challenges in seventeenth-century warfare is still more apparent, when we shift our attention from the consideration of prolonged sieges and military force concentrated against heavily-fortified places defended by large garrisons to a consideration of the conditions that

121

prevailed and the pattern of engagement that typified military action directed against lesser forces stationed in fortifications of the more modestly constructed type.

Ottoman combat (Part Two): operational realities during lesser campaigns as exemplified by the pattern of military engagements during the 1664 campaigning season

The story of seventeenth-century Ottoman warfare has been most commonly told from the point of view of major battles and decisive victories and defeats. The dramatic confrontation of the Ottoman and Safavid empires at Baghdad in 1638, and of Venice and the Ottomans between 1645 and 1669 in Crete are examples of full-scale, full-commitment warfare which was not altogether characteristic of the period. As we have already noted in an earlier chapter,[75] the typical pattern of engagement until the wars of the last quarter of the century rarely involved armies of mass mobilization and international assembly. The early sixteenth century witnessed to a degree the continuation of the medieval order and style of battle in which a season's activity typically culminated in a single, usually decisive, pitched battle. But a new pattern that became increasingly typical of the seventeenth century after the frontiers had been firmly established and to a large degree already solidified was marked by the clash of smaller forces dispersed between multiple fronts or engaged in a succession of rapidly-executed attacks across a wide band of territory. In the new period a more fluid, exploratory and opportunistic style of engagement emerged that shared many of the features of guerrilla warfare, and the concentration of huge opposing armies massed on a single battlefield became increasingly exceptional. While it is inevitable, perhaps even desirable given the easy availability and wider array of sources for analysis, that major conflicts and confrontations should form a focus for scholarly investigation, there is a danger that an exclusive focus on armies in concentrated modes of deployment may distort our understanding of the basic realities of military practice in the period. To gain a more accurate sense of the rhythm and pace of military activity associated with armies in dispersed modes of deployment, we will focus in the remainder of this chapter on contemporary Ottoman and Western narrative accounts of Ottoman army movements during a ten-month period stretching over autumn and winter 1663 to spring and early summer 1664. The period between the fall of Uyvar in late September 1663 and the confrontation between the Ottoman and Habsburg armies in early August 1664 at the battle of St Gotthard was full of a variety of military activity of a less chronicled and celebrated sort. The purpose of our narrative on the disposition of the Ottoman army during this period that lay between major confrontations will be to offer insights into the character of the low-impact, low-intensity warfare that was perhaps most characteristic of the period. Uyvar (1663) was, with the exception of Varad (1660) which immediately preceded it, the first siege on any scale to occur in this sector since the Ottoman capture of Győr in 1594, and St Gotthard (1664) was a pitched battle resulting more from accident than design after a similar hiatus dating from the time of the Egri campaign (1596). The intervening years were not always quiet, but military conflict in this period assumed different forms that are worthy of study in their own right.

In the short period between the banner events of Uyvar and St Gotthard military activity followed a common pattern of strike and counterstrike, with the difference that in this instance the reaction times were reduced to a fraction of the normal by the fact that instead of returning to Istanbul – the regular practice in the absence of any significant threat of off-season counter-attacks – the bulk of the Ottoman army, including a proportion of its Tatar allies, remained in the field throughout the winter season. The reaction to Ottoman successes in Slovakia, which had culminated in the end-of-season attack against and capture of Nógrád in early November, came swiftly in the form of a winter offensive led by the Ban of Croatia Nicholas Zriny. This attack was launched from his newly-established secure base at Zrinvár. The offensive was planned and carried out through his personal initiative with assistance from militias provided by the Batthany family who also had estates in the vicinity. These mostly local resources sufficed to raise an army of 30,000 men capable of undertaking the investment of Sigetvár, one of the Ottomans' principal bases in the region.[76]

After an initial attack against the smaller forts of Berzence and Bobócsa beginning on 21 January, the bulk of Zriny's forces moved quickly to the attack against Sigetvár which began on 25 January.[77] Gürcü Mehmed Pasha the Ottoman commander with winter headquarters at Ösek was charged with organizing a relief force drawing on local sources of manpower, but most of the army's main units had been assigned to winter quarters at a distance of over five to ten days' march.[78] Although the grand vezier moved quickly from Belgrade to set up field headquarters at Zemun across the Sava, his whole force amounted to little more than an escort troop of 4,000 men.[79] Support forces available to the field commander Gürcü Mehmed in his immediate vicinity at the front were, when the alarm was first raised, no more than half that number. Able to move more or less at will against his target or targets of choice, Zriny shifted the focus of his attack and, instead of concentrating his forces on Sigetvár, commenced a two-pronged attack aimed, on the one hand, against Pécs, another of the Ottomans' most important regional bases in southern Hungary and, on the other, against the bridge at Ösek which guarded the supply and communications lifeline between the front in Hungary and vital Ottoman resource and reinforcement bases strung out along the Danube.

The Ottomans could do little more than watch while the enemy systematically destroyed the outer defences of Pécs. The level of destruction was so great that Ottoman sources acknowledge that the holes resulting from the sustained enemy bombardment were "wide enough to allow grazing animals to pass in and out of the city walls without obstruction".[80] While Zriny's forces raised the siege of Pécs on the 6th of February without having captured the inner citadel,[81] the whole of the operation carried out between the last week of January and the first week of February cost the Ottomans dearly both in terms of expense for repairs and the inevitable delays that would result in their own spring mobilization. It was inconceivable that they should launch an offensive while their own border defences lay in ruins. This damage had been inflicted by a lightly-armed force of irregulars who advanced unopposed a distance of six stages into Ottoman territory at a time when the Ottoman regular army had disbanded. After a busy season of fighting on another sector of the front in Slovakia Ottoman troops were not very favourably disposed to listen to the grand vezier's urgent orders to reactivate. This pattern of uncontested or only minimally-contested offensives was not confined to the relatively unusual occurrence of winter offensives. It was, as our examination of the Ottoman counteroffensive of spring 1664 will show, a common feature of many military encounters even in the principal campaigning season.

In the spring of 1664 the first task of the full Ottoman army, reactivated and redeployed to the sectors where immediate action was required, was to make good the damage done in the winter raids carried out by the Croatian and Hungarian commandos. Their attacks had been so rapidly executed that by the time the Grand Vezier Fazil Ahmed Pasha had barely advanced beyond Sremska Mitrovica, the second stage after Belgrade, the guerrilla raiders had already withdrawn to their own bases beyond the Ottoman frontier. At the time of his return to Belgrade on 11 February Fazil Ahmed Pasha had already set in motion the plans for organizing works crews to carry out the extensive repairs that would be required before the critical bridge at Ösek could be restored to operation.[82]

The effect of the enemy's winter offensive in the early months of 1664 had been to eliminate the vitally important period of rest and recuperation that normally stretched over the whole of a four-and-a-half-month period beginning with the "Day of Division" (*Ruz-i Kasim*) on 6 November which marked the end of the summer season and the beginning of the winter months, and ending with the vernal equinox (*Nevruz*) on 21 March which marked the slow emergence from winter leading to active mobilization in springtime. As a result of Zriny's offensive, work crews were kept busy throughout this winter season and beyond just to restore the *status quo ante*, let alone attend to preparations for the Ottoman counteroffensive. Seventy-five days after the winter repair crews had been dispatched to Ösek, the arrival of the grand vezier with his assembled troops at the river crossing on 15 May 1664 still managed to coincide with a last-minute flurry of activity to complete the final phase of reconstruction.[83]

As the result of Zriny's sudden raid, the whole Croatian frontier was plunged into a state of panic, which was further heightened when, after a short pause while he sought backing from the imperial centre in Vienna, he resumed his offensive with an early-season attack on the strategic Ottoman frontier fortress of Kanizsa in the closing days of April 1664.[84] The previous attacks carried out against Berzence, Babósca, Pécs and Darány and, most important, on the bridge at Ösek had left Kanizsa effectively cut off, not just from its immediate hinterlands, but from all practicable routes of approach for purposes of supply and reinforcement.[85] Zriny's 36-day siege of Kanizsa ended in failure, but before they were able to move ahead with their own offensive plans the Ottomans were once again burdened with the task of repairing the damage done to this fortress, which formed a key element of their border defences in that sector of the frontier. The scale of these repairs was such that, according to Evliya Chelebi's account, even with input from civilian work crews mobilized – in open contradiction of normal Ottoman military practice – from seven outlying districts the work was not completed until 13 July, long after the normal start of seasonal operations.[86]

The immediate challenge facing the Grand Vezier Fazil Ahmed Pasha in the spring of 1664, before he could contemplate any active engagement of the enemy, was the remobilization of units earlier assigned to winter quarters in areas scattered throughout the Danubian region. Even after the bridge at Ösek had been finally restored to use and regular army units attached to the grand vezier had crossed the river on the 20th of May, Ahmed Pasha resolved to advance slowly so as to allow time for the army's ranks to swell to levels that would allow him to commence offensive action.[87] The news of Kanizsa's investment begun at the end of April was already four weeks old when the grand vezier's forces arrived at Sigetvár on 29 May to be joined there by bands of irregulars from Bosnia and Albania enlisted in place of members of regular units who, even at this late date, were still tarrying on their way from assigned winter quarters.[88] A swifter mobilization was ruled out in any case by the need for the mounts on whom the army would depend in later phases of the campaign to complete the spring pasturing before proceeding to the front.[89]

When the grand vezier arrived at Ösek on 20 May, a strategic decision had already been taken to leave behind most of the heavy siege guns and other bulky equipment to allow the army to advance as quickly as possible. In fact, only seven out of the 27 heavy guns stored in Ösek accompanied the army during its onward march.[90] This decision was based on a calculated risk but, given the fact that the four-week-old investment of Kanizsa was then entering its most critical phase, there was no real alternative. The decision was, moreover, based on a clear-headed assessment of the enemy's offensive capabilities and the design features and actual state of repair of local fortress defences in that sector of the frontier provided in detailed, up-to-the-minute scouting and intelligence reports. The Ottomans' decision to leave behind the heavy artillery was therefore an informed decision that rested on a pragmatic assessment of the likelihood (taking all factors into consideration) of its proving useful for Ottoman offensive purposes in the sector of the frontier they were about to enter. The decision was, of course, reversible should military developments take an unexpected turn, but for the army's immediate purposes the logic that suggested the shedding of unnecessary weight was irrefutable.[91] The wisdom of this decision was clearly demonstrated only a few days later when the thus-disencumbered Ottoman army was delayed for two days in covering the short distance of twenty kilometres separating the army's base of departure at Sigetvár and its "first" camp at Darány. In order to complete this, its first stage in the advance to relieve Kanizsa, it had to pause to construct bridges in four places to pass over marshy areas.[92]

Once the Ottoman army had reached its full strength and brought the Kanizsa relief operation to a successful conclusion, it was able to proceed with its real business which was to launch an offensive of its own. The fortress of Zrinvár situated only two hours' march to the west of Kanizsa was its first objective. Zrinvár's relatively sophisticated defences occupied Ottoman siege engineers for fully 21 days before it yielded to the Ottomans' frontal assault on 30 June 1664. The removal of this, the sole creditable obstacle between the Ottomans and "the rest of the West" gave them a relatively free hand in deciding where to turn next. After some further delays to oversee the demolition of Zrinvár, on the one hand, and the rebuilding of Kanizsa (see above) on the other, the Ottomans decided to move against a new, previously untested, region of the frontier extending to the north of Kanizsa towards the natural boundary formed by the Zala and Rába rivers. The Ottoman army set out on 14 July with its sights set on the lightly-fortified, central frontier zone that stretched for some 50 miles between Nagykanizsa in the south to Körmend in the north.[93] Including its numerous diversions during late July on both primary and secondary fronts – as for example in the subduing of Zalakomár which lay 18 km NW of Nagykanizsa, or for the capture of

Egervár situated 12 km N of Zalaegerszeg – the Ottoman *blitzkrieg* in fact ranged, in a series of closely co-ordinated attacks, over a considerably wider territory. Most of the encounters during this two-week period of intense activity were extremely brief. In fact, of the seven small-to-medium-sized forts which lay on or near the Ottomans' route of advance to the Rába in July 1664 only one, Pölöske, offered more than token resistance. The schematic chart which follows will give some indication of the pace and outcome of the fighting in this period of virtually unopposed Ottoman advance.

Chart Showing Ottoman Military Movements
and Outcomes in the period 14–27 July 1664[94]

Name of fortified place	Date of arrival	Method used in subduing	Action taken
Zalakomár	14 July	Voluntary surrender	Fortress demolished
Zalaegerszeg	17 July	Flight of garrison	Fort set on fire
Pölöske	20 July	Two-day siege	Fort set on fire
Egervár	22 July	Voluntary surrender	Fortress evacuated then demolished
Kemendollár	25 July	Voluntary surrender	
Nagykapornak	26 July	Flight of garrison	Fort set on fire
Zalaszentgrót	27 July	Flight of garrison	Fort set on fire.[95]

The prevalence of *aman* (voluntary surrender) as a means of ending conflict is a striking feature of the pattern of military engagement summarized in the above chart. Even Pölöske's initial determination to defend itself proved evanescent when the outbreak of fire along the walls forming its outer defensive perimeter rendered its continued resistance futile. Ottoman siege preparations for Pölöske had included siege technicians and miners standing by, equipped with a quantity of 5 kantars (620 pounds) of gunpowder whose use in the event proved unnecessary.[96] Fortuitously in the case of Pölöske, as in that of all the other attacks mounted during this phase of the season's operations, the Ottomans were able to achieve their military objectives with the application of a minimum of force, while committing only small numbers of their available troops.[97] The main purpose of this phase of the campaign was not to extend the Ottoman frontier or conquer new lands, but to neutralize their potential as a base for counterattacks aimed against nearby Ottoman settlements.

From the account of Ottoman army movements in late July 1664 outlined above it can readily be seen that the conclusion of a confrontation between seriously mismatched or, by some measure, disproportionate opponents by non-violent means, typically a conditional but otherwise voluntary surrender, was by no means unusual. Although the question has not yet been systematically investigated within the specific context of seventeenth-century Ottoman warfare, it has been persuasively argued with respect to the period in general that the application of overwhelming force in pre-modern warfare could have the (to us) unexpected result of actually reducing casualties.[98] In a seventeenth-century Ottoman-Habsburg context it seems clear that the conclusion of an encounter by the voluntary surrender of the obviously weaker side bore no stigma or implication of treachery. Instead it was regarded (on both sides) as a natural and everyday fact of military life. The Ottomans were themselves no more immune to such necessity than their adversaries. As an example of the normality, regularity and mutual acceptance of the conditions regulating the act of surrender one might cite the terms for the surrender of the Ottoman garrison of Esztergom in 1683 laid out in detail in a study by Majer.[99] The practical advantages which such non-violent means for concluding military confrontations offered, especially when the outcome was a foregone conclusion, were obvious enough. Typically, in addition to avoidance of unnecessary bloodshed, such arrangements provided wagons, often accompanied by a military escort, for the safe transport of the men and their personal belongings from the site they agreed to abandon to a nearby friendly fortress.

Another detailed account of the standard procedures in surrenders is provided in Mühürdar's history of the Uyvar siege. In this case the Grand Vezier Fazil Ahmed Pasha agreed to eight conditions of surrender requested by the garrison, despite the fact that the garrison commander Adam Forgács had relinquished any binding right to their enforcement by having offered a month-long and very determined resistance to the Ottomans after the terms had been agreed.[100] This prolongation of the conflict had greatly increased Ottoman casualties, but the grand vezier still retained his openness to all reasonable compromise that would help in securing a negotiated settlement. He agreed to draft a letter to the defenders' sovereign Leopold confirming the bravery and determination of the garrison's resistance to the Ottoman attack (Condition no. 4) and to provide adequate supplies of grain to cover them during their retreat (Condition no. 6). Although Ahmed Pasha reduced the provision of wagons from the 1,000 requested in Condition no. 3 of the surrender agreement to 400, still by general standards even this level of transport assistance was quite generous.

From the Uyvar example and a comparison with similar terms of surrender offered to lesser forts (e.g. the ones listed in the chart above) it is readily apparent that humane, even face-saving alternatives were routinely sought by the Ottomans as an alternative to the senseless continuation of the bloodletting on both sides that resulted from the needless prolonging of siege.

Aman was used not only as a means for terminating conflicts, but was also commonly offered to adversaries to avoid the inception of violence.

The example of the surrender of Egervár in 1664 is an interesting example of the Ottomans' offer of face-saving concessions to encourage local military figures to lay down their arms. According to information supplied in Mühürdar's history, the captain of Egervár was given leave to evacuate the fortress, not just with his personal belongings intact, but given exceptional allowance to come forth from the fortress bearing his own weapons. This concession, a point of honour not commonly agreed to, was granted by the Ottoman commander Ismail Pasha despite the fact that the garrison had, for a brief initial period, offered resistance.[101] Judging from the Ottoman army's pattern of engagement in summer 1664 as reviewed above it may be concluded that, although heavy fighting characterized some types of encounters in particular phases of the campaign (e.g. the Ottoman defence of Kanizsa and their attack against Zrinvár which followed it), at other times mutually harmful encounters were either avoided or brought to a swift conclusion through negotiated settlement.

Even in the context of Christian–Muslim enmity it should not be supposed that seventeenth-century warfare was always characterized by episodes of brutal, unyielding and bitter fighting to the last drop of the blood of soldiers on either side of the conflict. The defence of the honour and glory of their countries and even (in a pre-secular age) notions of the sanctity of their cause were not the only and by no means necessarily the overriding concerns in the minds of most soldiers. Although these concerns were never absent, there is clear evidence that such devotion still left plenty of room, not just for compromise and conciliation, but even for humanity on the part of participants from both sides.[102]

Ottoman combat (Part Three): the nature of combat and its part in war-related fatalities

In pre-modern warfare general mortality was not nearly as closely linked with combat-related casualties as it came to be in the more destructive mass mobilization wars of a later era. Exhaustion, exposure and disease resulting from poor nutrition (and still more from contaminated water supplies) had a much greater impact on general mortality than is the case in most modern armies. Conditions in the eastern theatre of operations were by all accounts particularly grim. The soldiers' general reluctance to take part in eastern campaigns is reflected in the complaints of hardships recorded in their letters sent home from the front.[103] The lives claimed through disease in Ottoman armies operating in the Iraqi desert outweighed the battle casualties by a wide margin. Iskandar Munshi, author of a contemporary Safavid chronicle who was himself with the royal party when the Shah visited Hillah and Kerbela in 1630, and in a good position to make accurate observations, counted the bodies of 8,000–9,000 Ottoman soldiers killed during the battle over Hillah, which in itself prompted him to compare it in terms of its wholesale destruction to the battle between Timur and Yildirim Bayezid in 1402. But, apart from this, he blamed disease for claiming the lives of 30,000 Ottoman soldiers over the two-year period covering Hüsrev Pasha's march to Hamadan, assault of Baghdad, and defence of Hillah during 1629–30.[104] Topçular Katibi also attributes a significant number of deaths to typhus (*huma-i muharrika*), which he says affected the army ranks most seriously, not during the period of siege, but during the six-month encampment of the army at Koç-Hisar after Hüsrev Pasha's retreat from Baghdad.[105] In describing the ravages caused by a combination of hunger, heat, and disease during the retreat to Kizilhan after raising of the siege in 1626, Knolles observed that in a single day 12,000 men's lives were claimed.[106]

Although the primitive state of medical treatment gave little scope for saving lives, the sultan was always concerned for the welfare of his troops and, in addition to providing surgical staff for emergency treatment of the wounded, he granted the wounded injury money (*merham beha*) of 40–50 gurush,[107] and even provided pensions to the families of soldiers killed in action.[108] While firmly establishing the credibility of any seventeenth-century casualty statistics is not possible, it is clear that, when the armies were mobilized for action, the number of soldiers recruited had to be twice as large as it would in a modern army, in order to ensure the availability of adequate supplies of healthy soldiers throughout the course of the campaign.[109] It was assumed as a matter of course that even those who survived the rigours of battle might well succumb to disease during the retreat, and even victorious armies returned from battle severely reduced in number.

Siege warfare of course contributed to steep rises in the death toll through disease both in the beleaguered city and the attacking army. The civilian population of Baghdad, apart from the garrison soldiers, apparently suffered a 70 per cent decline during Bektash Khan's governorship between 1632 and 1638,[110] quite apart from the casualties suffered in battle. From the besiegers' trenches likewise came constant complaint of dysentery (*iç agrisi*), dropsy (*istiska zahmeti*), influenza (*nezle*), and sudden deaths due to unknown causes (*mevt -i mufacat*).[111] But the prolongation of sieges beyond 30–40 days (Ottoman trench warfare in Crete between 1645 and 1669 being the obvious exception) was quite unusual in the seventeenth century, and it is not easy to determine the proportion of such civilian fatalities that should be causally connected with conditions directly linked with siege. The Ottoman siege of Baghdad in 1638 lasted 39 days, and came after a period of military inactivity in that sector lasting seven years. In the context of both major sieges (see above: Part one) and lesser campaigns (see above: Part two) it is important to remember that the direct contact between opposing armies was often confined to relatively brief encounters that followed long preparatory preludes. The destructive impact of these encounters is difficult to gauge, but from what we know of the rules of engagement and norms governing surrender, pitiless or needlessly prolonged attacks were relatively rare and indiscriminate or vengeful killing seriously frowned upon as an uncivilized aberration.[112]

Chapter Seven

Motivational and psychological aspects of Ottoman warfare

Of all the factors which affect the outcome of battle, one of the most decisive, yet least accessible for study, is the soldier's state of mind. The soldier's willingness to persevere in adversity is determined by a complex set of variables in which both tangible physical realities and personal perceptions play equally important roles. We have dealt in part already with some of the tangible aspects of a soldier's life, such as diet and general camp conditions (see Chapter 5 above), but to generate the sense of shared enterprise on which the army's success depended required that the commander do more than just meet the basic bodily needs of his troops. Apart from fulfilling their expectation of reasonable conditions of service, with special attention to the regularity and sufficiency of their wages, the successful commander had also to engage the hopes, aspirations and dreams (sometimes only illusions) of personal reward of the rank and file soldiery. Their ranks ran the whole gamut of military types from regular army and seasonally-mobilized permanent forces to mercenaries, auxiliaries, with equally important input from a motley assortment of tribesmen from a variety of vassal states. Each group had different expectations of service and hopes of reward. The application of those techniques most effective for motivating each of them in their turn required special insight and management skills. Apart from an unerring tactical sense, the successful general had to have the ability – through skilful diplomacy and psychological motivation – to elicit the maximum level of effort and enthusiasm from his troops, drawn as they were from diverse backgrounds. Although a fully comprehensive coverage of the wide-ranging topic of soldierly motivation cannot be attempted here, this chapter will provide at least a basic introduction to four principal dimensions of the subject: Ottoman traditions of leadership and command; troop motivation and loyalty; the role of army ceremony in promoting group cohesion; and, finally, the forms of

reward used for the ante-bellum encouragement and post-bellum acknowledgement of military service.

Leadership and command

The natural and, under most circumstances, most effective leader of troops
into battle was the sultan himself. Because of the absolute nature of his
authority and his complete fiscal independence, he was able both to punish
and to reward without restriction or fear of contradiction. Although the
sultan's presence or non-presence in battle had both symbolic significance and
practical importance, the simplistic division of Ottoman military history into
the era of sultan-led campaigns, ending with Mehmed III's heroic pose as
commander at Egri in 1596, and the seventeenth century when the responsibility was devolved mostly to the grand vezier is at the same time unjustified
and historically inaccurate. The six sultans whose reigns spanned the sixteenth
century and the nine who succeeded them in the seventeenth each had
independent and highly individual styles of rule, and the degree of their
involvement in military affairs and preference for the use of personally-
wielded executive as opposed to delegated authority was more subtle than
definitive. Effective command of the troops was in all periods the responsibility not of the sovereign whose role was at most complementary, but of his
appointed commander bearing the title *serdar* or *serasker*. The *serdar* was
invariably granted very extensive and explicit extra powers of decision in
tactical and other matters, and it was principally he who formed the immediate focus of the troops' loyalty. When things went wrong, it was he who
became the immediate target for the expression of their dissatisfaction. In the
context of operational realities, therefore, the distinction often drawn between sultanically-led and vezierial campaigns is rather artificial. In no sense
was the *serdar*'s authority over strictly military matters ever qualified.

Even the sultans most known for their generally forceful manner were
sometimes subject to troop rebellions over pay or general conditions. This
happened in 1446 at Buçuk Tepe when, although the exact sequence of
events is somewhat unclear, the dissatisfaction of the Janissaries over their
wages led to the removal of the young Mehmed II from the throne, and the
postponement of his definitive succession until his father's death in 1451.
Another example when the physical presence of the sultan failed to deter the
obstinacy of his *kuls* was the refusal of Selim I's battle-weary troops to follow
orders issued in spring 1515 to advance on Syria. The troops insisted that the
harshness of the conditions endured in the previous season's campaign, culmi-

nating in the decisive Ottoman victory at Chaldiran, exempted them from any obligation to carry out further service until the sultan had granted them their customary end-of-season leaves.[1] As these examples show, even the presence of a forceful sultan did little to cow the Janissaries, once they perceived an infringement of their privileges or a denial of their customary rights. The relationship between the sovereign and his *kuls* was never as simple and predefined as that between master and slave. Their working relationship was always strongly influenced by factors such as prevailing conditions at the time of a dynastic succession, and the degree of Janissary influence exerted to secure a particular candidate's succession and definitive installation in a position of power. For example, in the case of Selim I mentioned above, from the time he took the throne in 1512 until the mid-point of his brief eight-year reign he remained beholden to the Janissaries because of their role in securing his succession.[2]

Perhaps the best way of judging the notional as well as theoretical powers of the sultan-appointed commanders is to examine the wording used in their diplomas of appointment. While the tone in relations between commander and rank and file was formed in the crucible of real-life experience, the terms of reference used in the official documents serve as a useful guide to the typical range of functions and responsibilities assigned to top-ranking military leaders. Two examples are included in the Feridun collection of state correspondence. One of them was issued in February 1642 to confer the title of commander in chief on the former governor of Egypt Semiz Mehmed Pasha.[3] His brief was the recapture of Azak (Azov) which had fallen in 1637 to a coalition of Cossack forces at a time when the Ottomans were preoccupied on the Mesopotamian front. In a particular passage, the document gives express authority to the commander to grant revenue enhancements to timariots immediately upon the receipt of their district commander's recommendations without reference to higher authority for final approval. The rationale behind giving the commander independent powers to reward his troops is clearly expressed in the document:

> gladdening the hearts of the worthy by assigning them [timar] revenues in accordance with their merit so as to encourage them thereafter to perform even greater acts of heedless bravery (*serbazlik*) on behalf of his majesty the sultan.[4]

In addition to being granted full independence in decisions about rewarding his troops, Semiz Mehmed was also granted unrestricted powers to discipline and punish them up to the maximum penalties allowed by law. Any breaches of military discipline from minor derelictions of duty to committing of abuses against civilian populations came under his jurisdiction. In addition, the vezier was granted explicit powers over the administration of justice in the sultan's name for all districts through which the army passed on its way to the front. The catch phrase repeated in closely parallel form in the diplomas of appointment for all commanders was:

> you are to treat his every word as if it had issued forth in personal audience from my own (i.e., the sultan's) pearl-dispensing tongue forming part of our own auspicious utterances.[5]

Another case documented in the Feridun collection of state papers pertains to Süleyman I's preparations for the fourth campaign of his reign, which culminated in a brief investment of Vienna in autumn 1529. The appointment diploma for the Grand Vezier Frenk Ibrahim Pasha as *serasker* was issued by the sultan in early April 1529 just before their joint departure for the front in June.[6] The language in which the sultan expressed his delegation of absolute authority to the grand vezier-cum-commander in chief is no less forceful than that employed in the seventeenth-century diploma issued to Semiz Mehmed Pasha. Sultan Süleyman's diploma contains the following words defining the commander's status:

> Whatever he says and in whatever manner he decides to regard things you are to accept them as if they were the propitious words and respect-commanding decrees issuing from my own pearl-dispersing tongue. Hear them with the ear of confirmation, and give them your unqualified acceptance.[7]

An interesting difference between the documents representing the two periods is that, although even in the presence of the sultan decisions on preferments, dismissals and appointments are assigned to the commander, the administration of justice, especially punishment and most particularly capital punishment (*siyaset*) are reserved as the sultan's exclusive prerogative.[8] It is significant, however, that in both the document from 1642 and the earlier example drafted more than a hundred years previously, for the areas that most affected the leader's ability to command his troops' loyalty – most particularly his fiscal independence in the granting of rewards – the *serdar*'s authority was equally unrestricted.[9]

Contemporary commentators regarded the commanders' level of fiscal empowerment, coupled with a natural inclination to treat his subordinates generously, as a crucial element of his effectiveness in command. The sources are quite explicit on this score. For example, the historian Nihadî cites the niggardliness of the Grand Vezier Kara Mustafa Pasha who commanded a huge Ottoman army at Vienna in 1683 as a key factor in the undermining of his authority and subsequent failed leadership. According to Nihadî the vezier's neglecting to fulfil the troops' expectations through timely distribution of confidence-building and morale-boosting favours and bonuses (*inamat*) was instrumental in causing the collective loss of the soldiers' will to persevere when the Ottoman army was perched on the threshold of unprecedented success.[10] In a related passage, this time referring to Mustafa II's successful command of the Ottoman army at the battle of Cenei (near Temeshvar) in August 1696, Nihadî coined the telling phrase "*tergiben l'il cihad*", literally "encouragement to strive for the just cause", by which the author makes unmistakable reference to the importance of monetary reward as an underlying motive, if not the main driving force, behind the soldiers' devotion to their military mission.[11]

Concerning the different military circumstances of Koca Sinan Pasha's command in Hungary in 1594, the historian Mustafa Ali offered his own assessment and attributed the missed opportunities and lost potential of that season's unusually wide-ranging mobilization to the commander's mishandling of sensitive relations with the Ottomans' allies, the Tatars. His bungling of the negotiations over the terms of the Tatars' participation in the joint campaign, especially the inappropriately imperious tone he adopted in relations with their leader, the Tatar sovereign Gazi Giray Han II, together with his arbitrary denial to the common ranks of the Tatar troops of opportunities for booty, all served no strategic purpose and left a large contingent among his crucial auxiliaries with badly bruised feelings. The Tatar forces were most effectively employed when given independence of action in the carrying out of forward probing raids behind enemy lines. Denied this opportunity by the commander's intransigence and suspicion tinged – or so the author implies – with more than a little jealousy at their greater military prowess, their presence in the camp became more a source of irritation than a benefit to the team effort.[12] The term used by Ali to refer Sinan's leadership failure, apart from lack of skills in generalship, was lack (literally, deficiency) in generosity (*kem keremlik*).[13]

Whether it was the sultan himself or his absolute deputy (*vekil-i mutlak*) the grand vezier who fulfilled the role of distributor of imperial largesse and bounty was immaterial, but failure to perform the obligatory acts of symbolic and ceremonial generosity in the presence of the assembled troops seriously undermined the army's ability to work in unison towards the accomplishment of its shared goal. By insisting on the performance of these rituals it is not so much that the troops sought to make their loyalty contingent on specific terms of reward known and negotiated in advance, as an expression of their desire for some acknowledgement that, whatever the outcome of battle, they were entitled some form of recognition or reward for their services. To disregard these forms, or to pretend that they bore no relevance or importance to the troops' loyalty and enthusiasm for battle was a fatal error of judgement which even the sultans sometimes fell prey to.[14]

Because of the special powers granted to Ottoman military commanders as outlined in their diplomas of appointment, and the wide range of resources made available to them, the post of *serdar* was at the same time greatly coveted and highly insecure. The natural jealousy which resulted from the concentration of power, influence and control – at least in the first instance – over the distribution of the fruits of victory and conquest in the *serdar*'s hands meant that competition for such appointments was intense. Once installed in office, the *serdar* was also vulnerable to his rivals' continuing attempts to usurp his authority. These attempts were sometimes quite transparent, but they could also take the form of subtle gestures aimed at undermining the leader's influence, authority and credibility either with his patron the sultan or, even more disastrously, with the troops themselves.

Because leadership disputes and vezierial rivalries had a very real influence on the progress of battle, it will be useful if we consider here a few examples. The case of Koca Sinan Pasha is particularly instructive, since we are able to trace his effectiveness in a leadership capacity as tested through a series of leadership challenges mounted by a succession of rivals over the decade and a half between 1578 and 1595. The jealousy between Sinan and the first of his political opponents Lala Mustafa Pasha took shape as a rivalry over the terms of their simultaneous (and therefore potentially overlapping) commands on the eastern front during the opening phases of the Ottoman–Safavid wars. Competition between Lala Mustafa Pasha as commander of the northern sector of the front in Azerbaijan and his junior Sinan Pasha, who held the rank of third vezier in his capacity as commander in the southern sector, became so intense that during the pre-war preparatory phase in the spring of 1577 plans for a two-front attack aimed simultaneously against the Caucasian and Iraqi fronts had to be abandoned. The irrepressible animosity between the two veziers resulted in Sinan's dismissal in January 1578, and the setting-up of a single command centre at Erzurum with Lala Mustafa Pasha as sole commander on the Iranian front.[15] The hopes of each was pinned not just on glory and enhanced personal reputation, but on the anticipation both of promotion and significant material reward by the sultan that would follow any successful conquest of new territory.[16] Despite Lala Mustafa's successes in the Shirvan campaign of 1578 and his efforts at organizing a relief force to save the beleaguered Ottoman garrison at Tiflis in the following year, he was met on his return from the front to winter quarters at Erzurum in January 1580 with the news that he was being relieved of his command in a coup engineered by his rival Sinan Pasha.[17] Although he managed to resurrect his political fortunes after returning in April 1580 to the capital where he was better able to silence or at least soften the effect of doubts being sown in the sultan's mind through a whispering campaign organized by his rivals, the damage done in the meantime to the progress of the campaign was irrecoverable.[18] In the end it was only after the death of his bitterest rival Lala Mustafa Pasha in August 1580 that Sinan was able to achieve his double ambition of simultaneous appointment as sole commander on the eastern front and grand vezier. The first episode of Sinan Pasha's prolonged bid for power shows only too clearly how much a commander on a distant front was at the mercy of his "colleagues" who stayed behind in Istanbul.

The commander in the field was often required to do battle on a second undeclared front with his subordinates in Istanbul, who were busily engaged in undermining his credibility with the sultan, or doing their best to ensure his lack of military success by deliberately withholding either supplies or adequate funds for the soldiers' wages, or both. Although it was perhaps rare that these vezierial rifts should take such a blatant form as the deliberate sabotage of the current leader's plans and preparations for campaign, as happened in the case of Sinan and Mustafa Pasha during the first two years of the Iranian wars, they can nonetheless be clearly detected beneath the surface as a factor in many Ottoman campaigns. Leadership changes and leadership challenges had an immense effect on the unfolding of military events both in the sixteenth and the seventeenth centuries.

In a later phase of Koca Sinan Pasha's long career in politics he suffered a temporary reversal of fortunes when a new rival, Ferhad Pasha, took advantage of Sinan's absence at the front in Hungary in the seemingly unassailable double role as grand vezier and recently triumphant *serdar* to capitalize on the opportunity offered by the temporary power vacuum resulting from the death of Sultan Murad III in January 1595 and to propose his own candidacy for the grand vezierate to Murad's son and successor Mehmed III. Within a month of Sultan Murad's demise, Ferhad Pasha was firmly installed in Sinan Pasha's place, having dislodged a rival whose recent military record was not just untarnished but distinguished, judging by results if not by the quality of Sinan's generalship, with unprecedented success (that is, the Ottoman capture of Győr [Yanik Kale] the previous year).[19]

During the four and a half months' interregnum between his third and fourth terms as grand vezier, Sinan Pasha, while based at his estates at Malkara in the Thracian hinterland of the capital, did his own level best to discredit Ferhad and to ensure the collapse of the new commander's plans for a spring offensive aimed against Wallachia and the mouth of the Danube. Even before Ferhad had yet left the capital bound for the front on 27 April 1595,[20] the troops had become so polarized between the pro-Sinan and pro-Ferhad factions that violence broke out in the streets of Istanbul and reached such a pitch of intensity that it could be quelled only by the forceful intervention of Ahmed Agha commander of the Janissaries, who sanctioned a dangerously precedent-setting attack on the barracks of the sultan's standing cavalry regiments at the Porte.[21] Ironically and, in terms of the Ottomans' imperial prestige, wholly disgracefully, the first casualties in this campaign were suffered not at the front but inside the walls of the capital. Because of the long-standing, inter-service rivalry between Janissaries and Sipahis (members of the six permanent standing cavalry regiments at the Porte), there was always a barely suppressed tension between the two groups, but feelings at this time ran particularly high because of the recent distribution of the accession gratuity (cülus bahshishi) doled out only three months previously by the new sultan Mehmed III.[22] The selective awarding of gratuities by the sultan on these occasions was bound to leave one group or the other feeling ill-treated and neglected. Because Ferhad Pasha's priority at this time was to press on with urgent preparations for war in the North, he was obliged to leave such rankling differences still unresolved as he left for the front. Among the still unresolved complaints and grievances was the claim put forward by the former garrison troops at Ganja, a remote fortress on the northeastern frontier that had fallen to the Ottomans seven years previously in 1588 at a time when Ferhad was himself in command of the army in that sector. In their view Ferhad had reneged on promises made at the time to assign them permanent regimental homes in the cavalry regiments at the Porte in exchange for their agreement to complete a three-year term of service in provincial garrison duty at Ganja.[23]

The upshot of the accumulation of resentment against Ferhad Pasha resulting from the Ganja incident, the use of Janissaries to forcefully suppress the street-rioting in Istanbul, and a number of other unresolved complaints and grievances was that, when the grand vezier arrived at the vicinity of Razgrad just south of the proposed river crossing at Ruse (Ottoman Ruscuk), only 4,000 or 5,000 of the 40,000–50,000 troops called up for service in the campaign had reported for duty.[24] The gist of Ferhad Pasha's remarks on the situation are quoted by the historian Hasanbey-zade with the very strong implication that the Deputy Grand Vezier Ibrahim Pasha had contributed to the problem by deliberate delays in the dispatching of assigned units to the front.[25] Before Ferhad Pasha's sadly reduced force had yet completed work on the floating bridge at Ruscuk in preparation for the army's crossing, a messenger arrived in early July bearing news of the commander's dismissal.[26] The immediate effect of Ibrahim Pasha's connivance and Sinan Pasha's successful plotting was, apart from the latter's reinstatement as grand vezier, to create a disastrous leadership vacuum at the front at the most critical mid-season stage of its final preparations for battle. All the most objective contemporary observers agree that this last-minute change in personnel after the campaign was already under way served no purpose except to satisfy the seemingly limitless ambition of Sinan Pasha.[27]

Although the tactics and intrigues employed by Sinan (whether in confronting his first rival Lala Mustafa or his latter-day opponent Ferhad) to manoeuvre himself into a position of supreme power represent perhaps an extreme example of the triumph of personal ambition over the service ethic, it cannot be supposed that the Ottoman *serdar*'s position was ever very tranquil or secure. The source of challenges to his authority was not always his peers with vezierial status. Challenge could equally come from his subordinates with support from the rank-and-file soldiery. We know, for example, from a letter sent by a Janissary officer on the Mesopotamian front to a friend in Istanbul in 1626 that the army command of the Grand Vezier Hafiz Ahmed Pasha survived seven successive votes of "no confidence" before the army had even reached the Iraqi frontier.[28]

From the examples outlined above it can be inferred that divisions deriving from one source or another, whether the natural disposition of the troops themselves (Tatar, timariot or mercenary) or through factional infighting and leadership contests within the regular army ranks, must be considered as a primary factor influencing the army's performance. Such friction, though it was not always very overt or even discernible, often had very serious operational consequences. As the result both of latent jealousies and more open and specifically grievance-related hostility, the army rarely entered battle animated with the kind of unqualified unanimity of purpose and fullness of dedication needed to obtain quick or decisive results. That shared fighting spirit was a created not inherited ethos which could only emerge through common experience and shared risk will perhaps become clearer after we have completed our examination of the ultimate sources of the soldiers' diversity of motivation in the next section of the chapter.

Troop motivation and the role of ideology and religious inspiration

An unfortunate failing of studies on the Ottoman warrior has been the inability to distinguish clearly (or even to acknowledge any difference between) personal motivation and the individual's goals on the one hand, and corporate aims and state interest on the other. This avoidance of the issues of diversity of motive and conflict of interest among participants in war has so trivialized the role of the individual as to make the human contribution to war barely perceptible. The attitudes and aims of the state have so dominated our thinking that it has been blithely assumed that soldiers could have no other. While we cannot undertake here a systematic revision of the current thinking on the role of ideology in Ottoman warfare, it is important that we attempt to set the record straight. Only if we achieve some clarity in a definitional sense will it be possible to proceed with the far more difficult task of reconstructing the mental states and attitudes of the Ottoman warriors themselves. The most accessible views for us have always been those formulated by the propagandists and apologists for war, but the assumption that the wagers of and active participants in war shared such views unreservedly is far from safe. Distancing ourselves from the views of war as disseminated by "head office" is not easy and finding a means of approach to, let alone full comprehension of, the states of mind of the participants presents an even greater challenge. Human motivation is nothing if not complex, and the barriers of time and cultural difference limit our routes of access to understanding still further. Although this is not the place for us to enter into a philosophical discussion of the relative merits of different schools of historical analysis, it should be noted that, at least as far as the investigation of Ottoman social realities is concerned, the weight of argument supporting the principle that ideas have greatest determining power as the agent of human inspiration, and thereby of historical causation, has so dominated research in the last few decades that approaches emphasizing the countervailing importance of material determinants have hardly been given an opportunity even to enter the arena of debate.[29] While such momentous issues and research imbalances cannot be resolved or redressed here, by isolating some of the principal issues involved and presenting relevant illustrative evidence, we can at least hope to suggest some alternative lines of inquiry. The field of investigation relating to the mental frameworks, attitudes and motivations of the voiceless masses (including soldiers) who left only fragmentary literary evidence of their most cherished inner feelings remains a yet scarcely perceived, let alone adequately explored, new frontier of Ottoman studies. However, filling the gaps in our knowledge of the sentiments of the "common man" with information supplied by the Ottoman *literati* who least understood and appreciated them only serves to lead us further astray. What is required is a more balanced investigation which gives equal consideration both to the spiritual and the material motives governing Ottoman behaviour.

The first issue to be confronted is the role of the Ottoman warrior's faith and religious commitment as a source of his dedication to the task of waging war. A great deal has been written on this subject, much of it heavily reliant on simplistic cultural stereotypes and caricatured fixed assessments of the Ottoman psyche, without the least reference to changing historical circumstances during the empire's centuries-long existence.[30] While there can be no question that common religion served as one of the several unifying factors and bonding agents that produced a sense of *esprit de corps* amongst Ottoman soldiers, the tendency to place a strictly literal interpretation on the theoretical obligation of all Muslims to conduct Holy War (*jihad*) has placed a mistaken emphasis on a single source of the average soldier's motivation. One common source of confusion has been the assumption that *jihad* represented a universal and unlimited obligation for all Muslims at all times. In fact it was a rather more circumscribed and flexible concept that applied most fully when the Muslim community was itself at risk of invasion. This situation rarely applied to the Ottomans, whose borders were, for most of their 600-year history and particularly during their heyday in the years between 1500 and 1700, mostly immune from such threats.[31] It is important that we maintain a clear view of such more than purely legalistic distinctions, since by ignoring them we run the very real risk of reducing the Ottoman soldier to a mere agent of an abstract cause, a hollow figure deprived of the fuller range of normal human emotions.

Research on the modern army in the United States, based on interviews with more than fifty generals, has led one researcher to the, somewhat unexpected, conclusion that the religious views of soldiers (in this case officers), because they are always tinged with some degree of personal preference, sectarian bias or some other form of experiential preconception, can just as easily serve as a source of divisiveness as a focal point for unity.[32] In a different chronological context research on the early-modern French army has convincingly demonstrated that, contrary to general expectation and common belief, the French soldier of the Revolutionary period was inspired not so much by a sense of patriotic duty or revolutionary zeal as by more down-to-earth sentiments, such as regimental loyalty and feelings of comradeship created through a sense of shared labour, shared danger and an understanding of the need for mutual support to make the common enterprise work.[33] But the conclusion that the Ottoman soldier's ideological commitment to his master's cause had discrete limits only goes part of the way to filling the void left after decades of seemingly tireless debate on the *gazi* origins of the Ottoman state. The realization of a need to bring the Ottoman soldier down from the superhuman and up from the subhuman, restoring him to the merely human has only just now begun to dawn on investigators of Ottoman military matters.

It will perhaps best serve the cause of greater clarity if we outline in brief the historical context within which Ottoman military values and practices evolved over the longer term. In the fourteenth and fifteenth centuries the Ottoman empire was still a fledgling entity facing the very real possibility of sudden annihilation by its military peers (and sometimes superiors), especially in Anatolia and the East. However, by 1500 the empire's geopolitical circumstances had changed dramatically. Because of the empire's impressive and seemingly uncontainable expansion after 1480, it is an easily and often overlooked fact that the Ottomans' position until the critical events of the decade and a half between 1460 and 1475 was actually quite tenuous. Until the fall of Smederovo (Semendire) in 1459 and the definitive annexation of the Kingdom of Serbia which followed, the Ottomans cannot yet be considered as a firmly or yet permanently established European power. Their full hegemony in the East came even later with the final subjugation of Uzun Hasan and his followers at the battle of Bashkent (Otluk-beli) in 1473. The Ottoman dynasty's use of a strident ideology as a support to its sometimes faltering rule in this period of imperial growth and consolidation is neither unprecedented nor surprising.

During the so-called *Pax Ottomanica* of the sixteenth and seventeenth centuries after the definitive establishment of its world (or at least tricontinental) empire, the Ottomans came to have much to fear (especially internally) from the spread of fanaticism. The emergence of a more latitudinarian approach to religion and a greater internationalism in Ottoman foreign policy is forcefully felt, beginning with the reign of Süleyman I.[34] The Ottomans' firm establishment as a European power after the annexation of Serbia (in 1459) and Bosnia (in 1463), as well as the rapid transformation of these territories from borderland into hinterland and heartland as the Ottomans advanced past the Danubian frontier into southern Hungary after the fall of Belgrade in 1521, had a profound effect on the ruling ethos of the House of Osman. It was really only in the sixteenth century that the Ottomans came of age as an imperial power of truly international stature. The guiding principles for an empire which, by 1500, had come to assume such global proportions were tolerance, pragmatism and stability. These principles applied not just in the sphere of its foreign relations, but were also at the heart of its policies regulating the domestic affairs of the state, starting with the millet organization which guaranteed the communal autonomy of the non-Muslims, and ending with the universal scope of the paternalistic priorities which underlay its social, economic and judicial regimes.

In the sixteenth century Ottoman society made itself (for practical reasons) increasingly open to renegades or, to use the modern terminology, "defectors", "apostates" and "traitors" from neighbouring states in Europe. By placing too much stress on the religious identity of these migrant populations, who had so much to offer for the general enrichment of Ottoman economic and social life, the Ottomans risked upsetting the very dynamic which most attracted such settlers – i.e. the general tolerance of Ottoman society. Insisting on Muslim identity or public expressions of piety on the part of a majority of its citizens was for most Ottoman environments outside the Arab provinces a policy aim the Ottomans could no longer afford to embrace. The horizons of the Ottoman world had changed to something that would have been quite unrecognizable to the frontier *gazis* of the fourteenth and early fifteenth centuries. Ottoman imperial success in the sixteenth century no longer relied upon a combative fixation on the external Christian foe, but emphasized rather the smooth functioning of a co-operative ethos by which they could motivate all their diverse indigenous (both Muslim and non-Muslim) populations. Following the stabilization of the Ottomans' frontiers with Europe, an eventuality that could already be sensed as early as the closing years of Süleyman I's reign,[35] the relevance of an Ottoman imperial ideology based on strident religiosity became increasingly inappropriate, if not wholly inapplicable.

It is a scarcely acknowledged but fundamental fact influencing the evolution of the Ottomans' relations with mainland Europe (as opposed to peninsular Italy, where the era of peaceful coexistence began even earlier)[36] that between 1606 and 1660 no full-scale or openly declared war was waged on the Hungarian front. In this period not only did the relentless character of the Ottomans' war with Europe change, but its state-organized forms virtually ceased to exist. Light skirmishing and other localized forms of conflict associated with the so-called *klein krieg* phenomenon in European warfare had already begun to characterize the pattern of Ottoman–Habsburg relations in the immediate aftermath of the death of Süleyman I. Maximillian II's armistice with the Ottomans in 1568 marked the closing of an era in which war was pursued by the two sides as a kind of "final solution", and the renewed outbreak of war in the 1590s had as much to do with internal Austro-Hungarian politics – a maelstrom into which the Ottomans were drawn at their peril – than the resumption of the wars of conquest initiated by Süleyman.[37]

The unbroken period of Ottoman–Habsburg detente that lasted between 1606 and 1660 spanned fully two generations, and had a major impact on attitudes relating not just to the nature of war, but to the "foe" himself. Whether any true inter-cultural "dialogue" could have emerged during this period remains a subject of debate, but it is, nonetheless, clear that by the mid-seventeenth century the idea of mass mobilization for pursuit of the "Holy War" (*gaza*) against the "infidel" (*kafir*) retained little of its former dynamism, credibility and attraction and had begun to be regarded (even by idealistic Ottoman intellectuals, let alone the more practically-minded participants in warfare) as an anachronistic and impractical holdover from a bygone age.[38]

The all too prevalent view that the Ottoman *"gaza"* ideal was impervious to the effects of the empire's ups and downs over the centuries and remained the static (presumed at the highest pitch of intensity) and unchanging driving force behind all Ottoman wars, while at the same time dominating its norms and practices, is entirely ahistorical. In this context it is particularly important that the distinction between religion and religiosity be clearly maintained. Very often what is presented as the well-spring and internal motivation fuelling wars – that is, religiosity – should more accurately be described as the use (exploitation?) of religion in state ideology as the prop and *ex-post-facto* justification of its efforts to extend its territorial base by means of expansionist foreign wars.[39] Süleyman the Magnificent's (still more so his father Selim I's) use of religious propaganda as a justification for expansionist wars aimed at "schismatics" in the neighbouring state of Safavid Iran is only one of the most glaring examples of the exploitation of religion as a tool of foreign policy.[40] This assertion of religious identity by the state to meet its public policy needs has to be very carefully distinguished from other, more personally meaningful, manifestations of religious faith. Religion had unchallenged governance over the internal realms of conscience and belief where it served as the indispensable source both of spiritual values and individual piety. While *raison d'état* kept it alive for a part of the sixteenth century, in the Ottoman empire as in the West there was growing disenchantment with the demands that the, to many artificial, preservation of the ideals of the era of the Crusades imposed on them. By the end of the sixteenth century, the resource implications of protecting its wider territories, while at the same time maintaining its challenge to the West at a full level of intensity and credibility, were also beginning to dawn on the state itself.

When we turn to the viewpoints expressed by indigenous historians and commentators on the contemporary Ottoman social and political scene, we are confronted with a refreshing candour. In assessing the material motivations that urged people (most particularly soldiers) to participate in warfare, these authors make no attempt to disguise the participants' worldly concerns. The exclusive emphasis on spiritual values and the reluctance to acknowledge wider scope for the influence of normal human emotions is a purely modern misconception. In the view of the contemporary commentators it was wholly unrealistic to expect that soldiers in service should exhibit a level of pure and selfless devotion, or the strict observance of an elevated moral code undreamt of for the common run of mortals. The allying of the soldiers' efforts with the patriotic or pietistic aims of their masters and political spokesmen required, in the view of most realist (sceptic?) thinkers of the time, that the soldiers should be encouraged (tempted) by the offer of a full range of material incentives.

Contemporary Ottoman chroniclers' views
on the material motive in warfare

Katib Chelebi, a historian and polymath of the mid-seventeenth century, supplies us with some particularly astute observations on the connection between royal sponsorship and imperial largesse, on the one hand, and, on the other, the strength of the troops' enthusiasm for the expansionist projects set in motion by their sovereign. Concerning Murad IV's excursion to Erivan in 1635 the historian quotes the Arabic axiom which states "all men are in thrall to [their masters'] gratuity".[41] On the destructive influence of a ruler's failure to fulfil his subjects' material expectations on the depth of their devotion to his cause, the historian quotes another cardinal principle of political life: "the dominion and good fortune of the king who fails to provide his promised gratuity (*wahba*) will soon pass (*dhahaba*)."[42]

Writing of the Ottomans' attempts to generate enthusiasm for renewed offensives against the forces of the Sacred Alliance after the Ottomans had regained the initiative with Belgrade's recapture in 1690, the chronicler Mevkufatî makes open reference to mixed motives among at least some of the elements making up the Ottomans' fighting forces at the time. Mevkufatî is especially fierce in his condemnation of the army irregulars who had the habit of abandoning the effort as soon as they had performed the contracted minimum period of obligatory service, even if it ended before the enemy had yet been properly engaged. Speaking of the grand vezier and commander Chalik Ali Pasha's reluctant acquiescence to the irregular soldiers' demands that he grant them general leave in late October 1692, Mevkufatî remarks:

> Ever since the time of the Vienna defeat in 1683 when they first tasted its delights, the common ranks and soldiers of "diverse origins" [i.e. army riffraff] could not dislodge from their thoughts the delicious memory of the plundering of the imperial camp [an opportunity which arose as a hidden benefit when the whole army was forced to retreat following Kara Mustafa Pasha's defeat]. In the present year (1692) despairing of a renewed taste of these delights and offering the excuse "the end of the season (Ruz-i Kasim) is nigh" they broke ranks and scattered themselves across the countryside leaving the core of the imperial camp deserted and without protector.[43]

While careful to point out that this was abnormal and unacceptable behaviour confined to what he calls the lower elements (*erazil*) among the army ranks, the author strongly suggests that thoughts of personal enrichment were never far from the minds of soldiers of all ranks. Based on the premise *honi soit qui mal y pense*, the author implies that while it might only be the "contemptible ones" who had the effrontery to actually act out their fantasies and accumulate the maximum share of whatever profitable windfalls chance might bring their way, their companions in the ranks were no less tempted by such prospects of limitless material reward. In the realistic assessment of at least one unusually frank Ottoman commentator, the most active principle animating the soldier's behaviour in battle was not duty on behalf of the noble cause or sacrifice for the sake of his comrades, but basic human greed. Whether this was openly expressed or suppressed, instantly realized or temporarily deferred was, to Mevkufatî's mind at least, immaterial.

A third literary vignette relates not to soldiers and combatants, but to those who profited from war in another fashion. While it is perhaps dangerous to place too much store in the moralizing remarks of historians whose job was after all both to glorify the sultan and to sanctify his cause, the incidents of both private and official corruption they cite, and the negative role models they reveal, are clearly real-life examples drawn from actual events. The fact that their main preoccupation was the glorification of the sultan (and by extension also his wars), as well as the registering of honourable deeds performed to the sultan's greater glory, gives that much greater credibility and importance to the few recorded instances where historians let down their guard and expose the dishonourable or anti-social behaviour of their peers and contemporaries who held positions of public trust. One example comes from the official history of Mehmed Rashid, who drew in the first part of his narrative on the daybook entries of his predecessor as historiographer royal, Mustafa Naima.[44] It describes the case of a former head butcher and purveyor of meats to the imperial army named Kara Mehmed Agha, who was accused of presenting false accounts to the treasury in the aftermath of the disastrous Ottoman defeat at Senta in September 1697. According to this account Kara Mehmed, when summoned by the grand vezier in the field to give his estimation of the scale of the army's meat requirement for the forthcoming season of campaigning, had answered with the exaggerated figure of 60,000 head of sheep. Following the Ottoman defeat, he presented a claim to the treasury for the supply, not just of the 60,000 sheep making up the officially approved meat requisition, which, at the time of its mid-season defeat in early September, could by then have only partly been delivered, but a wholly implausible additional 30,000 head claimed as "lost in transit" to the front. The fabricated accounts, presenting an aggregated claim of payment for 90,000 head of sheep, which was bad enough in normal times, were made doubly dishonourable in the chronicler's mind by the fact that they represented the indulging of private greed at a time of grave communal loss and general suffering.[45] The no doubt exceptional case of Kara Mehmed is a striking example of a lack of public-spiritedness and social conscience during wartime (or, in this case, immediately post-war) crisis. But it is noteworthy that his conspiracy to defraud the treasury received crucial backing from a group of high-placed friends and backers in the capital. It cannot, therefore, be regarded as an isolated example. Apart from the issue of ultimate culpability the case serves as a useful reminder that it was not just the soldier who wished to minimize the loss and risks associated with warfare, while maximizing its potential for personal or corporate gain. To expect that soldiers should follow a different (especially a higher) moral code than that practised by their social betters is neither credible nor logical.

A rare literary document recording soldiers' impressions of war and the attitudes of the rank and file towards their commanding officers gives us a privileged glimpse at social divisions,[46] and how they affected the pursuit of war. These extracts reveal some of the personal and human dimensions of war which, especially in recent historiography on the Ottomans, has been regarded as an enterprise undertaken exclusively on behalf of the state and religion. The document records the deprivation suffered by the Ottoman garrison soldiers at Kamaniçe (Kamanetz-Podolsky) in 1673, when their own senior officers traded hoarded supplies of their rations to the enemy so as to realize disproportionate profits for themselves from grain sales at inflated wartime prices.[47] In examining the motives of simple Muslim soldiers and of their officers, as well as Ottoman grandees and magnates who also had an interest in the outcome of war, one needs to be very wary of placing too much faith in unexamined assumptions about cultural difference. Muslims were no more naturally predisposed to give predominance to spiritual values and motives over baser material concerns than were their Christian counterparts. On either side of the religio-cultural divide material interests remained a paramount concern of, and in many cases a principal justification for, the waging of war on both the personal and collective levels. War, certainly from the Ottoman point of view, was much more a matter of controlling land, resources and trade routes than a desire to impose its spiritual views on subject peoples. In any case, forced conversion was explicitly excluded as a motive for war by Islamic law.[48]

As far as the strictly material motives animating war are concerned, it is sensible to attribute the greatest interest and involvement to those who had the greatest stake in its outcome. We are reminded of the high economic stakes involved in conflict by the case of Nicholas Zriny, the semi-independent Ban of Croatia circa 1600, whose commitment to the continuance (if necessary by subventions from his privates resources) of war against the Ottomans is explained by his desire to protect border villages whose residents and revenues represented the mainstay of his family's fortunes.[49] In resisting the advance of the Ottomans, Christian magnates with estates in the border regions were defending the security of their personal wealth, assets and investments which were heavily tied up in the land and the peasants who cultivated it. The protecting of these investments was their overriding concern, and promoting the interests of the crown and abstract notions of general Christian welfare were remote and, at best, secondary priorities.[50]

Before concluding our account of the general scope of material motivation, it is perhaps appropriate that we consider one special category of participants in war who were drawn to it, not by contractual obligation, regimental loyalty or their own abstract perceptions of obligation or duty, but by an undisguised desire for booty. During the course of campaigns there often arose occasions for what may be termed "opportunistic attacks", aimed against civilian targets. The term by no means applies to all raids (akin) sent against enemy territory as, despite the outward appearance of disorganization, these were actually carefully planned to achieve specific military objectives. The principal aim of Tatar raids carried out behind enemy lines was not the accumulation of booty and riches for the Tatar cavalrymen, but to relieve pressure on Ottoman army supply by capitalizing on the foraging potential of the regions contiguous to the front, while at the same time maximizing disruption to enemy supply lines and restricting enemy access to all potential sources of food and forage. But it would be pointless to deny that some elements within these raiding parties regarded their participation as an open invitation to pillage. A share of the easily moveable and marketable property acquired in these raids, especially livestock and peasant captives, was reserved for the participants. Evliya Chelebi may be considered a reliable witness on the aims and organization of these raiding parties since his observations are based on his own participation in raiding on a secondary diversionary front that was timed to coincide with the grand vezier's siege of Zrinvár in June 1664.

Evliya's account makes it apparent that there were often two opposing schools of thought operating at cross purposes within such groups. The composition of these raiding parties was mixed, and might expand unpredictably with the inclusion of last minute volunteers (opportunists) pursuing their own agendas. It was characteristic of such raids that they were aimed at very poorly defended territories, whose militias and garrison forces had been removed to serve on a main active front. The fact that the likelihood of the raiders meeting any determined resistance in the enemy interior was remote made their recruitment that much easier.[51] It is clear from accounts of Ottoman slave-raiding expeditions organized during peacetime when local militias were in place that the participants ran a high risk of ambush,[52] but war

150

time raids were associated in the minds of the "volunteers" with minimal risks and the prospect of rich material reward.[53] In the case described by Evliya an informal alliance was formed between the Tatar forces under the command of the heir-apparent to the Crimean throne Ahmed Giray Han, whose military objective was to open up a subsidiary front behind enemy lines in Slovenia, and a small band of desperadoes gathered from the nearby Ottoman county of Pozega. Evliya himself bears witness to the later falling out of the erstwhile partners over the fair distribution of the spoils and optimal timing for their safe delivery to market. Evliya notes how one faction, made up principally of Tatars, favoured continuing their partnership until the operation's military objectives and potential had been more fully realized, while another, made up of the last-minute "volunteers" and opportunistic raiders from the borderland districts, preferred calling an immediate halt to activity so as to allow a swift return to base in time to dispose of their fair share of the booty at the seasonal fair held at Ösek.[54] Evliya himself openly avows an interest in the distribution of spoils deriving from his position as assessor and allocater of the shares (kassam).[55] Regardless of a person's education, social standing and devotion to high-minded ideals, it was natural that he should wish to defend his own stake in the sharing of proceeds gained through mutual effort. Soldiers were no exception to this rule.

While it would be wrong to suggest that the Ottoman warrior's allying of personal interest with devotion to an ideological or religious cause is in any way implausible or incongruous, it is hard to accept at face value, as many have suggested we should,[56] the suggestion that Ottoman soldiers as individuals were any more uninterested in the fruits of their labours than the Christian soldiers they confronted. Group solidarity and, if necessary, sacrifice for the communal good were values reinforced in Muslim society, but it cannot be supposed that adherence to these norms was achieved by the complete suppression of all individuality. Muslim and Christian soldiers both turned to their religious convictions as a source of inner strength in pursuit of triumph (or sometimes mere survival) in battle. But the extension of this inner and personal religious devotion to an unqualified dedication to the achieving of external goals such as inaugurating God's Kingdom on earth, or the collective triumph of the nation of Islam, was a remote consideration for all but the exceptionally devout and fearless. As far as Ottoman soldiers were concerned, especially the battle-hardened Janissaries, it is hard to believe that the promise of paradise in the afterlife as a reward for martyrdom in Allah's cause here on earth held much appeal. Their main concern was not the earning of such deferred and intangible rewards, but first ensuring their survival to the end of battle, and then the immediate securing of whatever tangible rewards and special bonuses their success entitled them to.

151

Army ceremonial

It must not be supposed that material motive alone was enough to inspire troops to endure the deprivations and dangers of campaign. Army commanders made use of an extensive range of other confidence-building and morale-boosting measures to maintain the soldiers' spirits in a state of battle readiness. They were subjected to constant reminders, through symbolic gestures and other sorts of blandishments, of the real rewards that awaited them at the conclusion of the campaign.

One pervasive element in the building of a group identity and sense of belonging was food, feasting and the soldier's everyday mess arrangements. To signal their withdrawal from active involvement with preparations for battle, the Janissaries' most extreme act of refusal was the overturning of their soup cauldrons. Its symbolic counterpart, the ritual sharing of food on the eve of campaign, was a clear reference to booty sharing which in the hopes of all present would mark the conclusion of the campaign about to commence. The obligatory pre-campaign feast occupied a central place in army routine, and it was often timed for maximum dramatic effect to coincide with the arrival of the commander in chief at the final gathering place, when the whole army was assembled near the front.

These festive occasions held on the eve of battle were important, not just as celebrations of present and future plenty, but also as reminders of the immediate prospect of hardship and deprivation during the course of the coming campaign. Any prolongation of battle was bound to entail some cutting back of food intake, an eventuality for which soldiers were made mentally prepared by ritual sharing of food in the calm before battle.

Pageantry in various other forms made up another important dimension of pre-battle preparations, and the carrying of banners and standards bearing either specific regimental or general religious and iconographic significance helped to foster feelings of primary group solidarity. The use of such emblems as external foci helped the soldiers to concentrate their minds, and distracted them from inner doubts and fears, offering relief from the general psychological tension associated with the imminent approach of battle.

The form which such pre-battle morale-boosting practices and rituals took had their source in pre-Ottoman Turkic custom, but it is important to remember that many of these ante-bellum rituals were universally practised. While the content might vary, all armies made use of similar forms and techniques to inspire bravery and lift the spirits of their troops. The suggestion that the exploitation of religious sentiments and iconography in Muslim armies as a consciousness-raising exercise was exceptional is contradicted by

4. Banquet given in honour of the commander before departure on the eastern campaign. *Source*: Hazine 1365, folio 34b.

5. Departure of Osman II's army from Istanbul on the campaign against Hotin in 1621/1030 H. Religious officials carrying banner of the prophet Muhammad, the *alem-i şerif*. *Source*: Hazine 1124, folio 54a.

the regularity and similarity (as well as universality) of such practices in contemporary Christian armies.

Ante-bellum prayers and other explicitly religious rituals played a central part in Western military practice. This was true not just of the Middle Ages, when it is best documented and studied, but also in later, ostensibly more secular, times. Prayers and supplications invoking the help of supernatural forces, whether by the direct intervention of God or through the miraculous powers invested by him in the saints, was a commonplace feature of both Eastern and Western military practice. The preference among the Ottomans for night-time ceremonies held around the camp fire and staged in a way to intensify feelings of awe and mystery among the participants may perhaps be considered a significant variation.[57] Religious justifications for the spilling of blood and notions of the "just war" were given explicit expression in medieval Western chronicle sources, but documenting the use of such rhetorical language in written sources should not lead us to the false conclusion that such pious expressions formed the only source of mental stimulus or inspiration to the troops as they entered battle. In the West, as in Middle Eastern practice of the same period, the theme of the holy or just war was only one, and not necessarily the most effective, of a much wider range of common motivational and rhetorical themes.[58]

The thirteenth-century chronicle of Robert of Clari gives an interesting example of the use of religion for justification of war waged against co-religionists that calls to mind similar efforts by the Ottomans in the early sixteenth century to justify their war against Shiite "schismatics" in Safavid Iran. Clari's account of the Fourth Crusade of 1204 contains the following passage:

> It was cried throughout the host that all should come to the sermons, (. . .) and the bishops said they absolved, in the name of God and of the pontiff, all those that should attack the Greeks. (. . .) When the bishops had preached and had shown the pilgrims that the battle was a righteous one, they did all freely confess themselves and receive the sacrament.[59]

The use of religious rites and especially spontaneous vocal prayers as a means of preparing the troops mentally to face the horrors of battle and to will themselves to ignore its obvious dangers was by no means a medieval relic. Such practices were still a living tradition in the time of Cromwell's New Model Army and formed an essential part of the social bonding that made for an effective fighting force.[60] Because the traditions had their origin in the period of the Crusades and are tinged with the particular religio-bellicose spirit of those times, it should not be supposed that they could not thrive in other historical circumstances. That concerns over the fate of their souls after death should be felt with particular immediacy and intensity by soldiers as they entered battle was only natural. The forms of reassurance which organized religion could offer in these circumstances are limited, and it should come as no surprise that they should be encountered repeatedly whatever the chronological and the religio-cultural context in which one is working. As an example of the universality of practice one might cite the reference in early medieval Western tradition to promises of eternal salvation extended to those who died (implied "in battle") as martyrs for the faith.[61] At the other end of the chronological spectrum in Colonial and Civil War America it can be seen from various printed examples that the tradition of pre-battle sermons (orations), preaching messages about the "just war" and delivered to the assembled troops or prospective conscripts on the eve of conflict, was kept vigorously alive.[62]

The beating of drums, the voicing of prayers and the carrying of both religious and non-religious banners into battle were seemingly an indispensable part of pre-battle ritual in both Eastern and Western traditions. Very similar versions of these practices are found everywhere in the medieval, early-modern and even modern eras of warfare. It would be prudent to regard these ritualistic aspects of warfare not as culturally determined *per se*, but as necessary elements whose form and content was imbued with specific religio-cultural meaning by the individuals who used them. The shape and decorative detail of battle standards used in the Ottoman army during the sixteenth and seventeenth centuries is an example of the flexibility in form encountered in these items of everyday use. The use of battle standards decorated with horse tails (*tugh*) among the pre-Islamic Turks of Central and East Asia is well documented. In later (i.e. Ottoman) times these standards were sometimes decorated with crescent-shaped finials by way of explicit reference to the Islamic emblem, but examples depicted in Ottoman miniature painting of the sixteenth century are by no means consistent in showing this feature.[63] The lack of clearly standardized forms is suggestive of practices which emerged over a protracted period of time. Over the long term an eclectic system developed in which pre-Islamic traditions and Islamic symbolism shared equal importance.

With regard to another frequently misrepresented or misconstrued Ottoman wartime practice, it is clear that the voicing of the war chant at the start of battle also served a practical purpose. The battle cry, often timed to coincide with the deafening roar of musket volleys fired in unison, was designed not just to daunt the enemy but also to raise the adrenaline levels of the Ottoman forces and stimulate feelings of self-confidence and the illusion of their own invincibility.[64] Like the visual symbol of the Prophet's standard (*alam-i sherif*), the initial battle cry and later the incessant beating of the battle drums formed an external aural focus for the troops, which helped prevent them from becoming overwhelmed by the morbid thoughts welling up inside them. Such external stimuli were an indispensable part of preparing the troops to engage the enemy and to put aside natural fears about their personal survival.

Morale-boosting measures were most needed to calm the army's nerves in the instant before battle. Once the soldiers were actively and physically engaged in fighting, instincts for self-preservation came automatically into play, and each man fought with the maximum of personal determination, courage and undistracted intensity he could muster. Aural techniques for stimulating the troops were developed to an elaborate degree by the Ottomans. As in other aspects of military tradition, the use of drums to beat out a rhythm for marching in formation and the employing of formal military bands were based on practices known and already quite developed in pre-Ottoman Turkic armies.[65] But the Ottomans, under direct palace patronage and supervision, advanced these inherited traditions to still higher levels of elaboration and perfection. Evliya Chelebi makes explicit reference to the usefulness of the corps of drummers as a means for lifting the flagging spirits both of battle-wary and (later on) battle-weary warriors.[66] The Ottomans set great store by the use of such devices to induce a state of psychological readiness for battle and the Janissary *mehter* band seems to have served as a model for European armies of the eighteenth century who sought to introduce similar practices.[67]

Ottoman army camp life also had its quieter moments, in which poets, story-tellers and narrators of oral folk history praised the great deeds of military heroes of past generations in order to draw the present company of warriors – in a spirit of friendly, though gently taunting, competition – to equal or surpass in the current campaign the exploits of their predecessors. One such hero whose praises were constantly sung in Anatolian folk poetry of the seventeenth century was a near contemporary Genç Osman, whose acts of rash heroism on behalf of his comrades at arms (*yoldash*) had cost him his life during the 1630 siege of Baghdad and made him a legend in his own time.[68] The act of reciting such tales of heroism incited the troops to similar gestures of self-sacrifice that would earn them not just personal honour but a permanent place in the pantheon of military fame. Naima, the founder of modern Ottoman historiography in the early eighteenth century, was well aware of the valuable role played by popular oral history as a consciousness-raising device for the common soldier.[69] The historian was fully aware that the less accessible and intellectually elevated works chronicling court activity of the sort that he himself wrote were of limited inspirational value to soldiers engaged in heavy fighting at the front.

Tales of Genç Osman's exploits reverberated throughout Anatolia in multiple versions, only a portion of which were later copied down and which have survived to the present day in manuscript versions. Similarly, in the European provinces of the empire the exploits of Tiryaki Hasan Pasha during the brave defence of Kanizsa against the fiercely-determined, enemy countersiege in 1601 were kept alive and told and retold until long after the Ottomans had ceased to have an imperial presence in the region. We know from the divergent versions and obviously wide distribution of such tales that they were told, not so much for the benefit of civilian populations or produced under court patronage to suit the convenience of opinion makers with close government ties, but to satisfy the tastes of warriors and active participants in ongoing conflict in the northern Balkan borderlands, who derived the most direct and powerful inspiration from them. In such texts intellectual concerns such as the defence of legal principles enshrined in the Islamic legal code (*sharia*) and even acceptance of the existing social order are noticeably absent. The story of war as told from the standpoint of the participants tells a wholly different tale from that related by the schoolmen, intellectuals, politicians and statesmen of the day. It is from these, until now, largely neglected folk sources that the anti-history of Ottoman warfare will eventually have to be written.

Although we have tended in the above account of motivational aspects of Ottoman warfare to give pride of place to material motivations and incentives, the mental state of warriors was by no means always or exclusively fixated on the concrete material plane. The greatest material rewards came when the war was over, but the soldier's more immediate worry was comfort and relief from the experience of battle itself. His most pressing need was for something to sustain his spirits and promote those feelings of self-esteem which were necessary to make him carry on. While it is difficult for us to grasp, and still more to document, what intangible factors most influenced the Ottoman soldier's state of mind and battle readiness, we can perhaps gain some insights from the relatively well-documented case of a soldiers' mutiny in Crete that took place in 1649. In this instance it appears that issues of fairness and equality of treatment were regarded by the Janissaries with equal seriousness to more openly mercenary concerns such as pay awards and bonuses. The dispute developed in the summer of 1649, when the soldiers felt that their reasonable expectations about leave had not been met. In July 1649 they had all completed 24 months of continuous service aimed at dislodging the Venetians from Candia (Heraklion) and, midway into their third successive season at the front, thoughts of much-deserved home leave occupied every mind. It was at this critical juncture that a fatal blow to general morale was delivered – against the advice of the commander in the field – by the decision to grant selective leaves (*icazet*) to a few privileged Janissary companies. Those not chosen for leave were expected to remain in their trenches, deprived not just of the benefits of leave, but forced to assume the burden of their released colleagues until new reinforcements arrived from Istanbul. The feelings of ill–will and general despair created by this unfortunate decision to grant leave to some while imposing double duty on others soon mounted to the point where a general mutiny could no longer be averted.[70] It is noteworthy that what was considered intolerable by the troops was not so much the conditions of service *per se*, but the inequality of treatment which implied that the service of some merited greater consideration (and reward) than others. By failing to meet their natural expectation that shared deprivation and shared danger merited shared reward, the bonds which tied them to the common and collective enterprise had been fatally compromised. Once the group's internal cohesion was broken, the step from general loss of enthusiasm in the fight to full-scale flight was easy enough for most to take.

The field commander Deli Hüseyn, leader of the troops since the early months of the landed invasion of Crete,[71] was fully aware, not just of the importance of gaining rest and relaxation for *all* his battle weary troops,[72] but of the damaging effect on general morale of decisions meant to apply only to a *part* of them. All commanders were aware of how difficult it was to restore morale once lost. It was for this reason that the best of them paid special attention, not just to the generous distribution of positive encouragement, but also to the issues of fairness and consistency. The honouring of the principle of like reward (whether monetary, promotional or personal) for like service was one way of ensuring that troop morale was never seriously compromised. While the 1649 mutiny, which resulted in the loss of a full season's potential for contributing to the Ottoman war effort in Crete, was perhaps an extreme example of the soldiers' collective loss of their will to fight, it serves as a useful reminder and – for those who doubt it – demonstration of the essential humanity of the Ottoman soldier.

It is important to recognize that the Ottoman soldier was not simply a machine to be driven by the conflicting urges of materialism and monetary concerns, on the one hand, and idealism and commitment to his faith on the other, but was guided in addition – perhaps, in combat situations, even principally – by his own emotions. The mission of rescuing the Ottoman soldier from his status as the impersonal agent of divine will or as victim – in a strictly deterministic sense – of uncontrollable materialistic urges to one of an individual able to exercise some degree of self-determination and personal choice is not easily achieved. But the recognition that Ottoman soldiers exhibited the same range of personal motivations, frailties, passions and psychological strengths and weaknesses as did their role-specific counterparts, the disciplined and trained regular forces or the unruly irregulars in the armies of contemporary Western states, must be the starting point if the task is to be undertaken at all. Whatever their perceived invincibility, patience and bravery under fire, Janissaries were in the final analysis still mere mortals. As an elite corps they had many special privileges, including judicial immunity, that set them apart from average civilians. Likewise they were able to endure (unlike the average man in the street) exceptional levels of privation, and had high thresholds for physical pain. But the fact that their limits, breaking points and perceptions of the tolerable and intolerable were different from the average, and defined by stricter codes of military discipline, made them no less real as absolutes. When Janissaries felt they had been denied due process or treated arbitrarily, they were as ready to protest, both on and off the battlefield, as the rest of mankind.

Pre-battle incentives, post-battle rewards

The last remaining task before our rapid survey of the motivational aspects of Ottoman warfare is complete is the consideration of the variety of forms used by the Ottomans to encourage and reward participation in battle. We began the chapter with a reminder of the diversity in motives which prompted different classes of warriors to take part in a campaign. The state and, even more, the commanders closest to the scene of action kept these differences uppermost in their minds when formulating the terms of reward and the timing of its distribution. For the timariots a key issue was the redistribution of incomes belonging to their colleagues who fell in battle, whereas for volunteers hopeful of an initial timar assignment it was the acquisition of a service-related living. For both members of this group the earning of a post-battle promotion, resulting from recommendations from their district commanders concerning their valour in battle provided a strong incentive for faithful service. If they merely registered their presence in campaign, this in itself was sufficient to prevent dismissal from their timar assignments, but the more active and distinguished a role they played, the greater was the likelihood of their sharing in the redistribution or, if new lands were conquered, in the first allocation of timar lands. On those occasions when the sultan was himself present in the army, there was a further behavioural check to discourage the various forms of shirking duty and encourage the performance of "brave deeds" – namely, the timariots' consciousness of the presence of the sultan's messengers called *chavush* who reported directly to him on the progress of battle. The cavalrymen were fully aware that the unsupported word of a *chavush* could bypass all other channels and lead either to summary dismissal or instant promotion.[73] The *chavushes* themselves were under surveillance by others in the chain of command for any signs of commendable acts of comradely behaviour (*yoldashlik*) that might recommend them to the sultan's attention for reward or promotion.[74] Battlefield promotions awarded by the sultan for acts of valour were a very effective auto-suggestive means of encouraging similar behaviour in others.

The transfer of title to the timars of colleagues who had fallen in action was often deferred to a time, especially in the immediate aftermath of victory, when it achieved maximum psychological as well as dramatic effect. For example, in a single sitting on Sunday 24 June 1565, the day immediately following the fall of the fortress of St Elmo in Malta after a siege lasting three and a half months, 80 petitions for promotions, transfers and initial timar assignments were heard together. This achieved the combined purpose of commemorating the war dead, celebrating the Ottoman expeditionary forces' initial success in the invasion of Malta and, at the same time, bolstering the troops' morale as they embarked on the next phase of the campaign.[75]

The distribution of compensation for losses suffered in battle formed another dimension of post-battle rewards used to build confidence and promote loyalty among the troops. *Ex gratia* payments to the wounded, based on five distinct levels of wounding each linked with payments in a fixed amount and other payments to the cavalrymen to compensate them for the loss of their mounts during battle, formed an expected part of post-battle rituals which was often performed on the battlefield itself. The historian Nihadî gives an account of these ceremonies held at Cenei in August 1695 after the Ottoman victory at which 33,853 gurush were distributed to cover the cost of replacing 2,172 horses lost in battle.[76] By such means, even those who had not earned material reward or gained permanent promotion were at least spared the indignity of incurring uncompensated losses by their participation in campaign.

Through an intricately woven pattern of awards, promotions, compensations, gifts and gratuities the sultan and his representative the *serdar* tried to ensure that no soldier suffered feelings of exclusion. The ritual performance of the expected bestowals (*ihsan*), most frequently in the form of cash bonuses, constituted a fundamental dimension of command. During the campaigning activity of summer 1664 (see above Chapter 6) the grand vezier marked the achievement of the two distinct milestones which headed his tactical agenda for that season's campaigning with the distribution of vezierial beneficence. The first occasion was upon his arrival at Kanizsa in early June, when he distributed ten purses (400,000 akçes) of *ihsan* to the garrison troops wounded during their unsupported defence of the city against a determined enemy attack lasting over one month.[77] The second distribution involved a sum double that of the first, which was distributed piecemeal to individual soldiers who had exhibited exceptional bravery on the day of the final assault against Yeni Kale (Zrinvár) which fell on 30 June.[78] The occasion was important as it marked the Ottomans' first offensive success of the season. Since these distributions took the form of discretionary largesse made only at the commander's order, he was able to time them so as to convey clearly to the troops his acknowledgement (as well as gratitude) for their extraordinary efforts and unusual sacrifices during battle. It cannot be said that the sums involved represented sufficient incentive for risking one's life, but beyond the tangible rewards for exceptional service, it was psychologically important that exceptional effort should be noticed and given official acknowledgement, if only in token form. To the recipient who had just risked his life the symbolic value of the award (of recognition) had equal importance to its intrinsic value (in monetary terms). The acquiring of merit and winning of honour were naturally important to the soldier's self-esteem but they also served as a model and example to his fellow-soldiers, causing them to redouble their efforts to acquire equal honour and merit. Behaviour modification had its cruder and subtler forms, but it appears from the character, diversity and acute sense of timing that distinguished Ottoman awards of distinction and remunerative reward that they were fully aware of the delicacy as well as the importance of the task.

Maintaining troop morale at a consistently high level was a much more complex matter than providing basic necessities, such as food, regular pay and conditions of relative comfort in camp: it required an elaborate celebratory and ceremonial aspect which gave public recognition to the troops' collective efforts and an honorific aspect which paid tribute to those whose efforts had earned them individual distinction. Material self-interest and desire for booty or other tangible reward formed only one dimension of the Ottoman soldier's motivation in battle. If the group dynamic was right, and appropriate tactical opportunities were in the offing, many if not most were also willing to fight to acquire the respect, gratitude and admiration not just of their commanders but also of their fellow soldiers.[79] Of the two categories (command as against rank and file) only the former was equipped to reward them in any tangible way for their efforts, but earning their comrades' esteem was also evidently important to Ottoman soldiers, especially those serving in permanent regiments. The soldiers' own code of honour prevented desertion, cowardice and other acts of disassociation with the common enterprise as much as the fear of punishment and the certainty of financial loss.

From the foregoing analysis it can be seen that, while ideological and material motivations were not absent in Ottoman warfare, loyalty (both to the sultan and to the *serdar*) was a highly personal matter, dependent on highly subjective judgements and the preservation of an attitude of mutual respect. The fact that four seventeenth-century sultans could be deposed, one of them, Osman II, at the hands of the Janissaries, without doubts being raised about dynastic loyalty or any serious disruption of established norms of government resulting is an indication that in the Ottoman empire the maintaining of paternal filial relations took precedence over ideological concerns. The sultan was not just a figurehead or the defender of an abstract cause: his leadership and charisma depended on his development of exceptional skills in inter-personal relations. Likewise the sultan's military representative, the *serdar*, used the dispersal of *ihsan* as a means of signalling his satisfaction with and appre-ciation of his subordinates' efforts. The acceptance of *ihsan* by the troops signalled their willingness to battle on in his cause.

Recruitment

On the most basic level of human motivation terms of recruitment carried more weight than after-the-fact recognitions of bravery and service dedica-tion. Soldiers did not sign up merely hoping for exceptional rewards, but were reassured by their knowledge (gained from experience in previous campaigns) of the normal and expected terms of service. Each service group had different expectations from, as well as motivations for, participation in battle, and, if recruitment was to be effective, special attention had to be paid to the particular requirements of each recruitment category. While it will not be possible to treat in full the particular recruitment and motivational techniques of each of the task-specific military groups employed in the Ottoman army, by focusing on two key categories of recruitment we hope at least to provide an illustration of how such recruitment mechanisms operated. Two groups that played key combat and general service roles were the special assignment commandos (*serden-geçtiler*) and reserve or de-activated members both of the Janissaries and of the highly-privileged, six cavalry regiments at the Porte who sought reinstatement as full members of their respective corps (*esame çalik yeniçeri ve sipahileri*).

The first of these two groups, the *serden-geçtiler*, were normally established members in good standing of regular regiments (either sipahis or janissaries) who willingly volunteered for especially dangerous assignments, attracted by the promise of exceptional and long-term rewards after their safe return. The terms governing such volunteer service were agreed in advance and consid-ered irrevocable.[80] Those who volunteered for high-risk, high-reward service

163

were exposed to exceptionally high casualty rates which, in exceptional circumstances, might rise to 80 to 90 per cent, but the fortunes of the lucky few survivors were permanently secure. For example, at the battle of the Dardanelles in July 1657 a landing party of 300 Janissary *serden-geçtiler* dispatched to Tenedos returned to the mainland with only 40 or 50 survivors, while only 200 of the 2,000 *serden-geçtiler* dispatched in early May 1686 to brave enemy lines and bring relief to the Ottoman garrison in Buda's inner citadel survived the attempt.[81] The level of the reward offered to the commandos varied in accordance both with the inherent danger and the urgency of the military mission. In the case of the last-minute sipahi recruits volunteering for Buda in May 1686 each was offered a permanent increase to their daily wage rate of twenty akçes, a rate that implied for all but the most senior recruits an effective doubling of their wages.[82] An incentive commonly offered to janissaries willing to volunteer as *serden-geçtiler* in the last phases of siege, especially during the final assault and scaling of the walls, was automatic promotion to one of the higher-paid permanent cavalry regiments at the Porte. These agreements amounted in effect to semi-contractual, guaranteed pre-enlistment in the ranks of the empire's most privileged regiments. While the notion of "contingent service" was nowhere explicitly mentioned, there is nonetheless a clear correspondence between these special recruits' willingness to serve and the size of the financial compensations being offered. What is interesting about the Ottoman system of recruitment for the most dangerous missions having the highest probability of ending in fatality is that they relied for the most part on the ranks of established soldiers with relatively secure positions, as opposed to desperadoes or the ill-trained and inexperienced. Securing the co-operation of the most experienced and effective elements in the army required that the level of reward be sufficiently generous to entice them. Rather than desperate and fearless adventurers, what was being sought from this category of recruitment were experienced men who, against all the odds, were capable of achieving success in the most hazardous missions.

The motivating of the second category of hopefuls, i.e. those who sought restoration to the permanent pay roll and reinstatement to the privileges and relative security of assignment to a permanent standing regiment, was a relatively straightforward proposition. The stakes for this group were higher, since for them it was not just a question as for others of earning incremental raises (*terakki*), but of their professional survival. Paradoxically it was the group who had greatest seniority and the highest level of pay and privileges – that is, the members of the six permanent standing cavalry regiments at the Porte (*alti bölük sipahileri*) – who had the least job security. The same applied, of course, to the ranks of the veziers: the higher they rose, the harder they fell.

Sipahis were the group most favoured with assignment to remunerative non-combatant administrative roles, the so-called *divanî hizmet* or service in the name of the imperial council. But they were also the most likely among all Ottoman military ranks to become the targets of disciplinary action, demotions and, in extreme circumstances, removal from the ranks and expunging from the rolls. As the military group with greatest seniority and experience they exercised considerable influence over weaker political leaders but, periodically, especially during the seventeenth century, they faced wide-ranging purges at the hands of more forceful leaders, such as the Grand Vezier Köprülü Mehmed Pasha. On a single occasion in 1658, two years after his elevation to the grand vezierate in September 1656 in the midst of a serious military crisis, Mehmed, still battling to establish his vezierial authority, struck several thousand sipahis from the rolls. The sudden reduction in their ranks by as much as a quarter of their total membership at a time when the empire was facing threats on more than one front had obvious strategic implications.[83] In Köprülü's view, however, taking a firm line with the "mutineers" (in Ottoman sources *zorba*) had a greater long-term significance than maximizing military opportunities in the short-term.[84] One may follow the detailed debate concerning the justice and doubtful defensibility of such savage cuts and summary dismissals in the Ottoman chronicles,[85] but our purpose here is not to try to unravel the root causes or describe the attempted resolutions of such intermittently repeated clashes between rival factions in Ottoman domestic politics. What is significant for our discussion of Ottoman military recruitment is the degrees of dependency in the relationship between the vezier as chief military recruiter (as well as dismisser) and his forces. The vezier's authority to offer regimental reinstatement to dismissed sipahis served as a powerfully persuasive tool when he sought the co-operation (military and otherwise) of the cavalrymen. In setting the limits of their influence and securing their compliance it was always he who had the greatest leverage. The chief term governing "contingent service" (see above) in this context was not the opportunity offered to the soldier to enhance his position by earning promotion and bonuses, but the withdrawal of punishment through reinstatement and reversal of previous disciplinary action. In other words, the chief motivating factor for dismissed sipahis was not the acquisition of honour, but the removal of dishonour.

As incentives to "good behaviour" the manipulation of human emotions such as greed and fear were both effective. But when a combination of positive and negative reinforcements were in operation, the results were doubly effective. Thus, for example, the timariot's fear of dismissal was enough to make him comply with mobilization orders, but provided only a weak motivation to fight. On the other hand, when he was sustained by the thought of earning additions to his timar assignment through valorous deeds in battle, his will to confront the enemy was, if not yet fully engaged, then at least stimulated. Once conflict with the enemy was under way, other basic instincts, especially the survival instinct, and learned behaviours such as primary group loyalty, came into play to see the individual through the trauma of battle. In the period leading up to battle, however, the creation of a positive mental outlook and the instigation of a desire within each soldier to contribute his maximum effort to the group enterprise was in the hands of the commander. The fulfilment of his desires (i.e. military victory) was contingent on his success in creating a sense of mutuality of interest endorsed by all his troops.

One might cite further examples of contingent service and contingent service agreements specific to the various categories of Ottoman soldier and types of military service. It is through the wider exploration of such difference and differentiation (especially in motivation) that the explanation for the Ottomans' consistent record of military success during the sixteenth and seventeenth centuries can best be discovered. In this period the Ottomans developed a unique system, not just of functional specialization within the military ranks in the traditional sense of infantry, cavalry, artillery, commissariat and transport services, but also of combining and maximizing the individual strengths of forces recruited from diverse sources, and developing individually appropriate, as well as effective, means for eliciting the best efforts from each and ensuring their loyalty. The military ethos and methods of Janissary and timariot were antithetical and – if allowed to become so – mutually hostile. But, in the right hands, with effective guidance from an all-embracing, neutral and universally nurturing leader they made a formidable, and for most of the period 1500–1700 virtually undefeatable, alliance. What made the Ottoman army in this period unusual for its time and quite distinct from fully-mobilized European armies, which tended to be composed mainly of last-minute conscripts filling in the ranks around a small core of permanent royal or imperial regiments, was that it was much better practised than any of its potential opponents at accomplishing an effective fusion of forces leading to successful team effort.

The focus of study in accounts of early-modern Ottoman warfare, whether by Europeanists or specialists in Ottoman history, has up to now rested very heavily on two particular themes. The first explores the connection between warfare and technological development, and raises questions about whether or not the Ottoman "Gunpowder Empire" joined or missed the "military revolution" beginning to take shape in Europe in the second half of the seventeenth century. The second concentrates on the relationship between warfare and ideology, and has been dominated by discussions, often taking the form of rather transparently circular arguments, concerning whether the Ottoman political entity is best described – both in origin and in its later evolutionary stages – as a "Gazi" state. As a principal focus of inquiry, questions about whether the state pursued or wished to pursue a policy of perpetual conquest justified by the need to expand the *Dar ul Islam* are only relevant to the sphere of military history if it can be clearly demonstrated that individual soldiers' pursuits and wishes coincided with those of the state. No such connection or coincidence of interest has yet been convincingly established.

Both of the above-mentioned approaches to the history of Ottoman warfare share the same inherent weakness in their emphasis on single-factor mechanistic explanations for what can only be properly understood as complex dynamic phenomena. Preoccupation with the precise philosophical content of official state doctrine of the day, and a, perhaps, too extreme belief in the "power of ideas" as source of historical causation has had the unfortunate result of reducing human agency to a bare and barely perceptible minimum in many analyses of Ottoman social reality. Once the human element is rescued from oblivion and reintroduced as a significant category of analysis, the precise nature of the relationship between men and machines in the study of the connection between technology and warfare as investigated by one school of thought can be more thoroughly explained and understood. A whole series of questions for study immediately suggest themselves: what were the attitudes of soldiers towards the use of particular weapons? How important was human error as compared to mechanical failure as a source of problems in reliability confronted by the Ottomans and their contemporaries? Without introducing the human element into the equation, the wider dimensions of the technology question cannot be satisfactorily addressed. Similarly, any exploration of the role of ideology as a source of soldierly motivation that fails to consider the "human factor" is doomed to superficiality.[86] As a starting point, the assumption that the individual's identity and persona were in any way as closely fused with state priorities as has become characteristic in the era of the modern nation-state is wholly anachronistic.

In this chapter we have sought to show the primacy of the individual as the driving force in battle, and his importance as a relevant unit of analysis for understanding the true character of pre-modern warfare. In earlier chapters our focus on Ottoman military institutions and organizational aspects of Ottoman warfare sought to clarify what enabled the Ottomans to wage war effectively. But the depersonalization of war as a result of a one-sided emphasis on the Ottomans' organizational effectiveness and a, perhaps, too rigorous concentration on the sophistication and elaborateness of the bureaucratic procedures developed by them to service the needs of their troops, provides only a distorted and incomplete picture of the realities of war. Leaving the mental states of Ottoman warriors out of the picture, and overlooking the individual's whole makeup in favour of uni-dimensional depictions of the Ottoman soldier based on the presumed strength of his political and religious convictions, deprives Ottoman military history of the very element which gives it depth and individuality. Neglect of such key issues as the Ottoman soldier's personal motivation for participation in war, once justified on the grounds that the relevant data is missing, is no longer so convincing or acceptable as it perhaps once was. The documentary evidence for this seemingly hidden dimension of human motivation is neither so sparse nor obscure as many have supposed.[87] There is no *prima facie* reason for supposing that Ottoman mentalities and motivations should be any less transparent than those of the rest of humanity. The main obstacle to better understanding of this important dimension of Ottoman warfare has not been so much a general lack of information, as a reluctance on the part of researchers to abandon once comfortable but too simplistic explanations and confront the whole question of Ottoman soldierly motivation in its full complexity.

Chapter Eight

The aftereffects of Ottoman warfare: a review of the essential elements of Ottoman pragmatism in the military sphere

The bulk of the evidence presented in this work (Chapters 1–5) has been concerned with the detail of Ottoman military organization and its role in advance planning for war. An attempt is made in this part of the book to assess both the range and effectiveness of the bureaucratic procedures employed by the Ottomans to prepare their armies for engaging military adversaries on a variety of fronts, and the case-specific flexibility and adaptability shown by the bureaucracy in meeting the challenges faced by the Ottomans as they engaged in warfare under a variety of geographic and topographic conditions and within the context of regionally-specific provincial administrative arrangements. Chapter Six was devoted to a general assessment of methods of combat employed during battle, while Chapter Seven pursued an analysis of the combined system of pre-battle incentives and post-battle rewards developed by the Ottomans to encourage full co-operation and elicit optimal performance from the soldiers both before and during military engagements. The focus in Chapter Seven was on the human element in warfare introducing the theme of the interdependency of state and individual in war. It presented as a working hypothesis the notion (as yet insufficiently supported and incompletely argued) that without mutuality of effort and the effective combination and fusion of the full array of disparate sources of material, animal and manpower resources representing its realizable but still unrealized potential, the state was unlikely to achieve much success in its "pursuit of power". The present chapter seeks to complete the argument by further pursuing the theme of mutuality of effort and the sharing of benefits and rewards in Ottoman warfare, focusing in particular on the post-engagement effects of war in the medium and long term.

The concentration of analysis in the first seven chapters on the "before" and "during" phases of warfare, and on the mechanics, has provided the essential backdrop to the assessment of war's aftereffects. Here we will examine some of the evidence offered to suggest a link between warfare and a seemingly unprecedented concentration of power in the hands of the state, and reassess the assumed connection between an overcommitment by the state to the pursuit of war, on the one hand, and social and economic decline, on the other. Our analysis will be presented under three principal headings: 1 The destructive capacity and demographic impact of seventeenth-century Ottoman warfare; 2 An attempt at an assessment of Ottoman military pragmatism; 3 The redistributive function of Ottoman warfare and an examination of military aspects of the challenge-response model of economic growth.

The destructive capacity of war

Assessment of the scale of physical and demographic damage associated with war in the sixteenth and seventeenth centuries is best pursued within the comparative context of the scope and destructive capacity of warfare in earlier and later eras. Typical patterns of engagement characteristic of "primitive" warfare before the introduction of firepower limited the destructive capacity of war in an absolute sense. However, this very lack of decisive weaponry and an inherent inability to achieve quick results led to the prolongation of conflict, with the net result that war's destructiveness was magnified. In the artillery age war's destructive capacity and also its destructiveness were greater, but typically this enhanced power was applied in restricted form during intense but relatively brief confrontations. The common siege reached its decisive phase within the first ten to twenty days and was directed chiefly against the enemy's brickwork and exterior defences. The civilian populations within a besieged city's walls were only secondary and sometimes accidental targets of attack. Once, normally within the first two weeks of siege, the irreversibility of outcome on a particular occasion (i.e. the attackers' success or failure) was mutually understood, an early cessation of hostilities, either by the defenders' voluntary surrender or the attackers' raising of the siege, was the most common result. In many cases the unsustainability of the attackers' assault because of the insufficiency of their powder supply or the inadequacy of their fire power was revealed by their artillery's performance in the opening phases of the siege. Prolonged sieges and repeated attempts at subduing stubbornly resistant and heavily-fortified sites, although dramatically recorded in the contemporary historical record, were in fact atypical of warfare in the period. War from the mid-sixteenth century took the characteristic form of a brief concentration of the besieging army's maximum destructive capacity against the confined space of a targeted city's walled defences. This offensive operation was carried out by a small fraction of the total armed force, consisting of the artillery units supported, in case of need, by a limited number of assault troops. Direct contact between defenders and attackers took place on any scale only in those cases when the artillery failed to achieve decisive results from the intensive first phases of bombarding the walls. The organization of army provisioning and supply, based on the presumption of success within the time span defined by a single season's mobilization, ensured that issues such as the billeting of armed troops in the provinces over the winter season arose infrequently and only when strategic considerations absolutely demanded.

The pattern of engagement described above stands in stark contrast to the pre-sixteenth-century era of Ottoman warfare when, for technological reasons, prolonged, inconclusive and geographically expansive conflicts commonly prevailed. The means for achieving success in "primitive" warfare was not concentration of fire power against a single target, but sustained raiding, gradual encirclement, harassment of enemy supply lines, embargo, blockade and other forms of what might be termed economic warfare. Although waged with primitive tools and limited personnel by comparison with the technical standards and army sizes common to warfare of a later era, the medieval style of combat, because it was less confined by the seasonal bounds which later came to govern the pace of Ottoman military operations, easily degenerated into messy and more broadly disruptive wars of attrition.

In the pre-artillery age Ottoman wars of attrition were capable of becoming extended on a single front over a period of more than a decade, as the example of Bursa's blockade by sustained Ottoman raids for the whole period between 1314 and 1326 shows. Contemporary sources report that Bursa was finally compelled to submit, not so much by new military developments as by the accumulated effects of a dwindling of its food supply and the laying waste over an extended period of the agricultural hinterland which had supported it. The gradualism, almost imperceptibility, of Ottoman military pressure in this era and the general absence of frontal attacks or other precipitating events that "explain" the success of Ottoman offensives is difficult to understand only if one disregards the enormous difference in timescale between campaigns of the pre-artillery and post-artillery eras. The pre-artillery era of warfare was characterized by the application of minimal force sustained over very long periods. The mounting of multi-seasonal campaigns was not just normal, it was the inevitable consequence of the primitive technical means at the disposal of early Ottoman warriors. While it remains questionable that primitive Ottoman warriors were lent compensatory strength by the ferocity of their commitment to a militant Islamic faith, it is a fact that what the Ottoman soldiers of the early imperial era lacked in capacity for destruction was made up for in their tenacity and perseverance.[1]

On the whole it may be judged that, though casualty rates and short-term disturbances associated with siege warfare of the early modern era were more extreme in terms of the disruption caused to normal economic life and the overall impact of war on civilian populations, warfare of the medieval pattern inflicted greater and more permanent damage. The post-siege recovery process was in many cases a straightforward matter of carrying out repairs to damaged masonry and other forms of state investment in urban renewal, while recovery from the effects of blockade tended to be as long-drawn-out and multi-dimensioned as the military operation itself had been. Paradoxically, at least if one assesses demographic data for the seventeenth century, the effect of an escalation in the destructive capacity of warfare in the period seems to have been a lessening of war's effect on net demographic loss affecting civilian populations. The net effect of the advance from low-intensity medieval warfare waged with spears and arrows to higher levels of potential violence through the introduction of cannon and muskets with their far greater capacity, when fired at close range, for inflicting fatal wounds was to give greater scope for the quick resolution of conflicts and the consequent overall reduction in war-related casualties. At the same time, the scope for negotiated settlements between unequally matched adversaries or the mutual acceptance of stalemate between adversaries who were too closely matched was greater in the warfare of early-modern times than in that of the extended medieval pattern.

Exclusive concentration on the technical and technological aspects of seventeenth-century warfare, and assumptions about the strength of conviction and unreserved ideological commitment on the part of the warriors has tended to overshadow the important role played by compromise and diplomacy in the termination of Ottoman conflicts. It is noteworthy, for example, that even uncharacteristically prolonged and bitter conflicts, such as that between the Ottomans and an alliance of European powers which ended with the Ottomans' defeat in 1699, were concluded with treaties that enshrined notions of conciliation and compromise.[2] In the context of its wars with Safavid Iran, especially those fought at the turn of the seventeenth century, it is clear that the Ottomans' intention in mobilizing large armies was not to deploy or use its maximum potential destructive force to achieve a military solution but, rather, by a show of its obviously superior capacity to encourage their imperial adversaries to sue for peace on terms favourable to the

Ottomans. Without the need to resort to actual violence, the threat was often enough to achieve Ottoman diplomatic objectives. In the same context of its periodically recurrent wars along the eastern borders of the empire, it is noteworthy that the basis of compromise formulated in the treaties of 1590, 1612, and again in 1619 with the Safavids was a return, relinquishing Ottoman claims to significant amounts of territory acquired during the intervening years of warfare, to the borders between the two states as defined in the Treaty of Amasya of 1555.[3] It is decidedly not the case that the Ottomans were in a military sense incapable of confronting the Safavids. Their reluctance to commit to full-scale war in the east was above all connected with the realization that engaging in prolonged sectarian warfare with their predominantly Shiite neighbours would have socially divisive effects within Ottoman society itself. Apart from Selim I (1512–20) Ottoman sultans, unlike the contemporary rulers of Reformation Europe, studiously avoided embroilment in what is often termed "wars of religion".

On the question of the demographic impact of seventeenth-century Ottoman warfare we have some figures relating to Hungary, which during the closing two decades of the century saw some of the heaviest fighting yet experienced in the long-standing imperial rivalry between the Ottomans and Habsburgs in Central Europe. One conclusion that seems inescapable based on the data compiled and analyzed up to now is that warfare, whatever its cumulative effect on demographic growth patterns which were as closely linked with other factors such as age of marriage, female fertility and general life expectancy as they were to the demonstrable effect of war, had a pronounced effect on the increased mobility of populations. The question of whether civilian populations were *driven from* their former homes by the destabilizing influence of armed conflict, or *drawn to* new places of residence by the opportunities offered (sometimes under the direct stimulus of war-related supply demands) is an open one which cannot be addressed satisfactorily here. As far as the impact of warfare on population growth (or decline) is concerned, it appears, for the limited context of the Danubian borderlands under Ottoman occupation in the sixteenth and seventeenth centuries, that the effect was relatively benign. Interesting research on border populations most exposed to the immediate dangers of war indicates that, while temporary flight and depopulation of the most perilous parts of the military frontier was the usual initial reaction of peasants in a threatened region, as soon as the heaviest fighting was concluded and relative security had been restored they expressed a preference for returning as rapidly as possible to their former lands. Furthermore, these "returnees" were often joined in their resettlement by significant numbers of new settlers.[4]

When divided into its three constituent parts comprising the Habsburg

West together with the northern counties, the Ottoman centre, and so-called "free" Hungary or Transylvania in the East, Hungary experienced only minor regional differences in locally prevailing curves of population increase in the seventeenth century, while sharing the same basic growth trajectory. According to data presented in the most authoritative studies, the collective population of all three regions grew from about 3.5 million inhabitants at the close of the sixteenth century[5] to about 4.0 million by the close of the seventeenth century.[6] While the precise regional distribution of population increases is still under investigation for the various areas that made up the seventeenth-century Ottoman empire, the findings in recent research on post-1600 demographic change in the Ottoman lands has tended to contradict long-held assumptions about the stark contrast between sixteenth-century growth and seventeenth-century stagnation. While the century does seem to have begun with several consecutive decades of either flat growth or modest demographic decline affecting most areas and both urban and rural populations, growth trends by the century's end had decisively resumed the upward trend of the previous century.[7] Revised research findings on the demographic effects of the Thirty Years' War, which lasted long enough to have a serious affect on the reproductive potential of two successive generations and encompassed a wider than usual geographical sphere, now agree that the post-1648 population of the Germanies amounting to some 16 or 17 million inhabitants represented a drop of between 15 and 20 per cent over pre-war levels of circa 20 million.[8] The Ottoman–Habsburg wars of the seventeenth century were fought on an intermittent basis and affected populations occupying a much narrower band of territory. Thus, apart from periodic but usually only temporary evacuations of border populations to clear the path for the advance and retreat of opposing armies in the most heavily militarized zones of the frontier, wartime dislocations in Hungary do not seem to have seriously affected mortality rates among the general civilian population. The most severe disruptions were experienced during the Hungarian time of troubles, when for the brief period between 1604 and 1606 the worst effects of the controlled confrontation between Ottoman–Habsburg forces were magnified many times over by Hungary's descent into civil war during the Bocskay rebellion. The breakdown of social order and of trading and other economic links between contiguous regions that is associated with prolonged warfare of the medieval pattern (see above) was largely absent in Ottoman warfare of the seventeenth century. In a later section (see below) we will explore some aspects of redistributive economic growth associated with early-modern warfare, but before turning to this phenomenon we must pause to consider the degree to which the Ottomans' successful mobilization of resources relied on the inherent richness of their base of raw materials, on the one hand, and their

174

ingenuity in devising strategies to tempt and coax both citizenry and soldiery into the fullest possible degree of co-operation, on the other. The issue of the Ottomans' use of co-optative versus coercive means in governance has both a military and an extra-military dimension. But the explanation of Ottoman efficiency in acquisition and deployment of the materials with which war was waged (see above Chapters 4 and 5 on provisioning and transport) lies not just in the sophistication of their bureaucratic apparatus and its use in identifying, extracting and allocating resources but also, perhaps even chiefly, in the willingness of most Ottomans (in a military context both officers and rank-and-file soldiers) to follow its dictates.

Ottoman military pragmatism

There is a well-established tradition in modern scholarship on the Ottoman state to assign cardinal importance to the divergence in political, cultural and religious values between the Ottomans and other Western states. This opposition of values is often presented in the form of rather crudely defined polarities, with the Ottomans consistently assigned to the negative pole.[9] This tendency in the secondary literature on Ottoman traditions of rule has led to seriously distorted views of sultanic power that convey a mistaken impression of the rulers's ability to dictate in the absence of consultation, and divorced from any need for compromise either with his own servitors in state administration (the *kuls*) or with his subjects at large.[10] Sultanic initiatives were of course difficult to ignore, but the view that the state always acquired what it demanded in the form and quantity that it had demanded grossly exaggerates the sultan's and his administration's real influence. With regard to Ottoman requests (demands) for the mobilization of civilian labour for war-related and other state-defined purposes, the implication that the taxpayers' performance of these expected services was either un- or undercompensated by the state needs reassessment.[11]

A typical feature of the Ottoman state's relations with taxpayers that is too often overlooked in the general literature, where a predominant role has been assigned to theoretical notions of Ottoman centralism and bureaucratic control, is the degree to which, in practice, the government remained flexible and open both to alterations of its expectations and to substitutions for the goods, services and cash assessments it imposed on the civilian population. The Ottoman state did not and could not express its needs in the form of fixed and non-negotiable demands, nor was it in a position to regard the unquestioning fulfilment of revenue or labour imposts as immutable.[12] The commuting of taxes from cash to kind and vice versa, and the substitution of military supplies for military service were matters which, though not left wholly to taxpayer choice, were clearly open to discussion, collective bargaining and extensive reformulation. Such redefinition of terms and balancing of interests to achieve a workable formula of give-and-take was unexceptional in the Ottoman state. Examples chosen at random may not add up to a convincing case for regarding such negotiated settlements as a routine feature of the Ottoman regime, but they do point to an aspect of Ottoman military pragmatism that bears wider investigation.

In what follows we will present a few examples of Ottoman flexibility in relation to its demands for taxpayer contributions to meet targets for military conscription and war-related supplies. These examples may be considered as representative of the wider phenomenon of reciprocal flexibility in the Ottoman state, although insufficient as demonstration that full reciprocity prevailed in all such transactions. In wartime circumstances the state was inclined to take more than it could give back in the short-term, but rewards for taxpayer compliance and co-operation were sometimes forthcoming even in the midst of military emergency. The example of the Ottoman tax reform of 1691 is a case in point.[13] To contend that the Ottomans never resorted to compulsion would be naive but, in practice, compulsion was not surrendered to as a first instinct but employed rather reluctantly as a last resort.

Our first example dating from 1691 relates to the commuting of commitments for provision of musket-bearing infantry by villagers in the vicinity of Elbasan in central Albania to an agreement to provide food supplies for army forces stationed at the front near Belgrade. Although the terms of the exchange and the nature of the mutual accommodation of interests might involve some pressure on the part of the state, as military priorities shifted from the filling of manpower shortages to the replenishing of food stocks for the support of the body of soldiers already under arms, the initiative for such exchanges did not always come from the state. It would appear from the Elbasan example at least that the state also acted in response to villagers' requests for military service exemptions.[14] The Elbasan example cannot be used to determine whether the terms of the such substitutions can be considered "fair" or "reasonable", but it does serve as a convincing demonstration of the Ottomans' responsiveness to credible counterproposals, even when these substantially altered the government's standard expectations and previously expressed wishes. What are often regarded by over-optimistic modern investigators as fixed assessments always represented for the practically-minded Ottoman administration optimal targets which had to be reassessed on a routine and continuous basis. The language used by the historian when describing the desirability of the Elbasan exchange conveys a strong sense that the state's willingness to consider the substitution was influenced by its wish to ameliorate the suffering which the villagers first experienced, and then unhesitatingly gave voice to in their petition for an alteration in the terms of their previous "agreement" with the state. That the substitution had also to suit the government's own convenience and meet other, perhaps more pressing and immediate needs goes without saying, but it is significant that the mechanism permitting such substitutions could be activated by the initiative of either side. It would be cynical to regard the recording of such mutually agreeable substitutions by the historian as mere rhetorical gesture, as such examples clearly represent a wider phenomenon of compromise in the arbitration of disputes between taxpayers and the state.[15] It is quite explicit both in the factual details presented and the descriptive language employed by the historian that, by entering into the new agreement, the state was relieving these particular taxpayers from a burden which they themselves regarded as less welcome, and replacing it with one that was, if nothing more, at least the lesser of two evils.

The next example exemplifies what, at various levels of seriousness and proportional significance, seems a universal feature of the Ottoman fiscal landscape. Non-compliance or only partial compliance with state revenue expectations began in some parts of the empire to assume growing proportions in the seventeenth century. In some outlying provinces this took the form of a near-chronic state of tax arrears. The Ottoman response to this development, where a combination of economic logic and political considerations left it no workable alternative, was to revise its expectations and renegotiate the terms of provision both with taxpayers at the village level and with governors at the provincial level. As an example of the downward adjustment of its revenue expectations based on economic logic and acknowledgement of a region's reduced capacity for shouldering its designated tax burden, Mevkufatî's account of a petition by villagers in the vicinity of Larissa (in Thessaly) gives evidence of a basic element in Ottoman fiscal realism. Reporting a decline in the region's village population due to the combined effects of brigandage and plague, the villagers proposed a reduction in their global assessment based on 444.5 tax households to a tax burden based on 364.5 households, representing a tax relief of 18 per cent.[16]

The collection of tax based on a rational assessment of taxpayers' ability to pay was a consistent feature of the Ottoman tax regime. Another dimension of Ottoman military pragmatism is exemplified by the government's offer of tax exemptions and tax abatements both to peasants and auxiliary military forces who either performed critical military-related tasks or, as civilians and cultivators, were willing to settle in unstable or as yet incompletely secured areas in the vicinity of active military fronts. Terms regulating settlement in strategic border areas as described in provincial law codes are quite explicit in identifying the purpose of Ottoman tax leniency and the logic behind the application of flat-rate taxation, as opposed to the more usual and (from a treasury standpoint) higher-yielding arrangements for the tithing of actual agricultural production.[17]

As far as the more strictly military sphere was concerned, the Ottomans' calculation of an optimal tax rate represented little more than a hypothetical target, and the taxpayers' full conformity to levels identified as "fixed" assessments was never realistically expected. As an example of the Ottomans' tolerance for non-compliance by taxpayers, one might cite the case of Ottoman efforts to requisition supplies for a planned campaign on the Caucasian front in 1590. In this case, while the level of compliance with government-set quotas for grain deliveries in kind varied between regions, even seemingly model provinces such as Aleppo managed to supply only about 65 per cent of the amount requested.[18] Increasing levels of taxpayer compliance with state demands was doubtless a government objective, but the Ottomans' preferred means for achieving a better tax yield was, characteristically, the identification of a common interest both with the taxpayers as producers and with other suppliers and transporters of goods. Fully aware that in the long run co-optation would yield better results than compulsion, the state sought to achieve enhanced co-operation with its war aims by making the waging of war, to the maximum practicable extent, a shared enterprise. This, in a nutshell, was the unaltering basis of Ottoman military pragmatism. In the next section we will explore further the connection between warfare and the unleashing of broader economic and market forces. As far as the more limited context of incentives and encouragements offered to individuals is concerned, it is clear that the Ottoman state relied on a subtle combination of psychological motivation and physical force to obtain its citizens'/ subjects' co-operation and to secure the release of goods and services when it most needed them. The government could not afford to stick rigidly to the enforcement of its fixed demands (whether for goods, services or taxes), since it was all too easy for peasants, soldiers and taxpayers at large to withhold their co-operation. No state in the seventeenth century was yet capable of enforcing its unilaterally-determined will, and this deficiency of power applied as much to the Ottoman sultan as it did to the emperors and other heads of contemporary European states. Many commentators remain sceptical that, even in the so-called "age of absolutism" during the later part of the eighteenth century, European states had yet developed sufficiently bureaucratized and centralized military systems to guarantee the enforcement of the sovereign's will.[19] Ottoman military pragmatism of the sixteenth and seventeenth centuries was firmly grounded in an implicit acknowledgement of the insufficiency of state power and the need for forging domestic alliances to achieve its ends.

The redistributive function of Ottoman warfare

The flip side of the coin of downward revision of government estimates and optimal expectations for revenue yield was the upward adjustment of cost estimates for military-related expenditures. While it had a natural preference for orderly acquisition in advance of basic campaign supplies such as grain at carefully controlled prices, army provision as a planned process could only ever secure a part of what was needed and consumed during war. Situations always arose, especially at the finish or in the immediate aftermath of battle, when stocks from easily available sources had dwindled, and the state was forced to pay top prices for grain to encourage the release of hoarded or previously withheld surpluses. A few examples taken at random from published and unpublished sources will suffice to illustrate the phenomenon. The most obvious price differential, and one of which peasants and other providers were themselves of course acutely aware, was the wide seasonal variation between summer and winter grain prices. Barley supplied as advance stock forming part of the army's planned provision during their spring season march to the front was typically acquired at a price significantly discounted from the one current in the state-controlled commodities market which varied, in the early seventeenth century, between 22 and 24 akçes per *kile*.[20] However, in the absence of such prior arrangement, or in the event of only partial compliance with government defined supply quotas (see above), prices fluctuated in accordance with local market conditions and reflected local availability. Thus, while it can be said the government underpaid for provisions in kind collected from taxpayers as part of the planned provision process,[21] it must always be remembered that the amounts successfully collected in this fashion always represented only a proportion of what was ultimately consumed. Unforeseen needs, prolongation of the campaign, wastage and countless other conditions, including the perennial uncertainty of harvests, conspired to make the most careful prior calculation of needs inadequate. When calculations erred on the side of undersupply, the state, in the same way as any other last-minute purchaser, was compelled to pay for supplies at, and in some circumstances at a premium above, the going market rate. To take one example from the Marmara region, a part of the empire which had a fairly developed commercial grain market because of its proximity to major population centres, it is recorded that in the winter of 1639 during the army's

179

return march from its victory at Baghdad a supply amounting to some 78 tons (about 3,000 kiles) of barley was to be requisitioned from a group of villages near the Marmara shores. The grain was being prepared in anticipation of the arrival, in a few weeks time, of the remaining army troops (especially the sultan's standing forces) proceeding towards the capital from central Anatolia. Of the 3,000 kiles requisitioned, a substantial quantity, 1,000 kiles, was provided from commercial suppliers at a free-floating price considerably above the then-current controlled market price.[22] Producers of grain in general and not just grain merchants stood to gain from such short-term fluctuations in grain prices, and the phenomenon was certainly not confined to the Marmara region where grain surpluses and transport conditions were unusually favourable. On its return march from Erivan in 1635, for example, it is recorded that the army was compelled to pay between 150 and 300 akçes for each *kile* of barley acquired from scarce supplies in the region around Harput.[23] None of these examples should be taken as indicative of the benevolence (or, conversely, malevolence) of the Ottoman regime towards taxpayers and producers. The conclusion that we must draw from the existence of such wide variation in prices and terms and conditions of supply is that, faced with factors such as seasonal availability and the urgency and scale of its own needs, the government was forced to put into suspension its own strict and seemingly universally-applied, price regulatory regime. It would seem that the state system of regulatory price controls did not represent a consistently enforced or inflexible and absolute standard, but functioned rather to provide suggestive guidelines, whose main purpose was the protection of retail consumers. It is also clear that the relaxation of or variation from the notional prices recorded in the *narh* registers was not always to the government's own benefit, yet the state itself, win or lose, yielded to price pressures which, given the vastly larger scale of its own purchases by comparison with other consumers of goods, were to a significant degree of its own making. In both market and extra-market exchanges we can clearly see the operation of an Ottoman economy in which a free price regime predominated over a fixed price one.[24]

Another feature of the Ottoman economy and other pre-modern economies that merits some discussion here is the relationship, as it applied to the agrarian sector of the economy, between supply and demand. Conventional wisdom holds that, for the whole era of pre-scientific and pre-mechanized agriculture, output remained highly inelastic and incapable of responding to significant or sustained increases in demand. Since, according to this logic, supply had a tendency to be fixed or only marginally expandable, increased demand represented not an opportunity but a threat to producers and implied a declining share of, and fierce competition for, the fixed supply of goods amongst average consumers. The logic of this argument holds good only if we accept that under the stimulus of increased demand agricultural production always remained flat. If, on the contrary, we assume the existence of even a modest, spare, untapped, productive capacity in seventeenth-century Anatolian and Balkan agriculture, the persistence of higher demand and the presence of relatively favourable prices for growers might well have stimulated production gains. If we accept this as our starting premise (equally hypothetical, but no less plausible than the inelasticity theory), the impact of increased demand would not be shared adversity but, rather, increased prosperity. The question of whether conditions of Ottoman expansion against Europe and the need to defend a widened frontier spurred or discouraged economic development has attracted more attention from Europeanist than Ottomanist historians. One preliminary conclusion of research on the effect of increased pressure on growers to supply increased amounts of grain to feed the expanding armies of Austria and its allies in the Ottoman–Habsburg wars of the sixteenth and seventeenth centuries is that, far from spelling the doom of southern German agriculture, it was actually instrumental in rescuing it from decades of stagnation and underproduction in which it had languished under the joint influence of a declining population base and steadily falling grain prices.[25]

There is also a clear relationship between war and the stimulation and expansion of trade. State demands for higher levels of basic commodities and for livestock, especially during war, were on such a large scale that they served to create market forces and new market opportunities that sustained economic activity in the longer term. While, in the first instance, goods were mostly channelled for use in the state sector and production was tailored to meet state-defined needs, such markets stimulated by occasional need could, if conditions were right, enjoy a considerable afterlife. Trade in some types of goods which benefited from the additional stimulus of demand on the international market and were easily transportable had a latent potential for exponential growth.[26] From study of the role of private contractors and imperial commissioners documented for the Habsburg case it is apparent that the mobilization of supplies for war provided opportunities for a class of intermediaries and middlemen to amass considerable fortunes in the seventeenth century.[27]

Although we are unfortunately not yet in a position to undertake a conclusive assessment of the position of Ottoman landlords and producers based on detailed monographic study, we cannot automatically assume, in the absence of confirmatory evidence, that the existence in the Ottoman lands of a different (more highly centralized) land tenure regime gave the state exclusive control of the land's products, or enough power effectively to stifle private initiative. Counterindications of an admittedly anecdotal but still suggestive nature are abundant enough to raise serious doubts about the state's ability to control even basic markets, such as those organized to regulate the food supply of metropolitan cities like Istanbul.[28] Another indication of private initiative in the realization of the full growth potential within the agrarian sector is seen in the general increase during the seventeenth century in peasant mobility. Although the evidence on this question is still far from complete, there are some indications that freer movement may have been prompted in part by heightened demand for peasant labour linked to substantial rises, on estates in selective areas, in agricultural output.[29]

The differential effects of Ottoman warfare on regional economic growth represent another understudied dimension of Ottoman economic life. What we do know as can be judged from the serious price instability already referred to above (see pp. 179–80) is that the presence of the army in a region was not just a source of depredation, but also of enhanced opportunities for local suppliers to realize, at least for the short-term, unprecedented profits. Such profits soared to still higher levels when locally available stocks of basic goods such as grain were affected by blockades or, though less dramatically, even by minor disruptions of normal supply patterns. Ottoman sources suggest that profiteering from war-time shortages was particularly rife during the time of the Venetian blockade of the Dardanelles between 1654 and 1656,[30] but the phenomenon was by no means confined to the Aegean or restricted to such unusual circumstances as the Ottomans' capital city being placed under a state of virtual siege.

It should be regarded as axiomatic that commercial activities in the Ottoman empire tended to migrate to those places where profits were greatest. The presence of the Ottoman army in a region for any extended period of time created business opportunities, not just for victuallers and provisioners, but for other trades as well. The spending power which soldiers represented (especially after their return from battle with a substantial accumulation of the spoils of war and victory bonuses paid in cash to dispose of) provided a powerful stimulus to local markets. The Ottoman writer Evliya Çelebi writes in detail of the feverish pace of activity generated at the periodic market of Focsani, located near the confluence of the three rivers Danube, Prut and Siret, by the occasion of the arrival of regiments of Ottoman soldiers both on their way to, and upon their return from, the Moldavian or Polish-Ukrainian fronts in the seventeenth century.[31] Although not exclusively dependent on the activity generated by the presence of soldiers, the location of markets like Focsani at convenient points near natural tarrying places for armies such as river fords is more than just accidental. Evliya's description speaks of 40 days of brisk activity at Focsani twice yearly, which served to rescue the region's economy from the doldrums it habitually experienced in the seasons between the annually repeated fair times. The presence of masses of soldiery and the release of their pent-up spending power magnified the scale and economic importance of the fairs for the rural economies, and allowed them to share, if only briefly, the economic status of cities as centres of consumption and loci for the creation and exchange of material wealth. The relative underdevelopment of rural (especially agrarian) economies was, in part, the product of the absence of sufficient stimulus to occasion the release of their full productive capacity. While the occasional arrival of the Ottoman army and the huge additional demand for goods and services it represented was insufficient stimulus to rescue rural economies from a condition of chronic underproduction, the mobilization of resources for war and the creation of spontaneous markets on a large scale served as a needed, if only temporary, spur to sluggish economic performance.[32] In sum, it can be said that the Ottoman rural economy suffered more from the effects of under- than over-stimulation. Although wartime requirements imposed exceptional resource demands with noticeable effects on the general economy, periods of war also offered exceptional opportunities for wider participation in economic activity.

Another feature of regional Ottoman economic life was the emergence of small- and medium-sized urban centres distributed throughout the extent of its stabilized border regions. The presence of cash-paid garrison troops, both Janissaries and locally-recruited forces, in these urban centres of the borderlands, while of course constituting an additional drain on local sources of food and other material resources, was welcomed by craft manufacturers and producers of smaller luxuries, who regarded them as their most reliable and creditworthy customers.[33] The capacity of war to act as a vehicle for the release and redistribution of wealth, and as a source of dramatic market expansion and economic growth, has been noted as a principal feature of medieval warfare.[34] In the seventeenth century the process worked differently, because, in addition to the release of goods and the redistribution and spreading of resources and wealth, there was the added feature of state investment, sometimes on a massive scale. By the seventeenth century Ottoman warfare had evolved beyond the typical fourteenth-century pattern of scattered and only partially coordinated raiding activity to a more orderly process in which the state had developed longer-term interests of its own. The purpose of warfare was by then not just to extract resources from the lands of the enemy for distribution among the warriors, but to provide the basis for a steady revenue stream from lands placed under permanent Ottoman administration. State investment in regional economic development including the building of roads, bridges, garrisons and other urban facilities to ensure regional security formed one dimension of the realization of its long-term interests. The commitment of state resources and investment in a captured region's post-war reconstruction also served as a catalyst to encourage settlement, while promoting the cause of further economic growth and development. Military subsidies paid with surplus revenues from other regions often helped on the fiscal side,[35] and with the growth of trade, commerce and more complete integration within wider Ottoman economic spheres and broader participation in mutually beneficial resource exchanges with other regions, the full benefits of the *Pax Ottomanica* began to be realized.

The added dimension of state investment in regional development in the seventeenth century distinguishes this period of warfare from the merely redistributive function of war as seen in the medieval pattern. In medieval warfare the release of goods and wider circulation of wealth in the immediate aftermath of booty raiding was not followed by investment in infrastructure development or "recovery" on any significant scale. Post-1450, as part of their elaboration of a more fully-developed imperial institutional structure, the Ottomans refined military organization. While state control over the use of violence was never absolute, an informal code of practice slowly developed which served in practice to eliminate some of the worst excesses of warfare of the diffused medieval pattern. Another difference was the shorter timescale of war in the early-modern era (see above), which meant that the normalization process after war could be more quickly and comprehensively achieved. Although the above-described differences between warfare of the medieval and early-modern pattern were of fundamental importance, assessing the precise effects of these changes is far from straightforward. The impact of war was felt most immediately and intensely in the border regions, but one must be very careful about extrapolating general effects from these localized and regionally-specific phenomena. Drawing inferences regarding long-term transformation on the macro-economic and trans-societal levels from the evidence of war's immediate impact is equally hazardous. In the concluding chapter we will explore briefly some of the complexities of the relationship between war and social transformation in the Ottoman empire.

Chapter Nine

Conclusion – war and social transformation in the Ottoman empire

The fact that the Ottomans preceded European states in their development of centralized means for the financing and administering of warfare has led some investigators of Ottoman social reality to the obvious, though not always very thoroughly argued, conclusion that expertise in the military realm had broader social consequences and led inevitably to the "militarization" of society. We have already spoken (see Chapter 2 above) of the dangers implicit in the use of all-encompassing typologies such as "Gunpowder Empire", "Conquest State" and the like, which give excessive emphasis to a single attribute (military prowess) in characterizing complex Ottoman social reality. The assumption that an overcommitment of the empire's resources by the Ottomans to the "maintaining of its military supremacy" resulted in a corresponding undercommitment to other, non-military forms of investment is a particularly prominent feature of Balkan historiography on Ottoman rule.[1] This assumption of an either/or dilemma, a guns or butter choice confronting the Ottomans is left unexamined by such investigators. The association of Ottoman rule with the militarization of society is not confined to the Balkanist historical perspective. The underlying assumption that, in order to be able to wage war effectively, the Ottomans were compelled by inexorable fiscal logic to take more out than they were in a position to pay back as imperial overlords in the empire's predominantly Muslim provinces is equally well-rooted in the literature.[2] Even with reference to the Anatolian heartlands, the notion that mounting Ottoman fiscal demands and changing recruitment needs led to a destabilization of rural society is implicit in many accounts. Before accepting that such widespread and sustained effects as these can have arisen directly from military pressures, we must take a closer look, first at the actual scale of increased manpower and material-resource demands that resulted from changes in the style of combat and new recruitment needs in

185

the seventeenth century and, secondly, at how these new burdens were geographically distributed and what effect they had on taxpayers at the local level.

Given the size of its population and resource base which, by the end of the sixteenth century, grew to more than 20 million inhabitants and some 800,000 square miles of territory,[3] neither increased recruitment demands nor temporary reallocation of grain surpluses for the support of armies at the front was likely to attain a level sufficient to cause permanent dislocation to economic life in the home provinces. Even when Ottoman war with Venice had entered its second decade and both fiscal and other resource pressures had mounted to unprecedented levels with particularly severe effect on the residents of villages near the western Anatolian coastline, who were heavily recruited to serve as oarsmen for the fleet, the wider impact of such war-related strains was only just beginning to be seriously felt. In a confidential letter addressed by Mehmed IV to his commander in the field in November 1668 the sultan expressed private reservations about the Ottomans' ability to continue their war with Venice in Crete beyond the upcoming season. It is worth recalling that the sultan wrote his letter at the conclusion of the second continuous season of full-scale and determined Ottoman assault against the walls of Candia and in the 23rd year of the Ottomans' intermittent struggle with Venice over the island's possession.[4] It is noteworthy also that the cumulative effect of rising demands for cash to finance this exceptionally intractable war were far more serious for the territorially-confined Republic of Venice than for the Ottomans. From a resource standpoint the Ottomans were relatively well-equipped to fight even inconclusive and long-drawn-out wars of attrition.[5]

In attempting to measure the global impact of war in the seventeenth-century Ottoman empire and to assess its effect on the home front we can achieve greater clarity by breaking the broader question down into its two constituent parts. We must address the impact, first, of the fiscal demands of warfare and, secondly, those of manpower and recruitment.

Fiscal pressures

The mounting fiscal pressure associated with the expansion of the ranks of the cash-paid permanent standing forces in the seventeenth century is frequently cited as one of the "social costs" of Ottoman warfare in the period. It is argued that, because a disproportionate share of the rising tax burden was shouldered by the taxpaying peasantry of the core provinces, the net effect of mobilization for war was increased pressure to produce more, so as to be able to meet their higher tax assessments. Our knowledge of the proportional share of average household income devoted to payment of taxes in successive imperial eras is not yet sufficiently developed for us to make confident judgments about the relative condition of the Ottoman peasantry in the sixteenth and seventeenth centuries. An important development in the seventeenth century, the social implications of which are still obscure, is the extension of cash payment as opposed to crop tithing as a method of tax assessment. The question of whether the peasant was better off paying in kind or, in a more fully monetized system, accepting the commutation of production quotas and other tax obligations to cash equivalents is a fundamental but still largely unanswerable question. The related question, whether the demands of war weighed more heavily on the peasantry in the seventeenth century as com-pared, for example, with the fifteenth, likewise remains open.[6] The effect of centralizing trends in sixteenth-century Ottoman taxation was still, according to one comprehensive data survey dating from a peak period of Ottoman military and naval involvements both in Hungary and the Mediterranean, to leave enough after-tax surplus capacity for investment in the village economy to allow peasants to undertake supplementary income-generating activities such as livestock raising and viticulture.[7]

In the absence of more detailed study, it cannot be assumed *ipso facto* that the *net* effect of the monetization of the Ottoman tax system in the seven-teenth century was greater hardship for the taxpayer or the general impover-ishment of the peasantry. We still need to know more about the after-tax, residual, average, disposable family income of seventeenth-century rural households before rushing to judgments about the effect of rising taxation expressed in akçe terms. The relevant figure is the proportion of average rural household income devoted to taxation, which would have to be calculated on the basis of fluctuating grain prices (see section 3 in Chapter Seven above), and more detailed knowledge of real production. Only this fuller picture would tell us whether tax burdens in a given period or region had become more or less supportable for the resident populations. At the present state of study we are still largely confined to hypothetical conjecture.[8] Indeed, a strong case can be made for regarding the commuting of peasant taxes from payment in kind to payment in cash, and the loosening of restrictions on peasant mobility that arose as a consequence of the abandonment of regular registration of timar lands in the late sixteenth century as socially progressive developments.[9]

A recent study by Darling of Ottoman provincial taxation in the seventeenth century, while noting the increased revenue demands of the state associated with the rising cost of warfare in an age of expanding armies and rapid technological advancement, has questioned the traditional assumption that this led inexorably to a consistent pattern of Ottoman overtaxation in the period. Darling concludes that, after accounting for the effect of inflation, the increase to the average taxpayer's tax burden in the seventeenth century was relatively modest.[10] It is also worth recalling that the increased yield to the treasury from "extraordinary" tax levies in the seventeenth century was achieved through a widening of the tax base the net result of which was a more equitable distribution of the tax burden. Because of its heavy reliance on taxes on agricultural production, the traditional tax system of the Ottoman empire in the sixteenth century had placed a disproportionately heavy burden on the empire's rural inhabitants. By including urban populations within its scope, the *avariz* revenue system was able to tap new sources of cash with which to finance grain purchases and other supplies requisitioned from the countryside. In the late seventeenth century, during the time of the European counteroffensive that followed the Ottoman defeat at Vienna, new taxes on urban consumption were introduced, which were designed to close growing and increasingly endemic budget gaps, while at the same time allowing the government to modify and make more tolerable traditional modes of taxation such as the non-Muslim poll-tax (*cizye*).[11] In addition, the Ottomans made increased use in the seventeenth century of revenue transfers (*havale*) and war subsidies from grain surplus and revenue rich provinces for the support of the least populated and most vulnerable borderland regions of the empire.

Changes in Ottoman fiscal practice in the period were designed at least as much to achieve a balancing and redistribution of tax burdens as to maximize the treasury's yield. Ottoman intentions in the sphere of taxation can be deduced from the persistence of widely divergent rates of assessment and collection present in different parts of the empire. The absence of consistent patterns and levels of taxation, permitting the application of a standard rate across the empire's whole extent, implies, not just the government's willing-ness to consider petitions for tax abatements where locally appropriate, but also indicates its general sensitivity to the wide disparity in average household income and levels of prosperity, as well as an awareness of the differential burden imposed by alternative forms of taxation in different provinces of the empire.

Although the *avariz* had by the mid-seventeenth century outgrown its original purpose to serve as a source of "extraordinary" revenue to meet unusual war-time expenses and become a fixed feature of Ottoman regular taxation, in practice it was rare for the same region to be heavily assessed in consecutive years. Periodic re-registrations and other adjustments provided some tax relief, and the government showed its readiness to act decisively when its intervention was needed to redress serious imbalances in the tax profiles of the empire's constituent regions.[12] In principle as well as in practice Ottoman *avariz* assessment was neither fixed, continuous nor universal in scope. It did, however, provide a practical means for balancing budgets, and secured a measure of financial stability for the empire in an era of rising costs. It is to be remembered that these rising costs affected all areas of the government's activities and not just the military sphere.

The positing of a direct connection between warfare and generalized socio-economic decline in the Ottoman empire remains problematic. The reconnecting of remote and underdeveloped regions of the empire with the economies of the core regions as a consequence of warfare concentrated in the border regions served as an economic stimulus to both core and periphery. Tax sacrifices fell most heavily on the core provinces, but it was they who were more capable of bearing them. Tax leniency in newly-acquired provinces was a key element of the Ottomans' imperial policy in all periods of their history. For example, the non-Muslim residents of the province of Uyvar in the period of Ottoman rule between 1663 and 1685 paid standard tax obligations, such as the Christian poll-tax (*cizye*), at a much reduced rate by comparison with provinces of the imperial hinterland. Such tax leniency under the newly-established Ottoman regime was intended in part to encourage loyalty, but also to promote the cause of full recovery and economic growth in the province.[13] It is also the case that in real money terms the government's spending power represented by its regular tax revenues was significantly eroded by the effects of wartime inflation. Thus, to take a hypothetical example, a static revenue assessment of 50 akçes in 1690 would have represented only about four-fifths of its pre-war value after taking the effects of the akçe's devaluation into account.[14] In such inflationary times, despite the seeming attraction of revenue maximization, the government actually preferred the peasants to pay their *avariz* obligations in kind (*nüzul*) to the commutation of these tax obligations to their cash equivalents (*bedel-i nüzul*).

The precise effects of war-induced revenue pressures on state–peasant relations is still too nebulously understood for us to conclude very much, but it is possible to state more categorically on the basis of examples like the Uyvar case cited above that the Ottomans were committed to introducing a post-war fiscal regime that, paired with other measures for reconstruction, significantly hastened the process of post-war recovery in the regions most exposed to wartime disruptions and devastation. In short, the Ottomans matched the military pragmatism followed in the "before" and "during" phases of warfare with a consistently-applied fiscal realism in the "after" phase.

Military recruitment and social transformation

A thorough assessment of the social consequences of war must give serious attention to its costs in human terms. To keep its expenditures and other resource commitments for military purposes within bounds sustainable by the tax-paying public, the state was obliged to meet a part of its troop needs with temporary recruits. While the use of these temporary recruits, consisting in the Ottoman case of the *sekban* infantry and *sarica* cavalry forces, was undesirable from the standpoint of military efficiency, since the presence of large numbers of irregulars tended to undermine army discipline, from a fiscal standpoint their employment was not just inevitable but desirable. Also, in judging the broader social impact of the Ottomans' increased use of *sekban* soldiers in the seventeenth century, we must not lose sight of the fact that conditions of universal conscription (*nefir-i am*) which led to their proliferation were temporary and unusual as opposed to endemic and normal circumstances. One cannot judge their impact on the balance of forces in a society based on mobilization levels at the height of a military crisis.[15] While it is quite true that at the conclusion of campaign the state frequently experienced considerable difficulty in forcing these temporary recruits to disband and return to their normal peacetime occupations, it is still perhaps disproportionate to speak of a "sekban domination of the empire" based on a wartime strength of between 4,000 and 10,000 men.[16] If such figures reflect their maximum strength at a time of serious military emergency, even a failed demobilization would have reduced them to no more than half that number. Taken over the whole of the Anatolian countryside, from which the majority of them were recruited, these numbers do not seem sufficient to account for the widespread social ills often associated with their presence in the provinces.

Historians focusing on eighteenth-century Ottoman warfare have observed, perhaps with some justice, that the scale of Ottoman reliance on *nefir-i am* soldiery to wage a near-continuous series of wars with Russia in the quarter century between 1768 and 1792 had a transformatory effect on Balkan society of the period.[17] But, neither on an absolute scale of recruitment nor in terms of their proportional significance in the balance of Ottoman military forces employed at the time can the Ottomans' use of such irregulars from Anatolia in the seventeenth century be considered similar. In the context of late seventeenth-century military emergency during the wars of the *Sacra Ligua* by drawing on mounted forces from among the tribes of Anatolia, and employing them as *sarica* to supplement the regular Ottoman army the Ottomans were not creating a new social type, so much as implementing a further dimension of their usual military pragmatism. While it can be agreed that the *sekban* phenomenon was different, the conclusion that heightened Ottoman manpower demands, induced by warfare and the consequent withdrawal of peasant labour from the countryside to fill the army's ranks, should be considered as a precipitant factor in the onset of a serious agrarian crisis in seventeenth-century Anatolia or of state fiscal crisis is too extreme. Both the scale of the recruitment demand and the size of rural society's response were too small to give rise to social or economic transformation of this order of magnitude.

Military conscription among the civilian population was, compared with contemporary European states, held at a minimal level in the Ottoman empire.[18] The Ottomans maintained large reserves in the ranks of both the permanent standing forces and the provincial timariot army. Undersupply of actives from domestic sources could also, on most fronts at most times, be compensated by participation with significant troop levels from vassal states and allies. Populations in the border areas naturally assumed a disproportionately high share of the responsibility for defence, and there was also a tendency for the less developed areas of the empire, such as Albania, where other employment prospects were relatively limited, to supply more military recruits than the most developed areas of the empire. Nevertheless, one must be very wary of judging the general level of militarization in the Ottoman empire by the standard and example of those restricted zones where military recruitment for emergency wartime service was heaviest.

The size of the Ottoman empire and the extensiveness of its resource base continued for the whole of the period 1500 to 1700 to serve as its main strength and protection. It was simply too big for Europe or any of the Ottomans' Middle Eastern neighbours to confront single-handedly. Without the effort, sacrifice, expense and risk involved in the creation of what often proved to be fragile anti-Ottoman alliances there was no hope of a successful military challenge against the Ottomans. For most of the sixteenth as well as the seventeenth centuries the Ottomans were able to achieve their geopolitical objectives by mounting a military operation themselves, using less than their own full capacity, or by enlisting support (particularly in the naval sphere) from friends and allies. On land it was the Tatars, Kurds and Caucasians who sometimes tipped the balance in the Ottomans' favour, especially by their lending of logistical, transport and reconnaissance aid to the main body of Ottoman combatant forces in the field. In the Mediterranean, when confronted by the combined fleets of its most redoubtable enemies, the Ottomans also relied on the invaluable help of their allies in the Barbary States and, for a brief period in the mid-sixteenth century, on France. In the waging of limited warfare of the more usual sort carried out on a single front, however, the Ottomans operated throughout this period of international

191

military challenges well within their own internal resource capabilities. This is not to say that the Ottomans never experienced economic strain induced by military overextension or the unfortunate, but sometimes unavoidable necessity of waging war on two fronts simultaneously. But barring such exceptional circumstances, the impact of Ottoman warfare, both in terms of its expense and its social costs, was kept within sustainable bounds. The mobilization of men and resources for war in the seventeenth-century Ottoman empire drew on a sufficiently wide geographical domain, and war's aggregate costs were kept to modest enough proportions that the Ottomans' transformation into "a near-perfect military society" was never threatened.[19]

Appendices

Appendix I

Chronological account of principal Ottoman military engagements in the sixteenth and seventeenth centuries

1514	Battle of Chaldiran, first major Ottoman confrontation with the Safavids in the east
1517	Battle of Raydaniyya, Ottoman conquest of Egypt
1521	Ottoman siege of Belgrade, opening of the gateway to Hungary
1526	Battle of Mohacs in southern Hungary
1534–5	Fall of northern Iraq and Baghdad to the Ottomans
1541	Ottoman capture of Buda and annexation of central Hungary
1543	Joint Ottoman-French fleet action against Spanish in coastal waters off Nice
1552	First Ottoman siege of Eğri (Eger) in northern Hungary ends inconclusively, but Ottomans secure firm control in the Banat of Temeshvar which serves as the nucleus of a new Ottoman province
1554–5	Resumption of the conflict with the Safavids in Azerbaijan with an Ottoman offensive aimed at Nahcivan; agreement of terms for settling the frontier at the Treaty of Amasya (May 1555)
1565	Ottoman siege of Malta
1571	Ottoman capture of Cyprus (August)
1571	Defeat of Ottoman naval forces at Lepanto (October)
1578–90	War on the Caucasus front with the extension of the Ottoman frontier to Kara Bagh and the incorporation of the western portions of Azerbaijan
1593–1606	Long War with the Habsburgs
	Significant campaigns included the Ottoman victory at Eğri (Eger) with the army led by Sultan Mehmed III in 1596 and the conquest of Kanizsa in 1600, resulting in the Ottoman annexation of the Croatian-Hungarian borderland.

Conflict brought to a conclusion by the Treaty of Sitva Torok which inaugurated a period of relative quiet on the Hungarian front lasting until about 1660

1603–12   Resumption of war on the eastern front ending with the restoration of Azerbaijan to Safavid control

1623–39   Intermittent war with the Safavids over the possession of Baghdad; Baghdad restored to the Ottomans after a 39-day siege concluded in late December 1638; other significant campaigns included the Ottoman offensive against Erivan (August 1635) which, after a brief possession by Ottoman garrison forces, was restored to Safavid control (April 1636)

1645–69   Intermittent war with Venice over control of Crete
Principal phases of the conflict were: the Ottoman capture of Hanya (Xania) (August 1645), the fall of Rethymnon (January 1646) and the siege of Candia (Heraklion), the latter stretching over three consecutive campaigning seasons concluding in September 1669

1660–1   Ottoman offensive against Transylvania; fall of Varad (Oradea) in July 1660

1663   Offensive of Grand Vezier Fazil Ahmed Pasha aimed at Slovakian stronghold of Uyvar (Nove Zamke); fall of Uyvar (late September 1663) and Nograd (early November 1663)

1664   Ottoman offensive in southwest Hungary; capture of Zrinvar (June 1661), Ottoman defeat at San Gotthard (August 1664) but conclusion of dual season's effort with a Treaty (Vasvar, August 1664) highly favourable to Ottoman interests in the region

1672   First of a series of Mehmed IV's offensives against Poland; fall of Kamanetz-Podolsk to the Ottomans (August 1672)

1673–4   Mehmed IV's second Polish offensive carried out over two successive seasons; first season ends with failed Ottoman attempt to take Hotin (November 1673) but second season's efforts are crowned with capture of Ladyzn (August 1674)

1675–6   Continuation of action on Polish front with Ottoman forces advancing as far as Lvov (August 1675); signing of Treaty of Zuravno (October 1676) formalizing Ottoman annexation of Podolia and western portions of the Ukraine

1678   Ottoman capture of Çehrin (Chyhyryn) in central Ukraine on the west bank of the Dniepr river (August 1678)

1683   Ottoman siege of Vienna in July–September ends in failure

1684–99   Pan-European offensive league (Sacra Ligua) formed to force Ottoman withdrawal from north of the Danube

Main events include:

1683   Surrender of Ottoman garrison at Esztergom (late October)

1684   Attempt by Europeans to recapture Buda (July–November)

1686   Fall of Buda

1687   Ottoman defeat at the second battle of Mohacs

1688   Surrender of the Ottoman garrison of Belgrade

1690   Ottoman recapture of Belgrade

1691   Ottoman defeat at the battle of Slankamen

1692–7 Relative quiet in Hungary as Leopold I pursues war with Louis XIV

1695   Failed siege of Azov by Peter the Great

1696   Russian capture of Azov (July); success of Ottoman forces at Cenei in the Banat of Temeshvar (August)

1697   Decisive Ottoman defeat at Senta (September)

1699   Signing of Peace Treaty at Carlowitz (January) by whose terms the Ottomans agreed to a wholesale evacuation of their territories in Hungary with the exception of the Banat of Temeshvar

Appendix II

Regnal Periods 1512–1703

Era of direct successions (succession of a son of the reigning Sultan), 1512–1617

1512–20	Reign of Selim I
1520–66	Reign of Süleyman I
1566–74	Reign of Selim II
1574–95	Reign of Murad III
1595–1603	Reign of Mehmed III
1603–17	Reign of Ahmed I

Era of mixed (direct and collateral) succession pattern – succession of brothers or sons of the reigning sultan, 1617–1703[1]

	Sultan's age at time of accession
1617 Accession of Mehmed III's son Mustafa (Ist) (first reign 1617–18)★	25
1618 Accession of Ahmed I's son Osman (IInd) (reigned 1618–22)★	13
1622 Re-accession of Mustafa I (second reign 1622–3)★	30
1623 Accession of Ahmed I's son Murad (IVth) (reigned 1623–40)	14
1640 Accession of Ahmed I's son Ibrahim (Ist) (reigned 1640–8)★	24
1648 Accession of Ibrahim's son Mehmed (IVth) (reigned 1648–87)★	6

1687	Accession of Ibrahim I's son Süleyman (IInd) (reigned 1687–91)	45
1691	Accession of Ibrahim's son Ahmed (IInd) (reigned 1691–5)	48
1695	Accession of Ahmed II's son Mustafa (IInd) (reigned 1695–1703)★	30

---

[1] In this period nine accessions took place (counting the re-accession of Mustafa I in 1622) and of the nine, six (marked with asterisk in the list) ended with the sultan's premature removal from the throne by forced deposition. Two other sultans, Suleyman II and Ahmed II had relatively short reigns because both were quite old (nearly 50) when they succeeded to the throne.

Appendix III

List of equivalents for weights of less than 150 pounds in standard measures[1] employed in the seventeenth-century Ottoman empire

okkas	pounds
0.25	0.707
0.50	1.414
0.75	2.121
1.0	2.828
2.5	7.07*
5.0	14.14
10.0	28.28
15.0	42.42
20.0	56.56
25.0	70.7
30.0	84.84
35.0	98.98*
40.0	113.12
44.0	124.43
50.0	141.4

* Note the close coincidences which are useful for rapid calculation (approximation) of larger quantities. 2.5 okkas was approximately equal to 7 pounds; 35 okkas was approximately equal to 100 pounds.

[1] The okka of 400 dirhems, the *kile* of 20 okkas and the kantar of 44 okkas were the main units of weight in this range. The dirhem weighed 3.207 grams. Thus, 100 dirhems (0.25 okka) was the equivalent of 11.3 ounces or 0.707 pounds. The standard okka weighed 2.828 pounds, the *kile* 56.56 pounds and the kantar 124.4 pounds.

Appendix IV

List of equivalents for weights between 150 and 7,500 pounds in Ottoman kile[1] and kantar units

kiles	pounds (long tons)
2.5 (50 okkas)	141.4
5.0 (100 okkas)	282.8
10	565.6
15	848.4
20	1,131.2
22 (10 kantars)	1,244.32
25	1,414.0
30	1,696.8
35	1,979.6★
40	2,262.4★
44 (20 kantars)	2,488.6
50	2,828.0 (1.263)
60	3,393.6 (1.515)
66 (30 kantars)	3,733.0 (1.667)
70	3.959.2 (1.768)
80	4,524.8 (2.02)
88 (40 kantars)	4,977.3 (2.222)
90	5,090.4 (2.273)
100	5,656.0 (5.525)★
110 (50 kantars)	6,221.6 (2.778)★
132 (60 kantars)	7,465.9 (3.333)

★ Note the close equivalents which are useful for making quick calculations. 35 *kiles* was approximately equivalent to a short ton (2,000 lbs) and 40 *kiles* to the long ton (2,240 lbs). 100 *kiles* was roughly 2.5 long tons, while 50 kantars (110 *kiles*) was roughly 2.75 long tons.

[1] The Ottoman *kile* equivalent for the larger metric weights was: 100 kg (1 quintal) = 3.897 *kiles*, 10 quintals (1 metric ton) = 38.97 *kiles*. The short ton of 2,000 lbs was 35.36 *kiles* and the long ton of 2,240 lbs was 39.6 *kiles*. A thousand *kiles* was approximately equivalent to 25.25 long tons.

Appendix V

Chart for converting small silver akçe coins (money of account) to large silver coins (gurush)[1] and gold (altun) equivalents for sums less than 1 million akçes

akçes	gurush	altun	kese[2]	yük
80	1.0	0.666		
100	1.25	0.833		
250	3.125	2.083*		
800	10.0	6.666		
1,000	12.5	8.333		
2,000	25.0	16.666		
3,000	37.5	25.0*		
4,000	50.0	33.333		
5,000	62.5	41.666		
8,000	100.0	66.666		
10,000	125.0*	83.333		
20,000	250.0	166.666		
30,000	375.0	250.0		
40,000	500.0	333.333	1.0	
50,000	625.0	416.666		
80,000	1,000.0	666.666		
100,000	1,250.0	833.333		1
400,000	5,000.0	3,333.333	10.0	4
500,000	6,250.0	4,166.666	12.5	5
600,000	7,500.0	5,000.0*	15.0	6

akçes	gurush	altun	kese[2]	yük
700,000	8,750.0	5,833.333	17.5	7
800,000	10,000.0	6,666.666	20.0	8
900,000	11,250.0	7,500.0	22.5	9
1,000,000	12,500.0	8,333.333		10

* Note the close coincidences. According to the "official" exchange, 250 akçes was the approximate equivalent of 2 gold pieces, 3,000 akçes equalled 25 gold pieces and 10,000 akçes equalled 125 gurush, and 600,000 akçes equalled 5,000 gold pieces.

[1] The value of the various coins and coin types which circulated rather freely in the Ottoman empire during the seventeenth century was subject to considerable fluctuation. The two most common types were the Dutch *rijksdaaler* and the Spanish *real* called in Ottoman the *esedi* and *riyal gurush*. For a summary account of these fluctuations, see Ş. Pamuk, "Money in the Ottoman Empire, 1326–1914", in Inalcik and Quataert (eds), *Econ. and Soc Hist.* (Cambridge, 1994), p. 964 (Table A: 6, "Exchange Rates . . . 1584–1731"). For a brief account of monetary trends in the seventeenth century, see H. Sahillioğlu, "The Role of International Monetary and Metal Movements in Ottoman Monetary History, 1300–1750", in J. F. Richards (ed.), *Precious Metals in the Later Medieval and Early Modern Worlds* (Durham, N.C., 1983), pp. 287–9. For some further detail on the principal coin types, see A. R. Frey, *Dictionary of Numismatic Names* (New York, 1947), s.v. "asadi ghurush" and "rijksdaaler" and F. von Schrotter, *Wörterbuch der Munzkunde* (Berlin, 1930), s.v. "Löwentaler".

[2] The standard kese (purse) in the seventeenth century consisted of 500 gurush or 40,000 akces.

Appendix VI

Equivalents of "loads" (yük) for sums from 1 million to 100 million akçes

yük	akçe (millions)	gurush	altun	kese[1]
10	1	12,500		25
20	2	25,000		50
30	3	37,500	25,000	75
40	4	50,000		100
50	5	62,500		125
60	6	75,000	50,000	150
70	7	87,500		175
80	8	100,000		200
90	9	112,500	75,000	225
100	10	125,000		250
150	15	187,500	125,000	375
200	20	250,000		500
250	25	312,500		625
300	30	375,000	250,000	750
400	40	500,000		1,000
500	50	625,000		1,250
750	75	937,500	625,000	1,875
1,000	100	1,250,000		2,500

[1] The standard equivalent of one purse (kese) for most of the seventeenth century was 500 big silver coins (gurush) or 40,000 akçes.

Appendix VII

Table of place-name equivalents for places frequently encountered in the text

Form most commonly encountered in Ottoman sources	Contemporary Hungarian form	Equivalents in other languages*
Ciğer Delen	Párkány	Štúrovo
Çehrin		Chigrin/Chyhyryn
Eğri	Eger	Erlau
Estergon	Esztergom	Gran
Fülek		Filákovo
Istolni Belgrad	Székesfehérvár	Stuhlweissenburg
Kamaniçe		Kamanetz-Podolsk
Kanice	Nagykanizsa	
Ösek	Eszék	Osijek
Senta	Szenta	
Sigetvar	Szigetvár	
Temeşvar		Timisoara
Uyvar	Érsekújvár	Nové Zámky
Vaç	Vác	
Varad	Nagyvárad	Oradea
Yeni Kale	Zrinvár	Neu Zrin
Yanık Kale	Györ	Raab

* E.g. English, German, Romanian, Serb, Ukrainian or form found on modern maps.

Notes

Preface

1. F. Szakály, "Early Ottoman Hungary", in P. Sugar, P. Hanak and T. Frank (eds), *History of Hungary* (London, 1990), p. 89.
2. M. Köhback, "Nemçe", in *Ency clopaedia of Islam*, Vol. 8, pp. 4–5.

Chapter One

1. See in particular G. Perjés, *The Fall of the Medieval Kingdom of Hungary* (Boulder, Co., 1989).

2. See the list of armistice and later treaty renewals with the Holy Roman emperors in J. von Hammer-Purgstall, *Geschichte des Osmanischen Reiches*, 10 vols. (Pest, 1827–35), Vol. 9, pp. 288–94. The 1568 agreements had been renewed four times by 1591 (in 1574, 1577, 1584 and 1591) and the 1606 Treaty of Sitva-Torok was reaffirmed six times by 1649 (in 1615, 1618, 1625, 1627, 1642 and 1649).

3. See, among others, V. L. Tapie, *Monarchie et peuples du Danube* (Paris, 1969); esp. p. 161 where he uses the phrase *"l'inachèvement de l'État"* to sum up the level of government success achieved at this early stage of Habsburg centralization efforts.

4. See M. Köhback, *Die Eroberung von Fülek durch die Osmanen 1554* (Vienna, 1994), pp. 183–4; esp. p. 183: *"nach den unterschiedlichen Angaben zwischen 4,000 und 8,000 mann"*.

5. See Thomas A. Barker, "New perspectives on the historical significance of the year of the Turk", *Austrian History Yearbook*, Vol. 19–20 (1983–4), p. 4. Despite the use of the word "new" in the article's title, this is essentially a repetition and defence of the views put forward by Barker in a book published seventeen years earlier; see Barker, *Double Eagle and Crescent* (Albany: SUNY Press, 1967), pp. 194–7: "inhumane behaviour", p. 280: "Ottoman barbarity", etc.

6. See R. Murphey, "Süleyman's Eastern Policy" in H. Inalcik and C. Kafadar (eds), *Süleyman the Second [i.e., the First] and His Time* (Istanbul, 1993), pp. 229–48.

7. The Ottoman occupation of Erivan began with a successful siege in August 1635 but ended a short eight months later, yielding to a determined Safavid countersiege mounted during the winter months of 1636. For its restoration to Safavid control on 30 March 1636 (22nd Şevval 1045), see Iskandar Beg, *Zayl-i Tarikh-i Alam-ara-yi Abbasi* (Tahran,1317), p. 180. Kâtib Çelebi records the surrender date as the 24th of Şevval (*Fezleke-i Tevarih* 2 vols. Istanbul, 1286–1287, Vol. 2, p. 180). The significant point is that, by this time, the Ottoman relief force had managed to advance only as far as Hasan Kale (mod. Pasinler) 40 km east of the Ottoman stronghold of Erzurum.

8. See R. M. Savory, "Safavids", *Encyclopaedia of Islam*, Vol. 8, p. 771 and R. N. Frye, "Ghalzay", *ibid.*, Vol. 2, p. 1001.

9. The most serious and protracted engagement was the 1638 siege of Baghdad which extended over 39 days between 15 November and 24 December. This is to be compared however with the timespan of the march from Istanbul to the front which extended over 197 days; see H. Sahillioğlu, "Dördüncü Murad'in Bağdad Seferi Menzilnamesi" in *Belgeler* 2 (1965), pp. 1–35.

10. It is noteworthy that the historian attributes the limited participation of the soldiers in this undertaking to the sultan's niggardliness. He faults Murad for the decision to use debased coin to pay the customary campaign bonus (*sefer bahşişi*) of 1,000 *akçes* per head to the household troops (*kapu kulu*); see Kâtib Çelebi, *Fezleke-i Tevarih*, Vol. 2, p. 170.

11. See the "Commentario della origine de Turchi", cited in C. Göllner, *Turcica: Die Europaischen Türkendrucke*, Vol. 1 (Bucarest, 1961), p. 158 and its nearly contemporary translation into English (facsimile of the London edition of 1562 entitled *Two Very Notable Commentaries*, Amsterdam and New York 1970).

12. See the account of the Venetian ambassador Lorenzo Bernardo who described the Ottoman land forces circa 1592 as consisting of 250,000 regulars (timariots and salaried

household troops) and further unspecified numbers of volunteers and raiders, L. Firpo (ed.), *Relazioni di Ambasciatori Veneti al Senato Vol. XIII, Constantinopoli, 1590–1793* (Torino, 1984), p. 73.

13. For a summary account of the collected works of Matrakci Nasuh, active to circa 1545, and of Arifi (d. 1562), see E. Esin, *The Age of Sultan Süleyman the Magnificent* (Washington, D. C., 1987), pp. 82–97 and J. M. Rogers, "Itineraries and Town Views in Ottoman Histories", in J. B. Harley and D. Woodward (eds), *The History of Cartography*, Vol. 2, Bk. 1 (Chicago, 1992), pp. 228–62.

14. *Tarih-i Peçevi* 2 vols. (Istanbul, 1283), Vol. 2, p. 125.

15. The historian Mustafa Ali draws a similar distinction in the *Kunh ül Ahbar* (Nuruosmaniye Lib., Ms. 3409), fols 400a–401a.

16. *Tarih-i Selaniki*, edition by M. İpşirli in 2 vols. (Istanbul, 1989), Vol. 1, p. 331.

17. See the *Tarih-i Peçevi*, Vol. 1, p. 130 which recounts the capture and recapture and the razing and rebuilding of both Petrinja and Sisak in quick succession over a two-year period between the summers of 1592 and 1593 (A. H. 1001–1002).

18. For the reservations voiced by the Sheyh ül Islam Bostan-zade Mehmed Efendi concerning the troops' readiness (and willingness) to engage a new foe so soon after the conclusion of a series of exhausting campaigns in Iran between 1578 and 1590, see *Tarih-i Peçevi*, Vol. 2, p. 133.

19. See the note on the emergency recruit of *maryol taifesi* (forced recruits from the peasantry) to defend the northern sector of the border between Esztergom and Hatvan in *Tarih-i Selaniki*, Vol. 1, p. 347: local commander's report dated Dec. 1593 (Rebi I 1002).

20. That is a siege in which the besiegers had amassed sufficient numbers of wall-battering guns to deliver a daily payload of 1,700 cannon balls. The numbers for the 1594 siege are provided by Kâtib Çelebi (*Fezleke* I: 92) and confirmed, with minor discrepancies, by Naima (*Tarih-i Naima* 6 Vols. [Istanbul, 1281–3], Vol. 1, p. 25). They imply (at the average rate of fire of 35 volleys per gun per day) a concentration of approximately 50 big guns called *bal yemez*. For an Ottoman description of the fall of Buda in 1686 as a "fifteen hundred shot siege", see *Tarih-i Nihadî* (Istambul University Ms., TY 6053), fol. 243a and 244b. In this latter siege the enemy deployed 43 *bal yemez* (divided between 5 batteries) each using the maximum size 24 okka (68 lb) shot. By comparison, the Ottomans when besieging Uyvar two decades earlier in 1663 established batteries of *bal yemez* totalling no more than 21 guns, of which only a part used the heaviest calibre shot. The three sizes in use at the Uyvar siege were 14, 18 and 24 okka shot, corresponding to 40, 51 and 68 pounders respectively; see Mühürdar Hasan Ağa, *Cevahir ül Tevarih* (Leiden University Lib., Cod. Or. 1225), fol. 23a. The average rate of fire of 35 volleys per gun per day was achievable if we assume the sustaining of fire over eight and three quarters hours at the average rate of four volleys per hour, or seven hours at the rate of five volleys per hour.

21. See the accounts by Kâtib Çelebi and Naima cited in *n*20 above.

22. See J. Spielman, *Leopold I of Austria* (London, 1979), p. 124 and compare the numbers suggested by R. R. Betts, *Cambridge New Modern History: Vol. 5* (Cambridge, 1961), p. 498, where the total size (including imperial regiments) of the force fielded and commanded by the Duke of Lorraine is put at 40,000. K. Péter, in Sugar, Frank and Hanak (eds), *History of Hungary* (London, 1990), p. 116, suggests that as many as 65,000 troops participated. The absolute numbers are unimportant and they all suggest that under more normal circumstances, in the absence of international co-operation on so massive a scale, mobilizations must have been much smaller.

23. This number in itself represented a huge increase over the 9,000-strong force that had existed in 1564 soon after the council's creation; see O. Regele, *Der Österreichische Hofkriegsrat, 1556–1845* (Vienna, 1945), p. 17. Writing in the 1670s, Montecuccoli still considered 50,000 troops (28,000 foot and 22,000 horse) as the "ideal" size of armed force for combating the Ottomans. That the standing regiments would account for even as much 50 per cent of this ideal force represents, to say the least, an optimistic expectation. For an assessment of Montecuccoli's views, see V. J. Parry, "La Manière de Combattre", in V. J. Parry and M. E. Yapp (eds), *War, Technology and Society in the Middle East* (London, 1975), p. 233 (fn. 3). It goes without saying that Montecuccoli's figure of 50,000 represents a mobilization target rather than an actual deployment.

24. John Shirley, *The History of the Wars in Hungary* (London, 1685), p. 95: "the grand vizier [i.e., Kara Mustafa Pasha] broke ground running his trenches with incredible speed [. . .] so that in six days 13,000 men were entrenched".

25. Charles Gerin, "Le Pape Innocent XI et le siège de Vienne en 1683", *Revue des Questions Historiques*, V. 39 (1886), p. 141 (fn. 1).

26. *ibid.*, p. 147.

27. See, H. F. Helmholdt, *The World's History: Volume 7, Western Europe to 1800* (London, 1903), p. 488.

28. On papal war subsidies, see Ludwig von Pastor, *Geschichte der Papste* (Eng. trans. by E. Graff, *A History of the Papacy from the Close of the Middle Ages*). In Pastor's estimation (*History of Papacy*, Vol. 32 [London, 1940], p. 167) by the end of Innocent XI's pontificate in 1689 the emperor (Leopold) had received sums equivalent to five million florins or (at the rate of 3.2 florins per ducat) 1,562,500 gold ducats. For contemporary exchange rates in Europe, see Pastor, *History of Pap.*, Vol. 32, p. 153, n. 3, (1 ducat = 3 florins and 12 kreuzer), and for the fixing of the *speciesthaler* at 90 and the *gulden* at 60 kreuzers by the ordnance of 1623, see Albert R. Frey, *Dictionary of Numismatic Names* (New York, 1947), p. 240. In Ottoman terms the equivalent sum at wartime exchange rates reaching 300 akçes per Venetian ducat (see *Tarih-i Raşid* [Istanbul, 1153], Vol. 1, p. 147 *sub anno* 1102/ 1690) was nearly 470 million akçes; a generous sum even by their own standards of campaign finance.

29. At Cenei the Ottomans faced an Austrian army numbering (at most) 60,000: 40,000 foot and 20,000 horse; see Silahdar, *Nusretname*, I. Parmaksızoğlu (ed.), 5 pts. in 2 vols. (Istanbul, 1962–9), Vol. I, pt. 2, p. 175. However, the following year at Szenta (after the redeployment of the Flanders army which preceded by some months the formal conclusion of peace with France in October) the Ottomans were confronted with the need for a massive mobilization to meet the threat posed by an international coalition of forces led by Prince Eugene. On this later occasion the Ottoman forces gathering at Belgrade (10 August 1697) were reckoned at 104,000 (*Nusretname*, Vol. I, pt. 3, p. 277) and an unusually large proportion of these (the actual number according to our source was 97,000) were actually present and accounted for in the trenches on the eve of battle in early September; see *Nusretname*, Vol. I, pt. 3, p. 291.

30. On the difficulty of coping with competing military demands during the period 1688–97, see L. Hobert, "Die Sackgasse aus den zweifronten Krieg: Die Friedes mit der Osmanen 1689", *Mitteilungen des Instituts für Österreichische Geschichtsforschung*, V. 98 (1989), pp. 329–80.

31. See R. Mihnea, "La participation de la Russie aux guerres de la Sainte Alliance", *Études Balkaniques* V. 15 (1979), pp. 94–103.

32. Evliya Çelebi gives figures for the minimal size of Tatar contingents joining Ottoman

campaigns, depending on the status of the commanders who led them, as ranging between 36,000 and 72,000 men. The minimal size of an army led in person by the reigning han of the Crimea was twelve *tapkir* regiments composed of 6,000 men each; see *Seyahatname*, Vol. 7, pp. 532–3: *"der beyan-i kanun-i al-i Gengiziyan"*.

33. See, *inter alia*, William H. McNeill *Pursuit of Power* (Oxford, 1982), esp. Ch. 4: "Advances in Europe's Art of War, 1600–1750", pp. 117–43 in which he develops the idea of emerging Western technical superiority in the seventeenth century. Recently a group of Europeanist historians has begun to suggest some qualifications to such arguments. Some regard their "technological determinism" as entirely untenable (see Mahinder S. Kingra, "Trace Italienne", *Journal of Military History*, 57 (1993), pp. 431–46, esp. p. 434), while others are inclined to push back the inception date of Europe's much debated "military revolution" from the mid-sixteenth to the late seventeenth century (see J. Black, *A Military Revolution?* (Basingstoke, Hants, 1991), esp. p. 33). The current consensus among the Europeanists seems to be that tactical and technical innovations did not play nearly as important a role in sixteenth and seventeenth-century warfare as was once generally believed.

34. See William B. Munson, *The Last Crusade* (Dubuque, IO, 1969).

Chapter Two

1. See P. Sugar, "A Near-Perfect Military Society: The Ottoman Empire", in L. L. Farrar (ed.), *War: A Historical, Political and Social Study* (Santa Barabara, CA, 1978), pp. 95–104.
2. For an account of the constraints under which European armies operated, see Frank Tallett, *War and Society in Early-Modern Europe, 1495–1715* (London, 1992), pp. 50–68.
3. See, *inter alia*, A. Goldschmidt, *A Concise History of the Middle East* 3rd edn (Boulder, CO, 18988), pp. 111–34.
4. See J. F. Pernot, "Guerre de sièges et places fortes", in V. L. Barrie-Curien (ed.), *Guerre et Pouvoir en Europe au XVIIe Siècle* (Paris, 1991), p. 132. For a comparative idea of Ottoman capabilities using both muskets and field artillery, see below Chapter 6, *n*25–6.
5. Mehmed Raşid (*Tarih-i Raşid* (Istanbul, 1153), fol. 52b) writing on the Ottoman siege of Candia in 1669 indicates that after 500 to 600 firings the cannons' touch holes (*falya*) were so collapsed that the guns had to be recast. Naima's account of Hüsrev Pasha's failed siege of Baghdad in 1630 describes a similar problem and attributes it to the poor quality of the gunpowder (*Tarih-i Naima*, III, 52: "*barutun alçaklığı ..*").
6. For an account of the principal manufacturing centres, see G. Agoston, "Gunpowder for the Sultan's Army" *Turcica* **25** (1993), pp. 78–9.
7. See T. Işıksal, "Gunpowder in Ottoman Documents of the Last Half of the Sixteenth Century", *International Journal of Turkish Studies* **2** (1981–2), pp. 81–91, esp. pp. 82–3.
8. See Naima, *Tarih*, III, 16 and Kâtib Çelebi, *Fezleke*, II, 118 on the execution of the officer in charge of the arsenal (*cebeci başı*) for his part in a bungled crossing of the Lower Zab near Altin Köprü in February of 1630.
9. Apart from the obvious examples of Uyvar (Nové Zamky) in 1663 and Candia in 1669 one might also include in this category relatively minor fortresses such as Novigrad (near Zara/Zadar) in Croatia which fell to the Ottomans in July 1646. See K. M. Setton, *Venice,*

Austria and the Turks in the Seventeenth Century (Philadelphia, PA, 1991), p. 143 (fn. 13): *"quasi inespugnable".* On the transformation of Uyvar from a reed-embrasured palisade (*çit palankası*) to a moated and stone-walled fortress (*kale*) over the six decades of peace following the signing of the Sitva-Torok Treaty in 1606, see Hasan Ağa [Mühürdar], *Cevahir ül Tevarih*, (Leiden University Lib., Ms Or 1225), fol. 31a: *"elli altmış seneye varınca toprak yığıp azim dağ etmişler, . . . ve dolayında azim metin duvar ki safi tuğladır".*

10. See the comments of Voltaire on Ottoman proficiency in the arts of trench warfare cited in R. Murphey, "Critica", *Archivum Ottomanicum* **13** (1993–4), pp. 377–8.

11. For the general code of practice in the late seventeenth century, see J. Black, *European Warfare 1660–1815* (London, 1994). For the limited context of gun founding there is still no reason to revise the judgement reached by A. R. Hall forty years ago. In his summary of the current state of research on military technology in the West (see "Military Technology", Charles Singer *et al.* [eds], *A History of Technology: Vol. 3: c. 1500–c. 1750* (Oxford, 1957) p. 363) Hall wrote: "the surviving evidence indicates that fundamentally the same methods were employed from the beginning (i.e. circa 1420) until about 1750".

12. See in this context, R. Murphey, "Ottoman Resurgence in the Seventeenth-Century Mediterranean", *Mediterranean Historical Review* **8** (1993), pp. 186–200, which argues that even in the sphere of naval technology, long considered an area of Ottoman weakness after their defeat at Lepanto in 1571, the Ottomans were both well-informed about, and able to keep pace with, evolving practice.

13. See the account of the siege by J. von Hammer-Purgstall, *Geschichte des Osmanischen Reiches*, **VI**, 471 which describes the opening of gaps in the walls "60 paces wide" after an accidental explosion in the Buda arsenal. The account in Silahdar's history (*Tarih*, II, p. 250) suggests that a cache of 36,000 quintals (over 2,000 tons) of powder exploded after receiving a direct hit from an Austrian grenade. For another account of the toll in Ottoman life resulting from this explosion, see G. Agoston, "The Baruthane of Buda", in G. David and P. Fodor (eds), *Hungarian-Ottoman Military and Diplomatic Relations in the Age of Süleyman* (Budapest, 1994), p. 159 (fn. 57).

14. See, for instance, the matching examples from the siege of Candia cited by Mehmed Raşid (*Tarih-i Raşid* (Istanbul, 1153) fol. 56a). Here Raşid relates that during the rainy season over the winter of 1668–9 the Venetians had spent six months preparing an elaborate counteroffensive mine which then failed to explode. The Ottomans' effort undertaken at the same time consisted of a land mine with a payload of 30 quintals, which also failed to ignite.

15. See Table I.31 in H. Inalcik and D. Quataert (eds), *An Economic and Social History of the Ottoman Empire, 1300–1914* (Cambridge, 1994), p. 99.

16. See Ayn-i Ali, *Risale-i Vazife-Horan* (Istanbul, 1280), p. 97 which gives the following breakdown:

	Men	(% of total)	Salary payments (in millions of akçe)	(% of total)
land forces	57,868★	96	257.2	97
naval forces	2,363	4	7.8	3
TOTAL	60,231	100	265	100

★ Of these 39,282 (roughly two-thirds) were Janissaries (see Table 2.1 in main text)

17. James B. Collins, *Fiscal Limits of Absolutism: Direct Taxation in Early Seventeenth-Century*

NOTES

France (Berkeley, 1988), pp. 163–4. At this time France was contributing approximately 15 million livres out of revenues of 30 million livres tournois to the cost of waging an internal war. Translated into Ottoman terms, using the multiplier of 26.666 akçes per livre tournois, the equivalent sum was 400 million akçes.

18. While one example cannot be taken as indicative of general trends, it is perhaps suggestive that participation in troop transport duties by the North African fleet during the early phases of the Veneto-Ottoman war in Crete is described by one Ottoman historian as minimal (see Naima V, 79–80 describing fleet activity in 1651). See also R. Murphey, "Resurgence", *Mediterranean Historical Review* **8** (1993), pp. 188–9.

19. J. Deny and J. Laroche, "L'expédition en Provence de l'armée de mer du Sultan Süleyman sous le commandement de l'amiral Hayreddin Pacha, dit Barberousse (1543–1544)", *Turcica* **1** (1968), pp. 161–211; esp. p. 187 (fn. 3).

20. See the budget for 1547 published by Barkan in *Iktisat Fakültesi Mecmuası* 19 (1957–58), pp. 237 and 251.

21. See the Tarhoncu budget of 1653 (A. Feridun, *Münşeat-i Selatin* (Istanbul, 1265), Vol. 2, p. 305, lines 26–34) which suggests the figure of 65 million akçes for the cost of maintaining (i.e. costs for crewing and provisioning but not for commissioning) a fleet of 50 galleys and 13 galleons. Only about 40 million akçes (61.5 per cent of the total) was provided by the treasury; the rest had to be met from extraordinary levies and other campaign contributions by taxpayers. To calculate the real cost of fleet mobilization, one would need to add roughly 600,000 akçes per vessel as the commissioning cost of the galleys and roughly eight times that amount (4.8 million each) for the galleons; see R. Murphey, "Resurgence", pp. 189 (tables) and 190 (fn. 9). Launching costs estimated at 4.8 million akçes per galleon represent an absolute minimum. Real costs probably ranged between 20 and 50 per cent higher; see I. Bostan, *Osmanlı Bahriye Teşkilatı: XVII. Yüzyılda Tersane-i Amire* (Ankara, 1992), p. 95 (fn. 149) which suggests that launching costs of between 5.9 and 7.5 millions per galleon were not uncommon.

22. See, for example, the Ottoman destruction of Pölöske near L. Balaton in Hungary in July 1664. Although the Ottomans had deployed miners supplied with a modest quantity of 5 kantars (620lbs). of gunpowder, once the fort's wooden outer palisades had been reduced to ashes its fate was already sealed, and the application of more violent (and technologically sophisticated) siege methods were rendered superfluous. See the description in Mühürdar, *Cevahir*, fol. 76b.

23. The upgrading of Mosul's defences in 1631, for example, occupied 3,000 locally-recruited men plus a significant portion of the army in the off-season over the better part of a year. For details, see R. Murphey, "Construction of a Fortress at Mosul", in H. Inalcik and O. Okyar (eds), *Social and Economic History of Turkey, 1071–1920* (Ankara, 1980), pp. 163–78.

24. See the *Tarih-i Selaniki* (edition in 2 vols by M. Ipşirli (Istanbul, 1989), Vol. 2, pp. 204–6. Mustafa Ali relates similarly ambitious construction work lasting 45 days following the Ottoman capture of Revan (Erivan) in 1583 and for 30 days following the fall of Tabriz in 1585. Erivan's defences consisted of an outer wall of 43 towers and 1726 embrasures and inner defences with 8 towers and 725 embrasures (M. Ali, *Kunh ul Ahbar*, Nuruosmaniye Lib., Ms.3409, fol. 358a). Tabriz's defences extended over 12,700 ells, equivalent to almost six miles (*Kunh ul Ahbar*, fol. 366a).

25. Ali, *Kunh ül Ahbar*, fol. 362a.

26. See F. Szakály, "The Hungarian-Croatian Border Defense System and Its Collapse", in J. M. Bak and B. K. Kiraly (eds), *From Hunyadi to Rakoczi: War and Society in Medieval and*

217

Early-Modern Hungary, Eastern European Monographs, No. 104 (New York, 1982), p. 149 (fn. 26).

27. See W. Bracewell, *The Uskoks of Senj* (Ithaca, NY, 1992), pp. 36–50. Bracewell (p. 40 and elsewhere) emphasizes the point that it was not before the 1550s that significant administrative centralization took effect. Nouzille (J. Nouzille, *Histoire de Frontières: l'Autriche et l'empire Ottoman* (Paris, 1991), p. 66) describes the essential autonomy enjoyed by the *grenzers* in even more striking terms: "*de l'origine ces refugiés vivent en tout indépendence sous les ordres de leurs chefs élus, les knez*". Nouzille (p. 72 ff) goes on to describe how the Croatian diet happily gave its approval to self-financing schemes and self-governing arrangements that lifted some of the fiscal burden of defence from its shoulders.

28. Recent research has shown that one of the consequences of the slow pace with which a centrally-funded system was emerging was that most of the border forts were poorly constructed *palanka* and *sharampo*-type structures whose inherent vulnerability was compounded by the fact that they were chronically undermanned. See R. Schoffer, "Festungsbau der Türkengrenze: Die Pfandschaft Rann in 16. Jahrhundert", *Zeitschrift des Historischen Vereins fur Steiermark* 75 (1984), pp. 31–59.

29. Concerning the Ottomans' reliance on local initiative and resources for the repair of fortresses, see P. Fodor, "Bauarbeiten der Türken an den Burgen in Ungarn im 16–17. Jahrhundert", *Acta Orientalia Acad. Scient. Hung.* 35 (1981), pp. 55–88: esp. the examples on p. 61.

30. M. S. Kingra, "The *trace italienne* and the military revolution during the Eighty Years' War, 1567–1648", *Journal of Military History* 57 (1993), pp. 431–46: esp. p. 439

31. Quoted by J. Stoye in "The English Ambassador at Istanbul and the Great Turkish War, 1681–1687", *Studia Austro-Polonica* 3 (1983), p. 321 (fn. 30).

32. In the context of the Ottoman military crisis of the late 1690s, for example, the Ottomans undertook an extensive expansion of the port facilities for the servicing of the Danube fleet at Belgrade during a seventeen-day army layover in the city in September 1696. For details, see *Tarih-i Nihidî* (Istanbul University Lib., Ms TY 6053), fols 259b–260a.

33. For the comments of the chief dragoman Alexander Mavrocordato concerning the Ottomans' ability to sustain prolonged conflicts, see J. Stoye, "English Ambassador at Istanbul", p. 327.

34. On the debate in the Ottoman camp on the eve of Hafiz Ahmed Pasha's siege of Baghdad in late autumn 1625 see Naima II, 360: "*Kasım günü geçti deyü sair seferlere kiyas olunmaya, zira Bağdadın mevsimi kışda dır*".

35. H. Inalcik and M. Oğuz (eds), *Gazavat-i Sultan Murad b. Mehmed Han* (Ankara, 1978), p. 30: "*Türk heman otu bakar. Hemen ki ot yerden çıktı, onlar öteden üzerimize gelir*" (*cf., facs., fol. 28a (lines 1–3)*.

36. See G. Perjés, "Army Provisioning, Logistics and Strategy in the Second Half of the 17th Century", *Acta Historica Acad. Scient. Hung.* 16 (1970), p. 15.

37. According to calculations made by Perjés the full support of infantry troops in the field required the presence of one horse for every two men. By this token (see Perjés, "Army Provisioning", p. 14, fn. 38) a force of 24,000 men composed of 18,000 infantry and only 6,000 cavalry still required the services of 13,600 horses. Likewise, a force of 60,000 men similarly composed needed 34,000 horses whose forage requirement could mount to as much as 90 tons of grass or hay per day; see Perjés, "Provisioning", pp. 11, 14 and elsewhere.

38. As an example one might cite the exceptional performance of the Tatar ponies used on

campaign in Poland in 1654, which managed to complete 59 hours of march in continuous stages over a three-day period with only one rest period, taken after the first day's march which lasted 13 hours; see R. Murphey, "Horsebreeding in Eurasia", *Central and Inner Asian Studies* **4** (1990), p. 11 (fn. 3).

39. For the Safavids' use of "scorched earth" tactics against the Ottomans in a mid-sixteenth-century context, see R. Murphey, "Süleyman's Eastern Policy", in H. Inalcik and C. Kafadar (eds), *Süleyman The Second [i.e., the First] and His Time* (Istanbul, 1993), p. 233.

40. See J. H. Pryor, *Geography, Technology and War: Studies in the Maritime History of the Mediterranean, 649–1571* (Cambridge, 1988), p. 177: "a slow, relentless and exhausting drive to gain possession of the bases and islands from which war galleys could control the sea lanes".

41. Kâtib Çelebi, *Tühfet ül Kibar* (Istanbul, 1329), p. 153. On the crewing requirements of the maona, see I. Bostan, *Osmanlı Bahriye Teşkilatı* (Istanbul, 1992), p. 88 (fn. 58).

42. Paul Rycaut, *The Present State of the Ottoman Empire* (London, 1668), p. 207. cf., Rycaut, *The History of the Turkish Empire From The Year 1623 to the Year 1677* [Knolles, 6th edn] (London, 1687), p. 156: "*It happened by God's Providence that that very night there fell such a deluge of rain (. . .)*".

43. On the Ottoman advance, see Silahdar I, 355: "*Be emrullah (. . .) ziyade yağmur yağıp*" and I, 363: "*yağan yağmur dahi esvabları ıslatmak hasebiyle ekseri atdan inip, kimi istirahat, kimi esvabın kurutmak (. . .) ile mukayyed iken (. . .)*". On the attempted retreat, see Silahar I, 365: "*nehr-i Raba gayet tugyan üzere ceriyan etmeğin, bir vechiyle uburu emr-i muhal olup (. . .)*".

44. *Tarih-i Nihadî*, fol. 249a: entry for Muharrem 1108/ August 1696.

45. See the *Nusretname* of Silahdar (a continuation of his history covering the events of 1696–1721), Vol. 1, pt. 3, p. 294.

46. *Tarih-i Raşid* (Istanbul, 1153), Vol. 1, fol. 231b: "*bu mahale gelince on kadar nehirden ubur ederek (. . .)*".

47. See, J. Mears, "Influence of the Turkish Wars in Hungary", in C. K. Pullapilly and E. J. Vankly (eds), *Asia and the West: Essays in Honor of Donald Lach* (Notre Dame, Ind., 1986), p. 138: "*The countryside north of the Danube and east of the Tisza [was] an area of desolate plains and vast swamps*".

48. See Mustafa ibn Molla Rizvan, *Tarih-i Feth-i Bağdad* (Oxford, Bodleian Library Ms Or. 276), fol. 255a. The Ottoman bushel of 37 cubic decimetres was marginally larger than the British imperial bushel of 36 cubic decimetres. The multiplier for converting from British to Ottoman imperial measure is 1.0277.

49. The "Ruzname" in A. Feridun, *Münşeat-i Selatin*, Vol. 1 (Istanbul, 1274), p. 569 records prices of 4, 5 and 6 akçes per kile for wheat (of intrinsically higher value than barley) at the beginning of the campaign as compared with prices ranging as high as 170 akçes per kile for barley by the conclusion of the campaign ("Ruzname", p. 576).

50. For an idea of the dangers associated with these foraging raids, see Feridun, "Ruzname", p. 570: "*azıkcıdan küffar ziyade adam aldı; azıkcı kapu halkından ve Sipah ve Yeniçeriden kafir 100 mikdar adam aldı*", and p. 574: "*otluğa ve azuğa giden kimselerden kafir bi-hadd adam aldı*".

51. Feridun, "Ruzname", Vol. 1, p. 569: "*kimse nimete bakmazdı*"; ibid., p. 572: "*şöyle ucuzluk oldu ki, orduda nimete kimse bakmaz oldu*". The meaning of *nimet* (favour) in this context is food, in particular the troops' daily bread rations.

52. See, for example, A. Balisch, "Infantry Battlefield Tactics", *Studies in History and Politics* **3** (1983–4), pp. 43–60, esp., p. 43.

53. Speaking of different places and times John Lynn treats "patriotism" as a purported source

of inspiration to troops with similar scepticism. See in particular, J. A. Lynn, *Bayonets of the Republic: Motivation and Tactics in the Army of Revolutionary France, 1791–1799* (Urbana, IL, 1984), p. 36: "*Such elevated concerns as patriotism and ideology cannot be entirely read out of the combat picture for all armies in all circumstances; however, for most soldiers (. . .) it seems that patriotism and the like are far from their minds*".

54. "Ruzname" in the *Münşeat* of Feridun, Vol. 1, p. 574.

55. See, for example, the eyewitness account (*An Historical Description of the Conquest of the City of Buda* (London, 1686), p. 43) which indicates that of 8,000 Janissaries who set out from Edirne as part of the Grand Vezier's relief force, only 5,000 remained in camp when the army arrived in Hungary.

56. See the chapter in Silahdar II, 243 entitled "*Bela-i Kaht*". Silahdar indicates that the price of a kile (56.5 lbs) of wheat in the years between 1684 and 1686 (1096–1098 A. H.) ranged between 200 and 240 akçes. Crop shortfalls in these years affected Anatolia with particular severity, but the overall effect was an empire-wide belt tightening.

57. On the attitudinal gulf that separated the Ottomans and their sixteenth-century allies of the steppe, see R. Murphey, "Süleyman's Eastern Policy", p. 237.

58. Kâtib Çelebi, *Fezleke-i Tevarih*, Vol. 2 (Istanbul, 1287), p. 352 (line 15).

59. See Çagatay Uluçay, *XVII,. Asırda Saruhan'da Eşkiyalık ve Halk Hareketleri* (Istanbul, 1944), p. 465 (Doc. dated Jan. 1698): "*yem ve yemek (. . .) be her nefere beş para*", and H. Inalcik, "Military and Fiscal Transformation", *Archivum Ottomanicum* 6, pp. 292–3 (fn. 23); rations allowance of one-eighth of a gurush = 10 akçes.

60. Mustafa Cezar, *Osmanlı Tarihinde Levendler* (Istanbul, 1965), pp. 355–6.

61. See Silahdar II, 270 (1098/1686–1687) on the extortionate terms demanded by the *levend* chief: "*altışar aylık ulufe ve yüzer guruş bahşiş verin, gidelim, ve ila ne denizi geçeriz ve ne sefere gideriz*".

62. In 1687, following the fall of Buda, 85 purses (42,500 gurush) had been set aside for the recruitment of *levends*. While under normal circumstances this should have sufficed to recruit more than 1,500 men, based on the extortionate rate of 115 gurush per man it would cover the costs for fewer than 400; see Silahdar II, p. 268.

63. The timing of these events is given as follows by Silahdar (see Vol. 2, pp. 268–70): arrival of *levends* to Üsküdar in mid-May 1687 (A.D.) = gurre-i Receb 1098 (A.H.); completion of negotiations on terms of pay on 16 June = 5th Şaban; departure for the front on 2 July = 21st Şaban.

64. For more detail, see below Ch. 5: Army Provisioning.

65. For a revisionist view, see R. Murphey, "An Ottoman View From the Top", in *Turcica* **28** (1996), pp. 319–38.

66. For an account of the policy shifts which accompanied Rüstem Pasha's succession to the grand vezierate in 1544, see R. Murphey, "Süleyman's Eastern Policy", pp. 245–6. Some contemporary Ottoman political commentaries suggest that Rüstem Pasha's policy shifts were motivated by pure self-interest; see Murphey, "Süleyman's Eastern Policy", p. 245 (n. 51).

67. The sources disagree on the exact date of Ibrahim Pasha's death. Naima, following Hasan Bey-zade, records the date as 9 Muharrem 1010/ 10 July 1601 (Naima I, 251), but Topçular Kâtibi says his death came in Zilkaade 1009 / May 1601 (see Vienna, ÖNB, Ms. Mxt. 130, fol. 143a), although the choice of a successor delayed the resolution of the matter until July (Ms. Mxt. 130, fol. 144a). As a result of this indecision it was not until 9 August (9th Safer 1010) that the new commander Yemişci Hasan Paşa was ready to leave for the front, and even his record-breaking speed covering the ground to Zemun

in just 27 days' march (Naima II, 253) brought him to the staging area for the campaign on the 7th of Rebiülevvel / 6th September, far too late to activate the complex machinery of war in time to take decisive action that season.

68. Hintze's periodization associates the development of a state capacity for military coercion with the period after 1800; see P. Paret, "Armed Forces and the State: The Historical Essays of Otto Hinze", in B. Bond and I. Roy (eds), *War and Society*, Vol. 2 (London, 1977), pp. 151–7, esp. p. 153. It is perhaps significant that in 1826, when European states were dedicated to the expansion of their military capabilities, the Ottomans were finally driven to abolish the Janissary corps because, far from representing or reinforcing state authority, it had increasingly (as had been shown in the context of the Serbian uprising of 1804–5) become associated with resistance to and undermining of the state.

69. See H. Inalcik, "The Socio-Political Effects of the Diffusion of Fire-Arms in The Middle East", in V. J. Parry and M. E. Yapp (eds), *War and Technology in the Middle East* (London, 1975), pp. 195–217. See also R. Jennings, "Fire-Arms, Bandits and Gun Control: Some Evidence on Ottoman Policy Towards Firearms and the Possession of the reaya from Judicial Records of Kayseri 1600–1627", *Archivum Ottomanicum* 6 (1980), pp. 339–58. On the relative accessibility of guns in the Ottoman Empire as compared with Moscovite Russia in the seventeenth century, see T. Esper, "Military Self-Sufficiency and Weapons Technology in Moscovite Russia", *Slavic Review* 28 (1969), pp. 185–208.

70. See Mustafa Ali, *Kunh ül Ahbar* (Nuruosmaniye Lib., Ms 3409, fol. 350a: "*eday-i hizmetde cust u çalak deprenmemişti*" and later on the same page: "*gönüllü gönülsüz deprenip, hoşnuddan hâli evzaı görülmemiş idi*".

71. The presence of the *han* in person according to Crimean rules of protocol implied the presence of a troop escort composed of at least twelve *tapkirs* (unit of 6,000 men); see Evliya Çelebi, *Seyahatname*, Vol. 7 (Istanbul 1314), pp. 532–3. Ali's recording of the arrival of 100,000 Tatars under their *han* at the Ottoman camp in early August 1594 (*Kunh ül Ahbar*, fol. 409a) describes more their ceremonial than their active presence in the Ottoman army. In actual deployments contingents of 30,000–40,000 men was more usual; see the example cited by Ali with reference to the 1594 campaign where he notes the dispatch of 30,000 Tatars across the Raba to chase and prevent the approach of an Austrian relief force advancing towards Györ (*ibid.* fol. 412a).

72. On Gazi Giray's participation in the Györ campaign, see Mustafa Ali, *Kunh ül Ahbar*, fols 409a–415a. In Ali's view part of the obvious incompatibility between Ottoman and Tatar forces in this battle was attributable to the commander Koca Sinan Pasha's high-handed treatment of the *han* which served to accentuate what were ordinarily bridgeable differences between the joint campaigners. On the conditions prompting Gazi Giray's rapid reinstatement to the hanate in 1596, see H. Inalcik, "Gazi Giray II", *Encyclopaedia of Islam*, Vol. 2, p. 1046.

73. The main divisions were Kartli in the centre, Kahketi in the East and Imereti in the West; see W. E. D. Allen, *Russian Embassies to the Georgian Kings (1589–1605)*, 2 vols. (Cambridge, 1972), foreword to the first volume, p. xvii.

74. See Rana von Mende (ed.), *Mustafâ Ali's Fursat-name* (Berlin, 1989), text facs., fol. 52b: "*sal be sal yüz bin sikke altun haraç . . .*".

75. See *Selaniki Tarihi*, Vol. 1, p. 152 which dates this diplomatic initiative to November 1584. See also, B. Kütükoğlu, *Osmanlı-İran Siyasi Münasebetleri, 1578–1590* (Istanbul, 1962), p. 139 (fn. 251).

76. Selaniki II: 835 places the arrival of Simon to Istanbul as a captive in December 1599.

77. See, for example, a case documented in volume three of the *Mühimme* in an entry (No.

1425) dated 28th September 1584. This entry registers the payment of a daily allowance of 100 akçes (the revenue equivalent of a medium-sized ziamet) to a certain Constantine who is identified as the brother of the ruler of Imeretia. The grant was in exchange for military and other services.

78. For the seven-month siege of Kutaisi by Ercil Han (i.e. Erekle I (r. 1688–91 and 1695–1703) beginning in April 1698 see the Nusretname of Silahdar (Parmaksizoğlu edn), Vol. 1, pt. 2, pp. 344–7. See in particular p. 346: "*Katayislilerle eyalet halkı serdarın otağına gelerek el öptüler. Memleketin ileri gelenlerine rütbelerine göre hilatlar giydirildi*".

Chapter Three

1. Writing circa 1630 Koçi Bey suggested only some 2,000 of the once legion *akıncı* remained; see A. K. Aksüt (ed.), *Koçi Bey Risalesi [Birinci Risale, 1041/1631]*, (Istanbul, 1939), p. 40.

2. Zarain, *A Relation of the Late Siege and Taking of the City of Babylon By The Turke* (London, 1639), p. 11. These numbers suggest that one-third of the troops taking part were infantrymen, but the obvious rounding of the figures may well exaggerate their actual presence in combat.

3. Estimates usually range within 50,000 of a total of 200,000. See the "breve relazione della miliza" in E. Albieri (ed.), *Le Relazione degli ambasciatori Veneti nel secolo XVI*, Seri III/ vol. 2 (Firenze, 1855), p. 311 which lists 230,000 (80,000 in Europe and 150,000 in the Asian provinces) for the year 1575. The number for the year 1634 given in Capello's account rises to 250,000; see L. Firpo (ed.), *Relazioni Di Ambasciatori Veneti al Senato, Vol. XIII: Constantinopoli, 1590–1793* (Torino, 1984), p. 684. See also Chapt. 1, n. 11 above.

4. Evliya Çelebi (*Seyahatname* I: 200) suggests a total of 166,200 men; 74,600 from the European provinces and 91,600 from Anatolia. But it must be remembered all these numbers represent full mobilization potential as opposed to real deployment figures.

5. For details of the geographical distribution of the 60,616 timariots who came from the core provinces (37,408 from Europe and 22,608 from the western districts of Anatolia) see Table 3.1.

6. The proportion in 1527 was 42 per cent and in 1631 it was 44 per cent of the total; see details in Tables 3.1 and 3.2, fn. 5.

7. Ayn -i Ali, *Kavanin Risalesi* (Istanbul, 1280), pp. 16–33.

8. See A. K. Aksüt (ed.), *Koçi Bey Risalesi [Ikinci Risale, 1050/1640]* (Istanbul, 1939), pp. 99–103.

9. Istanbul, Başbakanlık Arşivi, Tapu ve Tahrir Defterleri No. 727.

10. See *n*3 above.

11. Tafur's statement that the army of Murad II (1421–51) consisted of 600,000 horsemen is obviously based on impressions rather than detailed review; see M. Letts (tr. and ed.), *Pero Tafur: Travels and Adventures 1435–1439* (New York, 1926), p. 126.

12. The Ottoman chronicle record notes the Janissaries' participation in the Györ campaign of 1594 under Koca Sinan Pasha as a precedent-making turning point, and indicates the reluctance of the then commander of the Janissaries Mehmed Agha to agree to the grand

vezier's use of 4,000 of his troops; see *Peçevi Tarihi* II: 145 (lines 13–14): "*bu zamana gelince Yeniçeri ağalan serdarlara koşuntu olmak vaki olmamış idi*". See also A. K. Aksüt (ed.), *Koçi Bey Risalesi [Birinci Risale, 1041]* (Istanbul, 1939), p. 21: "*vüzera-i selef (. . .) padişah kullan kataen kullanmazlardı*".

13. As a method of recruitment the devshirme was finally abolished in the early part of Ahmed III's reign (1703–30); see V. L. Ménage, "devshirme", *Encyclopaedia of Islam*, Vol. 2, p. 212.

14. See the facsimile of the document in John K. Vasdravellis, *Klephts, Armatoles and Pirates in Macedonia During the Rule of the Turks, 1627–1821* (Thessaloniki, 1975), pp. 112–14 (doc. no. 10). The directive suggests that on this occasion, in contradiction to previous norms and practices, provision was made for the quota to be divided on an equal basis between Christian youth on the one hand, and Muslim volunteers from Albania and Bosnia on the other.

15. See Silahdar II: 264. By this date inflationary pressures had boosted the base pay rate for newly inducted Janissaries from the daily 3 akçes standard in the time of Ahmed I (1603–17) to 14 akçes per day (see Silahdar, II: 264, line 12). On the use of the white felt cap as the exclusive emblem of the Janissaries, see I. H. Uzunçarşılı, *Osmanlı Devleti Teşkilatından Kapukulu Ocakları*, Vol. 1 (Istanbul, 1943), p. 263.

16. For a comparative idea of global figures including Janissaries assigned to provincial garrison duty, see Table 3.5, fn. 4.

17. See TKSMA, D. 9619. The precise figures were as follows: Janissaries, 6,362; Sipahis, 3,670; Cannon Corps and Armourers, 1,666; staff of the Imperial Stables, 2,630 and other non-combatants, 1,284. The *Masar* roll call (for Muharrem, Safer and Rebiülevvel of 948) corresponds to the pay period May–July 1541.

18. The figure of 32,794 excludes 21,428 Janissaries assigned to provincial garrison duty; see O. L. Barkan, "1070–1071 (1660–1661) Tarihli Osmanlı Bütçesi", *Iktisat Fakültesi Mecmuası* **17** (1955–6), p. 310, *n*19.

19. See B. Brue, *Journal de la campagne que le Grand Vésir Ali Pacha a faite en 1715 pour la conquête de la Morée* (Paris, 1870 (repr. Athens,1986), p. 66 which records the arrival in the first instance of 40,000 of the Janissaries under their commander, but notes the later arrival of 10,000 stragglers, 15,000 under the separate command of the sultan's master of the hounds (*samsuncu başı*) and 2,000 belonging to the Cairo regiment, bringing the grand total to 67,000 men.

20. See Brue, *Journal*, p. 42 (diary entry for 11th August 1715): "*le nombre des Janissaires étoit réduit à peu de chose; on n'en comptoit guère plus de 10,000 dans le camp*".

21. Even in the most ambitious of all the Ottoman mobilizations – that undertaken for Vienna in 1683 – the Janissary component was 60 companies, 20 in the centre and 20 each for the right and left flanks (see Silahdar II: 45). With input from the armourers (*cebeci*), gunners (*topcu*) (for their registered numbers see Table 3.5), a host of casually employed trench diggers (an example from the 1638 Baghdad campaign records the recruitment of 4,400 trench diggers together with a few hundred drovers and carpenters to serve at the front in Iraq, see B. B. A., Kâmil Kepeci 2580), and a number of more specialized miners and sappers, the number of dedicated assault troops might rise to nearer to 15,000. However, it bears recalling that their most active participation was confined to the final stages of a siege.

22. Even in the late nineteenth century, urban agglomerations supporting populations in excess of 80,000 were still a relative rarity. See R. Murphey, "Patterns of Trade Along the Via Egnatia" in E. Zachariadou (ed.), *The Via Egnatia Under Ottoman Rule, 1380–1699*

(Rethymnon, 1996), p. 180 (Table 1) citing data which shows only three Balkan cities with more than 50,000 inhabitants.

23. See above Ch. 1, n21–2 and n30.

24. See Montecuccoli, *Memoires sur l'art militaire* (Paris, 1760), p. 58 describing the participation by 20,000 cavalry and 30,000 infantry in the Habsburg's successful siege of Gran (Esztergom) in 1595.

25. Only a quarter of the total (some 9,000–10,000 men) were directly under Montecuccoli's authority and under obligation to carry out his orders. For a brief but pithy account of the intricate wrangling that preceded the 1664 mobilization on the European side, see H. F. Helmholt *et al.*, *The World's History: Vol. 7 – Western Europe to 1800* (London, 1903), pp. 471–2.

26. For a summary of the current state of study on Ottoman demographic history, see H. Inalcik, "The Empire's Population and Population Movements" in H. Inalcik and D. Quataert (eds), *An Economic and Social History of the Ottoman Empire, 1300–1914* (Cambridge, 1994) pp. 25–9.

27. See C. Finkel, *The Administration of Warfare: the Ottoman Military Campaigns in Hungary, 1593–1606* (Vienna, 1988). See in particular the discussion of the difficulties encountered in the data of making the distinction (if any) between "budgets" relating to wartime (which included some general administrative expenditure) and peacetime budgets which incorporated extensive allocations, either for expenses related directly to war preparations, or for the payment of the salaries of military personnel; Finkel, *Military Administration*, pp. 218–35.

28. See Ö. L. Barkan, "933–934/1527–1528 malî yılına ait bütçe örneği", *Iktisat Fakültesi Mecmuası* **15** (1953–4), p. 277 (Table 7) and pp. 280–96. Compare Inalcik and Quataert, *An Economic And Social History* (Cambridge, 1994), pp. 81–2 (Tables I.20 and I.22). If we examine the figures for treasury revenues including timar lands of 477.4 million akçes, Egypt's role in subsidizing deficits of other regions of the empire is even clearer. The surplus after expenditure credited to the central treasury for Egypt and Syria alone came to 100 million akçes (161.1 in revenues against only 61.1 in expenditure). This surplus alone represented the equivalent of one-fifth of treasury revenues from all sources $(100.0 / 477.4 = 20.9\%)$.

29. See G. Orhonlu, "Khazine", *Encyclopaedia of Islam*, Vol. 4, p. 1184, where the mechanism governing transfers between the sultan's private "Inner" and the public "Outer" treasuries is discussed.

30. The remittance from Egypt in 1567 was 560,000 gold pieces; see Barkan, "974–975/1567–1568 malî yılına ait bütçe", *Iktisat Fakültesi Mecmuası* **19** (1957–58), p. 302. But levels around 600,000 were common in the seventeenth century; see *Suver-i Hutut-i Hümayun* (Istanbul Univ. Lib., Ms, 6110), fols 56a–56b. In 1596–7 (a war year) the level of 612,000 gold pieces is recorded; see S. J. Shaw, *Budget of Ottoman Egypt 1005–1006/1596–1597* (The Hague, 1968), text p. 82, trans., p. 206. It bears recalling that, while 600,000 gold ducats might cover 72 million akçes of expenditure at state-controlled rates of exchange, by taking advantage of open market rates in the period of shrinking treasury reserves during the 1630s a sum close to double the standard akçe amount could be realized. On the fluctuation of exchange rates for the Venetian ducat to levels in excess of 220 akçes, see H. Sahillioğlu, "Sikke Raici", *Belgeler* **2** (1964), p. 233. For the meteoric rise in the value of gold during the wars of the *Sacra Ligua*, see Ş. Pamuk, "Money in the Ottoman Empire, 1326–1914", in Inalcik and Quataert (eds) *An Economic and Social Hist.*

of the Ottoman Empire (Cambridge, 1994), p. 964 (Table A.6). Exchange rates for the Egyptian gold coin are given in *ibid.*, p. 963 (Table A.5).

31. According to Alvise Contarini writing in the late 1630s the balance in the Inner Treasury amounted to 15 million ducats (1.8 billion akçes), more than enough to close even the widest budget gap; see L. Firpo (ed.), *Relazioni di Ambasciatori* (Torino, 1984), p. 820.

32. See for example the "budget" for the year 1613 which shows revenues of 422 million akçes against expenditures of 420.7 millions, leaving a modest surplus of 1.3 millions (B.B.A., Maliyeden Müdevver Defterleri No. 2725). However, regular Outer Treasury revenues at this time amounted to only 392 million akçes, and without the 30 million akçe credit from the sultan, the operating budget would have shown a shortfall of 7 per cent.

33. In revenue terms treasury receipts increased from the 1527 revenue level (without timar) of 277.2 million akçes or ($\div 60$) 4.62 million gold ducats (see *n27* above) to the 5.38 million level recorded by Ottavio Bon in the early 1600s (see L. Firpo (ed.), *Relazioni*, pp. 467–8). Expressed in terms of the seventeenth-century silver exchange, a revenue level of 5.38 million gold ducats was sufficient to cover expenditures in excess of 645 million akçes.

34. See J. B. Collins, *Fiscal Limits of Absolutism* (Berkeley, CA, 1988), p. 156 where it is noted that much of the 180 per cent increase in state revenues from taxation over the two decades between 1620 and the early 1640s (121 per cent rise between 1620 and 1634, followed by renewed increases amounting to 60 per cent between 1634 and 1643) came from extraordinary tax levies, in particular military surtaxes. On the general practice of using military surcharges to close budget gaps in France, see Collins, *Fiscal Limits*, pp. 134, 141–2, 149–50, 156 and 164.

35. See A. Feridun, *Münşeat-i Selatin* (Istanbul, 1275), Vol. 2, pp. 304–7.

36. Fleet operations in Crete around this time placed a heavier than usual burden on the treasury. For the high costs associated with naval warfare, see above, Ch. 2: Cost Constraints.

37. The register BBA, Kâmil Kepeci No. 1927 provides a full summary of daily receipts and disbursements during the Grand Vezier Hüsrev Pasha's four-month march from Hamadan to Baghdad (June–September 1630), the two-month siege of Baghdad during October and November, the retreat from Baghdad to winter quarters at Mardin (December 1630 to January 1631) and the four months of army demobilization during the winter season (February to May 1631).

38. Compare this with the 8.3 per cent figure for 1653 (see *n35* above). The higher proportion in the data for 1630 is explained by the fact that here we are dealing with figures for the grand vezier's war chest (270 millions), not the full range of the treasury's revenues. The cash figure in the two cases is comparable: 48.1 million akçes in one case, 51.1 million in the other.

39. The prescribed daily rate of pay for entry level Janissaries in the time of Ahmed I (r. 1603–17) was just three akçes. By comparison promotion to a cavalry regiment implied a minimal salary of ten akçes per diem. See I. Petrosiian (ed.), *Mebde-yi Kanun-i Yeniçeri Ocağı Tarihi* (Moscow, 1987), fol. 39b (line 1) and 77a (lines 1–3): "*Yeniçeri yoldaşlarından hizmeti mukabelesinde, ve seferlerde dilaverlik edenlere Sipahilik verilmek lazım geldikte on akçe ile olur*".

40. On the significant drop shown in the data for 1609 and 1670, see above, Table 3.5, *n5*.

41. See Kâtib Çelebi, *Düstur ül Amel* (Istanbul, 1280), p. 132 (lines 15–17): "*zararsız kesret ve*

galebesine kail olmak lazımdır, nefer ziyadeliğinden ol kadar beis yoktur"; in loose English equivalent: "there is no great harm done by allowing small oversubscriptions in the military ranks as long as care is taken to maintaining the proper balances" [between high- and low-salaried ranks and between rival Janissary and Sipahi regiments].

42. On the Ottomans' use of emergency "loans" from normally tax-exempt funds such as the religious endowments as a source of short-term credit for the financing of war expenses, see R. Murphey, "Critica", *Archivum Ottomanicum* **13** (1993–4), pp. 379–80.

43. For details, see Maps 1 and 2.

44. Voltaire's views on Ottoman activity in the military sphere are summarized in R. Murphey, "Critica", pp. 377–8. For an idea of the scale and credibility of Ottoman military preparations for, and performance during, the Austro-Ottoman war of 1737–9, see L. Cassels, *The Struggle for the Ottoman Empire 1717–1740* (London, 1966), p. 184: "Trial of Strength". In a clear symbolic reference to the perilous and uncertain nature of the undertaking the Habsburg emperor had announced the inception of war by the traditional ringing of the *Türkenglocken*: see Cassels, *Struggle*, p. 126.

45. An isolated example of the recording of central treasury disbursements for fortress repair is the payment of a lump sum of 130,000 akçes made to the sancak bey of Stolni Belgrade (Székesfehérvár) in 1548; see Barkan, "954–955 Bütçe", *Iktisat Fakültesi Mecmuası* **19** (1957–8), p. 257 (item no. 18).

46. M. Ali, *Kunh ül Ahbar* (Nuruosmaniye Lib. Ms 3409), fol. 361a. Some of the 10,000 troops were transfers from nearby border fortresses such as Erzurum and Kars, but fully 8,650 men (82 per cent of the total), representing an annual wage bill of nearly 40 million akçes, were new recruits. Their wages had to be paid either by finding new resources or reallocating existing ones.

47. See above, this chapter, *n*31. Revenues nearly reaching the 600 million level are recorded in the Tarhoncu budget of 1653.

48. See B. B. A, Maliyeden Müdevver 18708 which documents the transport of 319 kiles of grain on 58 packhorses for a cost of 28,080 akçes.

49. The state-controlled market price for one kile of wheat according to the price regulations of 1640 was 55 akçes; see M. Kütükoğlu (ed.), *1640 Tarihli Narh Defteri* (Istanbul, 1983), p. 90.

50. Mevkufatî, *Vakiat-i Ruz-Merre*, Vol. 4 (Esad Efendi Ms 2437), fol. 132a.

51. The exact breakdown of these costs was as follows:

Purchase price of 43,872 kiles of grain @ 80 akçes per kile = 3,509,760 akçes
Shipping costs for 43,872 kiles of grain @ 14 akçes per kile = 614,208

Total annual cost for provisioning of Azak = 4,123,968.

52. See, *Suver-i Hutut-i Hümayun* (Istanbul University Library, Ms 6110), fol. 203b: an order in which the sultan requests the preparation of 80,000 kantars (4,515.5 metric tons) of dry biscuit for the sustaining of a force of 80,000 men on the march for a period of 80 days.

53. See, for example, the tax credits from several areas of the interior for the meeting of the wage payments of the Kars garrison in 1636, recorded in R. Murphey, *Regional Structure in the Ottoman Economy* (Wiesbaden,1987), p. 15 (items 21–2), 27 (item 14) and 199 (item e) amounting to a cumulative total of 6.7 million akçes. The size of the Kars garrison is revealed in a near-contemporary source to be 1,002 Janissaries and 301 local recruits for a total of 1,303 men (see BBA, Maliyeden Müdevver 7277, pp. 92–6). In the register for

1636 revenues amounting to 8.97 million akçes for wages and 3.06 million for meat supplies were contributed from Diyarbekir's tax revenues to meet the basic costs of maintaining the Van garrison; Murphey, *Regional Structure*, p. 216.

54. K. Hegyi, "Province Hongroise", *Acta Historica Acad. Scient. Hung.* **33** (1987), p. 212.

55. If we accept the higher figure of 22,000 men, then the three key garrisons of Buda and Pest (collectively 4446) and Esztergom (2775) whose troop complement amounted to 7,221 men accounted for nearly one third of the total. These troop concentrations are recorded in L. Fekete, *Buda and Pest under Turkish Rule* (Budapest, 1976), pp. 17–18. Similar figures are recorded in Gy. Kaldy-Nagy's *16. yüzyılda Macaristan'da Türk Yönetimi* (Budapest, 1974), p. 27. However, Kaldy-Nagy's figures are perhaps reflective of the different military conditions that prevailed by the 1560s when the Ottomans were more securely established in the province. He notes, for example, that while the Buda garrison in 1543 was almost 3,000 strong, by 1569 (after Maximillian II's Peace Treaty of 1568) the troop strength had been reduced to only about 1,600 men. On general Ottoman troop reductions in Hungary at the close of Süleyman I's reign, see Kaldy-Nagy, p. 43.

56. See B. B. A, Maliyeden Müdevver 6415, p. 4: "*icmal-i Yeniçeriyan-i Budin, Vaç, (. . .); nefer 8,239, al mukarrer fi sene-i kâmile, 26,773,558 akçe*". The information contained in this register applies to the hicri year 1052 (1642–3). Even at the height of Ottoman troop commitments for the initial period of Ottoman involvement during the 1540s the total for the four principal fortresses of Buda, Pest, Székesfehérvár and Esztergom came to just 10,200 troops (2,965 + 1,481 + 2,978 + 2,775); see L. Fekete, *Buda and Pest Under Turkish Rule* (Budapest, 1976), p. 17.

57. The notion of a static Ottoman military posture unresponsive to real military needs is proposed by Hegyi in a recently published study. But her suggestion does not seem to be be borne out in the evidence supplied by Ottoman documentary sources. Compare for example the statistics cited in *n*55 above. Hegyi's contention is expressed in the following form: "*Throughout Ottoman rule [in Hungary] the military force consisted of a large number of troops and (n.b.) they were not reduced in the relatively long period of peace either*"; see K. Heygi, "Ottoman Military Force in Hungary", in G. David and P. Fodor (eds), *Hungarian-Ottoman Relations in the Age of Süleyman the Magnificent* (Budapest, 1994), p. 147.

58. Barkan, "974–975/1567–68 malî yılına ait bir Osmanlı bütçesi", *Iktisat Fakültesi Mecmuası* **19** (1957–8), pp. 277–332.

59. The global figures for this period are: 1653–51,047 (Feridun, *Münşeat* II: 305); 660–54,222 (IFM 17: 310); 1665–49,556 (IFM 17: 216); 1670–53,849 (IFM 17: 263). The number recorded for the Istanbul based regiments in 1665 seems unrealistically low (20,468; see IFM 17: 216), but overall figures are consistent with what we know of global Janissary enrolment in the seventeenth century.

60. The breakdown provided by Hüseyn Hezarfen for this period shows the following division:

Geographical Region	Number of Companies	Number of Men
Asian Provinces	40	7,046
European Provinces	44	9,770
Crete	31	4,585
TOTALS	115	21,401

(average company size = 186 men)

See Paris, Bibliothèque Nationale, Ms A. F. 40, fol. 86b–87b.

61. See *n*52 above on the assignment of revenues from Diyarbekir to meet border defence needs in Van.

62. For Albania the short-term benefit of Ottoman military involvement in Crete in terms of wartime investment and increased circulation of goods was considerable, but when the conflict ended in 1669 and the principal source of economic stimulation was removed, the region's own development and its fuller integration with the economies of contiguous regions was cut short.

63. Kaldy-Nagy, *16. yüzyılda Macaristan*, p. 19 notes that the Egyptian subsidy to the Buda treasury for the year 1559–60 was 300,000 gold pieces.

64. See Topkapı Sarayı Müzesi Arşivi, D. 9619 dated 948 A. H. Most of the sum was distributed in gold from the sultan's private reserves.

65. For details, see Topkapı Sarayı Müzesi Arşivi [TKSMA], D. 2007.

66. See TKSMA, D. 2008, fol. 10b. The final disbursements were concentrated in the seven-day period between 14 and 20 Ramazan 1044 corresponding to 4–10 March 1635. Using then current exchange rates of 220 akçes per gold piece, the sum total of these advance disbursements came to nearly 83 million akçes.

67. For an attempt to reconstruct Ottoman costs in preparing for a joint naval campaign with France, see G. Veinstein, "Les préparatifs de la campagne navale Franco-Turque de 1552 à travers les ordres du divan Ottoman", *Revue de l'Occident Musulman et de la Mediterranée* **39** (1985), pp. 35–67.

68. See B. B. A., Maliyeden Müdevver 16,008.

69. For Tabanı-yassı's term of office as governor of Egypt between September 1628 and October 1630, see E. von Zambaur, *Manuel de Généalogie* (Hanover,1927 [Arabic edn, *Mu'jam al Ansab*, Cairo, 1951]), p. 252.

70. An imperial writ sent to Tabanı-yassı during his governorship of Egypt between 1628 and 1630 set the exchange rate at 72 paras for each gold piece: see *Suver-i Hutut-i Hümayun*, (Istanbul University Lib., Ms 6110), fol. 56a–56b. Using a multiplier of two, the result for the gold piece is 144 akçes, but since we know that during the period 1625–32 the gold exchange rate rose to levels as high as 220 akçes, it might be thought that the three-akçe multiplier for the para serves as a more accurate measure of real levels of expenditure. On the other hand, using the two-akçe equivalent translates the Egyptian purse of 25,000 paras into an equivalent value of 50,000 akçes which falls more closely into line with standard equivalents used in central treasury accounts. It seems likely, therefore, that for official accounting purposes and in currency conversions two akçes per para was the rate applied.

71. Kâtib Çelebi, *Fezleke-i Tevarih*, Vol. 2, p. 110: "*asker 1033 [=1624 A. D.] senesinden berü der-i devlete varmayıp, asitaneye gitmeğe talib oldular*".

72. The record of these events preserved in local histories suggests that Tabanı-yassı's mobilization came too late to save Sana, which fell to the rebel Zaidi Imam Muhammad Muayyed in March 1629 (Receb 1038). It was not until the first days of January 1630 that a sufficiently large force could be mobilized in Egypt to confront the Yemeni challenge. The most detailed account of these events is found in A. Raşid, *Tarih-i Yemen ve Sana* 2 vols. (Istanbul, 1291), Vol. 1, pp. 241–6.

73. The relatively modest charges for camel hire (1,500 paras = 3,000 akçes per animal) reflect particular conditions in Arabia where supply was plentiful. Overland transport costs were also kept to a minimum by the smaller size of the force deployed for the Yemen campaign. The largest group (500 camels) was assigned to transport the commander

Nasuh Pasha's baggage. The lower rates also reflect the fact that grain was shipped from Egypt via the Red Sea to coastal depots in Yemen. The overland trek to troops at the front was thus relatively short. For a comparison showing distance-related overland transport rates, see Ch. 4 below.

74. Gunpowder supply in Egypt was relatively plentiful and the Ottomans relied on it for use in other theatres of war linked by Mediterranean sea routes. The price, 1,000 paras per kantar (roughly 45 akçes per okka), corresponds to what we know from contemporary sources about the standard price for the lower quality range of powder. Prices recorded for Istanbul in 1640 ranged between 45 (for lowest quality) and 65 (for top quality) "black powder"; see M. Kütükoğlu (ed.), *1640 Tarihli Narh Defteri* (Istanbul, 1983), p. 228.

Chapter Four

1. As an indication of the relatively high cost associated with troop transport over water even (as for example across the Red Sea) when the distances involved were not very great, see the example of the 1629 Yemen campaign presented in Ch. 3 above. By themselves the payments made to Yusuf Agha for ship repairs at Bulak made up fully three-tenths of the amount budgeted for purchase of army supplies and equipment, totalling 14.3 million paras (28.6 million akçes); see p. 89 (Account No. II) above.

2. G. Perjés, *The Fall of Medieval Hungary: Mohacs 1526- Buda 1541* (Boulder, Co, 1989), pp. 33 (*n*18) and 37. The distance between Istanbul and Belgrade over the imperial highway system was perhaps marginally less than 1,000 km. Skrivanic ("Roman Roads", in F. W. Carter (ed.), *An Historical Geography of the Balkans* (London, 1977), p. 117) gives the distance over the *via militaris* as 624 Roman miles, equivalent to 924.5 km or 574.5 miles.

3. For details, see Kara Çelebi-zade Abdülaziz Efendi, *Tarih-i Feth-i Revan ve Bağdad* (Istanbul: Veliyuddin Lib., Ms 2424), fol. 28a for the outward and fol. 34b for the return march.

4. See the campaign journal inscribed in the margins of a copy of Kemal Paşa-zade's history of the Ottoman dynasty, Vienna: Österreichische Nationalbibliothek, Ms H.O. 46a, fol. 124a.

5. Compare the rate of advance of Süleyman I's army in 1529 during the final approaches to Vienna. Süleyman covered the last 12 halting stations (*menzil*) in 29 days. In other words, active march accounted for only about four tenths of the total time elapsed; see "Ruzname", Feridun, *Münşeat I*, p. 573. In the same source a stage of three and a half Hungarian miles (approx. 17.5 statute miles) covered by the army in a single day's march is described as exceptionally challenging; see Feridun I, 573: "*Estergom üç buçuk mildir. Gayet uzak konakdır, ve derbend dahi aşıldı*". On the equivalent of the Austrian postal mile of 7586 metres (4.7 English miles) and the Hungarian mile of 8335 metres (5.2 miles), see Horace Doursther, *Dictionnaire Universel des poids et mesures anciens et modernes* (Bruxelles, 1890), pp. 209–10.

6. See Vienna, ÖNB, Ms H. O. 46a, fol. 124a.

7. *ibid.* Departure from Edirne on the 6th of Ramazan 1073 (14th March 1663) and arrival in Esztergom in the first days of Muharrem 1074 (5–7 August 1663). The itinerary makes no mention of delays due to exceptionally heavy rains or other adverse weather conditions.

8. See S. Ünver, "Dördüncü Sultan Murad'in Revan Seferi Kronolojisi", *Belleten* XVI/ 64 (1952), p. 566.

9. See R. Murphey, "Horsebreeding in Eurasia", *Central and Inner Asian Studies* 4 (1990), p. 2 (fn. 3), citing an example from the Polish campaign of 1654.

10. Silahdar II, 362: "*bir mikdar deve ve 100 kadar çatal bargirli Tatar gönderilip, piyadeyi geçirdiler*".

11. Feridun, *Münşeat* I, 574: "*halk ekseri (. . .) çadırsız, esbabsız hayran ve ser-gerdan gezdi*".

12. Feridun, *Münşeat* I, 576: "*Sabah namazından mukaddem suvar olunup, yatsu namazı vaktinde konağa gelindi. Yolda bir mertebe davarlar durdu ki bi-hesab ve bi-hadd. Ve halkın ekseri ağruğun bulmayıp, yabanda yattı*".

13. Mühürdar, *Cevahir ül Tevarih* (Leiden Ms), fol. 27b: "*Islam padişahi ziyade te'kid ile vezir-i azama ısmarlamışki 'elli günden ziyade düşman vilayetinde eğlenmeyesin; zira sular taşgun olur'*".

14. Mühürdar, *Cevahir*, fol. 43a: "*Gayetiyle çamur ve bataklık olmağla, toplarımız iki güunde geldi*".

15. Mustafa ibn Molla Rizvan, *Fethname-i Bağdad* (Oxford, Bodleian Lib. Ms, Or 276), fol. 255a. Distributions from central stores were normally made only to regular army forces. Timariots were expected to provide for themselves. As a special exception, timariots who volunteered their services to assist in the task of dragging 25 siege guns overland from Mosul were promised as reward that they would receive grain rations from central stores for the duration of the campaign. See Kâtib Çelebi, *Fezleke-i Tevarih* (Istanbul, 1286), Vol. 2, p. 200.

16. For a summary of the argument supporting this assumption, see D. Engels, *Alexander the Great and the Logistics of the Macedonian Army* (Berkeley, CA, 1978), pp. 126–9.

17. The assigning of a 3.5 okka ration (9.9 pounds) for each horse from the daily total of 100,000 okkas would account for the dietary needs of 28,570 animals. Even if, based on a different assumption, each horse's ration was reduced to half measure dry fodder and the rest made up with straw and wet forage, the 5,000 *kile* figure would still only represent an amount sufficient to feed 57,000 of the army's mounts, whose collective strength (with auxiliaries and support staff included) was, for this particular campaign, probably double that number; see above, Ch. 3, p. 36 (*n*2).

18. One example documents the provision for 950 camels stabled at Hayrebolu (due E. of Çorlu in Thrace) of 190 *kiles* of barley and 190 kantars of straw to last for the 180 days of the winter season, starting with the Ruz-i Kasım and finishing with the Ruz-i Hızr of the year 1104/1692–3; see Mevkufatî, *Vakiat-i Ruz-Merre* (Istanbul, Esad Efendi Lib., Ms 2437), fol. 78b. Another document suggests that the standard daily provision of straw for camels was based on a sackful (*garar*) weighing 50 okkas, deemed sufficient to support a string of five camels. Based on this ration, the ratio of grain to straw was reduced to 1 : 2.5 (10 okkas straw to 4 okkas dry feed as compared to 8.8 to 4); see B.B.A., *Mühimme Defterleri*, Vol. 87, p. 18 (entry dated 15 R. 1046 = 10 Jan. 1637): "*her bir kıtarına [=5] günde birer kil-i Istanbulî arpa [20/5 = 4] ve ellişer vukiyye [50/5 = 10] alır bir garar saman*".

19. On the wide variety of camel loads in common use, see Table 4.3 below. In one source (TKSMA, D. 8702; undated but attributable to the early part of the reign of Süleyman I's reign during the grand vezierate of Ibrahim Pasha, 1523–36) load factors of 9 *kiles* (509

pounds) and 10 *kiles* (566 pounds) are used interchangeably. In this document 15 camels assigned to transport flour for use of the kitchen of the imperial household while on campaign were assigned loads of 9 *kiles*, while another group of 75 camels also carrying flour for bread baking were assigned 10 *kile* loads. The amounts carried (135 *kiles* in the first instance and 750 *kiles* in the second) represented only a 30-day supply. Once consumed, these quantities were replenished at various prearranged supply points along the army's route of advance.

20. See the discussion above in Ch. 3, p. 55, esp. *n*50. Another example indicates the allocation of 5 *kiles* of wheat and 2 *kiles* of flour to each of the *kapu kulu* participants in the Hotin campaign in 1621 (see Topçular Kâtibi, *Vekayi-i Tarihiye* (Vienna Ms, Mxt. 130), fol. 346b). Consumed at a daily rate of one okka, even accounting for losses during baking or processing, the 7-*kile* (140-okka) allowance would have sufficed to meet a soldier's basic needs for the four and a half months between mobilization in mid-May to demobilization at the end of September.

21. It will be recalled that this figure represents less than a third of the total force under arms. The bulk of the army was required to carry its own provisions or purchase them at halting stations along the route of march. See above, Ch. 3, p. 49.

22. This calculation assumes a hypothetical (and wholly unrealistic) army accompanied by 30,000 mounts (see *n*17) whose daily barley rations consisted of a transport equivalent of 500 camel loads and a fighting force of 20,000 men whose wheat rations consisted of a transport equivalent of 105 camel loads. By this token the total transport equivalent of grain supplies for 60 days of campaigning would consist of 36,300 camel loads and, for a more prolonged period of 90 days campaigning, of 54,450 camel loads.

23. On the arrival of the army in the vicinity of Baghdad on 8 Receb 1048 (15 November 1638) after an outward march from Istanbul lasting 197 days (121 in march, 76 at rest), see H. Sahillioğlu, "Dördüncü Murad'ın Bağdad Seferi Menzilnamesi", *Belgeler II/ 3–4* (1965), p. 27. For the arrival of the grain supplies courtesy of Tarpush and his tribal associates on 27 Receb (6 December), see Nuri, *Tarih-i Feth-i Bağdad* (Vienna Ms, H. O. 78), fol. 155a.

24. Rashid notes, for instance, the ready availability in the Belgrade storehouses alone, of a grain surplus amounting to 30,000 *kiles* (equivalent to 600,000 one-okka rations or 770 metric tons) of grain; see *Tarih-i Raşid*, Vol. 1 (Istanbul, 1153), fol. 231b).

25. For the purposes of this analysis we may assume the presence of a larger force consisting of 50,000 men (each with a daily ration of one okka) and 80,000 mounts (each with a daily ration of 3.5 okkas) of grain. Such an army's minimal daily requirement would thus consist of 330,000 okkas (423.32 metric tons) of grain; a cumulative amount of 6,350 tons for 15 days of operations, mounting to nearly 8,500 tons for 20 days. Based on his own reckoning for a smaller Austrian force, Perjés ("Army Provisioning", p. 11) calculated the transport equivalent of 11,000 ox carts (each carrying a load of 1,000 kg) was needed to carry a month's grain supply for the army. Perjés' calculation allowing a collective grain consumption rate of 11,000 metric tons per month or 366.66 metric tons per day is 15 per cent less than our figure, increased to 423.32 tons per day to allow for a larger force.

26. It would appear that at any given time the army was able to carry with it no more than a 30-day supply of basic provisions. See *n*19 above.

27. Hüseyn Hezarfen, *Telhis ül Beyan* (Paris, Bib. Nationale: Ms Turcs A. F. 40), fol. 117b.

28. Details of the loads distributed in the first instance to 158 strings (*kitar*) or 790 camels and in the second to 175 strings or 875 camels assigned to the use of the sultan's kitchen staff

are preserved in two registers from the Topkapi Palace Archives; TKSMA, D. 60176 and TKSMA, D. 8702.

29. See A. K. Aksüt (ed.), *Koçi Bey Risalesi [Ikinci Risale, 1050/1640]* (Istanbul, 1939), p. 86. A register from the early seventeenth century (for details, see below Table 4.1) records the requisitioning through purchases and "loans" of 4,600 camels for use in campaign transport, confirming in rough outline the figure suggested by Koçi Bey.

30. An account of what was taken from the Belgrade arsenal is given by the historian Silahdar (see I. Parmaksızoğlu (ed.), *Nusretname*, Vol. 1, pt. iii (Istanbul, 1964), p. 281). Silahdar's list of essential equipment accompanying the army includes the following: 15,000 kantars (847 metric tons) of gunpowder, 17 culverins using a variety of 3, 5 and 7 okka shot, 7 mortars using 35 and 40 okka shot, and 85 light field pieces using 1 okka shot.

31. For an idea of the general (i.e. non-military) transport conditions that prevailed in the Western Balkans, see R. Murphey, "Patterns of Trade Along the Via Egnatia", in E. Zachariadou (ed.), *The Via Egnatia under Ottoman Rule 1380–1699* (Rethymnon, 1996), pp. 171–91.

32. A document from the mid-sixteenth century (TKSMA, D. 8334 dated 962/1533) records that 90 camels were purchased from Syria at a total cost of 3200 gold pieces, an average price of 35.5 gold pieces per camel. Another document dating from 1013/1603 (from *Mühimme* Register No. 75, cited by L. Güçer, *Hububat Meselesi* [Istanbul,1964], p. 142, n249) records the offer of 30 gold pieces to be paid by the state as compensation to camel owners who had lent their animals for use during the Austrian campaigns. These prices (even adjusted for the mid-seventeenth-century increases in the exchange equivalent for gold), however, fall considerably below what we know from detailed accounts of the early seventeenth century (for example the register of 1635 summarized in Table 4.1 below) recording purchase prices in the range between 35 and 100 gurush with most purchases concentrated around the 80 gurush (8,000 akçe) mark.

33. B. B. A., Maliyeden Müdevver 2702, a detailed (*müfredat*) register covering the period from the beginning of Receb 1044 to the end of Muharrem 1045/ late December 1634 to early July 1635.

34. For example, in a register of camels assigned to transport supplies for the imperial kitchens in one of Süleyman I's campaigns (see n28 above) among the total of 875 camels 120 (14 per cent) were designated as "spare" (*yedek*). By allowing an increase in the margin of spares from 1 in 7 to 1 in 5, the apparent discrepancy in usage connected with the counting word *kitar* can be explained.

35. See above, n19.

36. According to this register (B.B.A., Maliyden Müdevver 15461) one consignment of 1716 okkas of gunpowder was loaded on to 16 horses (average load factor [ALF] = 107.25 okkas), while another consignment of 2287 okkas of lead was loaded on to 21 horses (ALF = 108.9 okkas).

37. See B.B.A., Maliyeden Müdevver 18708 which records the dispatch of 7,000 kantars of dry biscuit by pack horse divided into 2,800 "loads" of 2.5 kantars each.

38. The example from 1635 suggests that, for the transport of gunpowder along the relatively rough roads of eastern Anatolia, a consignment of 4715 okkas of powder should be packed into 50 sacks each weighing 94.3 okkas, to make 25 camel loads consisting of two sacks with a total weight of 188.6 okkas or 9.43 *kiles*.

39. See the passage from the Mühimme Register for the year 1244/1828 cited by L. Güçer (*Hububat Meselesi*, p. 29 [n93]): "*onar kileden ziyade tahmil olunmamak şartıyla . . .*").

40. The example is based on a register (B.B.A., Maliyeden Müdevver 4374) whose contents are summarized in Güçer's book; see *Hububat Meselesi*, pp. 138–9.

41. See above, *n*32.

42. Kâtib Çelebi (*Fezleke* II: 102) relates that, when a part of the water buffalo herd was lost after being caught by the flood waters of the Tigris during the course of the campaign to Hamadan and Baghdad in 1629–30, the commander Hüsrev Pasha requested the sum of 400,000 gurush (roughly 40 million akçes) to purchase replacements.

43. The cost of transporting one *kile* of flour overland by ox cart the 705 kilometres from Edirne to Belgrade was estimated at 20 akçes, representing 4/10ths of the value of the cargo itself valued at 50 akçes per *kile*; see Mevkufatî, *Vakiat-i Ruz-Merre* (Esad Efendi Ms 2437), fol. 118b. For an idea of comparable shipping rates, see R. Murphey, "Provisioning Istanbul", *Food and Foodways* 2 (1988), Table 2, p. 227.

44. The transport cost of 20 akçes per *kile*, while high in relation to the value of the goods (see *n*43 above), was still only a fraction of what it was in remote areas of the empire such as eastern Anatolia.

45. See the example given below in Table 4.3, *n*6.

46. See the example cited in *n*43 above in which the transport of flour to the army by ox cart was credited as part of the annual *avariz* obligation of 18,000 households belonging to twelve sub-districts (kazas) of the main county of Edirne. In such cases the transport fees were calculated at a greatly reduced rate.

47. In such cases the price was regulated by a concept fundamental to Islamic principles of economic justice based on the notion of like reward or recompense for similar work or service (Ottoman: *ecr-i misl* / Arabic: *ajr al-mithl*). For a brief discussion of "fair wage or rent", see J. Schacht, *An Introduction to Islamic Law* (Oxford, 1964), p. 154.

48. The order was sent on 25 Muharrem 1041/ 24 August 1631 (see B.B.A., Maliyeden Müdevver 8475, p. 114). In the event, the flurry of campaign preparations and ever-escalating expenditures came to naught, as the campaign was abandoned and the Grand Vezier Hüsrev Pasha sacked in October 1631.

49. The state faced the same need to engage in a process of collective bargaining when filling emergency troop quotas. See above, Ch. 2, p. 29.

50. The largest "contributions" (offered in exchange for tax credits as opposed to cash payment) came from the townships of Urfa and Ana, each supplying 300 animals. The burden (opportunity) of supplying transport animals was distributed (divided) between eighteen providers at a total cost to the treasury for the 179.5 metric tons in trans-shipments of 636,200 akçes (3181 $\times$ 200). The undated document is found in TKSMA, D. 9009. For an unexplained reason probably related to special account-ing procedures the unit of measurement used for calculating loads is not the pack load for horses consisting of 2 or 2.5 kantars, but a single kantar weighing 125 pounds. Carried by camel, the same shipments would have required only a fourth as many animals (roughly 800) each carrying a load of 4 kantars (8.8 *kiles*). The distance between Iskenderun (Alexandretta) and Birecik travelling via Kesikhan and Islahiye is today 244 kilometres. The per *kile* per kilometre transport cost in this case is therefore 200 / 2.2 = 90.9 divided by 244 or 0.3726 akçe p.*kile*/km. Compare the price data in Table 4.3.

51. For a reinterpretation of standard views on Ottoman absolutism, see R. Murphey, "A View from the Top and Rumblings from Below" *Turcica* **28** (1996), pp. 319–38.

Chapter Five

1. The weaving of the Janissaries' winter coats was organized in state-run mills concentrated most heavily in Thessaloniki. Their operation provided a substantial source of employment and stimulation to the local economy. According to a source for the year 1624 (B.B.A., Maliyeden Müdevver 1981, p. 10), funds amounting to a yearly sum of 14 million akçes were allocated for the purchase of woollen broad cloth for the Janissaries' winter uniforms. As the size of the Janissary corps expanded, the value of their custom for local industry increased. Thus, the sum allocated for purchase of broadcloth in 1078 / 1668 rose to 17.9 million akçes (see Barkan's budget for 1669–70 in *Iktisat Fakültesi Mecmuası* **17** (1955–6), p. 286). For a general account of the scale and economic importance of this activity, see H. Sahillioğlu, "Yeniçeri çuhası ve II. Bayezid' in son yıllarında Yeniçeri çuha muhasebesi", *Güney-Doğu Avrupa Araştırmaları Dergisi* **2–3** (1973–4), pp. 415–66.

2. This fund was established in the time of Gedik Ahmed Pasha, grand vezier 1474–77 when, based on his experience as chief cook to the twenty-first regiment (*Kanuni Devrinde Yeniçeri Ocaklarına Dair Bazı Merasim*, Istanbul University Library, Ms T. Y. 3293, folios 6b–7b [N.B.: In addition to the Istanbul and Bratislava manuscripts of this basic text cited here, there now exists a facsimile edition of the St Petersburg text; see I. Petrosiian (ed.), *Mebde-i Kanun-i Yeniçeri Ocağı Tarihi*, Moscow, 1987]), he decided that separate butcher's shops and a flour market (*unkapani*) should be established open only to the military, thereby guaranteeing a constant supply. Furthermore, a fund was started with 24,000 gold ducats (*Kavanin-i Yeniçeriyan*, Bratislava University Library MS, folio 37b) from which to meet fluctuations in the meat market. The ceiling price which Janissaries were required to pay was three akçes for 450 dirhems (1.125 okkas, a little over three pounds) of mutton, the balance being paid from the fund.

3. Janissaries received a sum of twelve akçes every three months for clothing incidentals (*yaka akçesi*) and thirty akçes for weaponry (*yay akçesi*), with an additional allowance for ammunition as well (*barut akçesi*); see *Kanuni Devrinde Yeniçeri Ocaklarına Dair Bazı Merasim* (Istanbul University Lib., Ms T. Y. 3293), fol. 3b.

4. *Düzen akçesi* and *seyisane akçesi* were provided for the purchase of horses and hire of grooms to attend the Janissaries (*Kavanin-i Yeniçeriyan*, Bratislava MS, folio 49b).

5. *ibid.*, folio 48a.

6. See C. Römer, "Die Osmanische Belagerung Baghdad's 1034–35/1625–26: Ein Augenzeugenbericht", *Der Islam* **66** (1989), p. 121 (line 27): "*Zahire gelmez oldu, beksemad beş guruşa vakiyyesi, arpanın on filoriye kilesi satılmağa başladı*".

7. Yasin ibn Khayrullah al-Khatib (al-Umarî), *Gayat al-maram fi tarikh muhasin Baghdad* (Baghdad, 1388/1968), p. 319. At the time Ottoman mints were producing 950–1000 akçes from 100 dirhems of silver. Based on the 10 akçes per dirhem valuation and the standard Iraqi *ratl* of 130 dirhems (130/400 = 0.325 okkas; see W. Hinz, *Islamische Masse und Gewichte* [Leiden, 1970], p. 31) the per okka price would have been 215 akçes (70 × 3.0769) and the per *kile* price 4308 akçes. If we apply the gold / akçe exchange rate of 1 to 220 based on a three-year average for the tumultuous (from a monetary point of view) years of 1624–6, which followed the accession of the minor sultan Murad IV (see H. Sahillioğlu, "Sikke Raici", *Belgeler* I/2 (1965), p.229) the equivalent sum in gold was 19.5 gold pieces. Although it is difficult to decide how much trust to place in uncorroborated narrative accounts of this type, the evidence is not implausible given the price of a

kile of barley cited in the precisely contemporaneous Ottoman sources. See the preceding note.

8. L. Güçer, *XVI–XVII Asırlarda Osmanlı İmparatorluğunda Hububat Meselesi*, p. 138.
9. To ensure that adequate grain supplies were paid for in full, the sultan had previously sent 44 million akçes to the vezier Tabanı-yassı Mehmed Paşa in two instalments; see *Suver-i Hutut-i Hümayun* (Istanbul University Lib., Ms 6110), fol. 194a.
10. For details on the undependability of the system used for provisioning troops by the Spanish army, and examples of disputes which arose from the system of delayed payment see G. Parker, *The Army of Flanders and the Spanish Road, 1567–1659* (Cambridge, 1972), pp. 86–96. The Janissaries' Spanish counterparts were expected to fight on a diet consisting mostly of bread, which according to one description contained in addition to a certain quantity of flour, "offal, broken biscuits, and lumps of plaster "(Parker, *Army of Flanders*, pp. 163–4).
11. Jean de Thévenot, *The Travels of Monsieur de Thévenot into the Levant*, Eng. trans. Roy LeStrange (London, 1686), Pt. 1, p. 71.
12. The size of the Danube fleet maintained by the Ottomans during the late seventeenth century wars was, it seems, 52 vessels manned by a total of 4,070 crew. Mevkufatî (*Vakiat-i Ruz-merre* IV: 128a) provides the following summary account:

Vessel type	Crew complement	No. of vessels	No. of men
galliotes (kalite)	227	4	908
frigates (firkata)	85	28	2,370
flat-bottomed river boats (shayka)	40	20	800
		52	4,078

13. See Chapter 3, *n*50.
14. A document in the Topkapi Palace Archives (D. 9672) shows a total of quantity of 82,972 kantars of hardtack supplied from depots in 11 locations. 20,000 kantars came from Birecik, 13,048 from Erzurum and 12,624 from Diyarbekir. A proportion of the remaining amount (10,300 kantars) was supplied from stocks on hand left over from a previous campaign and stored in Mardin near the army's winter camp. The exact coincidence of the amounts (10,300 kantars) makes it clear that the hardtack stockpile recorded in a near contemporary document (B.B.A., Maliyeden Müdevver 5907) refers in fact to the same residual supply.
15. In an example dated March 1640, two and half months after the army's return from the Iraqi front, surplus stocks of 7,599 *kiles* of barley requisitioned from the districts on the road between Seyitgazi and Ilgın in central Anatolia were released from state warehouses and offered back for the consumption of the local populace at the fair market price (see B.B.A., Kâmil Kepeci 2576, p. 43: *"baki kalan zahire (. . .) narh-i nızî üzere reaya'ya füruht (. . .)"*). State-controlled market prices took into account not just the "fair market price" for the time of year (i.e. the pre-harvest post-harvest price differential), but also allowed for the discounting of old grain that was approaching its "sell by" date.
16. See E. W. McHenry, *Basic Nutrition* (Philadelphia, PA, 1957), p. 49. A more exact equivalent for a full ration of one okka (1282 grams) of bread would be 3460 calories, but this calculation takes no account of the lower nutritional value of the average baked loaf of the period compared to modern bread. For the purpose of his calculations Perjés

("Army Provisioning", p. 12) assumes a basic nutritional value of 235 calories for every 100 grams of bread, reduced to 170 by the admixture of bran and other by-products of milling with the pure wheat flour. The later assumption is perhaps extreme, as the reduction of the caloric value of the standard daily bread ration to a mere 1700 calories would mean the ingestion of foodstuffs sufficient only to cover the body's average energy consumption during sleep (8 hrs = 500 calories) and non-occupational activities (8 hrs = 1500 calories) with nothing to spare for even light occupational activity, let alone the extreme energy requirements for active march (approx. 300 calories per hour). For average energy expenditures based on the 65 kg reference man (male person of average weight), see Robert S. Goodhart and Maurice E. Shils, *Modern Nutrition in Health and Disease*, 6th edn (Philadelphia, PA, 1980), p. 1261.

17. See Goodhart and Shils, *Modern Nutrition in Health and Disease* (Philadelphia, PA, 1980), p. 1245 (Table A-1a).
18. Goodhart & Shils, *Modern Nutrition*, p. 1261 (Table A-7a).
19. See Luigi Marsigli, *Stato Militare dell'Imperio Ottomano* (Amsterdam, 1732), p. 68.
20. In this diet 480 grams (approx. 1.4 pounds) was supplied in the form of baked goods made with wheat flour. This component of the diet was substantially increased during periods when the army was on the march. On the one okka (400 dirhems = 1282 grams = 3460 calories) per man per day ration (1/2 bread and 1/2 hardtack) allocated for soldiers during periods of march, see Ch. 4, p. 71 (n20).
21. For this conversion I have used the fixed rate of 270 calories for every 100 grams of ingredient material without distinction. Both the inherent quality of the ingredients and the conditions of their preparation varied considerably. In the absence of more exact data or evidence for the Ottomans it seems sensible to opt for the more generous calorie conversion rates, on the assumption that on the whole the Ottomans had an interest in reserving the best quality ingredients for use by the military performing critical and at the same time energy-demanding tasks.
22. Calorie conversion rates for the last two components of the diet were applied as follows: 320 cal. per 80 gm of cooked meats, and 50 cal. per 7 gm serving of butter; see E. W. McHenry, *Basic Nutrition*, p. 50.
23. I. Petrosiian (ed.), *Mebde-i Kanun-i Yeniçeri*, fol. 68b.
24. See B.B.A., Maliyeden Müdevver 18186, pp. 57–60.
25. See Mevkufatî, *Vakiat-i Ruz-merre* IV: 141b. This quantity, translated into number of sheep at the rate 12 okkas = 1 sheep would account for 55,510 sheep, almost a fifth of the annual total provided to the palace kitchens from Rumelia; see n23 above.
26. The annual quota of 300,000 head of sheep assigned to the sheep drovers of Rumelia had (according to K. Karpat, *Ottoman Population 1830–1914* (Madison, WI, 1985), p. 87) risen to an annual figure of 500,000–600,000 head by the eighteenth century. This rise reflects in part the empire's demographic growth and rising demand for domestic and civilian consumption. But figures from the sixteenth century compiled in detailed studies by Bistra Cvetkova suggest that the provision of a 250,000–300,000 head total remained the normal level of expectation for the period when Ottoman administrative control (and therefore presumably also its success in extracting the resources of its core provinces) was greatest; see in particular, B. Cvetkova, "Les celeb et leur role dans la vie économique des Balkans", in M. A. Cook, *Studies in the Economic History of the Middle East* (London, 1970), pp. 172–92, esp. p. 176 and pp. 182–3. In this study Cvetkova documents the activities of 7,931 sheep drovers (*celeb*) each providing an average of 36 head of sheep, making a total of approximately 285,000 sheep.

NOTES

27. See *n*24 above. The average price paid by the treasury of 1.7 gurush (136 akçes) for each sheep containing an average weight of 12 okkas of meat implies a per okka price of 11.333 akçes. This corresponds very closely to prices recorded in near-contemporary sources on Ottoman price structure; an indication that the sultan was bound by the same rules of supply and demand as the general populace. For contemporary mutton prices ranging between 10 and 12 akçes per okka, see M. Kütükoğlu, *Osmanlılarda Narh Müessesesi ve 1640 Tarihli Narh Defteri* (Istanbul, 1983), pp. 27–8.
28. At the end of the campaign 14 per cent of the total number requisitioned (29,521 out of 217,279 sheep) was still unused and available for ceremonial and celebratory use; B.B.A., MMD 1816: "*Bağdad'dan avdet buyurduklarında Matbah-i Amireye ve Tatar Sultanına ve Yeniçeri Ocağına kurbanlık ve Acem Şahi tarafından gelen elçi mesarifine ve Sipahi Meydanına ve gayra masraf olunup (. . .)*".
29. See B.B.A., Maliyeden Müdevver 18708, p. 21.
30. The event is described in a contemporary register (B.B.A., Kâmil Kepeci 1937, p. 80) in the following terms: "*beha-i erz ve rugan-i sade ve asel ve şeker ve gayrı beray-i ziyafet-i Yeniçeriyan ve Sipahiyan ki der vakt-i ameden an Diyarbekir ila ordu-i hümayun beray-i istikbal kerden-i hazret-i vezir-i azam ve serdar-i ekrem Bayram Paşa, der menzil-i Sivas ..*".
31. See Münir Aktepe, "Ahmed III Devrinde Şark Seferine İştirak Edecek Ordu Esnafı Hakkında Vesikalar", *Tarih Dergisi* VII/10 (1954), pp. 17–30.
32. See Aktepe, "Ordu Esnafı", p. 23.
33. See G. Veinstein, "Les inventaires après décès des campagnes militaires: Le cas de la conquête de Cypre", *Turkish Studies Association Bulletin* **15** (1991), pp. 293–305; esp. pp. 303–4.
34. See Veinstein, "Inventaires Après Décès", p. 303. The merchant from Bursa who was responsible for supplying olives and other foodstuffs to the army left an estate valued at 10,905 akçes, while the estate of the merchant from Tunis was valued at 13, 312 akçes.
35. A principal study making the argument for an inverse relationship between industrial output and the general level of military activity during the Russo-Ottoman wars in the late eighteenth century is M. Genç's article "L'économie Ottoman et la guerre au XVIIIe siècle", *Turcica* **27** (1995), pp. 177–89.
36. The relationship between war and economy for the pre-eighteenth century era of European warfare is explored by F. Tallett in his study *War and Society in Early-Modern Europe, 1495–1715* (London, 1992), p. 216 *et seq*. For this period Tallett emphasizes that the demands of war on manpower resources, agricultural stocks and its competition with the general manufacturing sector for use of basic raw materials were of a scale to provide stimulus rather than threat to general economic activity. See in particular his remarks on p. 222: "*. . . we need to bear in mind the relatively low level of demand from the military*". On the welcoming of the arrival of the Ottoman army as source of stimulation as opposed to unwelcome demand for local economies including regional grain markets, see Topçular Kâtibi, *Vekayi-i Tarihiye*, Vienna [ÖNB], Ms. Mxt. 130, fol. 334b: "*reaya taifesine sebeb-i ticaret*".
37. Aktepe, "Ordu Esnafı", p. 19: "*Isyana amil olan sebebler arasında (. . .) 1730 seferine iştirak dolaysıyla toplanan paranın 'ekl u bel' olunmasının da mühim bir rolu vardır*".
38. See M. Ali, *Kunh ül Ahbar* (Nuruosmaniye Lib., Ms. 3409), fol. 374a. Assuming a packload for horses to consist of 2 kantars or 88 okkas [see Murphey, "Via Egnatia", p.173 (fn. 6)] the equivalent of 300 packloads would be 26,400 okkas; not enough, even at half rations, to support more than the short-term needs of the horses and men within the city walls.

39. Ali, *Kunh ül Ahbar*, fol. 373b: "*Tebriz'de kapanan leşker . . . 80,000 nefer iken, 30,000 güzide Kızılbaş etraf-i kalede cilveger idiler*".

40. See Hüseyn Hezarfen, *Telhis ül Beyan* (Paris, Biblothèque Nationale, Ms. Turcs A.F. 40), fol. 115a.

41. See the imperial writ of Murad IV in *Suver-i Hutut-i Hümayun* (Istanbul Univ. Lib., Ms TY 6110, fol. 196a–196b: "*Iç Ahir-i Amire senevi 400,000 kile arpa sarf olunur. Ona göre üç dört kat müstevfi hazır edesin*". See also *n*9 above where the same sultan authorized the expenditure of 44 million akçes, largely for grain purchases. For the actual consumption of barley of 1,559,917 *kiles* (3.9 times the amount used by the Imperial Stables in a year) during the 1638 Baghdad campaign, see *n*42 below.

42. On the range of price per *kile* of barley in the period 1624–40 of between 16 and 24 akçes, see Kütükoğlu (ed.), *1640 Narh Defteri*, p. 51. For the allocation of 1,5559,917 *kiles* of barley for use during the campaign, see Güçer, *Hububat Meselesi*, p. 137.

43. See Ö. L. Barkan, "1079–1080/1669–1670 malî yılına ait bir Osmanlı bütçesi", *Iktisat Fakültesi Mecmuası* **17** (1955–6), pp. 232–4. The total sum disbursed represents a figure more like one-third of all campaign-related expenditures than the 5 per cent figure recorded in the observations by Hezarfen. See above, *n*40.

44. Equivalent to either 360 or 720 akçes depending on whether the pre- or post-akçe devaluation rate is applied. For the "normal" range of barley prices current circa 1600, see *n*42 above.

45. See M. Ali, *Nusretname* (Süleymaniye Lib., Ms. Esad Efendi 2433), fol. 91a.

46. See Ş. Pamuk, "Money in the Ottoman Empire, 1326–1914", in Inalcik and Quataert (eds), *Economic and Social History*, p. 960 (*n*39–40).

47. On the steady decline of the *nisfiye* (also called *şahi*) coin's value from a level of 12 per Ottoman gurush, to 18, and then to 30, see M. Ali, *Kunh ül Ahbar*, fols 378b–379a, who acknowledges the risk taken by Cafer Pasha in paying his troops' wages in the suspect coin while implying that, in the absence of real help from the government, he was left with little option. See in particular Ali's passage incorporating the phrase: "*kestirdiği akçe ancak nefs-i Tebriz'de revac buldu*". The local and wider effects of this monetary instability is noted in other contemporary sources; see esp., *Tarih-i Peçevi* 2 vols. (Istanbul, 1283), Vol. 2, pp. 115–21 and *Tarih-i Selanikî* [edited by M. Ipşirli in 2 vols. (Istanbul, 1989)], Vol. 2, pp. 284–5, events dated Zilkaade 1000/ August 1592. The latter events took place two years after the signing of the peace with the Safavids and too early for significant levels of remobilization for war in Austria which only reached a head with the Györ campaign in 1594.

48. London, Public Record Office, *Calendar of State Papers and Manuscripts Relating to English Affairs Existing in the Archives and Collections of Venice and in Other Libraries of Northern Italy*, Vol. 22 (1629–32), p. 57; *Suver-i Hutut-i Hümayun* (Istanbul University Library MS, T.Y. 6110), fols 63a–63b, letter of Murad IV to the governor of Egypt Tabani-yassı Mehmed Pasha sometime during his governorship during the years 1628–30: "*The provision of wheat to ships of the infidel in some coastal areas has led to the enrichment of the infidel nations and the impoverishment of the lands of Islam. A royal order has been issued to the effect that henceforth trade in grain with the infidel ships is strictly forbidden*".

49. See M. Todorova, "Was there a Demographic Crisis in the Ottoman Empire in the Seventeenth Century?", *Études Balkaniques* **24** (1988), pp. 55–63

50. See the example cited above in *n*15.

51. On holdovers from an earlier era of European systems for army provisioning that were prominently in evidence during the opening phases of the French invasion of the

Palatinate in 1688, see F. Redlich, *De Praeda Militari: Looting and Booty 1500–1815* (Wiesbaden, 1956), p. 62: "*During the winter of 1688–89 by way of contributions the French cavalry extracted from the region in which they were quartered 2 to 3 times as much as was needed for sustenance, the surplus going into the pockets of the captains commanding the squadrons*".

52. P. Rycaut, *The Present State of the Ottoman Empire* (London, 1668), Chapt. 11, p. 205.

53. See D. Chandler, "The Art of War on Land", *Cambridge New Modern History* Vol. 6 (Cambridge, 1970), p. 744: "*[Le Tellier and Louvois] imposed close government supervision at all levels, although there was a world of difference between practice and precept*". In a recently published study Lynn notes that the pace of administrative change in the seventeenth-century French bureaucracy lagged considerably behind what was needed to accommodate its rapidly expanding army. See John A. Lynn, *Giant of the Grand Siècle: The French Army, 1610–1715* (Cambridge, 1997), p. 547: "*changes in the institutions of central government never really matched the magnitude of army expansion.*"

54. Gaston Zeller (*New Cambridge Modern History* Vol. 5 [Cambridge, 1961], p. 215) points out the irony that the victuals and munitions purchased in advance of the French invasion of Holland in 1671 were acquired in the very country that had been targeted for attack.

55. F. Redlich (*De Praeda Militari*, p. 62) regarded this campaign and the decade of the 1690s generally as the turning point that hardened French resolve to abandon their outmoded supply systems once and for all.

56. Ö. L. Barkan, *Kanunlar* (Istanbul, 1943), p. 309: "*her haneden ellişer akçe 'sefer harcı' vermek adet-i mutadeleri olmağın (. . .)*".

57. See G. Veinstein, "L' hivernage en campagne", reprinted in Veinstein, *État et Société dans l'empire Ottoman* (Aldershot, 1994), No. V, pp. 109–43.

58. *Tarih-i Peçevi*, Vol. 2, p. 137 (lines 9–10): "*serhaddlu'ya müteallik hizmet iken bölük halkın gittiğin kimse makul görmedi*".

59. On the size and composition of the Ottomans' Danube fleet, see *n*12 above.

60. See A. Hertz, "Ottoman Ada Kale, 1753", *Archivum Ottomanicum* 4 (1972), pp. 104–5 which emphasizes the critical importance of river navigation to Ottoman support for its armies in Hungary during the sixteenth and seventeenth centuries.

61. G. Perjés, "Army Provisioning", *Acta Hist. Acad. Scient. Hung.* **16** (1970), pp. 1–51. See now also John A. Lynn (ed.), *Feeding Wars: Logistics in Western Warfare from the Middle Ages to the Present* (Boulder, CO, 1993).

62. Perjés, "Army Provisioning", pp. 10–11. Perjés assumes each cartload represented 500 kg for low density high volume cargo such as bread, and 1,000 kg for high density cargo such as grain.

63. The disproportion between animal and human food resources is even more striking if one takes into account the weight as well as the volume of the cartloads. The weight of the 7,600 cartloads of wet and dry forage came to a full 7,600 metric tons (2,400 + 3,000 + 2,200), while the bread rations came only to 1,480 metric tons ([0.5] × 2,660 + [0.5] × 300). Weight-wise thus the cargo for human consumption came to only about one-sixth of the total transported, 1,480/9,140 = 16.2 per cent; see Perjés "Army Provisioning".

64. This allows a perhaps overgenerous load factor of 253.333 kg. (197.48 okkas) for each camel. For a detailed discussion of these issues based on Ottoman evidence, see above Ch. 4, esp. p. 71 and *n*19–22.

65. A. N. Kurat (ed.), *The Despatches of Sir Robert Sutton*, Camden Society: Third Series, Vol. 78 (London, 1953), p. 59.

66. *ibid.*, p. 65.

67. *ibid.*, p. 66.
68. See the quotes from Voltaire's published works cited in R. Murphey "Critica", *Archivum Ottomanicum* **13** (1993–4), pp. 377–8. See also C. Finkel, "The Provisioning of the Ottoman Army During the Campaigns of 1593–1606", in A. Tietze (ed.), *Habsburg-osmanische Beziehungen* (Vienna, 1985), pp. 107–123. Finkel notes in particular the importance to the success of Ottoman armies operating in Hungary during the seventeenth century of their forward bases of supply at Belgrade and Buda; see *ibid.*, pp. 122–3.
69. For a single example, see the case of Kara Mehmed Aga described in Ch. 7 below, p. 148 (*n*45).
70. See below, Ch. 8, *n*18.
71. One example is identified in the lament of the Kamanice garrison soldiers; see below, Ch. 7, *n*47.
72. For a discussion of the danger of placing too much emphasis on the "rottenness at the centre" approach to Ottoman history in the seventeenth century, see the review of Kenneth Setton's *Venice, Austria and the Turks in the Seventeenth Century* in *Archivum Ottomanicum*, **13** (1993–4), pp. 371–83. The effects of dynastic change on basic state structure and administrative continuity in the Ottoman empire were not nearly as pronounced as portrayed in some popular accounts.

Chapter Six

1. See Ch. 2, pp. 13–16.
2. On attitudes towards technological change, see R. Murphey, "The Ottoman Attitude Towards the Adoption of Western Technology: The Role of the *Efrenci* Technicians in Civil and Military Applications", in J.-L. Bacqué-Grammont and P. Dumont (eds), *Contributions à l'histoire économique et sociale de l'Empire ottoman* (Louvain, 1983), pp. 287–98.
3. Von Kausler's book *Atlas des plus memorables batailles, combats et sièges des temps anciens du moyen âge et de l'âge moderne* (reprinted several times in 1831,1839 and again in Desau in 1847) was a widely read and influential source of opinion on the Ottoman practice of the martial arts whose chief weakness was that it grounded almost exclusively in European sources. By using Ottoman sources (especially the historian Mehmed Rashid) Nottebohm was able to suggest convincingly a substantial revision of his predecessor's views; see W. Nottebohm, *Montecucculi und die Legende von St. Gotthard an 1664: M. Reschid's Bericht über die Schlacht bei St. Gotthard* (Berlin, 1887).
4. Important advances have been made in the reassessment of once-standard views of Ottoman technical inferiority, including the supposed archaism of their metallurgical technique. But despite the importance of this work showing the standards of technical perfection achieved by the Ottomans, the issue of how applicable or indeed necessary this knowledge was to the practice of war has not yet been much considered. For the assessment (reassessment) of Ottoman technical skills, see especially B. Hall and K. Devries, "The 'Military Revolution' Revisited", *Technology and Culture* **31** (1990), pp. 500–7 and G. Agoston, "Ottoman Artillery and European Military Technol-

ogy in the 15th and 17th Centuries", *Acta Orientalia Acad. Scient. Hung.* **47** (1992), pp. 15–48.

5. The issue of the "applicability" of specific techniques and technologies to real conditions (prevailing wind patterns, currents and other unalterable navigational realities) in the context of naval warfare in the Mediterranean has been addressed in a work by John H. Pryor, *Geography, Technology and War: Studies in the Maritime History of the Mediterranean, 649–1571* (Cambridge, 1988). Unfortunately investigation of the environmental context of land wars has not yet been systematically undertaken.

6. See S. Christensen, "European-Ottoman Military Acculturation in the Late Middle Ages", in B. P. McGuire (ed.), *War and Peace in the Middle Ages* (Copenhagen, 1987), pp. 227–51.

7. On the timing of this transmission of knowledge, see P. Petrović, "Fire-arms in the Balkans on the eve of and after the Ottoman conquest of the 14th and 15th Centuries", in V. J. Parry and M. E. Yapp (eds), *War, Technology and Society in the Middle East* (London, 1975), pp. 164–94.

8. See W. Hassenstein (ed.), *Das Feuerwerkbuch von 1420* (Munich, 1941). Experts disagree about the precise dating of the spread of these techniques in Europe, but most would acknowledge that the critical decades for its dissemination were the 1430s and 1440s. For a recent discussion of the dating issue, see J. Needham *et al.*, *Science and Civilisation in China, Vol. 5, Pt. 7: Chemistry and Chemical Technology – Military Technology; the Gunpowder Epoch* (Cambridge, 1986), pp. 33, 349 and 421.

9. See the near-contemporary Ottoman account of these events in Kemal Paşa-zade's *Tevarih-i Al-i Osman* (Paris, Bibliothèque Nationale, Ms. Supp. Turcs 157), fols 19a–21a.

10. According to Paul Gille (in Vol. 2 of M. Dumas (ed.), *A History of Technology and Invention*, Eng. trans. by E. B. Henress (London, 1980)), though "discovered" much earlier, the flintlock system for firing muskets was: "not utilized until around 1630"; see Gille, "Handguns", in Dumas, *History of Technology*, p. 489). Gille concluded that, because of the questionable reliability and only marginal superiority of the earliest prototypes, the flintlock musket was not fully adopted as the standard weapon of war in northern Europe (e.g. France) until 1670.

11. The term "static" is used advisedly in preference to "stagnant" to convey a sense of the (seemingly universally) slow pace of advance in gun-founding techniques during the early modern period. For the opinion of one expert, see A. R. Hall, "Military Technology", in C. Singer *et al.*, *A History of Technology* (Oxford, 1957), Vol. 3, p. 363: "The surviving evidence indicates that fundamentally the same methods were employed from the beginning [in the early 15th century] until about 1750".

12. For the example of an Italian engineer named Vernada who served in successive phases of his career under Venetian, Ottoman and Maltese colours, see R. Murphey, "Critica", *Archivum Ottomanicum* **13** (1993–4), p. 375.

13. In this context see the remarks by Lynn (John A. Lynn, *Giant of the Grand Siècle* (Cambridge, 1994), p. 571): "*There is good evidence that Vauban introduced parallel [trenches] in imitation of the Turks who first used them in their siege of Candia in 1667–69*".

14. For the views of one scholar who excepts Moscovy from the general picture of parity between the other European countries (including the Ottomans) and argues for the relative underdevelopment (from a military and technological point of view) of Russia before the time of Peter the Great, see T. Esper, "Military Self-Sufficiency and Weapons Technology in Moscovite Russia", *Slavic Review* **28** (1969), pp. 185–208.

15. See G. Perjés, "The Zrinyi-Monteccucoli controversy "in J. Bak and B. Kiraly (eds), *From Hunyadi to Rakoczi: War and Society in Medieval and Early Modern Hungary* [Eastern European Monographs, No. 104] (Boulder, CO, 1982), pp. 335–49, esp. pp. 347–9, where Perjés emphasizes the general perception among the best military minds of the time that the most lightly-armed and most mobile military force was generally the most effective.

16. See Kâtib Çelebi, *Fezleke-i Tevarih*, Vol. 2, p. 197.

17. The range of requirements is specified (without any indication of the proportion for each category) in an order sent to the Ottoman governor of Semendire in 1568. A facsimile of the document was published by I. H. Uzunçarşılı, *Osmanlı Devleti Teşkilatından Kapukulu Ocakları* 2 vols. (Ankara, 1943); see plate no. 39 (illustration no. 114) at the end of volume 2 (lines 5–6): *22 vukiyyeden 11 vukiyye atar topa varınca (. . .) toplar lazım ve mühim olmağın (. . .)*".

18. This is confirmed in an account of the siege of Candia by M. Rashid. Rashid's account (*Tarih-i Raşid* [Istanbul,1153], fol. 52b] records that in the four-month period between late February and mid-June 1668, the winter season, 40,000 balls in the 16–30 okka range were fired. The slowing of activity during the winter season is reflected in the reduction of the average daily rate of fire to about 300 shots (see Ch. 1, *n*19 above).

19. A compromise middle category in the 11–14 okka range (30–40 pounds) seems to have been in particular demand for eastern campaigns. See the series of orders for melting down existing stocks of the heavier shot (especially the 18 okka balls) to produce 11 and 14 okka shot sent to the wardens of the Erzurum arsenal in 1631, B.B.A., Maliyeden Müdevver 8475, pp. 212 and 219.

20. For the casting of three new guns on the spot in the trenches around Candia in 1668 to fit the 30,000 surplus cannon balls fired by the defenders and collected from the battlefield by the Ottoman troops, see *Tarih-i Raşid*, fol. 51a: "*Küffar tarafından atılan 30,000 kadar gülle cem olup, ordu-i hümayunda olan toplara münasib olmadığından (. . .) müceddeden ol güllelere göre üç aded top döktürülmek üzere karar (. . .)*".

21. When the Ottomans captured Lippa (Lipova on the Mures R.) in 1695 they recovered five guns using 11 okka shot, as compared to only one using 14 okka balls; see Silahdar, *Nusretname* (Istanbul,1962), Vol. 1, Pt. 1, p. 77. An inventory of Ottoman Ada Kale for 1753 (see A. Hertz, "Armament and Supply Inventory", *Archivum Ottomanicum* 4 [1972], p. 139) shows the guns using 11 okka shot made up more than a quarter (25 out of 94) of the garrison's stock of guns in all sizes, including the omnipresent, lightweight *şahi* guns.

22. Uzunçarşılı, *Kapukulu Ocakları*, Vol. 2, p. 40 (*n*4): "*tûlu yedi karış, (. . .) her kıtası birer kantar, (. . .) ikisi bir bargire yüklemeğe kabil (..) zarbzen (..) top*". Assuming a span of approximately nine inches, the gun barrels would have measured a little over five feet.

23. The 21 "big guns" deployed by the Ottomans during the Uyvar siege used 14, 18 and 24 okka shot (40, 50 and 70 pounders). See Mühürdar, *Cevahir*, fol. 23b, where the author marvels at the unprecedented and awesome concentration of fire power in one place: "*böyle bir azim mehib toplar bir seferde dahi gitdiği yok imiş deyü nakl ederler*".

24. *Cevahir*, fol. 30b.

25. The suggestion is made by Parker; see his *The Military Revolution: Military innovation and the rise of the West, 1500–1800* (Cambridge, 1988), p. 126. An illustration showing the easy manoeuvrability of the Ottomans' field artillery is provided in the illustrated *Şehinşahname-i Sultan Murad Han* (Topkapı Saray Lib., Ms., Bağdad Köşkü 200, Karatay, *Farsça Yazmaları Kat.*, No. 792), fol 100a. In this illustration (see photographic reproduc-

tion, p. 112) groups of four men each are shown pulling the small field cannon into place to guard the entrance to the commander's tent.

26. See J. W. Wijn, "Military Force and Warfare, 1610–1648", *The New Cambridge Modern History*, Vol. 4 (Cambridge, 1970), p. 215.

27. P. Jaeckel, "Ausrüstung und Bewaffnung der Türkischen Heere", in H. Glasner (ed.), *Kurfürst Max Emmanuel: Bayern und Europa um 1700* (Munich, 1976), Vol. 1, p. 380.

28. Long overdue improvements at Győr, held briefly by the Ottomans between 1594–8, were postponed for six decades until the appointment (on 12 March 1611) of the celebrated and, perhaps more to the point, well-connected Montecuccoli as governor; see Mears, "Influence of the Turkish Wars in Hungary", in Pullapilly and Vankly (eds), *Asia and the West*, p. 132.

29. See V. Kopčan, "The Last Stage of Ottoman Rule in Slovakia", *Studia Historica Slovaca* **15** (1986), pp. 215 (n. 19) and 217 (n. 27).

30. On the blending of styles during the period of transition from "old style" to "new style" military architecture called by one researcher the "medieval-early-modern hybrid", see Mahinder S. Kingra, "The Trace Italienne and the Military Revolution During the Eighty Years' War, 1567–1648", *Journal of Military History* **57** (1993), pp. 431–41, esp., p. 439.

31. See L. Benczedi, "Warrior and State in the Seventeenth Century: Thokolly's Uprising 1687–1685", in Bak and Kiraly (eds), *From Hunyadi to Rakozi*, pp. 351–65.

32. Details on the style of construction found at Çehrin are provided by Silahdar (*Tarih* I: 685): "*Ak çam ağacından içi toprak dolma çatmalarıyla yapıp (. . .)*".

33. On the difficulties resulting from the sandy quality of the soil, see Silahdar, *Tarih* I: 685 "*kale lağım tutmaz bir kumsal yerde vaki (. . .)*". This same point is emphasized in an anonymous Ottoman account of the campaign; see Paris, BN, Supp. Turcs 927, fol. 32a: "*her koldan lağımlara mübaşeret (. . .), amma toprağı kumsal olduğundan ekser-i mevazide mümkün olmayıp (. . .)*".

34. See J. Redhouse, *Turkish-English Lexicon* (Istanbul, 1890), p. 836. For its resistance even under heavy enemy fire see the description of the Ottoman siege of Zrinvar in June 1664 by Evliya Çelebi (*Seyahatname* VI: 550, lines 21–4): "*duvarın düzme direklerin içi Horasanî nhtım kireç ile metin yapılmış olmağla, (. . .) nice bin aded balyemez topların kelle-kadar güllelerini bal gibi yeyip (. . .)*".

35. Naima (*Tarih* IV: 260): "*serdar-i ekremin şatırcıbaşı Muhammed Zaman Beg Acem ferzendi olup, çok geşt u güzar ve Acem cenklerde lağımcılık sanaatı tahsil edip, ol fende ziyade mahir (. . .)*".

36. On the source of the vezier's practical knowledge in the experiences of an earlier campaign, see the anonymous account of the Çehrin campaign (Paris, Supp. Turcs 297), fol. 32a: "*Ahmed Paşa mukaddem olan seferlerde sahib-i tecrübe ve kâr-azmude olmağla (..) ve Kandiye kalesi feth ve teshirinde müdebbir ve murur-dide olmağın (. . .)*". Before his elevation to the rank of vezier in 1086/1675 Ahmed had served for fourteen years as chief of the armourers (*cebeci başı*); see M. Süreyya, *Sicill-i Osmani* I: 223.

37. See Mühürdar, *Cevahir*, fol. 23b: "*Uyvar bir müstahkem kale, toplardan asla pervası yok*".

38. For Uyvar's designation as: "*die Vormauer der Christenheit*", see Mears, "Influence of the Turkish Wars", p. 134.

39. See, among others, J. B. Tavernier, *Les Six Voyages* 3 vols. (Paris, 1724), Vol. 1, p. 280; Matrakcı Nasuh, *Beyan-i Menazil-i Sefer-i Irakeyn*, edited by Hüseyn Yurdaydın (Ankara, 1976), fols 47b–48a.

NOTES

40. Nurî, *Tevarih-i Feth-i Bağdad* (Vienna, ÖNB, Ms. H.O. 78), fol. 140a.
41. Zarain Agha, *A Relation of the Late Siege and Taking of the City of Babylon* (London, 1639), p. 2.
42. Evliya Çelebi, *Seyahatname*, Vol. 4, p. 416.
43. Jean de Thévenot, *Travels* (London, 1687), p. 288.
44. According to Evliya Çelebi their resistance to heavy cannon fire was partly attributable to the terraced construction. The cannon balls often buried themselves ineffectually in the hollow spaces between the brick layers, *Seyahatname*, Vol. 4, p. 416.
45. C. M. de Salaberry, *Histoire de l'empire Ottoman* (Paris: 1813), Vol. 1, p. 240.
46. Zarain, *True Relation of the Late Siege*, p. 30.
47. Anon., *Fethname-i Bağdad* (London, British Library Ms, Add. 9704), fol. 6a.
48. According to Evliya, *Seyahatname*, Vol. 4, p. 416.
49. Mustafa ibn Molla Rizvan, *Tarih-i Fethname-i Bağdad* (Oxford: Bodleian Library, OR 276), fol. 257b.
50. *ibid.*, fol. 257a.
51. Except for the company mess officer (*vekil-i harç*), the cooks (*tabah*), and stable boys (*at-oğlanları*), all Janissaries were expected to serve in the trenches, Nurî, *Feth-i Bağdad* (Vienna Ms H.0. 78), fol. 143b.
52. *ibid.*, and Hüseyn Hezarfen, "Kavanin-i muhasere," *Telhis ül Beyan*, Paris (BN, Manuscrits Turcs), A.F. 40, fols 112b–114a.
53. Nurî, *Feth-i Bağdad*, fol. 35b.
54. See the collection of Murad IV's imperial writs *Suver-i Hutut-i Hümayun* (Istanbul University Library, Ms 6110), fol. 200a.
55. For details, see B.B.A., Kâmil Kepeci Defterleri, No. 2580.
56. According to the anonymous *fethname* (London, British Library, Add. 9704, fol. 39b) 25 days were spent in this process during the 1638 siege of Baghdad.
57. W. H. Bau, "Fortification," *Encyclopaedia Britannica*, 11th edn (1911), Vol. 9, p. 539.
58. Zarain, *True Relation of the Late Siege*, p. 14, describes the trench as being wide enough to allow thirty soldiers to march in file.
59. Karaçelebi-zade Abdülaziz, *Zafername* (Istanbul, Devlet Library, Veliyuddin MS 2424), fols 24b–25a: "*mah-i recebin ikinci günü Çubuk Köprü nam menzilde bir gün oturak olunup, çit vurmak için bi-nihaye çubuk kestirilip, boşalan zahire develerine ve sair yükü hafif olan seyisane ve katırlara tahmil olundu.*"
60. The translated passage is found on fols 146b–148a of the Vienna Ms of Nurî's *Feth-i Bağdad*.
61. One of the reasons for Sultan Osman's failure to capture Hotin during the 1621 (1030 A. H.) campaign against Poland was the ineffectualness of the cannon at long range. Since the Ottomans were unable to manoeuvre the guns close to the walls, they had little effect beside gouging huge craters in the ground short of the walls, E. Schütz, *An Armeno-Kipchak Chronicle on the Polish-Turkish Wars in 1620–1621* (Budapest, 1968), p. 73.
62. Another effective defensive measure was the construction of high mounds, glacis, in the vicinity of the trenches as an obstacle both to the forward progress and the line of fire of the cannons. See Alvise Contarini's account in N. Barozzi and G. Berchet (eds), *Relazioni degli Ambasciatori Veneziani: Turcica* (Venezia,1871), Vol. 1, p. 348 (cf. L. Firpo repr. (Torino, 1984), p. 802): "*il principal studio in caso d'attaco deve esser quello di tener lontani li Turchi dalle fosse con lavori di terreno in campagna all'uso moderno*". However, since the Safavid garrison was under almost constant military pressure from the Ottomans in successive

244

campaigns throughout the period 1623–38, there was little opportunity for constructing complicated defence works.

63. See Nurî, *Tevarih-i Feth-i Bağdad*, fols 158a–159a.

64. Knolles/Rycaut, *History of the Turks*, 6th edn (London, 1678), p. 28.

65. Nurî, *Feth-i Bağdad*, fols 156b, 160a, 163a–164a; Mustafa ibn Molla Rizvan, *Tevarih-i Fethname-i Bağdad*, Bodleian Lib., Or. 276, fol. 261b; British Library, Add. 9704, fol. 39b.

66. The illustration is taken from the collected poems of Nadirî illustrated by Ahmed Naksî. See Topkapi Palace Library, Ms Hazine 889, fol. 14a. On the work of Ahmed Naksî, see Esin Atil, *Turkish Art* (Washington, D.C., 1980), p. 215.

67. Nurî, *Feth-i Bağdad*, fol. 163a.

68. Mustafa ibn Molla Rizvan, Bodleian, Or. 276, fol. 152b.

69. Karaçelebi-zade, *Zafername* (Istanbul Devlet Library, Ms Veliyuddin 2424), fol. 26b.

70. Nurî, *Feth-i Bağdad*, Vienna H.O. 78, fol. 165a.

71. See A. Hertz, "Armament and Supply Inventory", *Archivum Ottomanicum* **4** (1972), p. 110.

72. B.B.A., Maliyeden Müdevver 5566, pp. 264–5.

73. B.B.A., Maliyeden Müdevver 403.

74. *Silahdar Tarihi*, Vol. 2, p. 705 (lines 18–20): "*metrislerinde olan Yeniçeri ve Cebeci ve Serden-geçtilerinin ve sair tevayif-i askerin birer yayılımdan sonra, seyl-i seyf üzerlerine havale ve hücum eylediklerinde yürüyüşler edip, mealin-i hasirinin ekseri kılıçdan geçirip (. . .)*".

75. See Ch. 2 above on the political context of the wars of the *Sacra Ligua*.

76. See *Silhdar Tarihi* Vol. 1, p. 311: "*Nemçe ve Macardan dirinti piyade ve süvar başına cem eylediği 30,000 mikdar melain (. . .)*".

77. *idem.*

78. *Silahdar Tarihi*, Vol. 1, p. 313: "*Osmanlı askerine uzak kışla verildiğinden, böyle şita vaktinde beş on gün içinde cem ve imdada erişmeleri muhaldır*".

79. The forces accompanying the grand vezier at this time had dwindled to 1,500 troops belonging to his own retinue, 2,000 Janissaries and a small number of local recruits; see Silahdar, Vol. 1, p. 313.

80. *Silahdar Tarihi*, Vol. 1, p. 312, lines 16–18.

81. The operation was halted on 9 Receb 1074; the 12th day of the siege (*Silahdar I*, 315, line 4).

82. By mid-February the task had already been assigned to Ismail Pasha, a senior commander and governor of Bosnia; *Silahdar Tarihi*, Vol. 1, p. 316, line 25.

83. *Silahdar Tarihi*, Vol. 1, p. 329, line 15. In Hammer's history (*Geschichte des Osmanischen Reiches*, Vol. 6, p. 123) the dimensions of the bridge are given as 8,565 paces (about 4 miles based on the "quick pace" of 30 inches) long by 17 paces wide.

84. The attack, originally planned by Zrinyi for launching on 8 April had to be deferred for several weeks due to the late arrival of key units supplied from the centre; see Knolles/Rycaut, *Turkish History* 6th edn (London, 1687), p. 148. Ottoman sources date the beginning of the siege to the 26th of April; see Silahdar I, 338 which notes the abandonment of the attempt on 31 May coinciding with the 36th day of the siege.

85. See Evliya Çelebi, *Seyhatname*, Vol. 6, pp. 522–3.

86. *Seyahtname*, Vol. 6, p. 525: "*Sadr-i azam kalenin termimine üç vezir, yedi sancak begiyle 20,000 reaya memur edip (. . .)*".

87. *Silahdar Tarihi*, Vol. I, p. 330 (lines 18–19): "*asakir-i cerrar gün-be-gün ordu-i hümayuna mülhak olmak tasmimiyle aheste aheste, ayak sürükleyerek gitmeği makul gördüler*".

88. Mühürdar, *Cevahir ül Tevarih*, fol. 70a: "*Arnavudlukdan miriden tutulan 1,000 tufeng endaz gelip erişti*".

89. See *Cevahir ül Tevarih*, fol. 67a where the timing of the grand vezier's departure from Zemun on 19 May is defended on the basis of the preeminent importance of meeting the horses' pasturing requirements. In the words of the chronicle: "*Ruz-i Hızrdan sonra on altıncı gün (i.e. 23rd Şevval) çayır gerçe müstevfi daha yoktur, amma yine bargirler doyacak kadar vardı*".

90. *Silahdar Tarihi*,Vol. 1, p. 330 (lines 19–20) and *Cevahir ül Tevarih*, fol. 74a.

91. This thought process is made explicit in a passage in Mühürdar's account; see the *Cevahir ül Tevarih*, fol. 74a: "*Bu tarafda Zrin-oğlu memleketinde bir müstahkem kale olmadığından, kale-kûb topları getirmedik, cümlesin Ösekte alı-koyduk*".

92. *Silahdar Tarihi*, Vol. 1, p. 334 (lines 19–21): "*Kılavuzlar bu menzili üç saat demişken, yedide güç ile gelinip, (. . .) askerin gerisi ikinci günde geldiler*".

93. The approximate distances covered in this military itinerary were as follows: Nagykanizsa to Zalaegerszeg (51 km), Zalaegerszeg to Körmend (29 km); total distance, 80 km, or about 50 miles.

94. The chart is a condensation of the information supplied in Silahdar (*Tarih* I: 347–56) and the *Cevahir ül Tevarih*, fols 74b–78b.

95. The final group of three forts all situated to the west of Egervár were attacked simultaneously over a three-day period; see *Silahdar Tarihi*, Vol. 1, p. 335 and *Cevahir ül Tevarih*, fols 77b–78b.

96. See *Cevahir ül Tevarih*, fol. 76b.

97. According to Silahdar (*Tarih*, Vol. 1, p. 350) the Ottoman forces assigned to the attack on Pölöske amounted to 1,000 foot and 1,000 mounted soldiers.

98. For an argument in this vein, see the article by George Raudzens, "In Search of Better Quantification for War History: Numerical Superiority and Casualty Rates in Early Modern Europe", in *War and Society*, **15** (1997), pp. 1–30.

99. H. J. Majer, "Zur Kapitulation des Osmanischen Gran (Esztergom) in Jahre 1683", in P. Bartl and H. Glassl (eds), *Südosteuropa unter dem Halbmond* (Munich, 1975), pp. 189–204.

100. See Mühürdar, *Cevahir ül Tevarih*, fols 32a–32b for a complete list of the terms of surrender.

101. *Cevahir ül Tevarih*, fol. 77a; Cf., *Silahdar Tarihi*, Vol. 1, pp. 351–2: "*Kapudanın niyazına müsaade edip, (. . .) 20 araba verip, (. . .) tekrar kapudan silahların rica eyledikte ancak kendiye silah verip (. . .)*".

102. Although written in the post-war era of reconciliation after the Ottoman withdrawal from Hungary dating from 1699, Osman of Temeshvar's memoirs stand as one striking example of such mutual acceptance and understanding of the basic humanity of the military "foe"; see R. Kreutel (ed.), *Die Autobiographie des Dolmetschers Osman Aga aus Temeschwar*, text in Ottoman Turkish published by Gibb Memorial Trust [New Series, No. 28] (Cambridge, 1980).

103. London (British Library Ms, Or 3482), fol. 277b. Abul Qasim Ev-oğlu, *Nusha-yi jamia-yi murasalat-i ulu'ul-albab*; letter from an Ottoman soldier at the front during the 1626 campaign. Similar sentiments are expressed in another letter from the same collection; (London, BL, OR 3482), fols 275a–277b.

104. Iskandar Beg and Muhammad Yusuf, *Zayl-i Tarikh-i Alam-ara-i Abbasí*, edn by Suhaylî Khwansarî (Tahran, 1317/1938), pp. 68–9.

105. Topçular Kâtibi, *Vekayi-i Tarihiye* (ÖNB, Mxt. 130), fol. 451a: June–November 1631/ Zilkaade 1040-Rebülahir 1041.

106. Knolles, *The Generall Historie of the Turkes*, 5th edn (London: 1638), p. 1469.
107. Kâtib Çelebi, *Fezleke-i Tevarih*, Vol. 2, p. 171.
108. Thévenot, *Travels*, p. 288.
109. Apart from the decimation of the ranks through disease, desertion was a common cause of significant loss in troop strength for all pre-modern armies. The precise effect of this factor on the outcome of particular battles is, however, difficult to gauge.
110. R. Mantran, "Baghdad à l'époque Ottomane", *Arabica* (1962), pp. 313–14 claims the drop in the city's population from its high of 40,000–50,000 in the late sixteenth century to 15,000 in the seventeenth century was more the result of epidemic diseases such as the plague than of the aftereffects of siege *per se*.
111. See Ev-oğlu, *Murasalat* (London, BL Ms, OR 3842), fol. 277b.
112. The historian Ali attributes such gratuitous acts of destruction to the irregulars and army riffraff who did not know any better. His tone of disapproval at the sacking of Tabriz in 1585 which, in his view, clearly went beyond the bounds of the acceptable is obvious in his chronicle; see *Kunh ül Ahbar* (Nuruosmaniye Library, Ms 3409), fol. 36a: *"avamm-i guzat (. . .) bulduklan hacegân be tuccarı ve gözleri gördüğü sadat (. . .) üç gün üç gece kılıçdan geçirdiler. Fi nefs al emr mürtekib-i fesad olanlar bir bölük bi-kâr levendler idi"*.

Chapter Seven

1. Unmistakable signs of the Janissaries' dissatisfaction with Selim had already been expressed when the army was camped at Amasya during the winter of 1514. Their clearest act in rejecting the sultan's authority took the form of personal attacks carried out against the residences of the sultan's chief advisers and favourites of the court such as Piri Mehmed Pasha and the sultan's private tutor Hilmi Çelebi. The targets were carefully chosen so as to cause maximum affront to the sovereign authority. For a brief account of the events, see Saadeddin Hoca, *Tac ül Tevarih* 2 vols. (Istanbul, 1279–1280), Vol. 2, pp. 287 (lines 19–23) and 298 (lines 14–15).
2. On the reasons for Selim's indebtedness to the Janissaries, see R. Murphey (ed.), *Kanunname-i Sultanî* (Cambridge, MA, 1985), pp. 6 and 45 (fn. 13).
3. Ahmed Feridun, *Münşeat-i Selatin*, 1st edn (Istanbul, 1265), Vol. 2, pp. 140–42.
4. Feridun, *Münşeat*, Vol. 2, p. 141 (lines 27–9): *"ziamet ve timar erbab-i istihkaka tevcihiyle hatırlarını tatyib ve min bad dahi uğur-i hümayunda serbazılık etmeğe tergib etmek için (. . .)"*.
5. Feridun, *Münşeat*, Vol. 2, p. 141–42: *"Onun sözü benim bil-müşafehe zeban-i dürer-barımdan sadr olmuş kelâm-i saadet-encamım bilip (. . .)"*.
6. Feridun, *Münşeat*, 2nd Edn (Istanbul, 1274), Vol. 1, pp. 544–6.
7. Feridun, *Münşeat*, Vol. 1, p. 546 (lines 8–12).
8. *ibid.*, p. 546 (lines 28–9): *"ferman-i şerife (. . .) muhalefet edenler kaç nefer olur ise, (. . .) südde -i saadetim canibine arz ve ilam (. . .)"*.
9. *ibid.*, p. 546 (lines 13–15): *"B'il-cümle havme-i sultanetimde olan küliyyen kullarımın azl ve nasbı onun rey-i saibine ve fikr-i safîsine müfevvaz (. . .)"*.
10. Nihadî gives the following assessment of Kara Mustafa's character (Istanbul University Library, Ms T.Y. 6453), fol. 239a: *"hem-cunud ve sipaha inam ve atada taksirat edip, onlar dahi müsamaha ve tekâsül üzere oldular"*.

NOTES

11. *Tarih-i Nihadî*, fol. 251b: *"kafirden yüz çevirme yüzleri olamayıp, bir vechiyle söyleyecek sözleri olmasın için 'tergiben l'il cihad' destur-i mükerremlere bin aded sikke-i hasene, ve mir-i miranlara ikişer yüz, ve mir-i livalara yüzer zer atiyye-i padişahî buyurulup, (. . .)"*.

12. On the size of the Tatar contribution to that year's mobilization Ali remarks (*Kunh ül Ahbar*, fol. 410a): *"Ol sene cemiyet eden leşker dahi bir tarihde (..) manzur-i beşer değil iken (. . .)"*.

13. Although one needs to be slightly cautious about the underlying motives that animated Ali's "character references", Sinan's oafish disregard for the common forms of courtesy in dealings with the Tatar Han and his general miserliness are noted among the pasha's character failings in other sources too. For Ali's views, see the *Kunh ül Ahbar*, fol. 414a–414b.

14. See above, Ch. 3 noting the effect on mobilization levels for the Erivan (1635) and Baghdad (1638) campaigns of changes in the form and the amount of sultanic largesse.

15. For a detailed account of this phase of Sinan Pasha's career, see Ş. Turan, "Lala Mustafa Paşa hakkında notlar", *Belleten* XXII/88 (1958), p. 584.

16. Ş Turan, "Lala Mustafa", p. 584: *"yeni ülkelerin fatihi olmak için harekete geçmişlerdi"*.

17. *ibid.*, p. 590.

18. On Lala Mustafa's attempts to restore his reputation with the sultan after returning to the capital, see *Selaniki Tarihi*, M. Ipşirli edn (Istanbul, 1989), Vol. 1, p. 128, events of Rebiül evvel 988.

19. *Selaniki Tarihi*, Vol. 2, p. 448.

20. *ibid.*, p. 474.

21. M. Ali, *Kunh ül Ahbar*, fols 430b–431a and *Selaniki Tarihi*, Vol. 2, p. 471: *"Yeniçeri taifesi yetişip, (. . .) Sipah taifesine kulaçlayu kulaçlayu girişmeğe başladılar"* ("the Janissaries waded into the Sipahis swinging their arms (and swords) at full stretch").

22. On the importance of these special distributions to the status and fortunes of the rival services, see R. Murphey, "Ulufe", *Encyclopaedia of Islam*, Vol. 10.

23. See *Hasanbey-zade Tarihi* (Nuruosmaniye Library, Ms 3105), fols 497a–497b.

24. *Selaniki Tarihi*, Vol. 2, p. 480.

25. See *Hasanbey-zade Tarihi*, fols 499b–500a: *"Ordu-i hümayunda asker kalil, onlar dahi alildir. Rusçuğa karib geldik, dahi askerin öşr-i aşiri erişmedi. Yanımızda asakir gayetiyle nadir olup, (. . . .)"*.

26. *Hasanbey-zade Tarihi*, fol. 500b; *Selaniki Tarihi*, Vol. 2, p. 491.

27. On Ferhad Pasha's undeserved dismissal and its highly disruptive effects, see *Hasanbey-zade Tarihi*, fol. 502a: *"bila istihkak zümre-i şehide ilhak eylediler"*. Ali, on the other hand, attributes Sinan's success in the unseating of his rival to his well-placed distribution of bribes to people of influence in the capital. See *Kunh ül Ahbar*, fol. 433b, where the sum of 30,000 gold dinars, the equivalent of 3.6 million akçes, is mentioned.

28. C. Römer, "Die Osmanische Belagerung Bagdads 1034–35/1625–6", *Der Islam* **66** (1989), p. 122 (lines 9–11): *"asker serdardan mührü alıp, çadır çadır gezdirip (. . .), bir defa mühür ondört gün Murad elinde kalıp, badehu getirip vermişdir"*.

29. On the two schools of historical thought, see the introduction to W. R. Roff (ed.), *Islam and the Political Economy of Meaning: Comparative Studies of Muslim Discourse* (London, 1987).

30. For an example of the historically distorting misuse of cultural stereotypes, see, in addition to Barker's views cited above in Ch. 1, *n*4, the article by A. Balisch, "Infantry Battlefield Tactics", *Studies in History and Politics* **3** (1983–4), pp. 43–60. In this article Balisch attributes the Ottomans' success in battle not to superior technique but to inspiration

derived from "a fanatically pursued mission to conquer Christian Europe". In another passage Balisch, disregarding the important distinction between regular army forces and the whole spectrum of opinions, ethnicities and sectarian views represented by the presence in the army of Tatar auxiliaries, Albanian irregulars and timariots drawn from provinces as widely divergent in their demographic, social and cultural makeup as Bosnia and Syria, states definitively (p. 49) that: "this obsession with their mission fired the Turks (sic!) with their spirit of aggressiveness".

31. For the distinction between "collective" and individual duty (*fard kifaya* and *fard 'ayn*) as one of the legal aspects which governed the limiting of individual responsibility, see Th. Juynbol, "Fard", *Encyclopaedia of Islam* Vol. 2, p. 740. See in addition the article "Djihad", *ibid.*, p. 539. On the origin of the misunderstanding of the term in the rhetoric of a later (colonial and post-colonial) age of East-West confrontation, see F. Rahman, *Major Themes of the Quran* (Chicago, 1980), pp. 63–4.

32. See J. J. Dowd, "The Faith of Warriors", paper presented at the annual meeting of the American Sociological Association (New York: August 1996).

33. See in addition to the passage cited above in Ch. 2, *n*54, a second passage in which Lynn places the whole question of the average soldier's devotion to the ideological goals of his masters (regardless of historical circumstances and cultural environments) into very clear perspective. John A. Lynn, *The Bayonets of the Republic: Motivation and Tactics in the Army of Revolutionary France, 1791–1794* (Urbana, Il, 1984), p. 179: "*The numerous and obvious assertions of intense nationalism in the army tempt historians to conclude that French troops were driven by something approaching fanaticism. The conclusion is too extreme, and it transforms the revolutionary soldier into a superhuman or subhuman being. Reality was more muted.*"

34. See R. Murphey, "Süleyman's Eastern Policy" in Inalcik and Kafadar (eds) *Süleyman the Second [i.e., the First] and His Time* (Istanbul, 1992), pp. 247–8.

35. It is significant that Süleyman's demise on the battlefield in Hungary, 40 years after the victory at Mohács in 1526 that had inaugurated his reign, was at a place (Sigetvár) removed from the scene of his former glory by a distance of only 45 miles (73 km).

36. One of the most often forgotten aspects of the aftermath of the flurry of activity that saw the Ottoman capture of Cyprus (1570–71) and their defeat at Lepanto in 1571, bringing a close to a long period of East-West conflict in the Mediterranean that had begun with the prolonged Veneto-Ottoman maritime wars of the 1460s, was that it inaugurated an unprecedentedly long period of peace (and even mutual co-operation) between the Ottomans and Venice that lasted from the Peace of 1574 to the outbreak of war in Crete in 1645.

37. On the renewals of this armistice in 1574, 1577, 1584 and 1591, see Hammer, *Gesch. des Osm. Reiches*, Vol. 9, pp. 289–90 (nos. 172, 176, 181 and 186).

38. For speculation concerning the emergence of a "spiritual interchange or dialogue" (*geistiger austausch*) in the seventeenth century, affecting most particularly the northern frontier zone where inter-communal conflict had formerly been most intense, see H. J. Kissling, "Betrachtungen über Grenztradition und Grenzorganisation der Osmanen", *Scientia: Revista di Scienza* **104** (1969), pp. 647–56, esp. p. 656. Whether this fraternization with the former enemy attained the kind of societal proportions that Kissling imagines, or was more isolated and confined to the experience of the individuals most directly involved (i.e. warriors and frontiersmen as opposed to civilians and residents of the Ottoman heartlands) cannot easily be determined.

39. For the role of religion (in its propagandistic and justificatory sense as distinct from its influence as a source of historical causation) see M. Bozdemir's article "Sources

historiques de l'armée Turque" in *Review of the Faculty of Political Sciences: Ankara University*, Pt. 1, Vol. 33 (1978), pp. 163–71 and Pt. 2, Vol. 34 (1978), pp. 147–75. Bozdemir expresses the view that (see Pt. 2, p. 158): "*La religion tient évidemment une place importante au sein de l'État, mais (. . .) plutôt qu'une véritable idéologie, la religion fait figure de slogan belliqueux pour suivre les guerres extérieures*".

40. See R. Murphey, "Süleyman's Eastern Policy", in Inalcik and Kafadar (eds) *Süleyman the Second [i.e., the First] and His Time*, pp. 230–32.
41. Kâtib Çelebi, *Fezleke-i Tevarih*, Vol. 2, p. 170 (line 6): "*al insan 'abd al ihsan*".
42. The rendition of the Arabic phrase in the printed edition of Kâtib Çelebi's history is flawed. In the printed version *dhahab* (gold) replaces *wahba* (grant, donation, "tip"); cf. *Fezleke-i Tevarih*, Vol. 2, p. 170 (lines 17–17). The manuscript version in the Topkapi Palace Library (Hazine 1341), fol. 238b (lines 3–4) reads as follows: "*Idha lam yakun al malik wahba wa'ada, wa dawlathu dhahaba*". In the printed version of Naima's history (*Tarih*, Vol. 3, p. 252), the second part of the quotation is omitted.
43. Mevkufatî, *Vakiat-i Ruz-merre* (Esad Efendi Ms, 2437), fols 44a–44b: "*Ecnas-i muhtelifenin garet-i orduya mutadı sene 1094 tarihinde (. . .) neşet edip, zuhur bulmuştur. (. . .) Erazil ve ecnas-i muhtelife makulesi firsat-i ganimet bulup, yağma-i ordu-i hümayun (. . .) lezzeti dimağlarında caygir olmuştur. (. . .) Bu sene [1104] (. . .) garet-i ordu-i hümayundan na-ümid olup, ve 'Ruz-i Kasım karib oldu' behanesiyle perakende ve perişan olmalarıyla, ordu-i hümayun hâli koyup, (. . .)*".
44. *Tarih-i Raşid* (Istanbul, 1153), Vol. 1, fol. 234b: "*Naima Efendi-i merhumun yevmiye ceridesinde (. . .) mestur*".
45. *Tarih-i Raşid*, Vol. 1, fol. 234b: "*30,000 koyun zayi olmak üzere iddia edip, Şeyh ül Islam Efendi tarafına kemal mertebe intisabından naşi zikr olunan 90,000 koyun miriye mahsub (. . .)*".
46. On the importance of typological divisions between soldiers performing different functions and drawn from different sources of recruitment, and factional and political divisions, see pp. 28–9 above.
47. See O. Ş. Gökyay, "Kamaniçe Muhafızlarının Çektiği", *Tarih Dergisi* **32** (1979), pp. 295–9.
48. See J. Schacht, *Introduction to Islamic Law* (Oxford, 1964), p. 130 (fn. 1).
49. See Knolles, *Gen. Hist. of the Turkes*, 5th Edn (London, 1638), p. 1133 where the Zriny family's ownership of 20 villages put at risk by the Ottoman commander Ibrahim Pasha's advance against Kanizsa in September–October 1600 is identified as a strong factor motivating his energetic participation in the counterattack aimed at relieving the fortress. Nicholas Zriny was the namesake and grandfather of the Nicholas (Miklos Zriny VII, d. 1664) who was still defending family interests in the region at the time of Köprülü–zade Fazil Ahmed Pasha's expedition in summer 1664. See above, Ch. 6 and, for further detail, R. J. Evans, *The Making of the Habsburg Monarchy, 1550–1700* (Oxford, 1979), p. 243 and elsewhere.
50. For a general assessment of the position of the magnates in the borderlands, see G. Rothenberg, *The Austrian Military Border in Croatia, 1522–1747* (Urbana, IL, 1960), p. 4: "*The dominant nobility was not only free from any national feeling, but the leading families (such as the Zriny and the Frangepani) had acquired lands in both (. . .) [Hungary and Croatia] and it was quite difficult to determine whether a particular individual was Hungarian or Croat*".
51. Evliya Çelebi describes the position with admirable clarity. See *Seyahatname*, Vol. 6, p. 545 (lines 19–21): "*Düşman Yeni Kalede cemiyetde iken vilayet-i kafiristan boşdur, ve 'zaman-i ganimetdir' deyü memalik-i düşman tahrib etmeğe çıkmışlar*".

NOTES

52. For example, in 1587 a group of overeager raiders from southern Hungary were caught unawares by enemy forces and themselves taken captive. See *Tarih-i Selaniki*, Ipşirli edn., Vol. 1, p. 189: "*Sigetvar serhaddından leşker ile doyumluk sevdasıyla tama-i ham'a düşüp, nice bin adem bile uyup gidip, (. . . .) giriftar olup, (. . .)*".

53. The organization of wartime raids as lightning strikes aimed against depopulated or lightly defended districts, followed by equally rapid retreats, further minimized the risk of significant loss of life. See the description given by Silahdar of one such raid (*Tarih*, Vol. 1, p. 301): "*vilayeti hâli kaldığı haberi mesmu (. . .) oldukta, memleketi vurup, (. . .)*".

54. Evliya Çelebi, *Seyahatname*, Vol. 6, p. 547 (lines 13–15): "*Serhadd gazilerimiz [devam etmeğe] nza vermedi. 'Ösek panayiri günleridir, kiymetli mal füruht ederiz' deyü Ösek kalesi tarafına revan (. . .)*".

55. See Evliya Çelebi, *Seyhatname*, Vol. 56, p. 549: "*Hakir kassam olarak (. . .) iki pay bir gulâm ve bir at ziyade verip, ve cümlenin nzasıyla huddamlarına dahi ikişer pay ziyade verdiler*".

56. See *n*30 above.

57. See B. Flemming, "The Sultan's Prayer Before Battle", in C. Heywood and C. Imber (eds), *Studies in Ottoman History in Honour of Professor V. L. Ménage* (Istanbul, 1994), p. 75.

58. For Western notions of the "just war" which involved both the invoking of God's support and the demonizing of the enemy (i.e. infidel), see J. Bliese, "Rhetoric and Morale: A Study of Battle Orations from the central Middle Ages", *Journal of Medieval History* **15** (1989), pp. 201–26. In this article (pp. 205–6 and summary on p. 220) Bliese compiles a list of the 17 themes most commonly encountered in battle orations from the West.

59. See Edward N. Stone (ed.), *Three Old French Chronicles of the Crusades* (Seattle, WA, 1939), pp. 220–21.

60. See I. Gentile, "Why Men Fought in the British Civil Wars, 1639–1652", *History Teacher* **26** (1993), 407–18.

61. See Bliese, "Rhetoric and Morale", p. 215 citing the work of Cowdry and Riley-Smith on the "First Crusade" of the early twelfth century. See also P. Contamine, *War in the Middle Ages* (Oxford, 1984), p. 298: "*A pitched battle was preceded by religious rites, confession, communion, mass and the sign of the cross which combatants made before risking death*".

62. Examples of this genre include: John Williams, *God in the Camp: . . . a sermon preach'd before his excellency and general assembly at a lecture in Boston, March 6th, 1706* (Boston, 1707) relating to the context of Queen Anne's War and W. Goodrich, *A Sermon on the Christian Necessity of War by William H. Goodrich, Pastor of the First Presbyterian Church Cleveland, preached April 21, 1861* (Cleveland, 1861).

63. See R. Ettinghausen, "Hilal", *Encyclopaedia of Islam*, Vol. 3, p. 384 and illustrations. For a collection of pre-twelfth century literary references to the form and uses of the horsetail standards by the Turks, see B. Ögel, "Tuğ", *Islam Ansiklopedisi* Vol. 12, pp. 1–5.

64. See the article "Gulbang", in *Encyclopaedia of Islam*, Vol. 2, p. 1135.

65. See I. H. Uzunçarşılı, *Omanlı Develtinin Saray Teşkilatı* (Ankara, 1945), pp. 449–52.

66. See E. Çelebi, *Seyahtname*, (Istanbul, 1314), Vol. 1, p. 620: "*Hususa cenk yerinde guzat-i muslimini tergib için yüz yiğirmi koldan cenk tablına ve kös-i hakanîlere tıralar vurmağa başlayarak (. . .)*".

67. See K. Signell, "Mozart and the mehter", *The Consort* **24** (1967), pp. 310–22.

68. For some remarks on the genre of folk history in general and its popularity among the military classes in particular, see R. Murphey, "Expression of Individuality in Ottoman Society", forthcoming in P. Dumont (ed.), *The Individual and Society in the Ottoman Empire*.

251

69. See the general introduction to Naima's history, Vol. 1 (Istanbul, 1260), p. 58 (lines 2–9): "*tergib edici sözler*". Compare Kâtib Çelebi, *Fezleke-i Tevarih*, Vol. 2, p. 353.
70. *Tarih-i Naima*, Vol. 4, p. 447: "*Askere fütur gelmeğin hizmetden soğudular. (. . .) Askere ye's -i tam gelmekle, gittikçe hizmetde tekâsül gösterir oldular*".
71. The first Ottoman troops landed in late June 1645 and Hüseyn Pasha assumed his command in early February 1646.
72. The commander's words in a letter to the Porte are clear in predicting a halt to significant further progress of the siege until all his tired forces were temporarily replaced and given a chance to return to home base on extended leave. See *Tarih-i Naima*, Vol. 4, p. 454: "*Bu asker vilayetlerine varıp bir mikdar dinçlenip gelmeyince, bir dahi muhasereye kadir değillerdir*".
73. See S. J. Christensen, "The Heathen Order of Battle", in S. J. Christensen (ed.), *Violence and the Absolutist State: Studies in Ottoman and European History* (Copenhagen, 1990), pp. 75–138, esp., pp. 115–16.
74. See the example of Ibrahim Çavush who received a 5,000 akçe increment to his timar for services rendered during the Caucasian campaign in 1579; Abdurrahman Şeref, "Özdemiroğlu Osman Paşa", *Tarih-i Osmanî Encümeni Mecmuası* IV/24 (1329), p. 1510 (no. 1): "*Menteşe, timar-i Ibrahim, Çavuş-i Dergâh-i Ali, 7,000 [akçe]. Ereş kurbunda bina olunan cisrda hizmet edip, asker ile geçildikte yoldaşlığı zuhur gelmeğin 5,000 [akçe] terakki verilmek buyuruldu; fi 12 Şaban sene 986*".
75. See the account of these distributions in A. Cassola, T. Scheban and I. Bostan (eds) *The 1565 Malta Campaign Register* (La Valletta, Malta, 1998), pp. 177–99.
76. See *Tarih-i Nihadî* (Istanbul Univ. Library, Ms T.Y. 6053), fol. 256b–257a: "*mutayyeb al hatır olmaları için (. . .) mecruh olanları yaralarına göre onar, onbeşer, yiğirmişer otuzar ve kırkar guruş ihsan olup (. . .), ve 2,172 reis helak olan fars behası 33,853 guruş ihsan buyurulup, (. . .)*".
77. Mühürdar, *Cevahir ül Tevarih* (Leiden, Cod. Or. 1225), fol. 71b.
78. *Cevahir*, fol. 73a: "*kelle ve dil getirenlere yürüyüş günü yiğirmi kise akçe ihsan (. . .)*".
79. On the importance of these subjective categories as sources of service loyalty and combat effectiveness among French soldiers in the late eighteenth century, see J. Lynn, *Bayonets of the Republic* (Urbana, IL, 1984), pp. 28 *et seq.*
80. On the difficulties encountered by Ferhad Pasha as a result of his perceived failure to carry out promises offered to servicemen to recruit their services in time of military emergency, see the Gandja episode referred to above in *n23*.
81. For the Tenedos landing, see *Naima Tarihi*, Vol. 6, p. 280 (lines 3–4). For the attempt to relieve Buda, see *Silahdar Tarihi*, Vol. 2, p. 249 (lines 15–17).
82. Initial pay rates for cavalrymen ranged between 13 and 20 akçes. See R. Murphey, "Ulufe", *Encyclopaedia of Islam*, Vol. 10 and I. H. Uzunçarşılı, *Osmanlı Devleti Teşkilatından Kapukulu Ocakları* (Ankara, 1943), Vol. 1, p. 349.
83. In addition to Crete, the Aegean and Dalmatia which were all active fronts connected with the Veneto-Ottoman war, going on since 1645, at the time of the 1658 purges Köprülü had only recently returned from Trans-Danubia where he had conducted a successful campaign against the rebellious vassal Principality of Transylvania (Erdel).
84. For an indication of the level of these cuts, see above, Ch. 3 (Table 3.5) and *Silahdar Tarihi*, Vol. 1, p. 147 (lines 23–4) which suggest that the number of muster roll tickets (*esame*) revoked by Köprülü reached as high as 7,000. For another, openly unfavourable, opinion citing the thinness of Köprülü's pretext for carrying out such extensive purges that amounted, in the author's opinion, to a kind of personal vendetta against the Sipahis, see Abdi Paşa, *Vekayiname* (Istanbul University Lib., Ms T.Y. 4140), fol. 48a: "*mevzi-i mezburde [i.e., the meadows of Kağıdhane in the vicinity of Istanbul where a part of the Ottoman*

army was camped in November 1658 after its late season return from Transylvania] Kasım mevacibi verilip, hazır bulunmayanlardan bir kaç bin adamın esameleri çalındı".

85. The historian Nihadî claimed the number of revoked pay-tickets mounted to 10,000 (cf. Silahdar's figure of 7,000 cited in *n*84 above), adding that the failure to attend a midnight roll call announced suddenly on 2 November (5 Safer 1069) was no justification for depriving so many veteran servicemen of their livelihoods. See *Tarih-i Nihadî* (Istanbul University Lib., Ms 6053), fol. 185a: *"Ol gece [vezir Köprülü Mehmed Paşa] on binden ziyade kimsenin esamisi çalınıp, kat-i erzak, zulüm-i sarih etmiştir".*

86. The term and its wider context are borrowed from the novel by Graham Greene (1st edn 1978) that bears the same title.

87. A still largely unexploited source are the folk histories which reflect the feelings and experiences of the men who actually fought in wars. The campaign diaries by the official historiographers, whose accounts have been used to-date as our nearly exclusive font of information on Ottoman warfare, reflect little of such frontline experiences.

Chapter Eight

1. See, for example, the assessment of Speros Vryonis who attributes the success of medieval Ottoman warriors to their commitment to proselytizing on a behalf of their newly adopted faith. In one passage Vryonis concludes (S. Vryonis, *Decline of Medieval Hellenism* (Berkeley, Ca, 1971), p. 273, fn. 764): *"the warlike mentality of the Turkmen [was] transformed by Islamic mysticism".*

2. The twelfth article of the Treaty of Carlowitz of 1699 made reference to the desirability on humanitarian grounds of organizing comprehensive prisoner exchanges. See Silahdar, *Nusretname* (ed. I. Parmaksızoğlu), Vol. I, pt. iii, p. 361: *"esirlerin tarafeynden merhamet ile tekayyüd oluna (. . .)".* Similar terms were provided in article seven of the Ottoman's 1606 Treaty with the Habsburgs; see G. Bayerle, "The Compromise at Zsitvatorok", *Archivum Ottomanicum* 6 (1980), pp. 19–21. Reference is also made in a subsequent renewal of the Sitva Torok Treaty in 1615 to the resolving of outstanding disputes between the two sides over the disposition of some border villages near Esztergom through a reconciliation of the two opposing viewpoints; see article three of this treaty as quoted by Kâtib Çelebi in the *Fezleke-i Tevarih*, Vol. 1, p. 371: *"Estergon'un nizalu 158 pare kariyesi görülüp (. . .) iki canibden uzlaştılar".*

3. For persistent reference in the later treaties to a return to the borders as they had existed at the time of Sultan Süleyman (the First) in the mid-sixteenth century, see, for the 1619 treaty renewal, A. Feridun, *Münşeat-i Selatin*, Vol. 2, pp. 170–73 and Kâtib Çelebi, *Fezleke -i Tevarih*, Vol. 2, p. 397.

4. On general peasant psychology and for an attempt to identify to what extent peasants were aware of and motivated by their knowledge of "growth centres" when making informed decisions about a preferred place of residence, see M. Vasic's study, "Der Einfluss der Türkenkriege auf die Wirtschaft des Osmanischen Grenzgebietes in Serbien und Bosnien", in O. Pickl (ed.), *Die Wirtschaftlichen Auswirkungen der Türkenkriege* (Graz, 1971), pp. 308–18.

5. G. David, "Demographische Veränderungen in Ungarn zur Zeit der Türkenherrschaft", *Acta Historica Acad. Scient. Hung.* 34 (1988), esp., pp. 82–3, where the regional breakdown

of Hungary's population in the late sixteenth century is given as follows: 900,000 for Ottoman Hungary, 1.8 million for "Royal" (i.e. Habsburg) Hungary, and 800,000 for "Free" Hungary, making a total of 3.5 million inhabitants.

6. G. David, "Demographische Veränderungen", pp. 86–7. David attributes the modest growth of Ottoman Hungary during the course of the seventeenth century – from a previous level of 900,000 to perhaps a million inhabitants – to the effects of boundary changes more than to biological increase, but the observed growth rate of 11 per cent in the Ottoman-administered region diverges only slightly from the average spread across the whole region whose net increase of 0.5 million from 3.5 to 4.0 million represents an average growth rate of 14.3 per cent. David is also careful in noting that the figure for Hungary's population circa 1700 represents its level before the effect of immigration to Hungary from other parts of the Habsburg empire, witnessed from the middle decades of the eighteenth century, had yet begun to take effect. See G. David (citing research by Z. David), "Demographische Veränderungen" p. 86: "es ist anzunehmen das Ungarns Bevolkerungszahl zu Anfang des 18. Jahrhunderts, also vor den grossen Einsiedlungen aus dem Ausland, 4 millionen betrug".

7. For some indications based on Istanbul's population and food consumption patterns, see R. Murphey, "Provisioning Istanbul: The State and Subsistence in the Early-Modern Middle East", Food and Foodways 2 (1988), pp. 217–63.

8. See C. R. Friedrichs, "The War and German Society", in G. Parker (ed.), The Thirty Years' War (New York, 1984), pp. 208–15.

9. For some examples, see R. Murphey, "Ottoman Administrative Theory and Practice", Politics Today 14/2 (1993), pp. 422–3. A new pair of polar opposites is proposed in an article by A. P. Martinez, "Atavistic and Negotiation States", Archivum Ottomanicum 12 (1987–92), pp. 105–74.

10. For a partial corrective to these views, see H. Inalcik, "Sultanism", Princeton Papers in Near Eastern Studies 1 (1992), pp. 47–72 and R. Murphey, "An Ottoman View From the Top", Turcica 28 (1996), pp. 319–38.

11. Relating to the context especially of guild workers, but with inferential attribution to more generalized conditions of labour S. Faroqhi offers the following assessment: "the Ottoman state relied extensively on drafted labor which was either paid below market rates or not at all", Faroqhi, "Labor Recruitment and Control in the Ottoman Empire", in D. Quataert [ed.], Manufacturing in the Ottoman Empire and Turkey, 1500–1950 [Albany, NY, 1994], p. 13.

12. The exploration of the immutable aspects of Ottoman warfare is found above in Ch. 2. The Ottomans would have included in the list of what they regarded as constant and unchanging the need for balancing of interests which could only be secured through continuous redefinition and refinement of the terms of taxpayer co-operation and co-optation.

13. See, on the reform of the Christian poll-tax, H. Inalcik, "Djizya", Encyclopaedia of Islam, Vol. 2, pp. 562–6. See also, B. McGowan, Economic Life in Ottoman Europe (Cambridge, 1981), pp. 80–82.

On wartime (1687–99) and post-war (1699–1703) administrative reforms including tax-reduction and tax reallocation schemes, see R. Murphey, "Ottoman Administrative Theory and Practice", Politics Today 14/2 (1993), pp. 426–36.

14. See Mevkufatî, Vakiat-i Ruz-merre, Vol. 4, fol. 117b. The terms of the exchange in this case were the replacement of the villagers' commitment to supply one musket-bearing foot soldier for every two tax households, with an obligation assumed by each registered

tax household to supply two *kiles* of barley and four *kiles* of flour and to provide transport overland as far as Belgrade.

15. See Mevkufatî, *Vakiat-i Ruz-merre:* "*her iki hanelerinden bir nefer piyade-i tüfenk-endaz ihrac olunmak üzere cümle tekâlifden muaf olan kazaların reaya fukerasına tüfeng-endaz ihracı müteessir olup, hallerine merhameten bu sene ref (. . .), teklifleri mukabilinde zahire ihrac ve Belgrad'a nakli fermanım olmuştur*".

16. See the entry dated 2 Cemazi II 1104 (9 February 1693) in the *Vakiat-i Ruz-merre*, fol. 176a–177a: "*Yenişehir sükkânı ayanından Kaftanî Hüseyn Ağa kullarından ve sair vukuf-i tamı olanlardan sual olundukta 'seksan haneleri tenzil olunur ise tekâlifleri tahfif ve ahvalları nizam bulur' deyü ihbar ettikleri (. . .)*".

17. See for example, the law code for Bosnia of 1542 published by Durdev *et al.* (*Kanun-ı Kanun-name* (Sarajevo, 1957), p. 64): "*Yeni feth olan yerlerde reaya (. . .) filoriye kayd olup (. . .) zikr olunan yerlerin ekseri Dar ul Harb'a mutassıl mahfuf yerlerde vaki olmağin, kemaliyle ziraat ve hiraset olunmaz (. . .). Ber vech-i nakd bedel-i öşr birer mikdar nesne tayin ve takdir olunmuştur. Kemaliyle ziraat ve hiraset olundukta (. . .) öşür [lerin] eda edeler*".

18. See S. Faroqhi, "Finances", in Inalcik and Quataert (eds), *An Economic and Social History* (Cambridge, 1994), p. 534 (Table II.18). The compliance rate for Anatolia generally was higher, rising to approximately 80 per cent of what had been asked for, but of course the achievement of even these higher levels still meant a shortfall in needed supplies amounting to one-fifth of the total.

19. For an assessment of the military power of the eighteenth-century state by a specialist on Habsburg institutional development, see R. Kann, "Conclusions", in Kiraly and Rothenberg (eds) *Special Topics and Generalizations on the 18th and 19th Centuries* (New York, 1979), pp. 146–7. Kann concludes that even in its final evolutionary stage when it is said to have developed a "bureaucratic army system", the Habsburg army was: "*governed as much by pragmatic considerations as by an imposition of what was theoretically best*".

20. See M. Kütükoğlu, *1640 Tarihli Narh Defteri* (Istanbul, 1983), pp. 48–51.

21. See remarks by S. Faroqhi, "Deliveries in Kind", Inalcik and Quataert (eds), *An Economic and Social History* (Cambridge, 1994), pp. 533–5.

22. See L. Güçer, *Hububat Meselesi* (Istanbul, 1964), p. 134: "*Izmit gemicilerinden Hasan Reis-'den serbest fiyatla kile başına 28 akçe, 1,000 kile*".

23. On the army's march through central Anatolia between Diyarbekir and Amasya in November and December 1635, see S. Ünver, "Sultan Murad'in Revan Seferi Kronolojisi", *Belleten* 16/64 (1952), pp. 555–6. A register of grain purchases is provided in B. B. A., Maliyeden Müdevver 18708 which records the purchase of one consignment of 40 *kiles* of barley for 6,000 akçes (150 per *kile*) and another at Harput of 458 *kiles* at a cost of 137,400 akçes (300 per *kile*).

24. For a discussion of the arguments for and against regarding the pre-eighteenth-century Ottoman economy as a "command economy", see R. Murphey, "Patterns of Trade Along the Via Egnatia", in E. Zachariadou (ed.), *Via Egnatia Under Ottoman Rule* (Rethymnon, 1996), pp. 171–2 and p. 189. Judging from the available evidence, it seems that, for most parts of the empire in the seventeenth century, the gap between the government's regulatory intent and enforcement success must have been rather great.

25. Citing the work of Igmar Bog on the economic stimulus linked with victualling Habsburg armies, Kristof Glamann reached the following conclusion: "*the agrarian depression came to an end more swiftly in Germany than in other regions of Europe*"; see the *Cambridge Economic History of Europe* Vol. 5 (Cambridge, 1977), esp., pp. 195–205.

26. The creation and expansion of an international trading network for livestock during the

period of the Ottoman-Habsburg wars of the sixteenth and seventeenth centuries has been studied by L. Ruzas, "Die Entwicklung der Marktflecke TransDanubiens", in O. Pickl (ed.), *Die Wirtschaftlichen Auswirkungen* (Graz, 1971), pp. 221–34.

27. For the Habsburg case, see J. Berenger, "Sammuel Oppenheimer (1630–1703) Banquier de l'empereur Leopold I'er", *Dix–Septième Siècle* 46/2 (1994), pp. 303–20. For an Ottoman example (albeit on a less grandiose scale) of the amassment of personal fortune through speculative involvement in the supply of war, see R. Murphey, "Historical Introduction", in R. Dankoff, *The Intimate Life of an Ottoman Statesman* (Albany, N, 1991), p. 23 (*n*2) and pp. 28–9 (fn. 9–11) where the legal and extra-legal activities of a certain Kudde Mehmed Agha as sultanic financier and army provisioner in the early years of the Veneto-Ottoman wars in Crete are detailed.

28. On the phenomenon of interloping (*madrabazlık*) in grain shipments and the government's only partial success in containing it, see R. Murphey, "The State and Subsistence", *Food and Foodways* **2** (1988), pp. 222.

29. See R. Murphey, "Labour Mobility", in M. Delilbaşı (ed.), *Studies on South-eastern Europe Under Ottoman Rule* (Ankara, 1998).

30. See the references to the boom in contraband grain trade during this period in R. Murphey, "Ottoman Resurgence", *Mediterranean Historical Review* **8** (1993), p. 195 (fn. 26).

31. Evliya Çelebi, *Seyahatname* Vol. 7 (Istanbul, 1928), pp. 489–90.

32. For the effect of the Ottomans' activation of resources for campaigns in Crete and on the Dalmatian front on the economic status of Albania and other parts of the Western Balkans which served as the principal supply bases for that theatre of war, see Ch. 3, pp. 58–9 and the text of *n*62 on p. 228. See also, R. Murphey, "Patterns of Trade Along the Via Egnatia" (as in *n*24), pp. 179 (fn. 21) and 185 (Table 3, fn. 2, 3 and 6).

33. For evidence showing the economic importance of garrison troops as consumers of urban manufactures, drawing mostly on examples from Anatolia, see Y. Oğuzoğlu, "Osmanlı şehirlerinde askerlerin ekonomik durumuna ilişkin bazı bilgiler", *Birinci Askeri Tarih Semineri* 4 vols. (Ankara, 1983), Vol. 2, pp. 169–76. The notion of the military's inherent "macroparasitism" has been suggested to describe its relation to society at large, but within a more localized and regional context their input and participation in reciprocal and redistributive economic activity was perhaps the most salient feature of their provincial profile. For the concept of "macroparasitism", see W. H. McNeill, *Pursuit of Power* (Oxford, 1982), p. viii and John F. Guilmarten, "Technology and Conflict: The Wars of the Ottoman Empire, 1453–1606", *Journal of Interdisciplinary History* **18** (1987–8), pp. 721–48; especially pp. 744–5.

34. For a summary account of the impact of war on the medieval economy, see G. Duby, *The Early Growth of the European Economy: Warriors and Peasants From the Seventh to the Twelfth Century*, Eng. Tr. by Howard B. Clarke (Ithaca, NY, 1974), esp. pp. 119–29. In his study Duby explores the effect of scattered raiding activity in bringing about the accelerated circulation of goods and forcing the redistribution of hoarded wealth.

35. In the provinces of the eastern borderlands such as Erzurum a relatively small proportion of revenues was actually remitted to the central treasury, and the net direction of capital flow was inward. On the net flow of investment, capital and revenue transfers from other regions inward for the sustaining of areas under threat of attack, based on data from the 1630s when the Ottomans were militarily active in the East, see J. Clark, "Computer Mapping of Maliyeden Müdevver Register 7075", in *Turkish Studies Association Bulletin* **13** (1989), pp. 79–90.

NOTES

Chapter Nine

1. The prevalence of such views among Balkanists is represented in the assessments found in a standard text on Balkan development (underdevelopment) under Ottoman rule; see J. Lampe, "The Economic Legacy of Ottoman Domination", pp. 21 et seq. in John R. Lampe and Marvin R. Jackson, *Balkan Economic History, 1550–1950* (Bloomington, Ind., 1982), esp. p. 23.
2. For an assessment of general views on the impact of Ottoman rule in the Arab lands, see R. Murphey, "The Ottoman Centuries in Iraq: Legacy or Aftermath?", *Journal of Turkish Studies* 11 (1987), pp. 17–29.
3. For a discussion of population figures, see H. Inalcik, *An Economic and Social History*, p. 29 and n13–16. For the empire's territorial extent, see D. Pitcher, *Historical Atlas of the Ottoman Empire* (Leiden, 1972), p. 134. By Pitcher's calculation the empire's three main territorial divisions extended by 1566 over 877,800 square miles as follows: 462,700 in Asia (53%), 224,100 in Europe (26%) and 191,000 (22%) in Africa.
4. The sultan's communication contained the following observation (*Tarih-i Raşid* [Istanbul, 1153], Vol. 1, fol. 55a): "*bir sene dahi kale ile cenk olunursa, asker ve cebehane ve sair alat [ve] mühimmat yetiştirmeğe memalik-i mahrusem aciz olmuştur*".
5. See R. Murphey, "Critica", *Archivum Ottomanicum* 13 (1993–4), pp. 379–80 on the spreading of the burden of war-finance through taxing (in the form of temporary exactions and "loans") of the tax-exempt foundations.
6. See S. Faroqhi, "Finances", in Inalcik and Quataert (eds), *An Economic and Social History*, p. 542: "*war-related demands weighed heavily on the Ottoman peasantry even in the fifteenth century*".
7. B. McGowan, "Food Supply and Taxation on the Middle Danube (1568–1579)", *Archivum Ottomanicum* 1 (1969), pp. 139–96.
8. One example of a plausible, but without corroborating evidence, insufficiently demonstrated hypothesis is the notion of the village economy's inherent inability to absorb increased grain and other basic agricultural production. However, it must be considered that the payment of taxes was only one of the uses to which surplus grain production could be put (see previous note). For the notion of malabsorption in the village economy, see C. Finkel, "The Costs of Ottoman Warfare and Defense", *Byzantinische Forschungen* 16 (1991), pp. 102–3: "*the local market was not big enough to absorb the extra agricultural produce they [the peasants in core provinces of the empire] were obliged to sell in order to raise the cash needed [to pay taxes]*".
9. For some further evidence on the socially progressive implications of the shifting of tax burdens from rural producers to urban consumers in the later part of the seventeenth century, see R. Murphey, "Administrative Theory and Practice", *Politics Today* 14 (1993), p. 430.
10. L. Darling, *Revenue-Raising and Legitimacy: Tax Collection and Financial Administration in the Ottoman Empire* (Leiden, 1996), pp. 113 et seq., Tables 7–8 and esp., p. 118: "*The actual rise of the cash avariz was only moderately greater than the rate of inflation*".
11. See R. Murphey, "Continuity and Discontinuity in Ottoman Administrative Theory and Practice", cited in n9 above and for cizye reform including the introduction of a graduated pay scale, H. Inalcik, "Djiyza", *Encyclopaedia of Islam*, Vol. 2, pp. 562 et seq.
12. See, for example, Darling, *Revenue-Raising*, p. 117: "*The number of avarizhanes in the empire*

257

[. . .] was halved at the beginning of the seventeenth century, effectively cancelling out much of [the] increase [due to rising tax rates]".

13. Residents of Uyvar paid 50 akçes per head for *cizye* as compared with the standard rate of one gold ducat (equivalent in the period to around 200 akçes, see *n*14 below) assessed in other areas. See J. Blaskovic, "The Period of Ottoman Turkish reign at Nove Zamky (1663–1685)", *Archiv Orientalni* **54** (1986), pp. 105–30. Blaskovic records (p. 118) the province's payment of a yearly sum of 1,009,150 akçes to the treasury by 20,183 non-Muslim *cizye* payers, amounting to 50 akçes per head.

14. For the steady decline in the akçe's value from 250 per gold ducat at the beginning of the wars of the *Sacra Ligua* to 300 at the end of the first seven years of the seventeen-year struggle between 1683 and 1699, see the *Tarih-i Raşid* (edn in 5 vols, Istanbul, 1282/ 1865) Vol. 2, p. 147 *(sub anno* 1102 A. H. / AD 1690): "*şerifif altun 270 akçeye, yaldız altunu 300'er akçeye alına*".

15. Even in the crisis of 1687–8 the emergency recruitment of *levends* to serve under Yeğen Osman Paşa only added a few thousand troops to the balance of Ottoman forces in the field. See above, Ch. 2, *n*61–3.

16. See H. Inalcik, "Military and Fiscal Transformation in the Ottoman Empire, 1600–1700", *Archivum Ottomanicum* **6** (1980), pp. 283–337; esp., pp. 299–300.

17. See Irwin T. Sanders, "Balkan Rural Society and War", in Kiraly and Rothenberg (eds), *Special Topics* (New York, 1979), pp. 151–62.

18. On the relationship between population and military recruitment in various European states at the turn of the eighteenth century, see A. Corvisier, *Armées et sociétés en Europe de 1494 à 1789* (Paris, 1976), Table on p. 126.

19. For the use of this designation with reference to the Ottoman empire, see P. Sugar's article in L. Farrar (ed.), *War: A Historical, Political and Social Study* (Santa Barbara, Ca, 1978), pp. 95 *et seq*.

Select bibliography

Primary sources

Abdi. Abdurrahman Abdi Paşa, *Vakaname-i Abdi Paşa*, Istanbul: Univ. Lib. Ms. TY 4140 [covers the period 1648–1682].

Ali, Mustafa (Gelibolulu). *Kunh ül Ahbar*, Istanbul: Nuruosmaniye Lib. Ms. no. 3409 [fols 286–459 relate to events of the years 1574–96].

Kâtib Çelebi. Mustafa ibn Abdullah [Kâtib Çelebi], *Fezleke-i Tevarih*, 2 vols. (Istanbul: Ceride-i Havadis Matbaası, 1286–1287) [covers the period 1592–1655].

Karaçelebi-zade. Karaçelebi-zade Abdulaziz Efendi. Nusretname, Istanbul: Devlet Lib. Ms, Veliyyudin 2424 [an account of the Ottoman siege of Baghdad in 1638].

Knolles, Richard. *The generall historie of the Turkes* (London, 1638). The Fifth Edn of 1638 contains the history of the dynasty to the year 1628 in 1499 pages of text with a separately paginated (pp. 1–31) "continuation" covering the years 1628–1637.

Mevkufatî. Abdullah ibn Ibrahim (al-Üskudarî, al-Mevkufatî). *Vakiat-i Ruz-merre*, in 4 vols. covering the period 1688–1693 [Vol. 4 – Istanbul: Suleymaniye Lib. Ms., Esad Efendi 2437 – covers the period Sept. 1692 to Sept. 1693].

Mühürdar. Hasan Ağa [Mühürdar]. *Cevahir ül-Tevarih* (Leiden: Univ. Lib. Ms., Or. 1225] [an account of the Grand Vezier Köprülü-zade Fazıl Ahmed Paşa's campaigns in Hungary (siege of Uyvar in 1663) and Crete (siege of Candia in 1669)].

Naima, Mustafa. *Tarih-i Naima* 6 vols. (Istanbul: Matbaa-i Amire, 1281–1283) [covers the period 1592–1660].

Nihadî (pseudonym for author b. 1065/1655). *Tarih-i Nihadî*, Istanbul: University Library Ms., TY 6053 [covers dynastic events up to the year 1096 A. H./AD 1685 but most detailed for the events of his own lifetime, esp. the 1680s and 1690s; see fols 237b–246b].

Nihadî, Seq. *Bin yuz sekiz senesinde Sultan Mustafa hazretlerinin ikinci seferinin tahrir olunan vekayiidir*, Istanbul: Univ. Lib. Ms, TY 6053, fols 246b–260b [a detailed account of the military manouevres carried out by the newly enthroned Sultan Mustafa II during A. H. 1107–1108 [AD 1696].

Nurî. Ziya'eddin Ibrahim [Nurî]. *Fethname-i Bağdad* Vienna: ÖNB Ms., H.O. 78 [account of Ottoman siege of Baghdad in 1638].

Peçevi, Ibrahim. *Tarih-i Peçevi* 2 vols. (Istanbul: Matbaa-i Amire 1283) [covers the period 1520–1640].

259

Rahmi-zade. Ibrahim Çavuş [Rahmi-zade]. *Kitab-i Gencine-i Feth-i Gence*, Istanbul: Topkapi Palace Lib. Ms., Revan 1296 [an account of Ferhad Paşa's campaign of 1588 against Gence (Gandja).

Raşid, Ahmed. *Tarih-i Yemen ve Sana* 2 vols. (Istanbul: Basiret Matbaası, 1291).

Raşid, Mehmed. *Tarih-i Raşid*, 2 vols. (Istanbul: Ibrahim Muteferrika, 1153) [covers the period 1660–1703].

Rizvan-zade. Mustafa ibn Molla Rizvan. *Tarih-i Fethname-i Bağdad*, Oxford: Bodleian Lib. Ms., Or. 276 [account of Ottoman siege of Baghdad in 1638].

Rycaut, Paul. *The Turkish history* [1623–1686] (London, 1687). The Sixth Edn [of Knolles, q.v.] printed in 1687 contains a continuation of Knolles to the year 1687 by Rycaut and others. The portions of the history covering the years between 1623 and 1686 are paginated continuously (pp. 1–338).

Rycaut, Paul. *History of the Turks* [1679–1699] (London, 1700).

Ruzname (Anon.) *Ruzname: 935–936 A.H.*, in Ahmed Feridun, *Münşeat-i Selatin*, Vol. 1 (Istanbul, 1274), pp. 566–74 [a campaign diary of the 1529 Vienna campaign].

Saadeddin. Mehmed ibn Hasan [Saadeddin], *Tac ül Tevarih* 2 vols. Istanbul: Tabhane-i Amire, 1279 [history of the Ottoman dynasty up to the year 1520].

Selanikî. Mustafa Efendi [Selanikî], M. Ipşirli (ed.). *Selanikî Mustafa Efendi: Tarih-i Selankî (971–1008/1563–1600)* 2 vols. (Istanbul: Edebiyat Fakültesi Basimevi, 1989) [the concluding portions of the work cover the period 1563 to 1600 in detail].

Silahdar. Fındıklı Mehmed Ağa [Silahdar], A. Refik (ed.). *Silahdar Fındıklı Mehmed Ağa: Silahdar Tarihi (1065–1106/1655–95)* 2 vols. (Istanbul: Devlet Matbaası, 1928) [covers the period 1655–95].

Silahdar. Fındıklı Mehmed Ağa [Silahdar], I. Parmaksızoğlu (ed.). *Silahdar Fındıklı Mehmed Ağa; Nusretname (1106–1133/1695–1721)* 5 pts. in 2 vols. (Istanbul: Milli Egitim Basimevi, 1962–9) [covers the period 1695–1721].

Solakzade. Mehmed Hemdemî [Solakzade]. *Tarih-i Al-i Osman* [Ottoman history up to the year 1657].

Temeşvarlı, Osman. Osman Ağa ibn Ahmed (Temeşvarlı). "Hatıra" edn in Arabic letters of London: British Library Ms., Or. 3213, R. F. Kreutel (ed.), *Die Autobiographie des Dolmetschers Osman Aga Aus Temeschwar* (Cambridge: E. J. W. Gibb Memorial Trust, 1980).

Topçular Kâtibi. Abdülkadir Efendi [Topçular Kâtibi], *Tevarih-i Al-i Osman*, Vienna: ONB Ms., Mxt. 130 [recounts dynastic events (with particular emphasis on military mobilizations and army supply questions) from 1591 to 1644].

Wratislav, A. H. (trans.). *The adventures of Baron Wenceslas Wratislav of Mitovitz . . . committed to writing in the year of our Lord 1599* (London, 1862).

Zarain, Aga. *A relation of the late siege and taking of the city of Babylon by the Turke as it was written from thence by Zarain Aga one of his captaines* (London, 1639).

Secondary works

Adanir, F. "Tradition and rural change in Southeastern Europe during Ottoman rule". In *The origins of backwardness in Eastern Europe*, D. Chirot (ed.) (Berkeley: Univ. of California Press, 1989), pp. 131–76.

Agoston, G. "Gunpowder for the Sultan's army", *Turcica* XXV (1993), pp. 75–96.

Agoston, G. "Ottoman artillery and European military technology in the fifteenth and seventeenth centuries", *Acta Orientalia Hung.* XLVII (1994), pp. 15–48.

Anderson, M. S. *War and society in Europe of the old regime, 1618–1789* (London: Fontana Press, 1988).

Bak, J. M. "Politics, society and defense". In *From Hunyadi to Rakoczi: war and society in medieval and early modern Hungary*, Bak and Kiraly. (Boulder, Co: Social Science Monographs, 1982), pp. 1–22.

Bak, J. M. and Kiraly, B. K. (eds), *From Hunyadi to Rakoczi: war and society in medieval and early modern Hungary* (Boulder Co: Social Science Monographs, 1982) [EEM, no. 104].

Balisch, A. "Infantry battlefield tactics in the seventeenth and eighteenth centuries on the European and Turkish theatres of war", *Studies in History and Politics* III (1983–4), pp. 43–60.

Barker, T. M. *Army, aristocracy, monarchy: essays on war, society and government in Austria, 1618–1780* (Boulder: Social Science Monographs, 1982) [EEM, no. 106].

Barker, T. M. "New perspectives on the historical significance of the year of the Turk", *Austrian History Yearbook* XIX–XX (1983–4), pp. 3–14.

Barrie-Currien, V. (ed.), *Guerre et pouvoir en Europe au XVIe siècle* (Paris: Veyrier, 1991).

Berenger, J. "La Diplomatie imperiale; personnel et structure". In *Guerre et pouvoir en Europe au XVIe siècle*, V. Barrie-Currien (ed.), pp. 57–77.

Betts, R. R. "The Habsburg lands", New Cambridge Modern History, Vol 5: *The ascendancy of France* (Cambridge: Cambridge Univ. Press, 1961), pp. 474–99.

Black, J. *European warfare 1660–1815* (London: UCL Press, 1994).

Black, J. *A military revolution? Military change and European society 1530–1800* (Basingstoke: MacMillan, 1991).

Boka, E. "Diplomatie à Constantinople et la siège de Vienne", *Südost Forschungen* LI (1992), pp. 65–104.

Bond, B. and Roy, I. (eds), *War and society*, 2 vols. (London: Croom Helm, 1975–1977).

Bracewell, C. W. *The Uskoks of Senj: piracy, banditry and holy war in the sixteenth-century Adriatic* (Ithaca: Cornell Univ. Press, 1992).

Cassola, A., Scheban, T. and Bostan, I. (eds), *The 1565 Malta campaign register* (La Valletta, Malta, 1998).

Cezar, M. *Osmanli Tarihinde Levendler* (Istanbul: Çelikcilt Matbaasi, 1965).

Collins, J. B. *Fiscal limits of absolutism: direct taxation in early seventeenth-century France* (Berkeley: U. Cal. Press, 1988).

Darling, L. *Revenue-raising and legitimacy: tax collection and finance administration in the Ottoman Empire 1560–1660* (Leiden: E. J. Brill, 1996).

David, G. "Ottoman administrative strategies in Western Hungary". In *Studies in Ottoman history in honour of Professor V. L. Ménage*, C. Heywood and C. Imber (eds) (Istanbul: Isis Press, 1994), pp. 31–43.

David, G. "Data on the continuity and migration of the population in 16th century Ottoman Hungary", *Acta Orientalia Hung.* XLV (1991), pp. 219–52.

Dickens, A. G. (ed.), *The courts of Europe: politics, patronage and royalty, 1400–1800* (London: Thames and Hudson, 1977).

Duffy, C. *Siege warfare: the fortress in the early modern world, 1494–1660* (London: Routledge, Kegan & Paul, 1979).

Duffy, C. *The fortress in the age of Vauban and Frederick the Great, 1660–1789* (London: Routledge & Kegan Paul, 1985).

Evans, R. J. W. *The making of the Habsburg Monarchy, 1559–1700* (Oxford: Clarendon Press, 1979).

Evans, R. J. W. "The Austrian Habsburgs: The dynasty as a political institution". In *The Courts of Europe: politics, patronage and royalty, 1400–1800*, A. G. Dickens (London) pp. 120–45.

Faroqhi, S. "Crisis and change, 1590–1699". In *An economic and social history of the Ottoman Empire, 1300–1914*, H. Inalcik and D. Quataert (eds.) (Cambridge University Press, 1994), pp. 411–636.

Farrar, L. L. (ed.), *War: a historical, political and social study* (Santa Barbara: ABC-CLIO, 1978).

Fekete, L. *Buda and Pest under Turkish rule* (Budapest: Lorand Eötvös University, 1976) [Studia Turco-Hungarica, no. 3].

Finkel, C. "Costs of Ottoman warfare and defence", *Byzantinische Forschungen* XVI (1991), pp. 91–103.

Finkel, C. "French mercenaries in the Habsburg-Ottoman War of 1593–1606", *BSOAS LV/3* (1992), pp. 451–71.

Finkel, C. *The administration of warfare: the Ottoman military campaigns in Hungary, 1593–1606* (Wien: VWGO, 1988) [WZKM, Suppl. no. 14].

Güçer, L. *XVI–XVII. Asırlarda Osmanlı Imparatorluğunda Hububat Meselesi* (Istanbul: Sermet Matbaası, 1964).

Hale, J. R. "Men and weapons: the fighting potential of sixteenth-century Venetian galleys". In *War and society*, B. Bond and I. Roy, Vol. 1, pp. 1–23.

Hegyi, K. "La Province Hongroise dans l'Empire Ottoman", *Acta Historica Hung.* XXXIII (1987), pp. 209–15.

Hegyi, K. "The Ottoman military force in Hungary". In *Hungarian-Ottoman military and diplomatic relations in the age of Süleyman the Magnificent*, G. David and P. Fodor (eds) (Budapest: Lorand Eötvös University, 1994), pp. 131–48.

Helmholdt, F. (ed.), *The world's history: vol. 7 – Western Europe to 1800* (London: William Heineman, 1903).

Hobert, L. "Die Sackgasse aus den zwei fronten Krieg: Die Friedens mit der Osmanen 1689" *Mitteilungen des Instituts für Österreichische Geschichtsforschung* XCVIII/2–4 (1989), pp. 329–80.

Hoppen, A. "Military engineers in Malta, 1530–1798", *Annals of science XXXVIII* (1981), pp. 413–33.

Hoppen, A. *The fortification of Malta by the Order of St. John, 1530–1798* (Edinburgh: Scottish Academic Press, 1979).

Hummelberger, W. "Die Bewaffnung, Ausrüstung, und Versorgung der Truppen der Heilige Liga bei der Belagerung von Buda 1686", *Acta Historica Hung.* XXX (1987), pp. 319–32.

Inalcik, H. "Military transformation in the Ottoman Empire, 1600–1700", *Archivum Ottomanicum VI* (1980), pp. 283–337.

Ingro, C. W. "Guerilla warfare in early modern Europe: the Kuruc war, 1703–1711". In *War and society in East Central Europe* No. 1, Kiraly and Rothenberg (eds), pp. 47–66.

Işıksal, T. "Gunpowder in Ottoman documents of the last half of the 16th century", *International Journal of Turkish Studies* II (1981–1982), pp. 81–91.

Kingra, M. S. "The Trace Italienne and the military revolution during the Eighty Years War, 1567–1648", *Journal of Military History* LVII/3 (1993), pp. 431–46.

Kiraly, B. K. "Society and war". In *From Hunyadi to Rakoczi*, J. M. Bak and B. K. Kiraly, pp. 23–55.

Kiraly, B. K. and Rothenberg, G. E. (eds), "Special topics and generalizations on the 18th and 19th centuries", *War and society in East Central Europe*, No. 1 (New York: Brooklyn College Press, 1979).

Kütükoğlu, B. *Osmanlı-Iran Siyasi Münasebetleri, 1578–1590* (Istanbul: Edebiyat Fakultesi Matbaası, 1962).

Lampe, J. R. and Jackson, M. R. "The economic legacy of Ottoman domination". In *Balkan economic history, 1500–1950*, Lampe and Jackson (Bloomington: Indiana Univ. Press, 1982), pp. 21–49.

Lucker, G. "Die Türkenzeit in den österreichischen Landern". In *Die Türken*, Wessely, pp. 7–23.

Lynn, John A. *Giant of the grand siècle: the French army, 1610–1715* (Cambridge: Cambridge Univ. Press, 1997).

McNeill, W. H. *The pursuit of power: technology, armed force, and society since 1000 A.D.* (Chicago: Univ. of Chicago Press, 1983).

Majer, H. G. "Zur Kapitulation des osmanischen Gran (Esztergom) im Jahre 1683". In *Südosteuropa unter dem Halbmond*, P. Bartl and H. Glassl (eds) (München: Troefenik, 1975), pp. 189–204.

Makki, L. "Istvan Bocskai's Insurrectionary Army". In *From Hunyadi to Rakoczi*, Bak and Kiraly, pp. 275–95.

Mears, J. "Influence of the Turkish wars in Hungary". In *Asia and the West: essays in honour of Donald Lach*, C. K. Pullapilly and E. J. Vankly (eds) (Notre Dame: Notre Dame Univ. Press, 1986), pp. 129–45.

Mihnea, R. "La Participation de la Russie aux guerres de la Sainte Alliance", *Études Balkaniques* XV/2 (1979), pp. 94–103.

Murphey, R. "Süleyman's Eastern policy". In *Süleyman the Second [i.e. the First] and his time*, C. Kafadar and H. Inalcik (eds) (Istanbul: Isis Press, 1993), pp. 229–48.

Murphey, R. "Review of Setton's Venice, Austria and the Turks", *Archivum Ottomanicum* XIII (1993–1994), pp. 371–83.

Murphey, R. "The Ottoman attitude towards the adoption of Western technology". In *Contributions à l'histoire économique et sociale de l'Empire Ottoman*, P. Dumont and Je.-Lo. Bacqué-Grammont (eds) (Leuven: Éditions Peeters, 1983), pp. 287–98.

Murphey, R. *Regional structure in the Ottoman Empire* (Wiesbaden: Harrassowitz, 1987).

Murphey, R. "Construction of a fortress at Mosul in 1631". In *Social and economic history of Turkey, 1071–1920*, H. Inalcik and O. Okyar (eds) (Ankara: Meteksan, 1980), pp. 163–78.

Murphey, R. "Horsebreeding in Eurasia", *Central and Inner Asian Studies* IV (1990), pp. 115–31.

Murphey, R. "The Ottoman resurgence in the seventeenth-century Mediterranean", *Mediterranean Historical Review* VIII (1993), pp. 186–200.

Murphey, R. "The Ottomans in Iraq: legacy or aftermath?", *Journal of Turkish Studies* XI (1987), pp. 17–29.

Nouzille, J. *Histoire de Frontières: L'Autriche et l'Empire Ottomane* (Paris: Berg International, 1991).

Oğuzoğlu, Y. "Osmanli şehirlerinde askerilerin ekonomik durumuna ilişkin bazi bilgiler" *Birinici Askeri Tarih Semineri: Bildiriler*, 4 vols. (Ankara: Genel Kurmay Basimevi, 1983), Vol. 2, pp. 169–76.

Pakalın, M. Z. "Akınlar ve Akıncılar", *TOEM* VIII/47 (1334), pp. 286–305.

Perjés, G. "Army provisioning, logistics and strategy in the second half of the seventeenth century", *Acta Historica Hung.* XVI (1970), pp. 1–51.

Perjés, G. "The Zrinyi-Montecuccoli controversy". In *From Hunyadi to Rakoczi*, J. M. Bak and B. K. Kiraly (eds) pp. 335–49.

Perjés, G. *The fall of the medieval kingdom of Hungary: Mohacs 1526 – Buda 1541* (Boulder: Social Science Monographs, 1989) [EEM, no. 255].

Paret, P. "Armed forces and the State: the historical essays of Otto Hintze". In *War and Society*, B. Bond and I. Roy (eds), vol. 2, pp. 151–7.

Pernot, Je.-Fr. "Guerre de sièges et places fortes". In *Guerre et pouvoir en Europe au XVIe siècle*, V. Barrie-Currien (ed.), pp. 129–50.

Péter, K. "The later Ottoman period and Royal Hungary". In *A history of Hungary*, P. Sugar, P. Hanak and T. Franks (eds), pp. 100–20.

Pickl, O. "Die Versorgung des Drau Corps . . . 1684–1687", *Acta Historica Hung.* XXXIV (1987), pp. 301–17.

Pickl, O. (ed.), *Die wirtschaftlichen Auswirkungen der Türkenkriege* (Graz, 1971) [Grazer Forschungen zur Wirtschafts- und Sozialgeschichte, Bd. 1].

Raab, T. K. "The effects of the Thirty Years' War on the German economy", *Journal of Modern History* XXXIV (1962), pp. 40–51.

Rebel, H. *Peasant classes: the bureaucratization of property and family relations under early Habsburg absolutism, 1511–1636* (Princeton: Princeton University Press, 1983).

Redlich, F. *De Praeda Militari: looting and booty 1500–1815* (Wiesbaden: F. Steiner Verlag, 1956).

Redlich, F. *The German military enterpriser and his workforce, 13th to 17th centuries*, 2 vols. (Wiesbaden, 1964–5) [Vierteljahrschrift fur Sozial- und Wirtschaftsgeschichte, Suppl. Nos. XLVII–XLVIII].

Refik, A. *Devr-i Sultan Süleyman Kanuni'de Birinci Viyana Muhasarası 926 h./1529 m.* (Istanbul: Ibrahim Hilmi, Kütüphane-i Islam ve Askeri, 1325).

Regele, O. *Der Österreichische Hofkriegsrat 1556–1848* (Wien: Österreichische Staatsdruckerei, 1949).

Rothenberg, G. E. *The Austrian military border in Croatia, 1522–1747* (Urbana: Univ. of Illinois Press, 1960).

Rothenberg, G. E. "Christian insurrections in Turkish Dalmatia, 1580–1596", *Slavonic and East European Review* XL (1961–2), pp. 136–45.

Ruzas, L. "The siege of Sigetvar of 1566: its significance in Hungarian social development". In *From Hunyadi to Rakoczi: war and society in medieval and early modern Hungary*, J. M. Bak and B. K. Kiraly (eds) (Boulder: Social Science Monographs, 1982) [EEM, no. 104].

Ruzas, L. "Die Entwicklung der Marktflecken Transdanubiens unter der Türkenherrschaft im 17. Jahrhundert". In *Wirtschaftlichen Auswirkungen der Türkenkriege*, Pickl (ed.), pp. 221–34.

Setton, K. M. *Venice, Austria and the Turks in the seventeenth century* (Philadelphia: American Philosophical Society, 1991).

Schimmer, C. A. *The sieges of Vienna by the Turks from the German of Karl August Schimmer and other sources*, Eng. Trans. (London: John Murray, 1847) [the first siege (of 1529) is described on pp. 7–53].

Schmidt, J. "The Egri Campaign of 1596: military history and the problem of sources". In *Habsburgisch-Osmanische Bezeihungen*, A. Tietze (ed.) (Wien: VWGO, 1985), pp. 125–44.

Sugar, P. "The Ottoman professional prisoner on the western borders of the empire in the sixteenth and seventeenth centuries", *Actes du Deuxième Congrès International des Études du Sud-Est Européen*, 6 vols. (Athens, 1972–6), Vol. 6, pp. 29–40.

Sugar, P., Hanak, P. and Frank, T. (eds). *A history of Hungary* (London: I. B. Tauris, 1991).

Sugar, P. "A near-perfect military society: the Ottoman Empire". In *War: a historical, political and social study*, L. L. Farrar (ed.) (Santa Barbara: ABC-Clio, 1978), pp. 95–104.

Szakály, F. "The Hungarian-Croatian border defense system and its collapse". In *From Hunyadi to Rakoczi*, J. M. Bak and B. K. Kiraly (eds) pp. 141–58.

Szakály, F. "Die Bilanz der Türkenherrschaft in Ungarn", *Acta Historica Hung.* XXXIV (1988), pp. 63–78.

Szakály, F. "Zur Kontinutatsfrage der wirtschaftsstruktur in den Ungarischen Marktflecken unter der Türkenherrschaft". In *Wirtschaftlichen Auswirkungen der Türkenkriege*, O. Pickl (ed.), pp. 235–72.

Tietze, A. (ed.), *Habsburgisch-Osmanische Bezeihungen* (Wien: VWGO, 1985) [WZKM, Suppl. no. 13].

Teply, K. "Vom Loss osmanischen Gefangener aus dem Grossen Türkenkrieg" *Südost Forshungen* XXXII (1973), pp. 33–72.

Vehse, E. *Memoirs of the court: aristocracy and diplomacy of Austria*, 2 vols. (London, 1856).

Veinstein, G. "Some views on provisioning in the Hungarian campaigns of Suleyman the Magnificent". In *Osmanistische Studien zur Wirtschafts-und sozial geschichte in memoriam V. Baskov*, H. G. Majer (ed.) (Wiesbaden, 1986), pp. 177–85.

Veinstein, G. "L'hivernage en campagne, talon d'Achille du système militaire ottoman classique", *Studia Islamica* LVIII (1983), pp. 109–43.

Varkonyi, A. "The reconquest of Buda in contemporary Hungarian political thought and public opinion", *Acta Historica Hung.* XXXIV (1988), pp. 3–16.

Vasić, M. "Die Einfluss den Türkenkriege auf die wirtschaft des osmanischen Grenzgebietes in Serbien und Bosnien, 1480–1536". In *Wirtschaftlichen Auswirkungen der Türkenkriege*, O. Pickl (ed.), pp. 308–18.

Wessely, C. *Die Türken und was von ihnen blieb* (Wien, Verband der Wissenschaftlichen Gesellschaften Österreichs, 1978).

Wojcik, Z. "King John III of Poland and the Turkish aspects of his foreign policy", *Turk Tarih Kurumu: Belleten* XLIV/176 (1980), pp. 659–73.

Zimanyi, V. *Economy and society in sixteenth and seventeenth-century Hungary, 1526–1650* (Budapest: Kiado, 1987).

Index

CPSIA information can be obtained
at www.ICGtesting.com
Printed in the USA
LVOW13s0727180418
573822LV00018B/275/P